A DICTIONARY OF
CANADIAN ARTISTS

A DICTIONARY OF CANADIAN ARTISTS

COMPILED BY

COLIN S. MACDONALD

VOLUME FIVE

CANADIAN PAPERBACKS PUBLISHING LTD.,
370 Queen Mary Street,
Ottawa, Canada, K1K 1W7

Printed in Canada

Catalogue No. L.C. 67-8044
SBN 0-919554-13-X

To

F/O ROYDEN GARFIELD BRADLEY

only son
of
CLIFFORD AND MAE (HAWKSHAW) BRADLEY

who died August 27, 1944 while piloting
a Lancaster Bomber over Danzig

———————————

and

my uncle

PTE. NEIL WATSON MACDONALD

PIPER

FIFTH ROYAL HIGHLANDERS, MONTREAL,

13TH BATTALION

killed April 22, 1915, with twenty of
his comrades from a Highland band of
twenty-four, during the Langemarck (St. Julien)
engagement of the Second Battle of Ypres.

I wish to express special acknowledgement
to the Canada Council and the Ontario Arts
Council for research and publication grants.

Colin S. MacDonald

ACKNOWLEDGEMENTS

I wish to express my indebtedness to all who have made possible this compilation:

To Dr. R.H. Hubbard, Chief Curator of The National Gallery of Canada for permission to use material from the National Gallery of Canada publications; the late Alan Jarvis and Mr. Paul Arthur for permission to use material from *Canadian Art* magazine; Prof. Melville W. Thistle, School of Journalism, Carleton University, for his vital constructive criticism; Mr. J. Russell Harper, author of *Painting in Canada/ A History and Early Painters and Engravers in Canada* for his key suggestions in the early stages of the manuscript; Mr. William Colgate, author of *Canadian Art, Its Origin and Development;* the late Graham McInnes, author of *Canadian Art;* Mr. Robert Ayre of *The Montreal Star;* Mr. Robert Fulford, Editor of *Saturday Night* and *The Toronto Star,* for passages from their writings on Canadian artists; *The Toronto Star, The London Free Press; Saturday Night; The Montreal Gazette; Globe And Mail* for permission to quote passages from their art reviews and columns; Mr. W. J. Withrow, author of *Contemporary Canadian Painting* and Director of The Art Gallery of Ontario; Mr. Lawrence Sabbath of Montreal, writer and critic; to Dr. William S.A. Dale, Chairman, and William S. Hart, Associate Professor, Art Department, University of Western Ontario for their vital moral support; to the following publishers: Burns and MacEachern Limited for excerpts from Paul Duval's *Canadian Drawings and Prints, Canadian Water Colour Painting, Group of Seven Drawings;* The MacMillan Company of Canada Limited for excerpts from *Canadian Art;* Clarke, Irwin & Company Limited for excerpts from *A Painter's Country* by A.Y. Jackson and *Growing Pains* by Emily Carr; to Ryerson Press for excerpts from their publications on Canadian artists too numerous to mention here (acknowledgements to their authors appear in the text); to *Maclean's Magazine* for excerpts from articles dealing with Canadian artists (acknowledgements to their authors appear in the text); *Weekend Magazine* for excerpts from their publications (acknowledgements to their authors appear in the text); to the Reference Department of the Ottawa Public Library; to Mrs. Mary N. Balke, Chief Librarian, National Gallery of Canada and Deputy Librarian, Miss J.E. Hunter, also former Librarian, Miss Christa Dedering; Reference Services Librarian, Maija Vilcins and Reference Clerk, James Kelly; former Art Documentalist Alexandra Pritz; summer assistants Lucya Yarymowich and Judy Kaminsky; to the following who have supplied information at various times and moral support: Mr. Jean-René Ostiguy, Research Curator and Lecturer, Canadian Art, and Mr. Dennis Reid Curator of Post-Confederation Canadian Art of the National Gallery of Canada; Mr. Paul Duval, author of many articles and books on art; Mr. Richard B. Simmins, author, lecturer, critic on art, and Miss Norah McCullough former Western Representative, National Gallery of Canada, and Mr. J. Stanford Perrot of the Southern Alberta Institute of Technology; to the following art societies: Royal Canadian Academy of Arts; Canadian Group of Painters, Canadian Society of Painters in Water Colour; Sculptors' Society of Canada; Nova Scotia Society of Artists; Ontario Society of Artists; Manitoba Society of Artists, Alberta Society of Artists; British Columbia Society of Artists; Federation of Canadian Wood Carvers; Young Commonwealth of Artists for information on Canadian artists abroad; to Mr. Raymond Poulin and Mrs. Moy Smith also Mr. Michel Champagne, Cultural Agent for the Department of Cultural Affairs of the Province of Quebec, who have provided information on Quebec artists; to over 400 Canadian artists from every province in Canada and scores of collectors and art dealers who have contributed information on art and artists in Canada.

Colin S. MacDonald
Editor

NADEAU, Albert

b. 1915

Born in St. François, Madawaska County, New Brunswick, he began wood-carving at the age of eight. Although financial difficulties forced him to work as a carpenter or a mechanic at times he kept to his carving during his spare time. By the age of twenty-one he had been discovered by Dr. J.A. Laporte, who helped him set up a workshop and arrange his first solo show in the New Brunswick Museum during February of 1946. His earlier carvings, realistic in style, were of animals and figures. His favourite type of carving however is done in bas-relief executed in wood and also clay. His "Water Carrier" for instance was acquired by a collector in the Philippines and other of his works are in collections in other countries. Nadeau has worked with Leonardo Ottina in Montreal and J.J. Bourgault at St. Jean Port-Joli, P.Q. A member of the Association Professionnelle des Artisans du Quebec, he lives at St. Jean Port-Joli.

References
Times-Globe, St. John, N.B., Feb. 1, 1946 "Exhibition of Albert Nadeau's wood carvings is opened at N.B. Museum"
Le guide des artisans créateurs du Quebec par Jean-Pierre Payette, La Presse, Mtl., 1974, P. 203
Document from artist

NADEAU, Marc Antoine

b. 1943

Born in Montreal, P.Q., he received his classical education at Collège André Grasset and studied sculpture at the Ecole des Beaux-Arts, Montreal, and worked at L'Atelier Libre de Recherches Graphiques (1965-66). His art consists of imaginative renderings of familiar objects, such as bicycles, sailboats and seaplanes. These sculptures in wood are delicately designed and sometimes painted, but nevertheless convey a statement about the complexity of our modern civilization exploring themes of flight, bicycle rallies, the sea and the American west. He has exhibited his work at many galleries in Montreal including Centre d'Art Mont-Royal, the Youth Pavillion of Expo '67, Museum of Contemporary Art and solo shows at the University of Montreal (1965), Galerie Nova et Vetera (1965), Boutique Soleil (1969). He is represented in the McGill Museum, the Quebec Ministry of Education and in private collections.

References
The Gazette, Mtl., P.Q., Sat., Mar. 20, 1971 "An Exploration into neglected fields" by M.W.
Vie Des Arts, Mtl., P.Q., Eté, 1970 "Marc Nadeau et Pierre Cornellier à la boutique soleil" par Claude-Lyse Gagnon, P. 62
NGC Info. Form rec'd 19 Sept., 1966

NAGY, Elena

Coming from Budapest, Hungary in January of 1957, the most important consideration for Elena Nagy was survival in a new and strange environment. With her well-founded experience in portraiture, she was able to make a living by soliciting

NAGY, Elena (Cont'd)

commissions from door-to-door, using the pseudonym "Cleopatra". Working in her studio at Notre-Dame-de-Grâce, Montreal, she has since become interested in landscape painting as well. Using her knowledge of the European styles, a vigourous brush stroke, and bright, vibrant colours, her skill is unmistakable. She has exhibited her work in Trois-Rivières, and in Montréal and has organized exhibitions at the Centre d'Art Stefanoff in the Laurentians.

References:
  L'Action, Québec, January 13, 1963
  "Deux Peintres" par Germaine Bundock
  Le Nouvelliste, Trois-Rivières, Sept. 25, 1964
  "Elena Nagy préfère les portraits et les paysages"

NAHANEE, David

"The Carving Post", North Vancouver, was opened in 1969 as a place where David Nahanee could work and at the same time display and sell his carvings. He works in wood, drawing from the legends and traditions of the Squamish clan of Indians for his subject matter, but his special interest is free form carving. He prefers to use wood that he has found along the Vancouver beaches for this type of carving because it lends itself so naturally to the work. Aside from "The Carving Post", his totems and wall plaques depicting British Columbia legends can be seen at the Three Greenhorns Restaurant in Denman Place.

Reference:
  Times, West Vancouver Lions Gate, B.C., July 17, 1969
  "Indian carver opens NVan shop" by Sherry Bie

NAKAMURA, Kazuo
b. 1926

Born of Japanese parentage in Vancouver, B.C., the son of Toichi and Yoshiyo Nakamura. In 1942 the Nakamuras were moved from the coast to the interior of B.C. because of the war. Following this period the family moved east to Hamilton, Ontario, in 1947. Young Kazuo about this time first became interested in painting while he was employed as a semi-skilled worker in a Hamilton box factory. He studied nights at the Hamilton Technical School with the hope of becoming a full-time artist. Finally he enrolled in the Toronto Central Technical School in 1948 where he took further studies for three years under Charles Goldhamer, Doris McCarthy, Peter Haworth, Elizabeth Wyn Wood, Virginia Luz and Jocelyn Taylor. He participated in his first exhibition at Eaton's unaffiliated artists show in 1950 then in November 1952 he held his first one-man show at the Picture Loan Society. The following year he held a solo show at Hart House and in October of that same year he was invited to participate in a group show, arranged by painter William Ronald in conjunction with Simpson's department store entitled "Abstracts at Home". Describing Nakamura's work not long after this event George Elliott in

Canadian Art noted, "Quietly impressive in this new group is a young Canadian of Japanese descent, Kazuo Nakamura, who paints alternately intellectual exercises in design and extravagant romance landscapes of elegant good taste and high decorative value . . . He has two recognizable sources of subject matter. One is what might be called a racial instinct for landscape. The traditional Japanese fragility, precision, simplicity, also a certain airy romance in landscape painting is in his work, although it is not especially Japanese in appearance. The other is his way of looking at man-made devices. He doesn't particularly care to see the whole, preferring to see a fragment, an upright and beam in a building repeating themselves, a turn in a pipeline or iron steps at a railway station. These sources provide him with all the visual material he needs to create landscapes which are fanciful, mistily abstract, full of calligraphic charm." Elliott went on to describe some of the methods Nakamura used to achieve his results which included application of paint by brush, razor blade, linoleum cutter, string, thread, wire screen and the edge of a piece of cardboard. An article by Jock Carroll in *Weekend Magazine* brought wider attention to Nakamura's work as a member of "Painters 11" and described him as an intellectual with an encyclopedic mind. In October of 1970 Nakamura held simultaneously solo shows at the Morris Gallery (of current work) and at Hart House (where a retrospective exhibition of his work between 1953 and 1960 was shown). Viewing these two shows the *Globe & Mail* critic noted, "To appreciate properly the thoughtful drive behind this 44-year-old artist's work, it's important to see Nakamura's retrospective at Hart House Gallery before his new painting at Morris Gallery. The span is less than 20 years, but it clearly proves the three-pronged drive behind his expression — still life, landscape, geometric — for he seems never to have stopped doing one in favor of another. Rather he has made them his interchangeable ally. Nakamura painted Plants and Moonlight, an almost figurative work, in 1952, and Winter in 1970, traditional snow and trees, but what is most interesting about the 20 years is that he has blended his three styles so imperceptibly into one — a kind of Nakamura school of abstract expressionism." Among the favourites of gallery goers and critics seem to be his 'string' paintings which Dennis Reid has described as 'beautifully profound'. Nakamura's awards include a prize at the Fourth International Exhibition of Drawings and Engravings, Lugano, Switzerland, 1956; purchase award, Fifth International Hallmark Art Award Exhibition, New York, N.Y., 1960. His one-man shows include: Picture Loan Society, Tor. (1952-56); Hart House (1953); Western Canada Art Circuit (1956); Gal. of Contemporary Art, Tor. (1956, 58); Jerrold Morris Int. Gal., Tor. (1962, 1965); Waddington Gallery, Mtl. (1967); Morris Gallery, Tor. (1970). He has exhibited in many group shows, national and international (see *Creative Canada*). He is represented in the following collections: Winnipeg Art Gallery, Man.; Art Gal. of Windsor, Ont.; University of Guelph, Ont.; Univ. of Western Ont., Lond.; Art Gal. of Ont., Tor.; Hart House, Univ. Tor.; Victoria College, Tor.; Nat. Gal. of Can., Ottawa; Embassy of Japan, Ott.; Dept. External Affairs, Ott.; Univ. Club Mtl.; Sir Geo. Williams Univ., Mtl.; Beaverbrook Art Gallery, Fredericton, N.B.; Dominion Foundries & Steel Coll., Hamilton; Imperial Oil Coll., Tor.; Toronto Dominion Centre, Tor.; Northern and Central Gas Coll., Tor.; C.I.L. Coll., Mtl.; Pirelli Cables Coll., Mtl.; Can. Imperial Bank of Commerce, Mtl.; Museum of Modern Art, NYC; Lugano Coll., Switz.; Hallmark Coll., USA; Philip Johnson Coll., NYC; and others. Lives in Toronto with his wife Lillian.

NAKAMURA, Kazuo (Cont'd)

References

Canadian Art, Vol. XI, No. 4, 1954 "Nakamura – Painter on the Threshold" by George Elliott, P. 136-139

Weekend Magazine, Vol. 7, No. 43, 1957 "New Accent To Canadian Art" photostory by Jock Carroll

Globe & Mail, Tor., Ont., Oct. 10, 1970 "Kazuo Nakamura"

A Concise History of Canadian Painting by Dennis Reid, Oxford, Tor., 1973, P. 250, 251

NGC Info. Forms, 1953, 1955, 1968

see also

Toronto Telegram, Ont., Oct. 28, 1954 "Artist Painted With Razor And String"

The Toronto Star, Ont., Apr. 24, 1956 "View From Train Wins Artist Famous Trophy" by Hugh Thomson

Mayfair, Tor., Ont., February, 1956 "The New World Of Pattern" by Robert Fulford

Globe & Mail, Tor., Ont., Apr. 5, 1958 "One-Man Show By Nakamura Poetic, Abstract"

La Presse, Mtl., P.Q., Sept. 27, 1958 "Nakamura s'affirme, Smith se révèle" par R. de Repentigny

Globe & Mail, Tor., Ont., Dec. 6, 1958 "Paste, Paper, Pigment in Watercolor Show" by Pearl McCarthy

The Montreal Star, P.Q., Oct. 31, 1960 "Toronto Artists' Works At Montreal Museum"

Le Devoir, Mtl., P.Q., Nov. 1, 1960 "Oeuvres de H. Town et de Kazuo Nakamura"

Globe & Mail, Tor., Ont., Aug. 5, 1961 "Pick Nakamura for Paris Biennial" by Ralph Hicklin

Ibid, June 2, 1962 "Nakamura Far More Than Mere Unskilled, Venturesome Carpenter" by Pearl McCarthy

The Gazette, Mtl., P.Q., 22 April, 1967 "An Artist Solves A Problem" by Paul Gladu

Toronto Daily Star, Ont., Oct. 16, 1968 "Kazuo Nakamura's paintings"

The Gazette, Mtl., P.Q., May 2, 1970 "At Waddington's – Nakamura geometry serious"

The Montreal Star, P.Q., May 2, 1970 "Kazuo Nakamura within the scientist, a poet" by Robert Ayre

Canadian Business, Mtl., P.Q., September, 1970 (cover and article on the cover)

Toronto Daily Star, Tor., Ont., Oct. 10, 1970 "Art Review – Artist has earned enviable reputation" by Paul Russell

Books

NGC Catalogue, Vol. 3 by R.H. Hubbard, Ottawa, 1960, P. 231-232

The Development of Canadian Art by R.H. Hubbard, NGC, Ottawa, 1963, P. 131

Sir Geo. Williams Univ. Coll by Edwy F. Cooke, Mtl, 1967, P. 145

The Hart House Coll. of Canadian Painting by Jeremy Adamson, Univ. Tor. Pr., 1969, P. 101

Art Gal. of Ont., The Canadian Collection by Helen Pepall Bradfield, McGraw Hill, Tor., 1970, P. 330, 552 (col. repr.)

Creative Canada, Vol. 2, 1972, McPherson Lib., Univ. Victoria, B.C., P. 202, 203

Canadian Artists In Exhibition, Roundstone Council For The Arts, Tor., 1974, P. 58, 284

Toronto Painting: 1953-1965, Introd. by B. Hale, Exhibition selected and organized by Dennis Reid

Four Decades, The Canadian Group of Painters and their contemporaries 1930-1970 by Paul Duval, Clarke, Irwin & Co. Ltd., Tor., 1972, P. 45, 131, 142-4 (ill.)

NAMER, Rosalie

b. 1925

Born in Montreal, P.Q., she studied painting and sculpture at the Montreal Museum of Fine Arts, Sir George Williams University, and École des Beaux Arts also ceramics at École des Arts Appliqués, Montreal. Teaching ceramics at MacDonald College (McGill University) since 1958 she is in charge of the ceramics department. She has held one-woman shows in Toronto and Montreal, and has exhibited in

NAMER, Rosalie (Cont'd)

group shows in Syracuse, N.Y.; Florence, Italy; Geneva, Switzerland; Brussels, Berlin, London and Tokyo. She has also participated in all of the Canadian Ceramics Biennial exhibitions. She received a Canada Council grant (1968-69) to search for suitable Canadian clays for ceramics and discovered such clays in use by west coast brick and tile manufacturing industries and also by firms in the Maritimes. In 1965 she was producing a hundred pieces of pottery a week.

References

Dimanche-Matin, Mtl., P.Q., June 7, 1970 "Exposition des oeuvres de Rosalie Namer à la Centrale d'Artisanat"
Pointe Claire Lakeshore News & Chronicle, P.Q., Sept. 11, 1969 "Mac teacher encouraging pottery growth"
The Montreal Star, Mtl., P.Q., Mar. 8, 1965 "Sales Don't Mean Quality, Says Artist" by Doris Giller

NANE-PIROCHE, Setsuko

b. 1933

Japanese-born, she was educated in the Japanese tradition by studying under a well-known and respected artist. She won first prize when she exhibited at the Tokyo Museum in 1958. She then continued to exhibit her work regularly in Japan until her move to Vancouver in 1967. In July of 1969, she held her first one-woman show at the Mary Frazee Gallery in Vancouver. Her paintings, described by Charlotte Townsend of the *Vancouver Sun* as "a decorative kind of expressionism" have been influenced by her travels in India, Australia and Tasmania. She has taken up weaving three-dimensional abstract hangings since her arrival in Canada, which are successful especially in texture and colour.

Reference:

Vancouver Sun, B.C., Jul. 19, 1969. "Her Expressionism Influenced by the Supernatural" by Charlotte Townsend

NANOGAK

b. (c) 1925

The fresh and humourous quality of Nanogak's prints and drawings is characteristic of the artists of Holman Island in the western Arctic. Her prints, exhibited at Vancouver's Images Gallery in February of 1972, explore aspects of Eskimo folklore and scenes from everyday life. They are fine examples of Nanogak's keen observation, fluid line and power to suggest movement. A series of about forty drawings, which she exhibited at the Eskimo Gallery of the Canadian Guild of Crafts (Montreal) in December of 1970, were executed with Ronald Melzack's versions of the Raven legends in mind. Her expressive use of colour and lively humorous touches beautifully complement the simplicity and directness of the stories.

NANOGAK, (Cont'd)

References:
The Vancouver Sun, B.C., Feb. 18, 1972 "New Eskimo prints fresh and humorous" by Joan Lowndes
The Montreal Star, P.Q. Dec. 9. 1970 "Melzack's Eskimo legends need Nanogak drawings" by Robert Ayre

NASBY, David
b. 1945

Born in Hamilton, Ontario, he studied at the University of Guelph where he received his B.A. in Honours Sociology in 1971 and took graduate studies there, also numerous short Museology courses at the National Gallery of Canada. Since 1969 he has been engaged in free-lance and commercial photography including fine art reproduction, photo-journalism, architecture, social research and documentation and been a panellist on professional development in the arts. He was a photographer for "Artists with Their Works", 1972 for the Ontario Arts Council and the Art Gallery of Ontario. He has taught at the Summer School "Edinburgh Arts '73" jointly run by the Richard DeMarco Gallery and the University of Edinburgh, Scotland where he was also a faculty member in charge of Photography Workshop; at Continuing Education Division of Mohawk College of Applied Arts & Technology, Hamilton, where he taught basic and intermediate photography. He has held solo exhibitions of his photography at Mount St. Vincent Univ., Halifax (1973); McMaster Univ., Hamilton, Ont. (1973); Richard DeMarco Gallery, Edinburgh, Scot. (1973); Baldwin Street Gallery of Photography, Tor. (1974); Univ. Guelph, Ont. (1974); Kitchener-Waterloo Art Gallery, Kitch., Ont. (1975); Wellington Co. Sch. Bd. (50 Schools, 1975-76) and several group shows. He was Oral Historian, Prov. of Ont. in Pickering Township (1972); Consultant to Ontario Association of Art Galleries; Social & Physical Survey of Art Galleries, OMA, Ministry of Culture and Recreation (1973-75); did catalogue design and production for Univ. of Guelph Art Exhibition Programme (1970-74); Operated Cardigan Fine Art Services (fine art, consulting, evaluations, reproduction photography, antiquarian books, photographica, prints, drawings and photographs (1970-75); Provincial Coordinator, Circus 1976; Corordination for, and liaison with, 20 Provincial arts organizations to instigate and promote multi-discipline cultural festivals in 25 communities in Ontario (1976); Director, Burlington Cultural Centre (1976); Member: Heritage Canada (1973-   ); Ont. Assoc. of Art Galleries (1974-   ); Can. Conference of the Arts (1974-   ); Assoc. of Cultural Executives (1975-   ); Director, New Chamber Orchestra of Canada (1976-77).

References
Document from artist, 1977
"Farm Auction". Guelph Alumnus, Mar-April, 1972 (12 photographs)
Permanence and Change: A Rural Ontario Document, House of Anansi Press, Tor., 1973
Photo Survey '74, Kitchener-Waterloo Art Gallery Exhibition (Catalogue Introduction)
Haldimand Norfolk Leader, Simcoe, Ont. "Lynnwood Photo Exhibit A Statement By The Artists" by Lynne Peterson

NAUMANN, Rose

Originally a laboratory technician in bacteriology, Rose Naumann became interested in art through a pottery course she attended at the Banff School of Fine Arts in 1963. In 1968, she graduated from the Vancouver School of Art and left for Mexico, where she spent almost a year studying weaving and the black pottery of Oaxaca, as well as teaching textiles at the Instituto Allende in San Miguel de Allende near Mexico City. In August 1969, she returned to West Vancouver where she began teaching weaving without a loom and pottery. Her pottery, glazed in bright blues and reds, batiks and mixed media were shown at the B.C. Arts and Crafts Show in October of 1969.

References:
  Lions Gate Times, W. Van, B.C., Aug. 28, 1969 "Technician turns artist, plans to teach weaving"
  Vancouver Province, B.C., Oct. 11, 1969 "The gentle creative arts in the world of handicrafts" by Kay Alsop

NEDDEAU, Donald Frederick Price
b. 1913

A native of Toronto, Neddeau graduated from the Ontario College of Art in 1937, where he had studied under J.W. Beatty and Franklin Carmichael. Prior to World War II, he worked as a commercial artist and art director, after which he joined the air force and later the army as a combat soldier. His first one-man shows were in Toronto at Woodsworth House in 1954 and Upstairs Gallery in 1960. He has since participated in many group shows and travelling exhibitions in Canada and the United States, and has an annual one-man show. His work consists mainly of figure and landscape paintings, in oil and water colour, which show fine draughtsmanship, a dependence on line and a concentration on the emotional quality of a subject. He also does graphic work and ceramic sculpture. Neddeau is a member of the Ontario Society of Artists, Canadian Society of Painters in Water Colour, Canadian Guild of Potters, Philadelphia Water Colour Society, Arts and Letters Club and a Fellow with the International Institute of Arts and Letters. He is a teacher with the Central Technical School Art Department in Toronto.

References:
  Observer, Dryden, Ont., Apr. 25, 1963 "Many Attend Art Showing" by E. Underhill
  Document from artist, Oct. 1960
  NGC Info. Form, 1960

NEEL, Ellen
-1966

Granddaughter of the late Charlie James of Alert Bay, who was the great totem carver of the Kwakuitl tribe, Ellen Neel was responsible for the revival of the art of carving among her people. Her totems, which were carved in her studios in Van-

NEEL, Ellen (Cont'd)

couver and Stanley Park, can be seen in North and South America as well as Europe. Such famous personalities as Queen Elizabeth and Bob Hope are owners of Neel's totem carvings. In 1949, the North Vancouver Squamish College, which is partly financed by the Department of Indian Affairs, sponsored a class in totem carving taught by Ellen Neel and attended by twenty-five students. The use of modern paints, rather than traditional clay colours and vegetable dyes, was introduced as a faster and easier method of colouring the carvings with exactly the same effect. Neel's work is carried on by her seven children.

References:

The Province, Van. B.C., May 20, 1950 "Ellen Neel Gains Recognition" by Palette

The Ottawa Journal, Ont., Dec. 30, 1949 "Granddaughter of Noted Carver Teaches Lost Art of Totem Making"

NFB Mat Release No. 203 "5th Generation Totem Carver"

NEESHAM, Robin Kenneth George

b. 1934

Lack of interest in his father's manufacturing business in his native Bristol, England brought Neesham to Calgary in 1957. During travels through Spain and Mexico, his work developed from water colour landscapes to non-objective works. In Spain, 1960, he met New York painter William Waldren, who taught him the plastic emulsion adhesive technique which became the basis for most of his paintings. He uses up to ten different sands, gravel, a concrete-like substance, pigment and the plastic emulsion to build up his pieces and give them sculptural strength. He describes his own work as "incisive and severe non-objective art, abstract in the fullest sense of the meaning"[1] *The Calgary Herald* has compared his work to the cave paintings of the German master Kurt Schwitters.[2] His first one-man shows were held at the Calgary Allied Arts Centre in 1962 and The Canadian Art Galleries in Calgary in 1963. He has participated in various other shows and is represented in private collections in Canada, United States, Algeria and England. He has written for *The Calgary Herald* as art critic, and has contributed articles to *Canadian Art* and *Art News and Review*.

References:

[1] *Oilweek*, Jul. 23, 1962 "CPA acquires two Neesham paintings"

[2] *The Calgary Herald*, Alta., Mar. 8, 1963 "Sand paintings Lend Gallery 'Fantastic' Cave Atmosphere"

The Albertan, Calgary, Alta., Jan. 30, 1963

The Albertan, Calgary, Alta., Apr. 28, 1962 "This Painting is Hard Work" by Linda Curtis

NGC Info Form 1963

NEGIN, Mark (Louis Mark Negin)

b. 1932

Born in London, England, Negin was educated at the Willesden School of Arts and Crafts there. In 1951 he settled in Winnipeg and began his career in theatre. He worked as designer for the Winnipeg Little Theatre in 1952, in the properties department of the Stratford, Ontario Festival from 1955 to 1957, as resident de-

NEGIN, Mark (Louis Mark Negin) (Cont'd)

signer for the London Little Theatre in Ontario from 1956 to 1958, and as assistant head of properties at Stratford from 1960 to 1961. While at Stratford, he won the Tyrone Guthrie Scholarship for studies abroad. This award enabled him to study in Paris at the École d'Apprentissage d'art dramatique in 1958 and in the Model-Room, Royal Opera House, Covent Garden, London, England in 1958 to 1959. In 1966 he was awarded a Canada Council Scholarship. He has since designed sets and costumes for the National Ballet Company of Canada, Toronto, Les Grands Ballets Canadiens, Montreal, Théâtre du Nouveau Monde, Montreal, the American Conservatory Theatre, United States and the National Arts Centre, Ottawa, to mention a few. He was a founding staff member of the National Theatre School of Canada in Montreal. His costume drawings for the National Arts Centre presentation "The Dybbuk" were shown at Roberston Galleries, Ottawa in 1974.

References:
Creative Canada Volume I, Reference Division, McPherson Library, U. of Vict. B.C., U. of T. Press, 1971 p. 231-2
Catalogue, Robertson Galleries, Ottawa, Ont., Oct. 29, 1974

NEHL-McLENNAN, Margarete
b. 1925

Born in Cologne, Germany, Margarete Nehl-McLennan came to Canada in 1952. Although she is primarily self-taught, she has taken sculpture from Italian sculptor Strabelle, and other courses from Kylliky Salmenhaara and John Reeve at the University of British Columbia. She has received a grant from the Theo Koerner Foundation. Her pottery has been exhibited at Canadian Ceramics in 1963, 1965, 1967, the Canadian Arts Pavillion at Expo '67, the Victoria Art Gallery and the Danish Art Gallery in Vancouver. Her work has been purchased by the National Gallery of Canada and the Department of External Affairs. She is a member of the Canadian Handicraft Guild, the B.C. Potters Guild, the World Craft Council, and the Victoria Art Society. She has taught in Port Alberni, Courteney and Victoria, British Columbia. She is the owner of Island Handcraft House-Gilmar Pottery Studio, in Victoria, where she is a supplier for all fine crafts and a teacher of pottery and weaving.

References:
Victorian, Vict. B.C., Mar. 15, 1972 "Back to basics with weaving and pottery."
NGC Info Form 1967

NEHRING, David

A painter from Smithers, British Columbia, David Nehring was commissioned to paint a portrait of Prince Charles Edward Stuart, the famous Bonnie Prince Charlie in 1966 for the Crest Motor Hotel of Prince Rupert.

Reference
The Prince Rupert Daily News, B.C., May 31, 1966 "Bonnie Prince"

NEILSON, Henry Ivan

1865-1931

Born in Quebec City, the son of John Neilson, explorer and land surveyor, Henry was educated at the Quebec Seminary and Nicolet College. He explored the Gander River, Nfd., in 1885, and was the following year appointed assistant to his father on Government Geographical Survey work at the Mecatina River, Labrador. He then studied mechanical engineering and entered the service of the C.P.R. Company in 1891 and travelled on steamers between Vancouver and the Orient and served with this company in several parts of the world receiving his 2nd class marine engineer certificate in December, 1894.[1] He was appointed superintendent of engineering for the Barbour Flax Company at Paterson, N.J. in 1895. An interest in art finally took him to the Glasgow School of Fine Arts in 1897 at the age of thirty-two. He studied there for one year then went on to the Académie Delécluze, Paris (1898), visited some Italian galleries then studied for two years at St. Gilles Academy, Brussels under Prof. Alfred Clausenaard. While living in Scotland during this period he exhibited at the Royal Scottish Academy, Royal Glasgow Institute, Walker Art Gallery (Liverpool) and other galleries in Britain and on the Continent. Returning to Canada in 1910 he achieved enough success in the next four years to be noted by E.F.B. Johnston[2] in *Canada And Its Provinces* as a painter "whose landscapes are exceedingly poetic." For much of his subject matter he drew upon the landscapes of Northern Quebec and Labrador where he had travelled earlier. Viewing a 1919 showing of his work a critic for the Toronto *Mail & Empire*[3] noted, "For most of his paintings, Mr. Neilson has found his inspiration in the scenery of the Province of Quebec where he has been living. There are several scenes round Cap Rouge, near his home, showing spots on the river and in the woodland . . . . There are one or two landscapes done in dark tones that are full of sombre feeling, and sharply contrasted are the views of Canadian fishing villages, picturesque in line and bright and restful in treatment . . . . In addition to the oil paintings Mr. Neilson is showing several water colors and a number of his etchings. The water colors are among the most attractive pictures in the gallery, and he also shows all sides of his talent as an etcher. There are the crowded harbor scenes, which contain plenty of virility. Industrial views are always treated by Mr. Neilson with the necessary amount of vigor and he gives satisfying interpretations of that side of modern Canadian life." One of his etchings was reproduced in Newton MacTavish's *The Fine Arts In Canada* (1925). In 1921 Neilson was appointed professor of drawing, painting and anatomy at the Ecole des Beaux-Arts, Quebec, and many of his students became well-known artists. He later became principal of the Beaux-Arts. He was elected A.R.C.A. (1915); Society of Scottish Artists and the Quebec Society of Artists (organizer). He died in Quebec City at the age of sixty-six.[4] He is represented in the Nat. Gal. of Can., the Art Gallery of Ontario, the Quebec Provincial Museum and elsewhere.

References

[1] *The Canadian Men & Women Of The Time*, Morgan, 1912, P. 846

[2] *Canada And Its Provinces, Vol. XII,* Tor., 1914 "Painting" by E.F.B. Johnston, P. 625

[3] *The Telegraph-Journal*, Saint John, N.B., May 23, 1919 (article from Tor. *Mail & Empire* "Quebec Artist's Exhibit in Toronto")

[4] *The Globe*, Tor., Ont. Apr. 28, 1931 "Outstanding Artist is Dead at Quebec"

see also

The Fine Arts in Canada by Newton MacTavish, MacMillan, Tor., 1925, P. 68, op. 145

Canadian Landscape Painters by A.H. Robson, Ryerson, Tor., 1932, P. 112, 117

NEILSON, Henry Ivan (Cont'd)

Canadian Art, Its Origin and Development by William Colgate, Ryerson, Tor., 1943, P. 130, 210
Canadian Art By Graham McInnes, MacMillan, Tor., 1950, P. 45
Early Painters and Engravers in Canada by J. Russell Harper, Univ. Tor., Pr., 1970, P. 235
Art Gallery of Ontario, The Canadian Collection by Helen P. Bradfield, McGraw-Hill, Tor., 1970, P. 332
NGC Catalogue, Vol. 3 by R.H. Hubbard, Ott., 1960 P. 232, 233

NELLES, Arthur Douglas
b. 1917

Born in Ottawa, he studied at the Ottawa Technical School under E. Fosbery, Allan Beddoe and Allan Brooks and also studied art under William Hoople in New York City. He was on the staff of *Canadian Nature Magazine* and the National Museum of Canada. He worked in Detroit for a period at the Blair Hospital making drawings of operations. Some of his illustrations appeared in *Saturday Night.*

References
NGC Info. Form
Saturday Night, Tor., Apr. 5, 1949

NEMISH, Bryan

A painter from western Canada, Bryan Nemish received his Bachelor of Fine Arts Degree from the University of Manitoba in 1967, and his Master of Fine Art Degree from the Instituto Allende, Mexico in 1968. He was awarded a Canada Council Grant in 1967 and 1968. He has exhibited his work at the Manitoba Society of Artists 44th, the Alberta College of Art Staff Show in 1969, a group show at the Calhoun Gallery in 1970, the All Alberta '70, Environment '71, West '71, and the Alberta College of Art in 1972. He is a member of the staff of the Alberta College of Art.

Reference:
Catalogue, Alberta College of Art Gallery, Mar. 6, 1972

NEON, John (John Edward Masciuch)
b. 1944

Born in Ottawa, Ontario, John Masciuch was raised in Edmonton and gave guitar lessons before deciding to work with electricity and art. In 1968 he went to Vancouver and while attending City College also attended the Intermedia workshop where he experimented with neon tubes and ended up with a collection of 5,000 of them. It was there that he picked up the nick-name of Neon under which he now does all of his artistic work. He held his first one-man show in March of 1968 at

NEON, John (John Edward Masciuch) (Cont'd)

the Douglas Gallery in Vancouver and subsequent shows at the Vancouver Art Gallery (May, 1968; Sept., 1968), Art Gallery of Ontario (Nov., 1968, Sept., 1970), Theatre event Toronto (Sept., Dec., 1970). He was appointed artist in residence at the Three Schools in Toronto in 1969 and worked in the Multimedia workshop where he also held many shows and theatre events. In his art he uses electricity, light and sound and his neon tubes are sometimes activated by heat or electrical waves from the viewer's body. He has completed a commission for Ontario Place, Toronto (1970) and made special tapes for Chum FM Radio Station in Toronto. Living in Toronto in 1972. He has shown his work at the Carmen Lamanna Gallery, Toronto.

References

The Province, Van., B.C., June 21, 1968 "What John Neon can and cannot do"

Globe & Mail, Tor., Ont., Nov. 9, 1968 "Triumphant threesome with a dynamic stamp" by Kay Kritzwiser

Artscanada, December, 1968 Issue No. 124-127 "Sculpture and light: Toronto and Montreal' by Nan R. Piene

Toronto Daily Star, Ont., Oct. 17, 1969 "Our arts people are taken to task" by Jim Beebe

NÉRON, Gertrude

Born in Chicoutimi, she studied interior design and painting at the Ecole des Beaux Arts, Quebec, taking her painting instruction from Jean Paul Lemieux and Jean Dallaire and graduating with her diploma in 1951. She worked as an interior designer at the Studio Roger Dussault in Quebec City (1952-54) and then in Chicoutimi while spending some time at Columbia University in New York (1954-58). During this period she exhibited her work in Quebec and took a study trip to Cuba and Haiti. In 1958, she left on a three year trip to Europe where she studied decorative arts in Paris at l'Ecole des Arts et Techniques (Palais du Louvre) and art history at the Musée du Louvre. Returning to Canada she studied for her professorship at Les Beaux-Arts, Quebec, under Jean Soucy for a year then taught at the Atelier-Ecole du Centre des Arts de Chicoutimi and at the Ecole des Beaux-Arts, Quebec (1965-68). She is known for her drawings, paintings and mobile sculptures which she creates from her imagination and impressions. They reflect her attempts to express spontaneity, vivacity and the joy of life. Her work has strong lines, bright and well-blended colours.

References

Chronicle-Telegraph, Que., P.Q., Mar. 4, 1971 "Neron Exhibit Characterized by Spontaneity and Movement" by R.D.

Le Soleil-L'Evénement, Que., P.Q., Mar. 13, 1971 "Gertrude Néron Expose"

L'Action, Que., P.Q., Mar. 4, 1971 "Exposition de Gertrude Néron au Foyer du Palais Montcalm"

La Patrie, Mtl, P.Q., Jan. 6, 1972 "Quand la peinture devient musicale" by Leon Bernard

NESBITT, John
b. 1928

Born in Montreal, P.Q., he studied French and English literature at Sir George Williams University and attended evening art classes at the College (1955-56) and evening instruction in drawing under Eric Byrd (1955) then he entered day classes at the Ecole des Beaux-Arts, Montreal, where he studied graphic arts under Albert Dumouchel and sculpture under Armand Filion (1956-57). He participated in the show Painters under Thirty in 1956, 57, 58, 59 and the Quebec Provincial Competition, 1957 and 1964 when he won the first prize for sculpture. He began to exhibit his work in the Spring Exhibition of the Montreal Museum of Fine Arts in 1958 and subsequently in 1963, 64 and 1965 when he won a prize for his sculpture. During 1960 and 1961 he had studied in Paris on a Canada Council Scholarship and received an additional Scholarship in 1961-62 to continue work there. Returning to Canada he moved toward prominence with his winning sculpture which took first prize at the Quebec Provincial Competition and the following year took another prize at the Spring Show. In the 1970's his sculpture has taken a futuristic streamlined look of smooth spheres, egg-like forms, cubes and other simplified shapes which he then etches with a single crestlike design. A photo reproduction of this work can be seen in the book *Canadian Artists in Exhibition* (1974). Nesbitt held his first one-man show in 1964 at Galerie Agnes Lefort, Montreal when Michael Ballantyne of *The Montreal Star* noted, "One gets the distinct impression that Mr. Nesbitt has an almost instinctive feeling for these raw materials, a sense of sympathy and also a sense of respect for their properties and for the great tradition stretching back into the centuries past . . . . Mr. Nesbitt's combination of metal and stone – in some cases pieces of pebble and polished semi-precious rocks – works wonders. He also uses silver, zinc and a variety of other minerals in the composition of his mysterious, totemish figures. As pure exercises in form and design, incorporating the products of our native earth, they are very satisfying and an almost unreserved pleasure. A private art, perhaps, but not so private that we cannot share in its delights. His achievement lies in the success with which he is able to combine his materials – bronze, onyx, ceramic, marble – so that they work together naturally and one has no suspicion that the artist is forcing them into an uneasy partnership. Their shape reflects Mr. Nesbitt's own interest in primitive art and reinforces the strong whiff of archaeology that was one of my first reactions." He has participated in several other group shows including International Exhibition, Granby (1958), Salon de la Jeune Peinture (1958, 59), Salon de la Jeune Sculpture, Musée Rodin, Paris (1965) and the Winnipeg Show (1961, Hon. Mention). His commissions include two sculptures for Expo '67, one of which was donated to the University of Moncton and placed between the Science and Arts Buildings. He is a member of the Quebec Sculptors' Society and the Sculptors' Society of Canada. Lives at Westport, Conn.

References

Le Devoir, Mtl., P.Q., 2 May, 1964 "John Nesbitt"
La Presse, Mtl., P.Q., 2 May, 1964 "John Nesbitt: d'insolites alliages naturels"
The Montreal Star., P.Q., 9 April, 1965 "Wrangling Good for Arts Playwright Gelinas Says" by Wouter De Wet
Ibid, 29 May, 1965 "New Exhibition – John Nesbitt, Sculptor" by Michael Ballantyne
The Gazette, Mtl., P.Q., May 29, 1965 "Jury's Choice" by Rea Montbizon
Moncton Transcript, N.B., July 16, 1969 "New Art Piece For UM Campus"
NGC Info. Form, June 30, 1953 also form undated.

NESBITT, John (Cont'd)

Books
Canadian Sculpture Expo '67 Introd. by William Withrow, Ed. Natan Karczmar, Graph, Mtl., 1967, Plate 21, 41
L'Art Au Quebec Depuis 1940 par Guy Robert, LaPresse, 1973, P. 252
Canadian Artists in Exhibition (1974), Roundstone Council for the Arts, Tor., 1974, P. 187

NESBITT, Prynce

Born in St. Catharines, Ontario, he is known as a Hamilton artist. Due to his fascination with people, his work consists mainly of portraits in charcoal and oil. He begins his work with large areas of light and shade then adds specific details and completes his painting in a little over an hour. He is also known for his interest and talent in music and astrology and is considered one of Toronto's thirty-two most interesting men. He once had a radio show on which he appeared as a pianist. He was an organist and choirmaster at St. James Anglican Church in St. Catharines. He has taught night classes in art at Winston Churchill secondary school in St. Catharines. Represented by the Beckett Gallery, Hamilton, in 1968.

References
Peterborough Examiner, Ont., Oct. 22, 1968 (CP) 'Artist Named After Family's Pet'' by Joan Phillips of *The St. Catharines Standard*

NESTOREL, Prince Monyo Simon Mihaelesque

Born in Bucharest, Romania, he employed court artists to decorate castles he once owned in prewar Romania. He was educated at the Sorbonne and in Florence, Italy. After the Second World War he was a political prisoner for seven years. Then he left Europe and worked under Rufina Tamayo in Mexico. He arrived in Toronto in 1963 with only three dollars in his pocket and began painting and sculpting many different subjects in several styles and in 1969 was reported to be worth a quarter of a million dollars. He owns his own gallery and foundry in Toronto's Yorkville where he executes and sells his work. He has exhibited in numerous cities in the United States as well as in Toronto and Montreal. He is also represented in many private collections. His sculptures have been commissioned by many large Toronto developers including John Ennis and C.H. Dolman.

References
Herald, Fonthill, Ont., July 12, 1966 "Prince Monyo holds One Man Art Exhibit"
Toronto Daily Star, Ont., Jan. 25, 1969 "An artist who's living like a king" by Gail Dexter

NEUENDORFF, Wilhelm
b. 1897

Born in Altwerpel, Estonia, he became interested in painting about the age of fif-

NEUENDORFF, Wilhelm (Cont'd)

teen however his talent was not discovered until he was twenty. He received his training at the School of Art in Tallinn, Estonia (1923-27) then took further studies privately under Prof. A. Laipman (1927-30). He held solo shows in Estonia and Germany and came to Canada in 1951 where he established himself as a painter of portraits, landscapes, still lifes and composition. He also taught painting in his former studio in Winnipeg. He works in oils, water colours, tempera, pastel, chalk and ceramics (Master of Ceramics). A member of the Manitoba Society of Artists and a former member of the Winnipeg Sketch Club, he lives in Winnipeg.

References
Winnipeg Sketch Club by Madeline Perry and Lily Hobbs, 1970
150 Years of Art In Manitoba, The Winnipeg Art Gallery, 1970, P. 96
Document from artist, 1963

NEUMANN Ernst
1907-1955

Born in Budapest, Hungary, he came to Canada with his Austrian parents in 1912 at the age of five. He studied at the Ecole des Beaux-Arts and life classes of the Royal Canadian Academy (at the Art Association of Montreal). He entered a lithography shop as an apprentice and during this period developed a personal interest in lithography, woodcuts, and other printed forms of the graphic arts. He was also a sculptor of note. He was inspired by the masters including Sir Joshua Reynolds, Rembrandt, Renoir, van Gogh and others. Early in his career Neumann became known for his fine lithographs, etchings and woodcuts. In the fall of 1936 he shared a studio with Goodridge Roberts and they founded the Roberts-Neumann School of Art. They had been students at the Ecole des Beaux-Arts around 1924. Viewing his work in 1939 *The Montreal Standard* noted "Etchings, lithographs and woodcuts in the Art Association print room make it clear that Ernst Neumann is a thoroughly metropolitan artist. He gets his pictures in the city streets and alleys and in the studio – nudes and painters and onlookers in the studio, down-and-outs on park benches or living on the grass of Fletcher's Field, lawyers gathered outside the courts, hymn-singers on the street corner, beggars on the pavement, urchins playing in back lanes – this is the stuff that appeals to his sharp eye, for registration by a skilled hand. He is at his best, I feel, in the detail of character, whether it be in a clump of old buildings or in the folds of a face or an old garment." Neumann exhibited his work at a number of places over the years including the following: Art Assoc. of Montreal/Museum of Fine Arts (Print Rm., 1939, Contemp. Art Room, 1950; Gal. XII, 1952); Arts Club of Montreal (1941, 1945); Temple Emanu – El. Mtl. (1942, 1943); Cercle Universitaire, Mtl. (1951); Henry Morgan Store, Mtl. (1953); Snowdon Y.M.-Y.W.H.A. (1954). He was delegated in 1954 by the Canadian Arts Council to attend the UNESCO sponsored congress which met in the Cini Palace on the Isle of St. Giorgio near Venice. He was awarded a government overseas fellowship by the Royal Society of Canada in 1955 to study in France and while at Venice died of a heart attack in his 48th year. Several showings of his work took place after his death: Art Gallery of Hamilton (1958), Montreal Museum of Fine Arts (1958), UNB Art Centre (1959) all sponsored by the National Gallery of Canada.

NEUMANN, Ernst (Cont'd)

References
The Gazette, Mtl., P.Q., 22 April, 1939 "Ernst Neumann Shows Etchings and Lithos"
The Montreal Standard, P.Q., Apr. 29, 1939 "Black and White"
Saturday Night, Tor., Ont., Jan. 27, 1940 "Satire and a Touch of Sentiment"
The Gazette, Mtl., P.Q., Feb. 22, 1941 "Ernst Neumann Shows Work at the Arts Club"
Ibid, April 28, 1945 "Ernst Neumann Holds Exhibit at Arts Club"
The Montreal Standard, P.Q., Mar. 4, 1950 "Self Portrait"
Ibid, Dec. 2, 1950 "An Artist Looks At The Law"
The Gazette, Mtl., P.Q., 8 Dec., 1951 "Ernst Neumann Shows Portraits and Scenes"
Ibid, Oct. 18, 1952 "Three Artists Showing At Fine Arts Museum"
The Montreal Star, P.Q., Oct. 25, 1952 "Art Notes – Three Types Of Paintings Now On View" by Robert Ayre
Le Petit Journal, Mtl., P.Q., Oct. 11, 1953 "Le peintre Ernst Neumann a reconstruit Montréal" par Paul Gladu
The Montreal Star, P.Q., Feb. 27, 1954 "Art Notes – Two Exhibitions: Scott, Neumann" by Robert Ayre
Ibid, Nov. 20, 1954 "Canada's Art Attitude Attacked by Delegate"
Weekend Magazine, Mtl., P.Q., 17 Sept., 1955 "Danger! Artist At Work" Photos by Louis Jaques
The Hamilton Spectator, Ont., 2 Oct., 1958 "Ernst Neumann Paintings Highlight Art Gallery's First Show Of Season" by Ian Vorres
The Gazette, Mtl., 20 Dec., 1958 "Ernst Neumann's Art In Retrospect"
Le Devoir, Mtl., Dec. 24, 1958 "Formes et Couleurs – A la mémoire d'Ernst Neumann" par René Chicoine
Daily Gleaner, Fred., N.B., Jan. 19, 1959 "Art Exhibition at UNB Said Interesting"
Canadian Jewish Congress Bulletin, February, 1959
The Montreal Star, P.Q., Oct. 30, 1968 "The Art Scene – Retrospective of Boultbee, Neumann" by Robert Ayre
NGC Info. Form rec'd May 4, 1932
Canadian Jewish Weekly, Tor., Ont. Mar. 28, 1959 "He Reaffirmed Humanity In Art" by Harry Mayerovitch
Books, magazines and catalogues
Canadian Art, Vol. 7, No. 2, 1949-50 "Ernst Neumann as a Painter" by Goodridge Roberts, P. 47-50
Canadian Art by Graham McInnes, MacMillan, Tor., 1950, P. 95
Canadian Drawings and Prints by Paul Duval, 1952, Burns & MacEachern, Tor., 1952, Plate 46
The National Gallery of Canada Catalogue, Vol. 3 by R.H. Hubbard, Ott., 1960, P. 233
Sir George Williams University Collection of Art by Edwy F. Cooke, Mtl., 1967, P. 146
A Retrospective Exhibition of Goodridge Roberts, catalogue by James Borcoman, NGC/Queen's Printer, 1969 (Chronology, P. 46)

NEUMANN, Manfred

A Collingwood, Ontario, artist who is a prolific painter with remarkable versatility. Much of his subject matter comes from around the Collingwood area district particularly landscapes. He has exhibited his work at the Skelton Galleries in Collingwood.

Reference
Enterprise Bulletin, Collingwood, Ont. April 2, 1970 (photo of artist and his work)

NEVILLE, Maureen (Mrs.)
b. 1921
Born in Hereford, England, she came to Canada in 1949 to Scarboro, Ontario, and has exhibited her work in one-woman shows in movie theatres and public places. She sold a seascape to Coutts Hallmark of Toronto for use in calendars.

Reference
NGC Info. form

NEVITT, Richard
b. (c) 1937
A Toronto artist and a member of the faculty of the Ontario College of Art he has completed commissions for the Canadian government to record activity of the Canadian UN force on the island of Cyprus (1968). Some of his paintings and etchings were acquired for the Canadian War Museum collection. His pen and ink and pencil etchings shown at the Art Gallery of Dunnville, Ontario, in 1971 consisted mainly of Maritime boat scenes of Toronto and Cobalt.

References
The Stag, Shilo, Man., Feb. 13, 1969 "Artists Brush Up On the Forces"
Welland-Port Colborne Tribune, Ont., Apr. 21, 1971 "One Man Show Feature At Dunnville's 'The Gallery' "

NEWCOMBE, William John Bertram
1907-1969
Born in Victoria, B.C., son of Mr. and Mrs. A.H. Newcombe he attended King Edward High School in Vancouver. He was largely self-taught in art although he took some private lessons from F.H. Varley for a short time. He did cartooning early in his career and also worked at commercial art as well as being staff artist for the Vancouver *Province*. He left B.C. in 1936 and settled in the Toronto area where he remained until the Second World War. He enlisted in the R.C.A.F. in 1941 and served overseas as an air-gunner and completed sixteen flights over Europe before his plane was shot down. He broke his leg in the parachute jump that followed and spent some time in convalescence when he did sketches of his experiences. Returning home he was discharged in 1945 with the rank of Flying Officer. He remained in Toronto where he held an exhibition of paintings at the Canadian Women's Art Association and at Vancouver Art Gallery (1946). He then left for Mexico where he lived for a year (1946-47) then returned to Toronto. He held a one-man show at Ferargil Galleries, NYC (1946) and other shows in Texas, St. Louis, Iowa and Connecticut. He exhibited with the American Water Color Society (1947, 48); The California Water Colour Society (1947); the Ontario Society of Artists; the Royal Canadian Academy; B.C. Society of Artists; Can. Society of Graphic Art (served as Pres.). In 1947 he became a member of the California Water Color Society. He made his home in Europe in 1955 and for the most part in England. He held one-man shows at the Obelisk Gallery, Lond. (1956);

1365

NEWCOMBE, William John Bertram (Cont'd)

Galerie El Corsario, Ibiza (1956); Galerie Iris Clert, Paris (1957); Stadtisches Museum, Wuppertal (1957) Duisberg (1959); Art Gallery of Toronto (1958); New Vision Gallery, London, Eng. (1958, 59, 62, 64, 65); Galeria El Corsario, Ibiza (1960); Portal Gallery, Lond. Eng. (1961); Grosvenor Gallery, Lon. Eng. (1961); Manchester City Art Gallery, Manch. (1961); Jerrold Morris Art Gallery, Tor. (1962); Reid Gal. Lond. Eng. (1962); Stone Gallery, Newcastle-on-Tyne (1962); Elizabeth Manor House Gallery, Ilkley (1962); County Town Gallery, Lewes (1964); Heal's Art Gallery, Lond. Eng. (1964); Arts Council, Karachi, Pakistan (1964); Nicholas Treadwell Gallery, Croydon (1965). He visited Canada in the summer of 1958 but returned to England where he remained. Viewing his 1962 showing at the Elizabethan Manor House at Ilkley, W.E. Johnson of *The Manchester Guardian* noted, "Newcombe comes closest to the work of the American Sam Francis in the moist images of his occasional watercolours. It is, however, in his canvases of oil, plaster, and graffiti that he communicates the most powerful of his experiences. From time to time he adds a profusion of burlap, bent matchsticks, and cut pieces of rope, but it is pointless to analyse the ingredients from which he fashions his work. And again, since the things he creates have no known point of physical reference, we can only describe the flavour of his work – its superb control, its forceful conviction, its quiet undemonstrative strength, and its essential 'rightness' which evokes a sensual pleasure somewhere midway between the coldly clinical pure mathematics of the constructivist and the passionate heat of the Fauve." Newcombe died at the age of sixty-two in London, England. He married Margaret Murphy of Vancouver, a former editor of the CCF News in Ontario. He is represented in the following collections: Boston Museum of Fine Art; Illinois State Museum (Springfield, Ill.); Philbrook Art Centre (Tulsa); Joslyn Memorial Art Museum (Omaha, Neb.); William Rockhill Nelson Gallery (Kansas); Manchester City Gallery; Wadsworth Atheneum, (Conn., U.S.A.); Leicester Education Committee; Whitworth Art Gallery (Manchester); Odessa Art Museum (Odessa, U.S.S.R.); National Gallery Of Israel (Tel Aviv); The Isaac Delgado Museum and Art Gallery (New Orleans, Louisiana); National Gallery of New South Wales (Sydney, Australia).

References

Beacon-Herald, Stratford, Ont., Nov. 15, 1938 "Bill Newcombe of Clinton Is Talented Cartoonist"

News-Herald, Van. B.C., Jan. 23, 1946 "B.C. Artists Hold One-Man Gallery Shows" by Browni Wingate

The Province, Van., B.C., Jan. 25, 1946 "Displays by Two City Artists Show Fine Creative Powers" by Palette

The Toronto Star, Ont., Mar. 15, 1948 "Painter Here Sells To Illinois Museum"

Globe & Mail, Tor., Oct. 30, 1948 "Art and Artists – Newcombe Finds Drama In Mexico" by Pearl McCarthy

The Province, Van. B.C., July 28, 1950 "Ex-City Man Now Tops As Artist"

The Toronto Telegram, Ont., Sept. 10, 1955 (article about his activities)

Manchester Guardian, April 11, 1957

The Toronto Telegram, Ont., Nov. 25, 1950 "At The Galleries – Strength And Clarity In Newcombe's Work" by Rose MacDonald

The Toronto Star, Ont., Feb. 4, 1955 "Solo Show Opens New Art Gallery" by Hugh Thomson

Globe & Mail, Tor., Ont., May 31, 1958 "Canadian Artist Back But Only for Summer"

The Province, Van. B.C., Mar. 10, 1959 "City Artist's works open London show"

NEWCOMBE, William John Bertram (Cont'd)

Manchester Guardian, Eng., 9 Oct., 1962 "William Newcombe Exhibition at Ilkley" by W.E. Johnson
The Toronto Star, Ont., Oct. 28, 1969 "William Newcombe Canadian Painter"
The Vancouver Sun, B.C., Nov. 5, 1969 "Former City Artist Dies In London"
The Colonist, Victoria, B.C., Nov. 9, 1969 "Victoria-Born Painter Dies at 62"
NGC Information forms

NEWFELD, Frank

b. 1928

A Toronto, Ontario, illustrator, typographer, book designer who has produced hundreds of designs and illustrations for which he has won 113 or more awards. He received his early training in costume design under Cochran in England and made costumes for the theatre then for many years was involved in design for the publishing industry. After serving as Vice-President of Publishing with McClelland and Stewart he returned to clothing design as joint president of Macpherson Newfeld Fashions Limited, a partnership he shares with Rose Macpherson, his mother. Newfeld has also been commissioned to design catalogues for the National Gallery of Canada and still handles two or three major designing projects a year despite the time he spends on fashion design. He lives at Agincourt, Ontario. Associate Royal Canadian Academy, and R.C.A.-elect (1973).

References
The Mirror, Downsview-Weston Edition, Ont., Oct. 7, 1970 "Rose Macpherson – where good design is relevant"
Winchester Press, Winchester, Ont., Sept. 3, 1964 "Ontario Reveals Official Symbol For Centennial"
Canadian Art, May 1960 (special issue of graphic design) Pages 140, 141, 147, 149, 150, 153
Royal Canadian Academy of Arts Membership List, 1974

NEWHOUSE, Max

An artist from Nanaimo, B.C., who is mainly self-taught in painting and sculpture. He has exhibited his work at the Discoveries Exhibition at the Burnaby Art Gallery and has made much of his own home furniture and is a plumber by trade. In 1971 he was planning to spend two months with his cameras travelling remote areas of B.C. accompanied by his wife Lillian and his son Zake. He was then to begin a new series of paintings based on what he had seen.

References
Nanaimo Free Press, Feb. 28, 1970 "City Can Have Statue – For About $3,500"
Nanaimo Times, B.C., Mar. 4, 1970 "Art Showing"
The Province, Van., B.C., July 2, 1971 "Art – An inner vision" by Ken Spotswood

NEWMAN, H.J.

A Georgetown, Ontario, painter Major Newman took his first instruction under F.S. Challener and F.H. Brigden. He then studied in Paris at l'Ecole des Beaux-Arts under Xavier Brichard and Paul Chabos; at the Polytechnic School of Art, London, England and privately under Leonard Richmond, Leonard Walker and a summer course under Sir Frank Brangwyn.

References
    Herald, Georgetown, Sept. 2, 1959 "Artists Newman, Schaap Prepare Exhibition, Sale"

NEWMAN, Jean (Mrs.)

She studied four seasons at the Doon School of Fine Art and exhibited her paintings at the Grenadier Restaurant, High Park, and at Simpson's Toronto. Her favourite subjects are landscapes in all seasons in Canada, U.S.A., Wales, Germany and Mexico. Controller for the City of Toronto in 1959.

References
    The Toronto Telegram, Oct. 2, 1957 "One-Woman Show By Mrs. Newman"
    Herald, North Toronto, May 29, 1959
    Free Press, North Toronto, May 29, 1959 "Con. Newman's Paintings On View This Week At Grenadier Restaurant"

NEWMAN, John Beatty
b. 1933

Born in Toronto, Ontario, he graduated from Parkdale Collegiate Institute (1952) and entered the Ontario College of Art where he graduated with honours (1952-56). In the year of his graduation from O.C.A. he won first prize in an international paintings competition "Sports Hall of Fame" at the Canadian National Exhibition. He did post-graduate studies at the Academy of Cincinnati (1956-57) where he won a drawing prize and a graduate division scholarship (1957). He worked closely with Harley Parker and Marshall McLuhan on the staff of the Royal Ontario Museum as an exhibit designer and continued to paint and exhibit in group shows. He joined the faculty of the Ontario College of Art in 1964 and in the same year participated in the exhibition "Surrealism in Canadian Painting". In 1966 he was awarded a Canada Council Grant and travelled in England, France, Belgium, Holland, Germany, Spain and studied 15th and 16th Century Flemish painting. In 1971-72 he travelled and studied in Europe for four months in Belgium, France, Germany and Austria. During this period he lived and painted in England and had two works accepted by the Royal Academy. At home he won the Honour Award of the Canadian Society of Painters in Water Colour and the A.E. Ames Purchase Award of the same society. He also became a member of the Canadian Society of Graphic Art (1957) and the Royal Canadian Academy. His one-man shows include: Victoria College, Univ. Tor. (1964); Rodman Hall Arts Centre,

NEWMAN, John Beatty (Cont'd)

St. Catharines, Ont. (1969); Lefebvre Gallery, Edmonton, Alta. (1971); St. Michael's College, Univ. Tor. (1971); Althouse College, Univ. Western Ontario (1973); Art Gallery, Erindale College (1973); Art Gallery, Gander International Airterminal, Nfld. (1974); Corner Brook Arts & Culture Centre (1974); Grand Falls Art & Culture Centre (1974); Memorial University Art Gallery, St. John's (1974). Viewing his 1973 show at Erindale College, Kay Kritzwiser of the *Globe & Mail* noted, "As paintings, they are a tender assessment of people – in this case, of little girls, balancing tentatively on that delicate line between childhood and adolescence. In this aspect, Newman's paintings do have a compositional resemblance to the strange, crowded humanistic works of Spencer . . . . To capture this natural process of growth, Newman leans on legends and symbols, some treading a fine line between realism and surrealism." He is represented in public and private collections in Canada, United States and England.

References

Catalogue with chronology, Scarborough College, Univ. Tor. show Jan. 10 - Feb. 3, 1974
Catalogue for travelling exhibition, 1973-74
Globe & Mail, Oct., 1973 "Art – A tender look at little girls" by Kay Kritzwiser
NGC Info. Form rec'd July 7, 1958

NEWTON, Alison Houston (Mrs. Stanley Newton)
b. 1890

Born in Edinburgh, Scotland, she studied at Trinity Academy, Edinburgh (1900-05) and privately under David Wallace. She won many prizes when in high school and for her teachers' studies in Edinburgh. She came to Winnipeg, Manitoba in 1910 and worked as a commercial artist with the T. Eaton Company (1910-1916). She married Stanley Newton in 1916 and in 1918 joined the Fashion Art Department of Brigden's in Winnipeg. She continued her studies at the Winnipeg School of Art under Alex Musgrove and Frank Johnston and also took private lessons under W.J. Phillips for water colour and wood block print work. She won a medal for the Winnipeg Sketch Club for landscape painting in 1929. She became an Associate member of the Manitoba Society of Artists in 1928, full member in 1932, Secretary, Vice-President, and President (1943-45); member Federation of Canadian Artists (1943) on the Executive; delegate to Canadian Arts Council and National Council of the Federation of Canadian Artists in Toronto, 1947. She exhibited at the National Gallery of Canada, Ottawa, 1932 and with the Royal Canadian Academy; Art Association of Montreal; Canadian Society of Painters in Water Colour; Canadian Society of Painter-Etchers and Engravers. Living in Winnipeg in 1947.

References

NGC Info. Forms rec'd Oct. 1, 1930; May 17, 1947
Winnipeg Sketch Club by Madeline Perry and Lily Hobbs, 1970
Winnipeg Tribune, Man., April 21, 1945 (photo of artist and her work)

NEWTON, Garry
b. 1939

Born in York, England, he emigrated with his family to Medicine Hat, Alberta. He graduated from Medicine Hat High School (1957); studied zoology at the University of Alberta. He started painting and sketching while on a geological survey team one summer near the Arctic Circle. He visited Greece where he was immediately captivated by the beauty of the land. He returned to university in Canada but finally decided to go back to Greece. In 1964 he concluded his affairs in Canada and settled in the village of Lindos of the Aegean Islands. He started painting and creating sculptures in the Byzantine tradition using scrap iron and metal pieces either welded, nailed, or hooked together. He received a commission to build a ten foot Byzantine sculpture near Athens. His parents live in Medicine Hat where Garry makes periodic visits.

Reference
Medicine Hat News, Alta., Aug. 27, 1968 "Local artist sets up studio on Aegean Island"

NEWTON, Lilias Torrance
b. 1896

Born in Montreal, P.Q., daughter of Forbes and Alice (Stewart) Torrance, she began painting at the age of twelve.[1] She received her formal education at Miss Edgar and Miss Cramp's secondary school, Montreal. Then she enrolled in the School of The Art Association of Montreal where she studied under William Brymner (c. 1914) and won two scholarships. During the First World War the Torrance family became fully involved when three of her brothers went to the Front and she herself, with her mother, joined the Red Cross and served overseas.[2] At the conclusion of the war she studied painting for a few months under Alfred Wolmark, a Russian artist who was living in London. Wolmark stimulated her sense of colour.[3] Returning to Canada she began to paint on her own. Then in 1920 with Edwin Holgate, Randolph Hewton, and Mabel May she discovered rooms on Beaver Hall Hill which they rented for use as studios.[4] For a short period, a group of former students of the Art Association of Montreal made it their headquarters. In 1921 Lilias Torrance married Fred G. Newton. Her husband gave her the encouragement and freedom she needed for artistic development. She travelled to Europe in 1923 and studied four months in Paris under Alexandre Jacovleff. Jacovleff, a Russian artist, was considered to be an exceptionally fine draughtsman and was recommended to her by Edwin Holgate. Jacovleff was a member of a group of painters, musicians and dramatists who made their home in Paris following the Russian Revolution.[5] Working many hours each day on chalk drawings from life she was able to develop a new technique and a better understanding of picture construction which she was later to incorporate into her painting.[6] She exhibited in the Paris Salon in 1923 and received honourable mention for her life size painting of Miss Denise Lamontagne of Montreal, the painting was simply entitled "Denise".[7] Returning to Canada the same year she was elected an Associate of the Royal Canadian Academy becoming the youngest member of this society. She received her full membership in 1937 and became the third woman member of the Academy. By 1921 two of her paintings had been acquired by the National Gallery of Canada,

"Nonnie" and "The Little Sisters" and at the Panama Pacific Exhibition of 1925 "Yvonne" was awarded Honourable Mention and purchased for the permanent collection of the Los Angeles Museum. In 1926 her son Forbes was born. In 1927 praise of her work by the *Saturday Night*[8] went as follows, "It is the successful combination of qualities in Mrs. Newton's work that makes it outstanding. She is not only a fine draughtsman, with a keen sense of form and line, but a colourist who can achieve the most charming decorative effects by simple means. And she is by no means merely a decorative artist, but a student of human nature, with an insight which has left its impress upon some of her fine portraits, — portraits that are a genuine contribution to the world's gallery of personalities. Her work has been likened to Sir William Orpen's in England. Like him, she has style, and she faithfully records what she herself has truly seen." In 1933 she became a founding member of the Canadian Group of Painters. Graham McInnes[9] describing her work in the 1950's added "Lilias Newton, adopting the pure colour and flat areas of the Group (of Seven) to a more sophisticated and personal approach, became Canada's leading portraitist. Her simplified use of bold planes enabled her to effect subtle characterizations and to take the curse off 'official' portraiture." It is in her portraits of friends and associates that she has achieved her warmest results. Charles Hill in his catalogue *Canadian Painting In The Thirties* (1975) points out that this success is due to a greater personal identification between the sitter and artist when friends or models are chosen. She gave private classes during the early thirties and in 1934 she teamed up with Edwin Holgate to teach for two years at the School of the Art Association of Montreal until funds ran out (the artists bore full financial responsibility). Then in 1938 they teamed up again when the school was re-opened this time under the Art Association's support and the school flourished with an added distinguished staff. Newton and Holgate departed from the school in 1940. In the meantime she had been doing portraits of members of the Southam family, and many of her friends and associates including two members of the Group of Seven. She was a friend of A.Y. Jackson almost from the time she first began to paint and her portrait of him is one of the finest done (in NGC). Lawren Harris was so pleased with her portrait of him that he would offer it for a substitute every time someone wanted his photograph.[11] It too was acquired by the National Gallery of Canada. In that period and the years that followed she also did portraits of others including: Queen Elizabeth; Prince Philip; Earl Alexander; Frère Adelard; Air Vice-M.L.S. Breadner (R.C.A.F.); André Biéler (artist); Eric Brown (Dir. NGC); Newton Brett (airman); John E. Brownlee (Premier Alta.); Mrs. Bongard (Tor.); Mr. & Mrs. Brooke Claxton; Sr. Wm. Clark (British High Comm.); Dr. Chas. Camsell (Min. Mines & Res.); Miss Cramp (former teacher of Mrs. Newton); Gen. H.D.G. Crerar; The Rev. F.H. Cosgrove (Prov. Trinity College); W.F. Chipman, K.C., D.C.L.; Mrs. Tandy Davoud; J. Shirley Denison, K.C.; Miss Edgar (former teacher of Mrs. Newton); R.Y. Eaton (Pres. AGT); Dr. C.S. Fosbery (Principal, Lower Can. College); Dr. John Falconbridge, K.C.; Dr. Hamilton Fyfe (Princ. Queen's Univ.); Col. G.R. Geary (M.P. Tor.); W/C A.H.S. Gillson (R.C.A.F.); Henri Hébert (artist); Hon. A.G. Hardy (Spkr. of Senate); Edwin Holgate (artist); Major Holgate (Mtl.); Eric Kierans (financial advisor & former Fed. Cabinet Minister); Frances Loring (artist); Vincent Massey; Alice Massey; Louis Muhlstock (artist); Frances McCall; Col. R.S. McLaughlin; Gen. A.G.L. McNaughton; W. Ross MacDonald, K.C.; Dalton L. McCarthy, K.C.; Mrs. T.W.L. MacDermot; Chas. McRea, K.C.;

NEWTON, Lilias Torrance (Cont'd)

F.E. Meredith, K.C.; Dr. Norman MacKenzie (UBC); Mrs. W.J. Northgrave (Tor.); Forbes Newton (son); Lieut. Susan O'Reilly (WRCNS); Mr. Alan Plaunt; Mrs. Alan Plaunt; Albert Robinson (artist); Mrs. Savage (Mtl.); Miss Ethel Southam; Miss Janet Southam; H.S. Southam; W.S. Southam; Mrs. Wilson Tory (scientist); Miss Josette Vaillancourt; Dr. R.C. Wallace (Principal, Queen's Univ.). In all, she has done over three hundred portraits of which the above are only a few. She is represented in the following collections: Edmonton Museum, Alta.; Calgary Museum, Alta.; Art Gallery of Ontario; Hart House Univ. Tor.; National Gallery of Canada, Ott.; Montreal Museum of Fine Arts; Musée du Quebec; Canadian War Collection, War Museum, Ott. and elsewhere. She lives in Montreal.

References

[1] *The Herald*, Lethbridge, Alta., Aug. 30, 1946 "Foremost Canadian Woman Artist Visits City on First Trip West"

[2] *Saturday Night*, Vol. XLII, No. 52, 12 Nov., 1927 "Canadian Woman in the Public Eye" P. 35

[3] Ibid

[4] *The Beaver Hall Hill Group* (catalogue), NGC, Introduction by Norah McCullough

[5] *The Gazette*, Mtl., P.Q., May 9, 1923 "Canadian Artist At Paris"

[6] *Sat. Night* see[2]

[7] Ibid

[8] *Sat. Night* see[2]

[9] *Canadian Art* by Graham McInnes, MacMillan, Tor., 1950, P. 73

[10] *Canadian Painting in the Thirties* by Charles C. Hill/NGC, 1970, P. 40

[11] *The Nude in Canadian Painting* by Jerrold Morris, New Press, Tor., 1972, P. 12

Newspapers

The Gazette, Mtl., P.Q., May 9, 1923 "Canadian Artist At Paris – Mrs. Torrance Newton, Montreal, Exhibits at Salon"

The Toronto Telegram, Tor., Ont., May 17, 1930 " 'Group of Seven' Portrait Painter at Work Here"

Saturday Night, Tor., Ont., May 31, 1930 "A Gracious Artist"

The Gazette, Mtl., P.Q., Oct. 18, 1932 "Lilias T. Newton Shows Portraits – Montreal Painter Reveals Possibilities of Charcoal at Arts Club"

The Montreal Star, P.Q., April (?), 1934 "Art Association Classes To Re-Open – Edwin Holgate and Lilias Torrance Newton, A.R.C.A. to Be in Charge"

The Ottawa Journal, Ont., Nov. 20, 1937 "Artists Honor Third Woman – Academy Elects Mrs. L.T. Newton to Membership"

The Montreal Standard, Dec. 17, 1938 "Canadian Art and Artists – Lilias Torrance Newton, R.C.A. – Well Known Montreal Portrait Painter and Teacher" by Richard H. Haviland

The Gazette, Mtl., P.Q., Oct. 28, 1939 "Portraits by Lilias T. Newton, R.C.A., Form Interesting Exhibition" by St. George Burgoyne

Ibid, Mar. 7, 1941 "Portraits Of Noted Educationalists" (Miss Edgar, Miss Cramp)

The Ottawa Journal, Ont., Feb. 24, 1945 "Unique Style Marks Newton Portraits"

The Ottawa Citizen, Ont., Feb. 24, 1945 "Portraits By Lilias Newton Seen In Important Exhibition" by E.W.H.

The Herald, Lethbridge, Alta., Aug. 30, 1946 "Foremost Canadian Woman Artist Visits City on First Trip West"

The Vancouver Sun, B.C., Oct. 11, 1946 "Successful Portrait Painter Must Know Human Nature" by Frank Rasky

The Ottawa Citizen, Ont., Nov. 19, 1951 "New Vision In An Old Art" by Carl Weiselberger

The Toronto Star, Ont., Sept. 27, 1956 "Montreal Woman Will Paint Queen and Duke"

The Montrealer, Mtl., February, 1957 "Arts – Lilias Torrance Newton Painter Of The Queen"

NEWTON, Lilias Torrance (Cont'd)

La Presse, Mtl., P.Q., Jan. 25, 1958 "La première Canadienne à peindre la reine et le duc, à Buckingham Palace"
Calgary Herald, Alta., Aug. 30, 1961 "Painter Prefers Restricted Field" by Martin Gerwin
London Evening Free Press, Ont., Sept. 27, 1958 "Lilias Newton Commentator On Canvas" by Lenore Crawford
Victoria Colonist, Victoria, B.C., Aug. 24, 1965 "At the Gallery – Clock Goes Back For Newton Show" by Ina D.D. Uhthoff
NGC Info. Form, Aug. 22, 1946 & form undated
Books
Canadian Art, Its Origin And Development by William Colgate, Ryerson, Tor., 1943 (Paperback, 1967), P. 133, 228-230
A Painter's Country by A.Y. Jackson, Clarke, Irwin, Tor., 1963, P. 38, 61, 84, 120
Canadian Paintings In Hart House by J. Russell Harper, Univ. Tor. Pr., 1955, P. 56
NGC Catalogue, Vol. 3 by R.H. Hubbard, NGC/Univ. Tor. Pr., 1960, P. 234-236
Painting In Canada by J. Russell Harper, Univ. Tor. Pr., 1966, P. 319
Check List of The War Collections by R.F. Wodehouse, NGC, P. 186-187
Art Gallery of Ontario, The Canadian Collection by Helen Pepall Bradfield, McGraw-Hill Co., Tor., P. 332-333
Creative Canada, Volume One, Ref. Div. McPherson Lib., Univ. Victoria, 1971, P. 233
Four Decades, The Canadian Group of Painters and their contemporaries 1930-1970 by Paul Duval, Clarke, Irwin, Tor., 1972, P. 14, 40, 42-3, 81
A Concise History of Canadian Painting by Dennis Reid, Oxford, Tor., 1973, P. 187

NEWTON-WHITE, Muriel Elizabeth
b. 1928

Born in Robillard Twp., Temiskaming, Northern Ontario, she received her public school education through the Ontario Department of Education Correspondence Courses and she attended the Ontario College of Art through scholarships and bursaries. Her speciality is landscape in oils somewhere between traditional and modern in style. She has done other work including designing and processing of religious greeting cards and signwriting. She has given private art lessons and taught art for Adult Education Night School in Kapuskasing and later at Englehart. She lives at Charlton Station, Ontario.

References
NGC Info. Form

NG, Betty Shuet-Wah

Born in Hong Kong she attended university there and in London where she also studied painting. Coming to Canada she received her Master of Arts and teacher training at the University of British Columbia. A painter of scrolls and traditional Chinese scenes she held her first solo show at the Banff School of Fine Arts in 1961. She was teaching at Maple Grove Elementary School, Vancouver, in 1963.

Reference
Weekend Magazine, No. 40, Oct. 4, 1963 "Canada Through Chinese Eyes"

NGAN, Wayne G.

b. 1938

Born in China, he came to Canada in 1952 and studied at the Vancouver School of Art under R. Weghsteen and graduated with honours; he also studied at the University of British Columbia under John Reeve and in Northwest Seattle where he studied pottery under Paul Solderer. A painter, sculptor and potter his principal activity seems to have been in pottery which he tries to make as simple as he can in what he calls the "naturalistic style" but he also makes pottery which he calls "Raku", a particular technique of firing in the kiln associated with a Japanese tea ceremony and Zen Buddism. Living on Hornby Island with his French-born wife Anne, a weaver of wool fabric, and his daughter Goya, he shares his small pottery with Heinz Laffin, a German Canadian whom he met at the Vancouver School of Art. Ngan has exhibited his work at the Campbell River museum near the Central Plaza, and has participated in the following exhibitions: "B.C. Craftsman, 1962, 1964 (Van.); "The New Ceramic Presence", 1964 (Fine Arts Gal., UBC); Canadian Travel Exhibition abroad, 1964; Canadian Fine Arts, National Gallery of Canada, Ottawa, 1967; Canadian Handicrafts Guild, Montreal, 1967. He taught ceramics at the Vancouver School of Art (1965-67) and at the University of British Columbia.

References

The Vancouver Sun, B.C., Sept. 19, 1964 (photo of artist with his work)

Comox Dist. Free Press, Courtenay, B.C., Mar. 4, 1970 "They like different kind of pot" by Bob Blakey

The Daily Colonist, Vic., B.C., April 15, 1970 "Wayne Ngan – Artistry Reflects Nature" by Bill Thomas

Alberni Valley Times, Port Alberni, B.C., Sept. 16, 1970 "Pottery Brings Man Closer To Nature"

NGC Info. Form rec'd July 5, 1967

NIBLOCK, Hugh

Born in Toronto, Ontario, he was interested in art in his youth but in his later teens turned to writing. He studied at the University of Toronto and as a member of the staff of *Varsity* he did cartoons. During this period he worked on the staff of newspapers in Toronto and also for the CBC. After graduation he taught two years in England then served with the R.C.A.F. mainly in Manitoba. He taught at Fort Frances where he met his wife. He studied and travelled in Spain and England, then specialized in teaching art. He teaches art at Penetanguishene Secondary School and also opened an art gallery in 1970 in Midland, Ontario, named The Gallery of Contemporary Art which doubles for his home. In his own work he has done abstract expressionistic paintings, wall constructions, realisitic pen drawings and other work. He completed a large mural in Hart House, University of Toronto and is represented in private collections in a number of countries.

References

Georgian Tourist, Midland, Ont., August, 1969 "PSS art teacher opens new gallery in Midland"

Midland Free Press Herald, Midland, Ont., April 3, 1970 "Local artist's work will appear at gallery"

Ibid, May 6, 1970 (photo of artist and his wife in their gallery)

NICHOL, Peter
b. (c) 1912

Born in Slavgored, Siberia, he emigrated to Canada as a child. He lived in Western Canada in the 1930's where he saw a ranch cook fashion juniper and other roots into works of art and became interested in this craft himself. He moved east to Hamilton but in 1955 settled in Deep River, Ontario, where he took up his duties as a machinist at the Chalk River Nuclear Laboratories. His interest in driftwood carving was revived when he discovered numerous forms of wood along the shores of the Ottawa River. He selects shapes of wood which suggest subjects to him, then he makes minor changes by trimming excess branches or roots from the main form after which he sands the wood to reveal the grain and varnishes it to bring out the various colours. Some of his creations are abstract in nature but nevertheless resemble birds or animals. One of his works measured eight feet. By 1970 he had created five hundred pieces of work which he has presented to the public as a museum in his own home. None of his works are for sale but his name and address are listed in the official Ontario brochure of artists and craftsmen. He directed a course in driftwood at the Haliburton School of Fine Arts (1970) which drew pupils from as far away as Buffalo and Florida.

References
> *Pembroke Observer*, Ont., Aug. 12, 1969 "Deep River Artist Displayed"
> *Whig-Standard*, Kingston, Ont., July 15, 1968 " 'Nature's garbage' turns beautiful"
> *North Renfrew Times*, Deep River, Ont., Dec. 10, 1969 "Driftwood Exhibition"
> *The Toronto Telegram*, Ont., Sept. 2, 1970 "Driftwood sculptor's work 'an assistance with nature' "
> *The Ottawa Citizen*, Ont., Aug. 21, 1970 "Natural Art — Shoreline driftwood sculptor's medium" by Brenda Lee-Whiting

NICHOLAS, Frederick (Joseph George Frederick Nicholas)
b. 1891

Born in Windsor, Middlesex, England, he came to Canada in 1913. He studied painting under Frederick Stubbings, R.I.; at the School of Applied Art, Michigan, U.S.A.; and summer courses at Mount Allison University, Sackville, N.B., under Stanley Royle. Mainly a landscape and seascape painter in water colours he has also done work with mixed media (water colours and polymer with pen and ink). His subject matter is mainly found in the Maritimes especially at Parrsboro, N.S. and Grand Manan Island, N.B. He has held one-man shows at the following places: East York Public Library (1966); Kelowna Public Library, B.C.; Brantford Public Library, Ont. (1966); Scarborough Public Library; Amherst Branch Library, N.S. (1970). A member of the Maritime Art Association (1941), the Amherst Art Association (1950, former Pres.) and the Nova Scotia Society of Artists (1941, former Vice-Pres., 1966) he has participated in many group shows of the above societies. Lives at Amherst, N.S.

References
> *Chronicle*, Halifax, N.S., Apr. 10, 1943 "Gallery Accepts Nicholas Work"
> *Amherst News*, Amherst, N.S., Apr. 27, 1965 "Has Paintings Accepted"
> *Brantford Expositor*, Brantford, Ont., Jan. 7, 1966 "Art Exhibit Displays New Touch"

NICHOLAS, Frederick (Joseph George Frederick Nicholas) (Cont'd)

East Toronto Weekly, Tor., Ont., Oct. 20, 1966 "Nicholas exhibition at library"
Amherst Daily News & Sentinel, N.S., Sept. 11, 1970 "Exhibition Of Paintings"
Maritime Artists, Vol. 1 by Mary W. Hashey, M.A.A., 1967, P. 60
NGC Info. Forms July 26, 1955; June 11, 1959; 26 July, 1966

NICHOLS, Dale

His oil painting "Grains of Wheat", a harvest scene, appeared in the Toronto *Saturday Night* in 1939. There seems to be no other reference to this artist in literature on Canadian painting. His work seems to be quite good and has a definite style which might be described as a decorative realism.

Reference
Saturday Night, Tor., Ont., Jan. 21, 1939
Ontario Index Of Canadian Artists by J.N. Watney/Louise Chenier, Toronto, 1973

NICHOLS, Jack
b. 1921

Born in Montreal, P.Q., his parents died while he was still a child and by the time he was fourteen he had worked at a wide variety of jobs.[1] When he had saved enough money he painted until just about every cent was spent then returned to work and saved again for more painting time.[2] With few alternatives during The Depression, he was never able to afford formal art studies. He taught himself drawing and painting and received considerable guidance in figure drawing from Louis Mulstock. Mulstock would suggest sketching at the local Turkish bath where both artists were allowed to sketch whenever they wanted and good subjects were to be found in its vaporous atmosphere.[3] Much of their subject matter recorded the daily activities of the poorer people of Montreal. Nichols then lived in Ottawa with his brother from 1931 to 1939 and there received instruction in drawing from F.H. Varley who was in the city as a teacher at the Ottawa Art Association (1936-40). Having received guidance from Mulstock and Varley, both superb draughtsmen, Nichols made rapid progress. He spent several summers working as a deck hand on ships of the Great Lakes and when time permitted in his off duty hours he made charcoal, crayon and pencil wash drawings which caught the feeling of humanity he had found in the people of Montreal.[5] By 1940 he was living in Toronto where his work was seen by Douglas Duncan owner of the Picture Loan Society Gallery who was so impressed with his talent that he arranged for a one-man show in 1941. The following year a solo show of his work was held at Hart House. Nichols was commissioned by the National Gallery of Canada in 1943 to execute paintings of the Canadian Merchant Navy. He sailed from Halifax to the Caribbean with Canadian artist Michael Forster also on assignment. In 1944 Nichols joined the Royal Canadian Navy and was then appointed Official War Artist (Apr. 1944 to Aug. 1945) and crossed the Channel on "D" Day with the British assault forces painting scenes of the Normandy landings and destroyer actions near Brest. He spent some time in Normandy until the fall of Caen then returned to London to develop his work. Many of his drawings (36 in mixed techniques of varying proportions in charcoal, chalk, pencil and turpentine wash) are now in the Canadian War Museum in Ottawa. He did many fine paintings during his years at sea and won a prize for "Rescue at Sea" shown at the Canadian Group of Painters exhibition in 1946. In 1947 he was awarded the unusual honour of a Guggenheim Fellowship for creative painting. This fellowship enabled him to study lithography in the studios of American printmakers and work with muralists. Then he did research on the application of synthetic resins to the fine arts at the National Polytechnical School in Mexico City. Returning to Canada he taught at the Vancouver School of Art and began producing lithographs (1948) and held a one-man show of lithos and drypoints at the Picture Loan Society, Toronto, in 1950. Viewing this show Pearl McCarthy[6] noted, "He draws like a master and this collection proves that he can exploit a variety of figures and countenances as well as the tragic, or lean-and-hungry types which dominated his earlier work. There is a drypoint of two figures (one with a clown-like rotundity and with indolently humorous face, the other with longer curves), in which both line and composition are breathtaking in their beauty. Yet it is done with supreme economy of expression. Girl with Folded Hands and Cowboy are excellent pictures in the now rare medium of stone lithograph. Nichols differs from some sensitive younger artists in not making a stew about his sensitivity, about feeling contemporary or being independent of influences. He just is. And this period away on Guggenheim fellowship broadened his concepts, but left him Jack Nichols. It is beautiful art." In 1955 he completed his large mural for the Salvation Army headquarters building designed by the Parkin architectural firm. He received a Canadian Government Overseas Fellowship to study lithography in France (1956-57) and a Canada Council fellowship to continue his study of the graphic arts there in 1957 and then in 1960-61. Commenting on his lithographs in 1960 Kathleen Fenwick[7], then Curator of Prints and Drawings for the National Gallery of Canada, noted, " . . . with the release of himself from this restraint he has produced with the greatest freedom prints rich in emotion and feeling, exploiting the whole magnificent range of lithographic blacks and achieving new textures which have interested even the experienced craftsmen-printers with whom he has been working. In this latest and so far most successful series of lithographs, . . . he has turned for his theme to the circus, a theme to which he naturally responds. For he finds in the sadness which pervades the sparkle and transient brilliance of circus life that melancholy which to him underlies all humanity and which moves him so deeply." During his career Nichols has done considerable teaching at: Northern Vocational School, Tor.; University of Toronto; Art Gallery of Toronto; Vancouver School of Art and the Ontario College of Art. His one-man shows include: Picture Loan Society, Tor. (1941, 1950, 1953, 1956, 1963, 1965); Art Gallery of Ontario, Tor. (1942); Hart House, Univ. Tor. (1942, 1954, 1960); Art Gallery Springfield, Mass. (1952); London Public Library and Art Museum, Ont. (1952); University of Massachusetts (1952); Montreal Museum of Fine Arts, P.Q. (1952); Victoria College, Univ. Tor. (1955); travelling exhibition through western Canada (1955-56); Contemporary Art Assoc., Ottawa (1958); Roberts Gallery, Tor. (1965, 1968) and many group shows national and international (see *Creative Canada*, P. 206). He is represented in the following collections: Vancouver Art Gallery, B.C.; Art Gallery of Hamilton,

NICHOLS, Jack (Cont'd)

Ont.; London Public Library and Art Museum, Ont.; Agnes Etherington Art Centre, Queen's Univ., Kingston, Ont.; National Gallery of Canada, Ottawa, Ont. and the Public Archives of Canada. He is a member of the Canadian Group of Painters, Canadian Society of Graphic Art, and the Royal Canadian Academy. His awards include Guggenheim fellowship, 1947; C.G.P. exhibit. 1945; purchase prize, International Exhibition of Black and White, Lugano, Switzerland, 1952; Coronation medal, 1953; purchase prize, National Annual Exhibition, Hamilton, Ont., 1954; Canadian Government overseas award, 1956-57; Canada Council fellowship 1956, 1960-61; Royal Society of Canada fellowship. Lives in Toronto.

References
[1] *Canadian Art*, Vol. 4, No. 4 Summer, 1947 "An Artist To Watch" by Andrew Bell P. 140
[2] Ibid
[3] *The Growth of Canadian Painting* by Donald W. Buchanan, Collins, Tor., 1950, P. 79
[4] *The Ottawa Citizen*, Ont., Feb. 15, 1946 "Jack Nichols Working On D-Day Paintings" by James B. Roe
[5] Ibid
[6] *Globe & Mail*, Tor., Ont., Jan. 28, 1950 "Art and Artists – Nichols' Art Is Mature; New OSA Show Bright" by Pearl McCarthy
[7] *Canadian Art*, Spring, 1958 Vol. XV, No. 2 "The Recent Lithographs Of Jack Nichols" by Kathleen M. Fenwick, P. 104, 105
see also
Canadian Art by Graham McInnes, MacMillan, Tor., 1950, P. 80, 83, 85, 90
Canadian Drawings And Prints by Paul Duval, Burns & MacEachern, Tor., 1952 Plates 80 and 81
Canadian Water Colour Painting by Paul Duval, Burns & MacEachern, Tor., 1954
The Arts In Canada, Ed. by Malcolm Ross, MacMillan, Tor., 1958, P. 27, 30
The Development of Canadian Art by R.H. Hubbard, NGC/Queen's Printer, 1963, P. 113, 114, 115
Painting In Canada/A History by J. Russell Harper, Univ. Tor. Pr., 1966, P. 336
Great Canadian Painting/A Century of Art by E. Kilbourn, F. Newfeld, Ken Lefolii, Wm. Kilbourn, Marjorie Harris, Sandra Scott M&S/*Weekend Magazine*, 1966, P. 24
Three Hundred Years of Canadian Art by R.H. Hubbard and J.R. Ostiguy, NGC/Queen's Printer, Ott., 1967, P. 185, 245
Agnes Etherington Art Centre, Queen's Univ., Permanent Collection by Frances K. Smith, 1968
Check List of The War Collections by R.F. Wodehouse, NGC, Ottawa, 1968, P. 135, 136
Art Gallery of Ontario/the Canadian collection by Helen Pepall Bradfield, McGraw-Hill Co. of Can., 1970, P. 333
Gift from the Douglas M. Duncan Collection and the Milne-Duncan Bequest by Pierre Théberge, NGC/Info. Canada, Ott., 1971, P. 82, 93
Four Decades, The Canadian Group of Painters and Their Contemporaries 1930-1970 by Paul Duval, Clarke Irwin, Tor., 1972, P. 22, 69-70, 72, 75, 79-80
Creative Canada, Volume Two, Reference Division, McPherson Lib., Univ. Victoria, B.C., 1972, P. 205, 206
A Concise History of Canadian Painting by Dennis Reid, Oxford, Tor., 1973, P. 238-9
NGC Info. Forms Aug. 9, 1946; May 8, 1939
Newspapers
Globe & Mail, Tor., Ont., Feb. 10, 1945 "Art and Artists – New Show of War Art Revives Hope for Memorial Building" by Pearl McCarthy
The Ottawa Citizen, Ont., Feb. 15, 1946 "Jack Nichols Working On D-Day Paintings" by James B. Roe
The Province, Van., B.C., Apr. 11, 1946 "Nichols' Work Outstanding In War Artists' Display" by Palette
Globe & Mail, Ont., Apr. 14, 1947 "Guggenheim Fellowships Awarded Toronto Men"

NICHOLS, Jack (Cont'd)

Saturday Night, Tor., Ont., June 21, 1947 "Canadian Artist Prefers Humans To Landscapes"

The Evening Telegram, Tor., Ont., Jan. 28, 1950 "At The Galleries — Lithographs Show Feeling For People" by Rose MacDonald

La Presse, Mtl., P.Q., Oct. 25, 1952 "Deux peintres montréalais et un graveur de Toronto"

The Montreal Star, P.Q., Oct. 25, 1952 "Art Notes — Three Types Of Paintings Now On View" by Robert Ayre

Globe & Mail, Tor., Ont., 10 April, 1952 "Canadian Artist Wins Italian Prize"

The Windsor Daily Star, Ont., Jan. 10, 1953 "Willistead Show Varied" by David Mawr

Ibid, Jan. 21, 1953 "Jack Nichols Will Lecture — Noted Artist To Speak at Willistead"

The Evening Telegram, Tor., Mar. 7, 1953 "At The Galleries — Solid Cast Statuette Gives Goddess Grace" by Rose MacDonald

Globe & Mail, Tor., Ont., Jan. 9, 1956 "Two Canadian Artists Provide Major Works" by Pearl McCarthy

The Toronto Telegram, Ont., Feb. 25, 1956 "Two Young Canadians Exhibit Water Colors" by Rose MacDonald

Globe & Mail, Tor., Ont., May 10, 1958 "This Week's Openings Are Uneven in Appeal"

Ibid, 1958 "Art and Artists — Gained Persuasive Sense in Paris" by Pearl McCarthy

The Toronto Telegram, Ont., Dec. 13, 1958 "Accent On Art — Travel And Art Technique" by Paul Duval

Globe & Mail, Tor., Ont., Dec. 13, 1958 "Why Nichols Admired"

The Ottawa Journal, Ont., Dec. 17, 1958 "Jack Nichols' Lithographs Exciting Show"

The Toronto Telegram, Ont., Nov. 21, 1959 "Accent on Art — Time Tamed These Rebels" by Paul Duval

Globe & Mail, Tor., Ont., Mar. 12, 1960 "Nichols' Handsome Simplicity"

The Toronto Telegram, Feb. 4, 1961 "Accent On Art — Jack Nichols: Direct And Dynamic Color" by Paul Duval

Globe & Mail, Tor., Ont., Feb. 3, 1963 "Paris Ousting Abstracts" by Carol Chapman

The Toronto Star, Ont., Feb. 23, 1963 "Printmaker With Night Vision"

The Toronto Telegram, Ont., Feb. 20, 1965 "Art & Artists — The Urban Inspiration" by Harry Malcolmson

Ibid, Jan. 27, 1968 "Art — Jack Nichols artist on stone" by Bernadette Andrews

---

NICHOLSON, Christian M.

A Saint John, N.B., painter who has studied art at the Mount Allison School of Fine Art where he won several scholarships. His exhibition of pencil drawings, pencil sketches, water colours and oils at the Morrison Art Gallery, Saint John, was well received.

Reference

Evening Times Globe, Saint John N.B., July 13, 1971 "Artist Said Promising — One-Man Show Opens"

NICKELL, Ruth

A Richmond, B.C., artist who has been instructing at the Peace Arch Summer School of the Arts at White Rock. Formerly of Vancouver and of Sydney, Australia, she is a well known commercial artist.

NICKELL, Ruth (Cont'd)

Reference
Richmond Review, B.C., Feb. 13, 1970 "Richmondite Will Instruct At Summer School Of Arts"

NICKERSON, Forrest C.

b. 1929

Born in Richfield, Digby County, Nova Scotia, he graduated from the Halifax School for the Deaf (1948) then took a course in commercial art, designing and cartooning (1949-51). Through his interest in hunting with his father, a forest ranger, he became interested in wildlife art. He has done illustrations for *Sportsman's Province, Hunting and Fishing in Canada* and *Wildlife Crusader*. In recent years he became interested in western specimens such as the big horn sheep, mountain goat, woodland caribou, antelope and grizzly bear. He spends much time outdoors observing and sketching bird and animal life.

Reference
An unidentified clipping from a magazine

NICKERSON, Vivian

Born in Yarmouth, N.S., she studied two years drawing at the Massachusetts School of Art, Boston, and at the Schneider School of Fine Arts, Ontario. She has painted land and seascapes and genre subjects in oils, water colours and acrylics, exclusively in the Maritimes. She has exhibited her paintings at the Dartmouth Heritage Museum and in a one-woman show at Bridgetown. Lives at Bridgetown, N.S.

Reference
Halifax Mail Star, N.S., Aug. 6, 1971 "Nova Scotia artist's work praised"

NICKLE, Lawrence

b. 1931

Born in Toronto, Ontario, he graduated from the Ontario College of Art in 1954. He lived in Kenora and Dryden, Ontario, with his wife Olga and taught on a northern Ontario Indian reserve. In 1965 the Nickles went to Europe where they visited galleries and Lawrence painted. Returning to Canada they lived at South Porcupine and later Wawa. Working in water colours, oils and acrylics he has painted the landscapes of Northern Ontario often in the company of artist Michael Cleary; both men are full-time painters. His outdoor work is done in oils on wooden panels, his larger canvases in acrylics and he sometimes works in water colours

NICKLE, Lawrence (Cont'd)

to keep his approach fresh. He has exhibited his work in Calgary, Montreal, Buffalo and in Ontario at Liz's Boutique, Birk's Falls (1970); Markham Centennial Library (1970); the Public Library, Sault Ste. Marie (1971) and the Muskoka Arts & Crafts Exhibition. He has taught painting to private groups and to night classes in high schools at Wawa, Sutton, Newmarket, King City, Markham, North York and a workshop at Bracebridge. Lives with his wife at Huntsville.

References
> *Timmins Daily Press*, Ont., Apr. 18, 1958 "Says Appreciation Of Art Is Waning"
> *Tribune*, Stouffville, Ont., Aug. 10, 1967 "Gormley Artist – Dreams Of 'Schoolhouse' Studio" by Mollie Stewart
> *Economist & Sun*, Markham, Ont., Jan. 8, 1970 "On exhibit at Library"
> *Almaguin News*, Burks Falls, Ont., Mar. 25, 1970 "Avid Interest In Canadian Artist"
> Ibid, Mar. 18, 1970 "Lawrence Nickle . . . . "
> *Huntsville Forester*, Ont., Mar. 26, 1970 "Huntsville artists' work praised"
> Ibid, Mar. 14, 1970 "Landscape workshop to be held for district artists in Bracebridge"
> *Sault Ste. Marie Star*, Ont., Nov. 19, 1971 "Muskoka artists show Algoma"
> Ibid, Nov. 24, 1971 "Cleary, Nickle, linear and organic painters" by Linda Richardson

NICKMANN, G.H.

Decorated the walls of a wine-cellar at Val d'Or with a Canadian scene.

Reference
> *L'Echo d'Amos*, May 4, 1966 (photo of artist painting his mural)

NICOL, Louisa

Her canvases show a fresh young humourous perception with compositions in the manner of Chagall and at times reminiscent of the canvases of Jean Paul Lemieux. Her colours are surprising because of the unusual combinations and the vigorous care of their application. She has exhibited her paintings and drawings at Maison Routhier, Quebec, and her drawings at La galerie Kaleidoscope, Montreal.

Reference
> *Le Soleil*, Quebec, P.Q., Aug. 31, 1968 "Louisa Nicol, le talent et la fantaisie"

NICOL, Luc

Born in Granby, P.Q., he exhibited his paintings in a retrospective show at Maison des Arts, Granby, P.Q.

References
> *La Voix de l'Est*, Granby, P.Q., Apr. 19, 1962 "On désire la création d'un comité d'enquête"

NICOL, Nancy

b. 1951

A young Gananoque, Ontario, painter who studied at the Banff School of Fine Arts on a scholarship and has exhibited her paintings at the Up and Down Gallery in Kingston.

References

Gananoque Reporter, Ont., July 3, 1968 "Painting of bandshell wins mention for local artist"
Whig-Standard, Kingston, Ont., Aug. 31, 1968 "She has a painting at the 'ex' "
Gananoque Reporter, Ont., Sept. 4, 1968 "Local Artist returns from Banff School of Fine Arts"

NICOLETTI, Rodolfo

b. 1914

Born in Toronto, Ontario, he later lived in Italy from 1922 to 1929 then returned to Canada. He studied four years at the Danforth Technical School where he graduated with honours then studied nights at the Central Technical School and at the Ontario College of Art. He worked for the Vincent de Vita Studios where he became assistant art director. He also worked on the Canadian Pavilion for the World's Fair of 1939 and other projects. He joined the Royal Canadian Navy in 1941 and was attached to the Special Service Branch of the R.C.N.V.R. and decorated naval barracks with murals. No recent information.

Reference

The Gazette, Mtl., P.Q., June 27, 1944 "Navy Man's Murals of d'Iberville Adorn New W.R.C.N.S. Barracks"
NGC Info. Form rec'd June 16, 1943

NICOLL, Jim McLaren

b. 1892

Born in Fort Macleod, Alberta, he graduated from the University of Alberta, a civil engineer and worked for the Canadian Pacific Railway for many years. He became interested in painting around 1935 when he joined the Calgary Sketch Club but no doubt his drafting experience necessary in his profession prepared him well for his drawing and painting. Later he became associated with the Calgary Allied Arts Centre. He provided illustrations for books and became the founding editor of *Highlights*, a magazine published by the Alberta Society of Artists. His early landscapes were realistic in style and then took on a mosaic-texture-like surface pattern. He also uses a linear technique of intricate lines of colour. Two of his pen and black ink drawings appear in Lorne E. Render's *The Mountains and the Sky*. Nicoll has done portraits and other subjects as well. He has exhibited his work with the Royal Canadian Academy, the Canadian Society of Painters in Water Colour and at the Vincent Price Gallery, Chicago, and has held solo shows at Banff at the Archives of the Canadian Rockies (1971), the University of Calgary (1971) and the Peter Whyte Gallery, Calgary (1971). He is represented in the col-

NICOLL, Jim McLaren (Cont'd)

lections of the University of Edmonton; the University of Calgary; University of St. John's Nfld.; and the Calgary Allied Arts Centre. A member of the Alberta Society of Artists (former Pres.) he is married to Marion Nicoll, painter.

References

Calgary Herald, Alta., Jan. 11, 1971 "Alberta artist on exhibit in Banff's Rockies Archives" by Carrie Hunter
Calgary Albertan, Alta., Jan. 23, 1971 "Local artist at Banff" by Danny L. Gannon
Ibid, Mar. 13, 1971 "Man and wife art integrity demonstrated" by Helen McLean
Calgary Herald, Alta., Mar. 18, 1971 "Art works of Calgary husband and wife team on display in U. of C. Mezzanine Art Gallery" by Derek G. Whyte
The Mountains and the Sky by Lorne E. Render, Glenbow-Alberta Inst. M. & S. West, 1974, P. 199, 200

NICOLL, Marion Florence (Mackay)
b. 1909

Born in Calgary, Alberta, she drew as a child and never contemplated any career other than that of a painter. She took extra curricular painting classes during high schools years at St. Joseph's Convent, Red Deer Alberta (1925-26); attended the Ontario College of Art, Toronto, where she studied under J.E.H. MacDonald (1927-29) but her study there was interrupted by an illness. Then she studied at the Provincial Institute of Technology and Art, Calgary (1929-32) under A.C. Leighton in an exhaustive academic training in water colours also attended the summer school under him at what is now known as the Banff School of Fine Arts (1932, 33, 34). She studied figure painting under Duncan Grant at the Central School of Arts and Crafts, London, England (1937-38); under Will Barnet, Emma Lake Seminar, Sask. (1957); Art Students' League, NYC (1958-59). She studied under J.W.G. Mac-Donald, a friend, who introduced her to automatic drawing. She began teaching art in 1934 at the Provincial Institute of Technology and Art/Alberta College of Art, Calgary (1934-37, 1938-40, 1946-58, 1959-61, 1961-66); also summer school of the University of Alberta (1937, 1938); extension classes (1946-48); Banff School of Fine Arts (1946); Cultural Development Board, Government of Alberta (1948-49). Around 1946 she became associated with painters in Calgary working toward a personal expression (J.W.G. MacDonald, Maxwell Bates, several others). In 1964 her work was described by Ken Winters during a solo show at the Yellow Door Gallery as follows, "Perhaps the special validity for us in Miss Nicoll's 14 severe and monumental gestures in paint is something more parochial and more personal than her splendid reconciliation of the abstract and the elemental. To be sure she says basic things with a minimum of fuss, and this is the source of the dignity and honesty of her work. But for Canadians it also will be significant that she says these things in a particularly Canadian voice. Her designs have their roots in the marvellous designs of native Indian art; her colors have their source in the unsentimental colors of the fruits of our native earth; her thoughts have the stern, unostentatious sense that we like to believe is the best characteristic of the workings of our national mind. Not flashy, not futuristic, not flossy nor phony nor flip, Miss Nicoll's hard-won, hard-painted, distilled observations of life and the world are enormously worth our attention and our respect." Her solo shows include

NICOLL, Marion Florence (Mackay) (Cont'd)

the following: Alberta College of Art, Cal. (1959); Bowness Town Hall, Alta. (1960, 1965); Studio 61, Edmonton, Alta. (1961); Bowness Recreation Centre, Alta. (1961); Focus, Edmonton (1962, 63, 64); Upstairs Gallery, Tor. (1963); Yellow Door Gallery, Winn. (1964); Western Canadian Art Circuit, Vict., B.C. to Winnipeg, Man. (1966); Bonli's Gallery, Tor. (1967); Sear's Vincent Price, Chicago, Ill. (1968). She received a Canada Council grant, 1958-59; and a senior fellowship in 1966. Her other awards include six honour certificates (for teaching) from the Royal Drawing Society, Lon., Eng. (1929-34); honourable mention for jewellery design, Stratford, Ont., and Vancouver, B.C. (1962). She has exhibited in the 5th, Sixth and Seventh Biennials of Canadian Painting. She is represented in the collections of Memorial University, Nfld.; University of Alberta; Edmonton Museum; Poole Collection, Edmonton; Winnipeg Art Gallery. She designed a wall for the Trans-Canada Highway between Tilley and Brooks, 1967-68. Member of the Alberta Society of Artists, she is married to James Nicoll, noted western Canadian painter. Lives at Bowness, Alberta.

References

Canadian Art, Vol. XX, No. 2, March/April, 1963 "Clement Greenberg's View of Art on the Prairies" by C.G. P. 96
5th Biennial Exhibition of Canadian Painting, 1963, P. 52
6th Biennial Exhibition of Canadian Painting, 1965, P. 34
7th Biennial Exhibition of Canadian Painting, 1968, P. 50
Painting In Canada/A History by J. Russell Harper, Univ. Tor. Pr, 1966, P. 350, 391-4
Creative Canada, Vol. 1 Ref. Div. McPherson Lib., Univ. Victoria, 1971, P. 234
A Concise History of Canadian Painting by Dennis Reid, Oxford, Tor., 1973, P. 268
Document from artist, 1960
NGC Info. Form, 1966
Newspapers
The Gazette, Mtl., P.Q., Dec. 30, 1957 "Calgary Woman Masters Ancient Wax-Painting Art"
North Hill News, Calg., Alta., Dec. 3, 1959 "Exhibition Of Paintings"
Albertan, Calgary, Alta., Dec. 8, 1959 "Artist Shows Oil Paintings"
Edmonton Journal, Edmonton, Alta., Jan. 26, 1963 "Gallery Exhibition Thursday"
Ibid, Oct. 19, 1963 "Exhibit By Nichol (sic) Last For Gallery" by Dorothy Barnhouse
Calgary Herald, Alta., Dec. 10, 1963 "Art Show Features Boldness Of Nicoll's Abstract Works" by Robin Neesham
Winnipeg Free Press, Man., Jan. 30, 1964 "14 Monumental Gestures" review by Ken Winters
Calgary Herald, Calgary, Alta., Jan. 27, 1965 "Life And Painting Synonymous For Calgary Artist-Teacher" by Adeleine Flaherty
Ibid, Apr. 18, 1966 "College of Art Display – Marion Nicoll Work Praised" by David Thompson
Calgary Herald, Apr. 26, 1966 "Canada Council Fellowships – 2 Calgary Artists Win Awards"
Leader-Post, Regina, Sask., Jan. 4, 1966 "Gallery features Calgary artist"
Globe & Mail, Tor., Apr. 29, 1967 "Bonli Gallery"

NIEDOJADLO, Jersey

A Hamilton, Ontario, sculptor whose work is permanently displayed in the city hall plaza at Oslo, Norway; Place des Arts, Bais, Belgium and in the lobby of the National Arts Centre, Ottawa.

NIEDOJADLO, Jersey (Cont'd)

Reference
　Kitchener-Waterloo Record, Ont., Jan. 21, 1970 "$8,000 in Steel Art on Display"

NIELSEN, Kaj
b. 1909

Born in Copenhagen, Denmark, he drew, modelled, carved, made model coaches, sailing ships during his school years. He left home at the age of fourteen to sail the seven seas on a windjammer. He came to Canada in 1927 and got a job on a prairie farm near Brandon, Manitoba, and for several succeeding summers worked on dairy farms, grain farms doing all types of work. Then he worked in logging camps ending up in the Queen Charlotte Islands, B.C. In the evenings he carved on a small work bench he built at the end of his bunk. Finally he settled near Victoria, B.C. He has been working mainly on art representative of British Columbia but has been influenced in his sculpture and carving by C.W. Jefferys. He completed relief panels of Canadian historical scenes, figures of Canadian birds and animals in realistic style in four plywood murals (4 ft. x 8 ft.) located at the B.C. Forestry Department's Douglas Hotel; did a large carving of Henry Fuller Davis (Twelve-Foot Davis) who was a trader, explorer and prospector. This large work was commissioned by the Town of Peace River, Alberta, and erected near the grave of Davis, overlooking the Peace, Smoky and Hart Rivers. Nielsen exhibited his work at the Pacific National Exhibition in Vancouver in 1952 and won all the major awards including the gold medal. Fire destroyed his workshop in 1964 but he rebuilt and has continued with his fine work. A member of the Federation of Canadian Woodcarvers, he teaches woodcarving and lives on the Trans-Canada Highway near Victoria with his wife Florence.

References
　Document from artist, 1961
　Victoria Colonist, B.C., April 14, 1968 "Kaj Nielsen – Master Carver – Has hit comeback trail after fire destroyed his home – museum – workshop" by Wilmer H. Gold

NIEMANN, Fritz (Friedrich C. Niemann)
b. 1936

Born in Duisburg, West Germany, where he studied drawing and painting and won two scholarships. He worked and exhibited there extensively before coming to Canada. He took further study at the Ontario College of Art, Toronto, and after graduating settled in St. Catharines with his wife and children. He has exhibited his work in solo shows in Brampton; Gallery Sol, Georgetown, and at Niagara-on-the-Lake and has taught painting to students in St. Catharines and Niagara-on-the-Lake. He was commissioned in 1967 to do a mural (21 x 7 ft.) for the Delphian House, St. Catharines. In his mural work he has combined the best of the old with the best of the new like using layers of gesso (a favourite of Florentine schools and others) to give his work the same standard of finish and luminosity

NIEMANN, Fritz (Friedrich C. Niemann) (Cont'd)

which the old masters achieved. He uses a modern plastic binding agent with oil paints (instead of egg yolk which was used with tempera by the Masters) to give the paints more security from moisture thus protecting their brillance.

Reference
Independent, Grimsby, Ont., Nov. 24, 1966 "Art centre to open December 1"
St. Catharines Standard, Ont., Nov. 8, 1967 "Fritz Niemann, St. Catharines Artist – Combines Old And New Techniques While Preparing Huge Wall Mural" by Stephen Carlman

NIEMININ, Jorma
b. (c) 1940

Born in Finland, he first visited Canada in 1969. His paintings which are surrealistic in nature, have wide areas of clear, clean colour which convey a feeling of lyricism and sometimes power. Space and time are the themes he is concerned with using Greek mythology mingled with 20th Century symbols. Pearl Oxorn described his "Anno Domini 1977" series in 1977 as follows, "The ruins of an ancient world, remnants from the dawn of Western civilization, are juxtaposed with the broken and decaying detritus of an auto graveyard: 'Industrial sculpture', the artist calls it. Derelict autos dot the environment, the inevitable result of an assembly line economy; they are the waste products of our consumer society. This theme carries through the fresh, open, sky-filled landscapes which are light and airy in feeling, echoing their dream-like evanescence. Birds symbolize the living present and as the bird flies, so time flies too." Jorma has shown his work with his brother Martti at the Collectors Gallery (Ottawa) and the Randall Gallery, Ottawa (1970), Wallack Galleries, Ottawa (1977).

References
Exhibition sheet, Collectors Gallery, Ottawa
The Ottawa Citizen, Ont., June 9, 1970 "Finnish brothers paint in contrasts" by Jenny Bergin
The Ottawa Journal, Feb. 12, 1977 "Finnish artists stress pollution and ecology" by Pearl Oxorn

NIEMININ, Martti
b. (c) 1943

Born in Finland, he is one of the well-known primitive artists there and has exhibited at the Modern Art Museum of Tampere, the Salo Gallery, Tampere and his works are admired in Helsinki. In his paintings he uses wide areas of bright clear colour especially the green of his pastoral scenes which are peopled with zoo creatures and all kinds of Noah's Ark animals. Pearl Oxorn in the *Ottawa Journal* noted, "Animals in Martti's paintings have disarmingly human countenances, like the lions and monkeys that inhabit Rousseau's jungle. They stare out at us with pleading, uncomprehending eyes, imploring us to halt their extinction. We have disrupted the ecological balance between the wildlife and the environment and

NIEMININ, Martti (Cont'd)

there is no road back." Shepherds are seen as the central theme of many of his canvases. He has exhibited his paintings in Canada at the Collectors Gallery, Ottawa, and the Randall Gallery, Ottawa (1970), Wallack Galleries, Ottawa (1977) and elsewhere. Brother of Jorma Nieminin.

References

Exhibition sheet, Collectors Gallery, Ottawa

The Ottawa Citizen, Ont., June 9, 1970 "Finnish brothers paint in contrasts" by Jenny Bergin

The Ottawa Journal, Ont., Feb. 12, 1977 "Finnish artists stress pollution and ecology" by Pearl Oxorn

NIESSEN, Wolfram

b. 1923

Born in Krefeld, West Germany, he studied modelling and pottery in high school followed by studies in art at the Academies at Mannheim and Karlsrube, Germany (1946-50). He did free lance work from 1950 to 1952 and held his first solo exhibition in 1952. He was awarded a full scholarship in 1952 by the State to study sculpture at the Academie Mainz (1953-54) under Prof. Emy Roeder. He came to Canada in 1954 and in 1956 joined the staff of the University of Saskatchewan, Regina, where until 1961 he taught drawing and sculpture. At the same time he was also a Museum Artist with the Saskatchewan Museum of Natural History, Regina. He took further study at Michigan State University, majoring in sculpture and received his Master of Fine Arts Degree in 1963. He joined the staff of Stout State University, Menomonie, Wisconsin, as Assistant Professor in design, drawing and sculpture. In Canada he has done several commissions including a Canadian Government commission of a 9 ft. high metal sculpture of a single whooping crane entitled "Taking to Flight" for the Regina Airport. In 1966 Niessen held a one-man show of his sculpture at the Yellow Door Gallery, Winnipeg. Living in Menomonie in 1966.

References

Biographical information sheets filed with NGC Documentation Centre

Winnipeg Free Press, Man., Feb. 25, 1966 "The Yellow Door – Niessen's 'Uncluttered Style' " by Frances Cohen

NIEUWENHUIS, Douwe (DOW)

He studied at the Royal Academy of Fine Art in The Hague and worked in the Netherlands, England, West Indies as KLM illustrator and decorator. He came to Canada in 1955 and finally settled in Ottawa to become staff artist and cartoonist with *The Ottawa Journal*. In his painting he favours abstraction for its greater freedom, both in mixed media construction pieces and abstract expressionistic canvases.

Reference

The Ottawa Journal, Ont., Mar. 13, 1971 "Ottawa Artist (22) – Finds Art in Everything" by Valerie Knowles

NIGNUIK, Davidee
b. 1925

A resident at Apex Hill, Frobisher Bay, with his wife and children, he supported his family by hunting in the Port Harrison area of Arctic Quebec. With a crippled foot from birth coupled with the fact he had earlier been a patient in a tuberculosis hospital, hunting became an increasingly more difficult occupation as he got older. He decided to move to the Rehabilitation Centre at Frobisher Bay operated by the Department of Northern Affairs and there began to carve. After a year at the Centre he was producing exceptionally fine work in stone. Taking his subjects from the traditional Eskimo way of life usually centered around the human figure he has become a prominent artist. The National Gallery of Canada acquired one of his black soapstone heads in 1963 which was reproduced in George Swinton's *Sculpture of The Eskimo.*

References
> Press release, Dept. of Northern Affairs and National Resources #5411, Feb. 26, 1963
> Biographical sheet, March, 1969
> *Sculpture of The Eskimo* by George Swinton, M&S, Tor., 1972, P. 196

NINCHERI, Guido

Born in Florence, Italy, an artist creating frescoes in the tradition of the great Italian renaissance masters. He came to Montreal, Canada, where he decorated churches with frescoes, stained glass and other work, including the Church of Our Lady of Defence (stained glass, fresco) and St. Leon Church, Westmount (frescoes) and fifty or more churches in United States and Canada including St. Anne's at Woonsocket, R.I., an eight-year project which he himself considers to be his masterpiece.

References
> *The Gazette*, Mtl, P.Q., June 20, 1940 "Mural of Il Duce Stirs Storm Here" (mural to commemorate Lateran Treaty between Pope and Mussolini)
> Ibid, Sept. 30, 1947 "Mussolini Mural Again Displayed – Church Painting of Ex-Italian Leader, Covered During War, Now on View"
> *The Hamilton Spectator* (AP, Woonstock, R.I.), Ont. Aug. 21, 1950 "Church Project Completed – Visitors Flock To View Canadian Artist's Work"
> *The Canadian Citizen* (Italian), Mtl., P.Q. 24 July, 1953 "Guido Nincheri: Neo-Renaissance Artist" by Lucio Salverio

NIND, Jean

Born in Borneo, she travelled on several continents and studied art in England. Coming to Canada she taught children's art classes at the Saskatoon Art Centre while in her free time painted scenes of the prairies exhibited at the Bonli Gallery, Toronto in 1967.

References
> *Globe & Mail*, Tor., Ont., Nov. 18, 1967 "Bonli Gallery"
> Exhibition notice, Bonli Gallery, Nov. 7, 1967

NINGEWANCE, Pat

An Ojibway artist from Lac Seul, Ontario, who illustrates legends of her people (as told to her by her mother) in oil and oil pastel paintings. She studied art with other courses for four years at Korah Collegiate. During her last year at Korah she wrote a play based on an Ojibway legend which was presented by the Ojicree Club. Later she attended Algoma College for a short period then turned to full-time painting. She held her first solo show at Shingwauk Hall, Algoma College, Sault Ste. Marie in 1971.

References
> *Sault Ste. Marie Star*, Ont., May 3, 1971 "Indian week opened officially today"
> Ibid, Dec. 16, 1971 "Young artist paints Lac Seul Legends" by Linda Richardson

NISBET, Florence (Mrs.)
b. 1913
Born in Toronto, Ontario, she studied painting at the Mary Schneider School of Fine Arts at Actinolite, Ontario, but is mainly self taught. Her main medium is oils but she also works with collage, acrylics, water colours and fabric hangings. Her subjects include buildings, street scenes, waterfalls and rocks. A member of the Niagara District Art Association she has exhibited her work at a number of juried shows including those at the Glenhyrst Galleries, Brantford; the Welland Public Library; Old Fire Hall Galleries, Niagara-on-the-Lake and elsewhere. Lives at St. Catharines, Ontario.

References
> *The St. Catharines Standard*, Ont., Aug. 29, 1967 "Dream Is Now Truth For Oil-Happy Widow" by John Gibson
> *Niagara Falls Review*, Ont., Jan. 2, 1971 "St. Catharines artist believes in experimenting in new forms"
> NGC Info. Form 30 Oct., 1967

NISHIMURA, Mikko Barbara

Canadian-born Japanese painter who studied six months in Japan on a Canada Council grant and returned home to hold an exhibition of abstract expressionistic paintings at 123 Gallery in Toronto in 1967.

Reference
> *Globe & Mail*, Tor., Ont., Oct. 28, 1967

NISKA (François Lortie)
b. (c) 1940
Born in Montreal, P.Q., he has been painting since the age of fourteen. He lived in Ottawa for eight years during which period he married Germaine Albert (1961)

NISKA (François Lortie) (Cont'd)

and graduated from the University of Ottawa with his Phy. Ed. (1963). He turned to full time painting developing a technique which Guy Robert in his *L'Art Au Quebec Depuis 1940* has described as lyrical and joyous, high in colour and rhythm and although really non-figurative has a landscape appearance to it. He was elected a member of l'Académie Internationale Leonardo da Vinci de Rome in 1970. He has exhibited at the Musée d'Auvillar and the Salon de l'Action d'Art, Bordeaux, France (1970) the Ligoa Duncan Gallery, NYC (1971) and elsewhere internationally. His exhibition at the Valleyfield City Hall in 1970 was opened by the French Ambassador to Canada. He was selected Laureate at the 7th Grand Prix International de Peinture de Côte d'Azur, Cannes France. Lives in Mont-Tremblant with his wife and two daughters.

References

La Vallée De La Diable, St. Jovite, P.Q., 24 Mar., 1967 "Niska, un peintre libéré des conventions"

The Ottawa Journal, Ont., Aug. 1, 1968 " 'Niska' Returns to U of O for One-Man Art Show" by W.Q.K.

La Gazette, Valleyfield, P.Q., Apr. 2, 1970 "Le Peintre Canadien Niska Exposera A Valleyfield"

Ibid, Apr. 15, 1970 "Exposition A Valleyfield D'un Peintre Plein De Promesse Et De Grand Talent"

St. Lawrence Sun, Que., Apr. 22, 1970 "Peintre, une situation où je peux être moi-même"

The Ottawa Citizen, Ont., Dec. 10, 1970 "Niska art unchanged – natural" by Jenny Bergin

L'Echo du Nord, St. Jerome, P.Q., June 24, 1970 "Niska A Paris"

Annuaire National des Beaux Arts, France (1969-70) Mar.

Réaliser, August, 1970 "Niska, peintre cosmique" par Pierrette Paré

Les Cahiers d'Action d'Art, September, 1970 "Niska, Peintre Canadien" par Georges Joran

L'Art Au Quebec Depuis 1940 par Guy Robert, La Presse, 1973, P. 187, 190

NIVERVILLE, Georges de

b. 1928

Born in Ottawa, Ontario, he studied at the Montreal Museum of Fine Arts under Goodridge Roberts, Arthur Lismer and Jacques de Tonnancour (1946-49) and at the Académie Ranson, Paris under Goetz, Manessier and Singier on a Canadian Government Scholarship (1953-55). Employed by the CBC graphics department in Ottawa he has painted abstract and humourous personalized expressionistic portraits of people and events which have interested him. His one-man shows include those at the Robertson Galleries, Ottawa (1958, 1960); Le Cercle Universitaire, Ottawa (1961); Blue Barn Gallery, Ottawa (1964); Denise Delrue Gallery, Mtl. (1968, 1969); Lofthouse Gallery, Ottawa (1969) and in a two-man show with Duncan de Kergommeaux on a travelling exhibition sponsored by the National Gallery of Canada (1967-68). He is represented in the Confederation Centre Art Gallery and elsewhere. Lives in Ottawa.

References

The Ottawa Citizen, Ont., Mar. 26, 1958 "Three Distinct Realms In Painting Exhibit" by Carl Weiselberger

NIVERVILLE, Georges de (Cont'd)

Ibid, May 12, 1961 "Abstract Photo Works Show Art's Versatility" by Carl Weiselberger
The Ottawa Journal, Ont., May 24, 1961 "Local Artists' Works Shown at Le Cercle Universitaire" by Jill Mulkins
Ibid, Oct. 8, 1964 "De Niverville Display Opens"
The Ottawa Citizen, Ont., Oct. (?) article by Carl Weiselberger
Guardian, Charlottetown, P.E.I., Oct. 27, 1967 "New Painting For Gallery"
The Ottawa Journal, Ont., Feb. 3, 1969 "One-Man Exhibit Opens"
The Gazette, Mtl., P.Q., Mar. 8, 1969 "De Niverville exhibit trip through memory" by Anna McGarrigle
La Presse, Mtl., P.Q., Mar. 8, 1969 "Des photos qui trichent"
NGC Information form (undated)
5th and 6th Biennials of Canadian Painting (catalogues)

NIVERVILLE, Louis de

b. 1933

Born in Andover, England, one of thirteen children (12 brothers and 1 sister) of Air Vice-Marshal Albert de Niverville of the R.C.A.F., Louis came to Canada with his parents in 1934 and settled in Montreal, P.Q.[1] He began drawing at an early age and most of his work until he was fifteen was representational.[2] In 1953 the de Niverville family moved to Ottawa where his father took up a position with the Department of Transport. From his middle teens Louis became interested in the humourous side of drawing.[3] In 1957 he worked as an office clerk in the Department of External Affairs and in his spare time did set designs and advertisements for the Ottawa Little Theatre for the play 'East Lynne'. His encouragement came from Ottawa architect and director of amateur theatricals, Stan White and free lance art director and designer Paul Arthur.[4] He also received considerable help from his brother Georges de Niverville, a professionally trained artist. On a trip to Toronto Paul Arthur urged de Niverville to take a portfolio of his drawings with him to show to various art directors. The result was that he received work from *Mayfair* magazine and was hired two or so months later by the CBC graphics department headed by David Mackay. Even the drawings in his portfolio which he took to Toronto were used in an animated film entitled "The Pounding Heart" produced by David Mackay and Warren Collins. This film was described by Robert Fulford[5] as follows "Put together to a surrealistic, plotless script, enhanced by recorded scraps of Beethoven and Offenbach, this delightful, eight-minute essay in incongruity — full of triumphant men riding past, playing clarion trumpets while riding Vespas, and glum women working out with barbells — is, like all of de Niverville's work, a unique and welcome addition to the Canadian scene. We should all be grateful for it. After all, how else could we have seen a baroque motorcycle?" For three years de Niverville drew twelve sketches a week for the programme "Fighting Words" and he contributed to several other T.V. productions. In the 1970's he has explored the theme of nightmares and dreams and exhibited this work at the Jerrold Morris Gallery which Sol Littman[6] described as follows, "In a series of large, dramatic paintings, de Niverville describes a private hell populated by stupified children, stalking animals and terrified princelings. The exhibit serves both to display his skill and explain his neglect." Nick Johnson in an article on de Niverville in 1973 noted that his paintings evoked the mystery of the subject but did not name it.[7] Some of his close admirers longed to see him return to the happier images of the 1960's but Littman in his review pointed out that even in these happier images there was the "vague element of threat." De Niverville's main influences have come from American cartoonists Saul Steinberg and James Thurber, and his paintings show the influence of French artists Henri Matisse and Pierre Bonnard. His first solo was held at the Gallery of Contemporary Art (1957, 1959) and subsequent solo shows at the Here & Now Gallery, Tor. (1959, 1967); Dorothy Cameron Gallery, Tor. (1963, 1964); Jerrold Morris Gallery, Tor. (1967, 1973); Owens Art Gallery, Sackville, N.B. (1968); two-man show with James Boyd at the Wells Gallery, Ottawa (1973, 1975) Galerie de Montreal (1973) and elsewhere. He participated in a number of group shows including Surrealism in Canadian Painting at the London Public Library and Art Museum. He completed murals for the Ontario Architecture Building Centre, Tor. (1957); two murals for the Toronto International Airport (1963); Mrs. Alan Skaith Memorial Painting for the Toronto Crippled Children's Centre (1963) and a mural for the Expo Theatre in Montreal. He exhibited his paintings in the 4th, 5th, and 6th Biennial Exhibitions of Canadian Painting, 1961, 1963 and 1965. He is represented in the following collections: University of Western Ontario; Agnes Etherington Art Centre, Kingston; McMaster University, Hamilton, Ont.; Sir George Williams University, Mtl. and elsewhere. He received two Canada Council grants (1964, 1968). He is represented in the private collections of Joseph H. Hirshhorn (NYC); Mr. & Mrs. Percy Waxer (Tor.); Mr. & Mrs. Paul Arthur (Tor.); Mr. & Mrs. Clair Stewart (Tor.); Mr. & Mrs. Meredith Fleming (Tor.); Mr. & Mrs. Ben Wise (Tor.); Mr. & Mrs. Mort Rapp; Mr. & Mrs. David MacKay (Tor.); Mr. & Mrs. Leonard Sachter (Tor.); Mr. & Mrs. G.G.R. Harris (Tor.); Mr. & Mrs. Michael Taylor (Tor.); Dr. Alexander Best (Tor.) and many others. He illustrated the books *Mice in the Beer, The Fully Processed Cheese* and the film "Lady B." Lives in Toronto.

References
[1]*Toronto Daily Star*, Ont., Jan. 26, 1963 "This Is The Way of A 'Way Out' Painter" by David Cobb
[2]*Canadian Art, Vol. 16, No. 3,* 1959 "Louis De Niverville" by Robert Fulford, P. 177
[3]Ibid
[4]Ibid, P. 177, 180
[5]Ibid, P. 181
[6]*The Toronto Star*, Ont., Mar. 30, 1973 "Brilliant artist's work describes a private hell" by Sol Littman
[7]*Artscanada*, May, 1973 "Louis De Niverville: the focus of ambiguity" by Nick Johnson, P. 24
see also
Globe & Mail, Tor., Ont., July 5, 1958 "Artists Rule the Day In Souvenir Program"
What's What For Children compiled by Eve Kassirer, Ctiizen's Committee On Children, Ottawa, 1958, 1959 (ill. by L. de Niverville)
The Hamilton Spectator, Ont. Feb. 18, 1961 "De Niverville"
Globe & Mail, Tor., Ont., Mar. 4, 1961 "Niverville Is Bigger but Gayer" by Pearl McCarthy
Globe & Mail, Tor., Ont., Jan. 19, 1963 "Painter's Characters Desert Hothouse" by Carol Chapman
Toronto Daily Star, Ont. (1964) "Art And Artists – A witty illustrator" by Elizabeth Kilbourn
Globe & Mail, Tor., Ont., Mar. 7, 1964 "Abstractionist Turns on Light"
On the Enjoyment of Modern Art by Jerrold Morris, M&S, Tor., 1965, P. 51
Agnes Etherington Art Centre Permanent Collection, 1968, by Frances K. Smith, No. 102
Creative Canada compiled by Reference Division, McPherson Lib., Univ. Victoria, 1971, P. 235

NIVERVILLE, Louis de (Cont'd)

Four Decades, The Canadian Group of Painters and their contemporaries, 1930-1970 by Paul Duval, Clarke, Irwin, 1972, P. 180, 181
Globe & Mail, Tor., Ont., 6 Jan., 1973 "Elusive realism in Artschwager work" by Kay Kritzwiser
Le Droit, Ottawa, Ont., 31 Mar., 1973 "De Niverville et Boyd à la galerie Wells" par Michel Dupuy
The Gazette, Mtl., P.Q., 27 Oct., 1973 "Gallery Round-up — Something strange from Toronto and a Quebecois magic realist" by Virginia Nixon
Canadian Artists In Exhibition, Roundstone Council for the Arts, Tor., Ont. 1974, P. 241
NGC Info. Form rec'd Feb. 25, 1969
Catalogues of 4th, 5th and 6th Biennial Exhibitions of Canadian Painting

---

NIXON, Andy

Born in Toronto, Ontario, he attended the children's art classes under Arthur Lismer at the Art Gallery of Toronto. Later he studied and graduated from the Toronto Central Technical School and took further studies at the Doon School of Fine Art. A painter and sculptor he has travelled and painted in Canada's western arctic and in Australia and Greece and won the Centennial Art Award, Toronto, for his contribution to the fine arts (1967). Working free lance he has completed projects for *The Globe & Mail* and has taught art for the Eastview Secondary School in Barrie. He has been cited for his proficiency with oils which he works with varying techniques of thick or impasto brush strokes to the loose style of the turpentine washes. He is also known for his mixed collages. In his Australian paintings for instance he delights in the use of tropical colours. He has held one-man shows at the following: Canadiana Gallery, Tor. (1963, 1964, 1966); Gallery of Contemporary Art, Midland, Ont. (1969, 1970); Orillia Public Library and Art Gallery (1972, 1974); Gallery Green, Barrie, Ont. (1973). He has participated in a number of group shows including: 14th Annual Winter Show at the Art Gallery of Hamilton (1963); St. Catharines, Rodman Hall, Jury Show (1963); Robert McLaughlin Gallery, Oshawa, Jury Show (1968); Tom Thomson Memorial Gallery, Owen Sound, Jury Show (1969); CNE Better Living Exhibition, Tor. (1970); Art Gallery of Hamilton CKOC Exhbition (1971, 1972, 1973, 1975); Stratford Art Festival, Ont. (1974); Art Gallery of Vancouver (1974); Orillia Public Library & Art Gallery, Jury Show (1975); Ontario Society of Artists, Tor. (1975). He is represented in the following collections: Art Gallery of Vancouver; Public Archives of Canada, Ottawa and the rental collections of the Tom Thomson Memorial Gallery, Owen Sound; Barrie Public Library; Art Gallery of Hamilton and his work can also be seen at the Picture Loan Gallery, Tor.; Canadian Arts Gallery, Stratford, Ont.; Green Gallery, Barrie, Ontario. He lives in Barrie with his wife Cathy and their three daughters.

References
Midland & Penetang Free Press Herald, Ont., Aug. 15, 1969 "Exhibits at Oshawa gallery"
Ibid, Oct. 24, 1969 "Art Gallery features works by Midlander"
Midland Georgian Tourist, Ont., August, 1969 "Exhibits at Oshawa gallery"
Barrie Banner, Ont., Nov. 11, 1970 "Barrie artist in jury show"
Info. from artist, Jan. 26, 1976

NIXON, Donald Allan

b. 1928

Born in Hamilton, Ontario, he began painting seriously at the age of fifteen and studied art while attending Westdale Secondary School under Miss Eleanore Fiennes-Clinton and Ida G. Hamilton and also under F.H. Varley at the Doon School of Fine Arts. He has produced a number of important collages and has held four one-man shows in Hamilton at the Wesdale Gallery also a solo show at McMaster University. He has participated in group shows at McMaster University, at the Blue Barn Gallery, Ottawa, at the Four Seasons Outdoor Exhibition sponsored by Carling where he won the Mixed Media Award, and in group shows elsewhere. In 1969 he sold off nearly one hundred pieces of his work (oils, acrylics, brush drawings, sketches and collages) at his home in Hamilton before moving to smaller living quarters with his mother Mrs. B. Marie Nixon. He has written several articles for the Hamilton Society for Education through Art and the Ontario Society for Education through Art. He has also lectured to the Art Appreciation Group of the Women's University Club of Hamilton and has given demonstrations at the Art Gallery of Hamilton.

References
> The Hamilton Spectator, Ont., Sept. 25, 1969 "15 years of his life up for sale Saturday"
> Ibid, Sept. 29, 1969 "Teacher buys pupil's art"
> NGC Info. Form, 9 Mar., 1967

NIZAMI, Harris M.

b. 1943

Born in Pakistan, he received his formal education in the University of Karachi, Pakistan, and in the U.S.A. at Minnesota and came to Canada in 1966. A teacher at the Gull Lake High School, Saskatchewan, in 1968 he held a solo show of his paintings at Gull Lake with the intention of holding exhibitions at Swift Current, Regina and Saskatoon. An objective and abstract painter his work was well received. Sculptor and photographer as well.

References
> Gull Lake Advance, Sask., July 3, 1968 "Teacher Holds Painting Exhibition"
> Ibid, July 10, 1968 "Artist Presents Abstract and Life Paintings"

NOEH, Anna

She studied mural design and painting at the Academy of Applied Arts of Budapest where she won several prizes for wood-batik murals, a medium which she invented. She entered the Academy of Fine Arts in Vienna in 1956 where she studied for a year before coming to Canada in 1958. She exhibited a collection of her painted batiks at the two-craftsmen show at the Galerie des Artisans of the Canadian Handicrafts Guild in Montreal. She used the usual wax technique but painted instead of dyed her designs on Indian raw silk. She was planning to study the technique of weaving in France.

NOEH, Anna (Cont'd)

References
La Patrie, Mtl., 11 June, 1967 "De la beauté dans la maison: tapisserie et poterie"
The Montreal Star, June 5, 1967 "Folklore Designs — Fresh Vistas In Art" by Doris Giller

NOËL, Jean
b. 1940

Born in Montreal, P.Q., he received his B.A. from Worcester, Mass., U.S.A., and became interested in painting, then sculpture about 1961 studying at the Ecole des Beaux-Arts under Louis Archambault (1960-63). He did his early sculpture in wood and metal then became interested in plastics with which he has carried out experimentation. He received assistance from the Canada Council for his work in sculpture. His solo shows include those at Ecole d'Architecture de Montréal (1965); Galerie L'Art Français, Mtl. (1965); Galerie Le Gobelet, Mtl. (1967); Galerie Soixante, Mtl. (1968); Galerie du Siècle, Mtl. (1969) Carmen Lamanna Gallery, Tor. (1969) and elsewhere. Commenting on his work in 1968 *Artscanada* noted, "The vibrant colours of plastic came as a sudden revelation to Jean Noël whose earlier work had been in wood and metal. The latter media had been sufficient until he discovered what pleasure he took in the intensity and subtle gradations of colour possible in plastics. He uses colour and form in his airblown work with a unique lushness of expression. One large piece, resembling a human aorta, is blood red; behind it pulses a light, effecting a highly sensuous, irregular breathing movement. Noël sees his work — both the organic and geometric pieces as an exploration of " . . . essential masses, shapes, colours, their relationship to each other, their relationship to and effect on people. The works are not to be framed and hung on walls but to become primarily non-functional containers, non-functional architecture, see-through packaging for people." He was appointed titular head of the International Arts Studio in Paris for the Quebec City section in 1970. His work has been displayed at the Contemporary Art Museum in Montreal, the Youth Pavilion of Expo '67, the Canadian Pavilion, Expo '70, Osaka, Japan, the Seventh Biennial of Canadian Painting and others. He is represented in the collection of the National Gallery of Canada and elsewhere.

References
La Presse, Mtl., P.Q., April 6, 1968 "L'oeuvre ramenée à des éléments visuels primaires"
The Toronto Telegram, Ont., July 4, 1968 "Art . . . on anything BUT canvass" by Bernadette Andrews
Ibid, "Art — Age of big sculpture, but where will it hang?" by Bernadette Andrews
Quebec Le Soleil, Quebec City, No. 8, 1969 "Le sculpteur aux prises avec les problèmes de la création et de la technique"
The Montreal Star, P.Q., 3 January, 1970 "Back To Square One: A Discussion" by Arthur Bardo
Quebec Chronicle-Telegraph, Mtl., P.Q., July 11, 1970 "Mtl. Sculptor Assigned Post"
Le Droit, Ottawa, Ont., July 22, 1970 "Le sculpteur Jean Noël, nouveau titulaire du Studio du Québec à la Cité des arts de Paris"
Le Devoir, Aug. 8, 1973 "Oeil pour Oeil — Doigt pour doigt' au Musée d'art contemporain"
La Presse, Mtl., P.Q., 2 Aug., 1973 'Oeil pour oeil, doigt pour doigt"
The Montreal Star, P.Q., 25 Aug., 1973 "Look . . . and Do touch" by Chaterine Bates

NOËL, Jean (Cont'd)

Artscanada Nos. 120/121 "Plastics" P. 23
                122/123 "Exhibition Reviews" P. 41, 42
                138/139 "Exhibition Reviews" P. 59
                148/149 "Lausanne & Venice, Summer '70"
                150/151 "the Concours artistique du Quebec 1970" P. 61
L'Art Au Quebec Depuis 1940 par Guy Robert, La Presse, 1973, P. 423, 446
Seventh Biennial of Canadian Painting, 1968 (catalogue), P. 52-53
NGC Info. Form rec'd 1968

NOËL, Roland

Born in the Gaspé area, he drew from the time he could hold a pencil in his hand and at thirteen won a prize for a sketch he did in coloured pencil. He studied for a time under François Coutellier then at Mount Allison University, Sackville, N.B., before attending the University of Moncton part time under Claude Roussel. He studied next under Sid Dobson. A landscape painter and commercial artist he was intending to study at the Nova Scotia College of Art. Lives at Moncton, N.B.

Reference
    Telegraph-Journal, Saint John, N.B., Feb. 6, 1970 "His Life Is Prettier Picture Now" by Vera Ayling

---

NOLTE, Gunter
b. 1938

Born in Germany he made his first stone and bronze sculptures in 1956 and in 1959 came to Montreal, Canada, where he studied drawing and etching at the School of Art and Design of the Montreal Museum of Fine Arts. From 1964 he has participated in Canadian group shows and received an Honourable Mention from the Canadian Society of Graphic Art (1966) and First Prize in Sculpture at the Winnipeg Show (1968). Viewing his 1972 show at the Martal Gallery, Montreal, Michael White of *The Gazette* noted, "He uses very simple materials, plaster, cement, fired terra cotta, stone and plastics. He also uses white latex molding material as a special means of bringing out some of the qualities. The key to the show is to allow yourself the maximum of pleasure from the simple things of the show. The awareness that one can achieve is almost universally transferable. The slightly bulging roundness of a molded bag is the quality of any container from a vegetable to a human form like a breast. The sculptures remain as touchstones or standards of the qualities. The overall field of this modern contemporary sculptural experimentation, Nolte's work is gentle and gentile . . . . His pieces have fineness and fragility that demand a rather tense respect, that may limit the actual transfer of awareness of qualities. On the other hand this will make them fit more easily into the already rather scuplturally refined modern home interior . . . . " Nolte is represented in the collections of the Winnipeg Art Gallery, Musée d'Art Contemporain (Mtl.). He received assistance from the Canada Council and the last year he spent in Germany was awarded a scholarship from the Kulturkreis im Bundesverband der Deutschen Industrie. He has as well exhibited his work at Galerie Sherbrooke, Montreal, a number of times.

NOLTE, Gunter (Cont'd)

References

La Presse, Mtl., P.Q., Jan. 17, 1970 "Concept ou sculpture"
The Gazette, Mtl., P.Q., Jan. 17, 1970 "Variations on original make up Nolte exhibit"
The Montreal Star, P.Q., Jan. 19, 1970 "Plastic sculpture exhibit by Nolte" by Arthur Bardo
The Gazette, Mtl., P.Q., Mar. 22, 1972 "Year's first modern sculpture show" by Michael White
Biographical Info. by NGC.

NONCOURT, Michel de
b. 1941

Born in Grand-Mère, P.Q., he studied at the Ecole des Beaux-Arts, Montréal, and specialized in sculpture. He held his first one-man show at Sept-Iles, Quebec in 1964 and subsequent shows at Galerie La Masse, Mtl. (1965); Galerie La Rocaille, Mtl. (1965); Centre Culturel de Longueuil (1967) and Biosphère, Terre des Hommes, Mtl. (1968). His sculpture erected in a park in Longueuil, has the solidity of iron combined with spatial lightness. Sometimes he uses light filtering through water, in his search for a natural approach which shows itself as much in his works as in his love for the country and the open air. He has participated in the following group shows: Sculptures of Quebec at Musée d'Art Contemporain, Mtl. (1969); Pavillion de Monaco, Terre des Hommes, Mtl. (1969); La Maison des Arts La Sauvegarde, Mtl. (1969). Has been co-ordinator of arts at la Régionale Le Royer de Montréal-Est.

References

Montreal-Matin, Mtl., P.Q., Sept. 30, 1968 "Des arts et des hommes − La Sculpture, C'est Comme Une Plante Dans Un Jardin" par Denis Tremblay
Ibid, Aug. 28, 1969 "Des arts et des hommes − Une sculpture à Longueuil et pas encore de protestations!" par Denis Tremblay
Biographical Info., NGC

NONNAST, Paul
b. 1948

Born in Philadelphia, PA., he studied at the Tyler School of Art under sculptor Italo Scanga (1968) and at the Vancouver School of Art (1968-70) and has exhibited his work at the Bau-Xi Gallery, Van., B.C. (1969) and the Burnaby Art Gallery, Burnaby, B.C. (1972). Lives in Vancouver, B.C.

Reference

NGC Info. Form rec'd 1969

NOORDHOEK, Harry Cecil
b. 1909

Born in Moers, Germany, of Dutch parentage, he came to Canada with his parents at the age of five and they settled on a prairie farm near Duhamel, Alberta. At

NOORDHOEK, Harry Cecil (Cont'd)

eighteen he went back to Europe to study at Gamaldegalerie, Kassel, Germany (1927-30). He returned to Canada and settled in Montreal to live and work in 1930. He held his first solo show of landscape paintings in 1934 at the Top of The Hill Gallery (Beaver Hall Hill). In 1939 he joined the Canadian Army and served with the R.C.E.M.E. as an instrument mechanic until 1946. In 1950 he visited Paris, Cologne, Frankfurt, Cassell and Amsterdam. Returning home he entered his most active period producing many fine pieces of sculpture and moving into prominence with the winning of several honours including The Sir Otto Beit Medal for Sculpture of Special Merit in the British Commonwealth (1965); Concours Artistiques-Acquisition Prize, Provincial Museum of Quebec; Canadian Arts Award to study one year in Great Britain (1967) at Cornwall near St. Ives where he worked in native British stone; and a short term Canada Council Award to spend three months in Carrara, Italy (1968) where he lived and worked with local marble and imported onyx (4 mo.). He has participated in numerous exhibitions throughout Canada and Europe. In an Arp-like tradition Noordhoek has added his own individualism to his fine work gaining him an international reputation. In 1969 he represented Canada in the 6th International Biennial in Carrara and exhibited a three-ton sculpture in white Carrara marble at the International Open-Air Sculpture Exhibition in Milan, Italy. A member of the Société des Arts Plastiques (Mtl.); the Association of Quebec Sculptors (Mtl.); Associate of the Royal Canadian Academy. Represented in the collections of the City of Alma, Quebec and the Quebec Provincial Museum. Lives at Dorval, P.Q., with his wife Lorraine.

References
Nat. Gal. of Can. Info. Form (see detailed list of writings about artist)
L'Art Au Quebec Depuis 1940 par Guy Robert, La Presse, 1973, P. 240, 248, 250
Vie Des Arts, Winter, 1965-66, P. 47

NORBURY, Frank H.

(c) 1871-1965

Born in Liverpool, England, he studied at the Liverpool City School of Art; the Lambeth Model School and the School of Art, Architecture, Liverpool Univeristy. He was instructor of carving at the School of Architecture where he had studied and taught as well at the Liverpool School of Art. During the First World War he served in the Royal Army Service Corps and rose to the rank of Major receiving the O.B.E. and the Croce di Guerra (Italy). He came to Canada in 1920 and for twenty years was art critic for *The Edmonton Journal*. As a sculptor he worked in wood, bronze and stone and completed war memorials for Red Deer and Holden Alberta, and did hand carved wooden furniture for the Central Masonic Temple in Edmonton.

Reference
The Edmonton Journal, Alta., Mar. 11, 1922 "Red Deer's War Memorial Statue, an Epic in Stone, Is Nearing Completion" by W. Everard Edmonds
Ibid, Dec. 28, 1965 "Prominent Sculptor Dies Sunday In City"

NORD, Heather

Born and educated in Picton, she is well known in Prince Edward County as a skilled and talented potter. She was always interested in this art form but only had time to devote to it after her marriage. While living in Timmins, she studied pottery with the Department of Recreation and became President of the Timmins Potters' Guild.

Reference
   Picton Gazette, Ont., July 15, 1970 "Skilled Potter in Barrie Widely Known in County."

NORGATE, Robert Maxwell
1920-1956

Born in Toronto, Ontario, the son of Ernest and Maria Norgate he received his education at Danforth Technical School under Fred Haines, Emanuel Hahn and C.J. Travers and at the Ontario College of Art, Toronto, where he won a Junior Scholarship, a Student's Club Scholarship and two books for his studies in sculpture given by Emanuel Hahn who was also a teacher there. He then attended the Cranbrook Academy of Arts (near Detroit) where he studied under Carl Milles on a scholarship. He returned to Canada to begin his career. He gained prominence as a sculptor and in the years that followed produced a wide variety of work in the media of marble, limestone, bronze, aluminum and beaten lead. In 1948 his "Swimmer Disrobing" was chosen as Canada's entry in the Olympic Games Art Competition held in the Victoria and Albert Museum, London, England. He opened a studio in Ottawa in 1952 which he intended to establish as an art centre. This same year his "Unknown Political Prisoner" was one of three models chosen out of twenty-four submitted by Canadian sculptors for the international competition sponsored by the Institute of Contemporary Arts, London, England. In 1954 he was curator and demonstrated at the exhibition of the Sculptors' Society of Canada at the Stratford Shakesperian Festival. He taught at the Northern Vocational School, Art Association of Montreal, Carleton College (Ottawa), Fisher Park High School (Ottawa) and was a member of the staff of the Ontario College of Art. He visited London and Paris in 1949 and 1953 and was a member of the Royal Canadian Academy, the Ontario Society of Artists and the Sculptors' Society of Canada. He died at the age of thirty-six and was survived by four sisters, Mrs. Art Barnes (Staten Island, NYC); Mrs. E. Irving (Owen Sound, Ont.) Mrs. Paul Lowe and Mrs. Norman Young (both of Tor.) and four brothers, Raymond (Hamilton, Ont.) Kenneth, William and Lee (all of Toronto).

References
   The Ottawa Citizen, Ont., May 29, 1952 "Drawings By Sculptor Reveal Fine Technique" by Carl Weiselberger
   The Ottawa Journal, Ont., Sept. 13, 1952 "Bearded Ottawa Sculptor Showing Work in New Studio" by W.Q. Ketchum
   The Ottawa Citizen, Ont., Sept. 10, 1952 "Sculptor May Establish New Art Center in City"
   Ibid, Nov. 4, 1952 "Small Exhibit By Norgate At The Odeon"
   Ibid, Sept. 17, 1952 "Unusual Sight At Art Show" by Carl Weiselberger
   Le Droit, Ottawa, Ont., Jan. 27, 1953 "Le sculpteur Robert Norgate"

NORGATE, Robert Maxwell (Cont'd)

The Ottawa Journal, Ont., Jan. 27, 1953 "Milton's Poem Inspiration For Sculptor's Contest Model"
Globe & Mail, Tor., Ont., Aug. 17, 1954 "Canadians' Sculpture On Show in Stratford" by John Kraglund
Ibid, Sept. 26, 1956 "Artist, Sculptor Displayed Works Across Canada" (obituary)
NGC Info. Form rec'd June 19, 1942

NORGROVE, Trev

This Toronto artist was commissioned by a group of Niagara Falls citizens to paint the portrait of former Mayor F.J. Miller. The painting is now hanging in the Niagara Falls City Hall.

References
Niagara Falls Review, June 22, 1965 "Portrait Honors Merged City's First Mayor" by Robin Moore

---

NORMAN, William
b. (c) 1942

Born in Ontario, he has been living in Keswick, New Brunswick since 1965. After graduating from a three year art education programme affiliated with the Central Technical School in Toronto and studies in pottery under Gordon Barnes, he was invited to come to New Brunswick as an instructor in pottery with the New Brunswick office of Economic Growth, Handicrafts Branch. In 1965 three of his pieces were chosen for "Ceramics 65" and later bought by the Ontario government. More pieces were chosen for "Ceramics 67"; also by External Affairs for a Canadian exhibition in Paris; and at the Atlantic Pavilion, Expo '67, others at Habitat '67; C.N.E. shows in Toronto; the O'Keefe Centre Flower and Garden Show (1968). His work is also represented in the Canadian Gallery of Art and the Chatelaine House of Tomorrow. Norman was awarded the "Craftsman Award 1967" by the Canadian Guild of Crafts. In November, 1969 he held a one-man show at the University of New Brunswick Art Centre, Fredericton and he exhibited thirty-three pieces in the Confederation Centre Gallery, Charlottetown in February, 1970. He was awarded a Canada Council bursary for study of visual arts in April, 1971.

References
Fredericton Gleaner, N.B., May 21, 1968 "Keswick Resident Is Master Craftsman" by Dave Gibbs
Ibid, Nov. 5, 1969 "UNB Art Centre" (photo and caption)
Telegraph Journal, Saint John, N.B., Nov. 10, 1969 "A One-Man Exhibition" (photo and caption)
Charlottetown Patriot, P.E.I., Feb. 5, 1970 "Centre gallery has new exhibition"
Fredericton Gleaner, N.B., April 20, 1971 "Area Artist To Get Council Bursary"

NORMANDEAU, Pierre-Aimé

1906-1965

Born in Outremont, P.Q., he studied at the Ecole des Beaux-Arts, Montreal, l'Ecole Nationale Superieure de Céramiques de Sèvres, France and the Royal Ceramic School of Faenza, Italy. He was a professor for many years at both the School of Fine Arts and the Institute of Applied Arts of Montreal. In 1953 he won the first prize in the Quebec provincial contest for sculptors. He was a member and former President of the Sculptors' Society of Canada. He died in his 59th year and was survived by his wife Gilberte, his mother, a brother, Roland and a sister Mrs. Dante Mallozzi.

References

Chronicle Telegraph, Quebec, P.Q., Sept. 18, 1953 "Provincial Sculpture Contest Won By Pierre Normandeau"
The Montreal Star, P.Q., Nov. 4, 1965 "Obituaries"

NORMANDIN, Richard

b. 1934

Born in Shawinigan, P.Q., he studied at the Ecole des Beaux-Arts, Montreal (1953-58) then worked as an interior decorator and graphic artist for CKTM-TV (1958-61) and also studied engraving under Albert Dumouchel. He opened his own advertising agency in 1961. A graphic artist, painter and muralist his painting moved into the non-figurative hard edge area. Early in his career he worked in inks on various colours also in pastels, gouaches, oils and quick drying plaster. Later he chose acrylic on masonite. In 1966 he created an outdoor mural for the Institut de Technologie, Shawinigan, in two sections each measuring 23 ft. x 26 ft. These two sections were made up from a total of 84 aluminum panels each measuring 46 include: Cultural Centre, Trois Rivières (1968, 1970, 1973); Galerie Les Gens de Mon Pays (1973); Galerie Fantasmagorique, Trois Rivières; Galerie Lacroix, Chicoutimi; two-man show at Galerie du Vieux, Trois Rivières (1969); Four-man show, Galerie du Parc, Trois Rivières (1972). He was winner of a competition for the logo (insignia) representing Caisses d'Epargne et d'Entraide Economique de Quebec (awarded by the Administration Council) and he has created logos for other organizations. He has also exhibited his work at Maison des Arts La Sauvegarde, Montreal and in Quebec Provincial Competitions.

References

La Presse, Mtl., P.Q., Nov. 26, 1966 "Une sculpture toute d'aluminium" par L. Gagnon
Shawinigan Falls Les Chutes, P.Q., Sept. 11, 1968 "Exposition du peintre Richard Normandin au Centre Culturel"
La Voix de Shawinigan, P.Q., Sept. 18, 1968 "Exposition de tableaux de Richard Normandin au Centre Culturel"
L'Echo du St. Maurice, Shawinigan, P.Q., Sept. 11, 1968 "Richard Normandin au Centre Culturel"
Le Nouvelliste, Trois Rivières, P.Q., Sept. 21, 1968 "L'artiste explique ses méthodes de travail lors d'un colloque pendant l'exposition"
Grand' Mère-Le Laurentien, P.Q., Oct. 11, 1968 "Exposition du peintre Richard Normandin au Centre Culturel"
Le Nouvelliste, Trois Rivières, P.Q., Feb. 8, 1969 "Exposition conjointe de Pierre Landry et Richard Normandin"

NORMANDIN, Richard (Cont'd)

Ibid, July 10, 1969 "Un sigle soumis par M. Richard Normandin choisi à l'unanimité"
Ibid, Sept. 24, 1969 "L'art d'environnement compte de plus en plus d'adhérents" par Jocelyne Milot
Ibid, April 9, 1970 "L'espace et la lumière pour Richard Normandin"
Ibid, Feb. 5, 1972 L'ouverture de la Galerie du Parc est un événement marquant"
Ibid, Feb. 14, 1972 "Quatre artistes de grande classe présente la première exposition" par René Lord
Ibid, Feb. 8, 1973 "La Carrière de Richard Normandin"
Le Soleil, Que., P.Q., 13 Mar., 1973 "Les formes géométriques de Richard Normandin"
L'Art Au Quebec, Depuis 1940 par Guy Robert, La Presse, Mtl., P.Q., 1973, P. 157, 159, 385

NORRIS, George

A sculptor, he graduated from the Vancouver School of Art. He then studied with the Yugoslav master Ivan Mestrovic at Syracuse University and studied in London on a British Council Scholarship. He has taught night school classes for the UBC extension and the Vancouver School of Art, although he has been a full-time working sculptor for many years. He has worked in various media and on a wide range of buildings. Believing that "sculpture is essentially a public art form", he has closely collaborated with architects Ian Davidson, Barry Downs, Blair Mac-Donald and Gerald Hamilton during the 1957-70 period. Several of his sculptures are famous for their exhibition in public locations. The 1961 Salmon Fountain in Nanaimo and the 1961 symbolic sculptured screen "City of Lead and Zinc" presented to the town of Trail by Consolidated Mining and Smelting Company for display in the city offices are two examples. Other works in Vancouver include the crucifix, Stations of the Cross, and exterior decoration for the Holy Name Roman Catholic Church and three beaten copper reliefs for East Asiatic House. The lobby sculpture in the Pacific Press Building, a male figure of welded and beaten copper is also Norris' work. Perhaps his most famous piece, however, is his 1968 crablike stainless steel fountain sculpture in the reflecting pool in front of Vancouver's Centennial Museum – H.R. MacMillan Planetarium complex at Vanier Park, a gift of the women of Vancouver to the city to celebrate the 1967 Canadian Centennial. Mr. Norris also had sculptures on display in an October 1970 exhibition for the H & S Canvas Art Gallery, Vancouver.

References
Hamilton Spectator, Sept. 16, 1961 "Salute to the Salmon" by Stephen Franklin
Nelson Daily News, B.C., Dec. 20, 1961 "Mayor-Elect Unveils Newest Sculpture for City of Trail"
Vancouver Sun, Mar. 14, 1964 "Spirit of Lent Captured by Station" by Martha Robinson
The Province, Van., B.C., April 7, 1966 "World of Art – Sculpture dramatic from any angle" by Joan Lowndes
Vancouver Sun, Oct. 4, 1968 "Sculptor Had Fun Creating Museum's Showpiece" by Mike Jessen
The Province, Van., B.C., Oct. 20, 1970 "Death Transfixed in Driver" by Richard Simmins

NORRIS, Len (Leonard Matheson Norris)

b. 1913

Born in England, he came to Canada in 1926. His family settled in Southern Ontario. He received his schooling in Port Arthur and was then employed as a draftsman in the offices of the Port Arthur City Engineers. In 1953 he moved to Toronto where he worked first for the Elias Rogers Coal Company and in his free time began turning out occasional cartoons which he sold to the *Toronto Daily Star*. By the 1940's he was in the advertising business as an illustrator and art director. During the war, he served in the Canadian Army and created a new kind of cartooned army technical instruction manual and received an M.B.E. for his efforts. In 1945 he left the army and was hired by the Maclean-Hunter Publishing Company working as art director of *Canadian Homes and Gardens* and as cartoonist for *Maclean's* in Toronto. In 1950 he moved to Vancouver as staff cartoonist for *The Vancouver Sun*. In 1951 he received first prize in the National Newspaper Awards for caricature. In 1957 the Art Gallery of Toronto exhibited twenty-five of his cartoons. In the tradition of other leading cartoonists his work has appeared in book form.

References

Saturday Night, Tor., Ont. Apr. 12, 1952 "Cartoonist of The Year" by John Creed
Maclean's Magazine, May 10, 1958 "Len Norris' B.C. Sketchbook"
Le Droit, Ottawa, Ont., Feb. 14, 1959 "Len Norris, caricaturiste!"
Johann's Gift to Christmas by Jack Richards, illustrated by Len Norris
19th Annual Collection, Norris 101 Cartoons From The Sun
The Best of Norris, as selected by himself, M&S, Tor., 1955

NORWELL, Graham Noble

1901-1967

Born in Edinburgh, Scotland, the older of two sons of Captain John Craigie and Mary Helen Norwell. He came to Canada with his parents and brother Ian in 1914 aboard the "S.S. Grampian" (Allan Lines). After a short period in Montreal the Norwell family moved to Kingston, Ontario, where Graham's father took a position as Provost Marshal for the Military District No. 3 from 1914 to 1918. There the Norwell brothers completed their education. In 1920 Graham and Ian went their separate ways. Graham went to South America, Europe and the United States and during his stay in New York visited Greenwich Village where he saw artists and writers at work. On his return to Canada that same year he entered the Ontario College of Art where he studied under Arthur Lismer, G.A. Reid, J.W. Beatty and Robert Holmes and won a scholarship and Honourable Mention in Design. He seems to have studied only a year at the College then went on to Paris and then London where he met Augustus John and became his pupil. Travelling to the United States he was hired in 1922 as a well-paid commercial artist for a large industrial firm in New York City. After several weeks with this firm he went on a holiday in the mountains and was enjoying himself so much that he overstayed his leave. The company sent him a cheque for $100 for the first week, $50 for the second week, and $10 for the third week and the fourth week a ham sandwich with a note which read "Please return to work at once." Reluctantly Norwell did return to work. Probably lonesome for Canada he returned there and settled in Ottawa for a period where he did some serious painting. Now twenty-one he received

NORWELL, Graham Noble (Cont'd)

favourable reviews in the Ottawa papers during his showing at James Wilson and Company when *The Ottawa Citizen* noted, "There are about 75 pictures on view. There are some water colors and some pastels, but the majority are oils. The whole indicates an unusual finish and maturity, but a finish and a maturity that hold promise of something more distinguished in the future. Mr. Norwell's work possesses courage and conviction. He handles any scene in almost any medium with confidence and ease. His conceptions are well imagined and are well carried out. There is freedom in his lines and forms, and his handling of color and his composition are excellent to a degree." In 1924 he was elected a member of the Ontario Society of Artists. Much of his early work was done in oils but later he did many more water colours. In 1925 when he was living in London, England, Neville Chamberlain then Minister of Health, visited his studio and bought two of his paintings. Norwell married the niece of Austen Chamberlain, half brother of Neville. Later however the marriage was dissolved. After he had returned to the United States Norwell married a young lady writer from Rochester, New York, but this marriage failed after Norwell's repeated solo trips to the countryside where he painted to his heart's content and enjoyed a brew in his relaxation. Many of his difficulties in life developed because of his liking for seclusion and alcohol. Eventually he took up residence in the lower-end of Montreal renting space in various run-down apartments. His poor diet led to his poor health. He painted and sold many of his paintings in exchange for a few pleasurable hours in his favourite tavern. From time to time he managed to escape from the city to his beloved Laurentians where he painted pure landscapes in which he seldom included the human figure. But on occasion he would add skiers or campers to his landscapes and he also painted city scenes but landscapes were his main interest. He spent the last six years of his life in the Laurentians north of Montreal first at Ste. Agathe and finally at the Village of Val David where he died in his sixty-sixth year. He was survived by his brother Ian (John Craigie Norwell) also a painter who lives in Ottawa. Graham was probably at the height of career between 1925 and 1930 as evidenced by his success in London, England, and the inclusion of a reproduction of one of his canvases in Newton MacTavish's *The Fine Arts In Canada*. A year earlier the National Gallery of Canada had acquired its second painting by him entitled "Autumn, Ottawa Valley" and the Art Gallery of Toronto (Ontario) purchased one of his winter landscapes in 1930. During those years he had exhibited with the Ontario Society of Artists, the Royal Canadian Academy and at the Canadian National Exhibition. Some of his one-man shows include: James Wilson & Sons, Ottawa (1922), Montreal Museum of Fine Arts (1934); Johnson Art Galleries, Mtl. (1937), The Little Gallery (Photographic Stores), Ottawa (1947). He is represented in the collections of Hart House (Univ. of Tor.); the Art Gallery of Ontario and the National Gallery of Canada as mentioned. An unpublished biography on him was written by Gerald Shebib in 1970 and deposited in the National Gallery of Canada Library.

References

The Ottawa Citizen, Ont., Oct. 25, 1922 "Exhibition of Paintings by G.N. Norwell" by E.W.H.

The Ottawa Journal, Ont., Oct. 27, 1922 "Graham Norwell Has Exhibition Of Art"

The Ottawa Citizen, Ont., Oct. 28, 1922 "Ottawa Artists' Fine Work"

The Fine Arts In Canada by Newton McTavish, MacMillan, Tor., 1925 (ill. between 144 and 145)

NORWELL, Graham Noble (Cont'd)

The Gazette, Mtl., P.Q., Jan. 31, 1934 "Works By Norwell" (shown at Print Room of Mtl. Museum of Fine Arts)
Ibid, Oct. 18, 1937 "Graham Norwell Show At Johnson's"
The Ottawa Citizen, Ont., Aug. 8, 1947 "Art Display Inspires Genuine Appreciation" by W.M.A.
The National Gallery of Canada Catalogue, Vol. 3 by R.H. Hubbard, NGC, 1960, P. 236
The Gazette, Mtl., P.Q., Sept. 1, 1966 "His Only Landscape – 'His' Laurentians" by David Tafler
Ibid, June 23, 1967 "Artist Norwell Dies; Well-Known Here"
The Ottawa Citizen, Ont., June 24, 1967 "Painter dies" (CP Mtl.)
The Hart House Collection of Canadian Paintings by Jeremy Adamson, Univ. Tor. Press, 1969, P. 102
Art Gallery of Ontario, The Canadian Collection by Helen Pepall Bradfield McGraw-Hill, Tor., 1970, P. 339
The Canadian Art Auction Record Vol. V, 1973 compiled by H.C. Campbell, Chief Librarian, Tor. Pub. Lib., Bernard Amtmann Inc., Mtl., 1974, P. 49-50
Canadian Art Auction 1968-1975, Edited by Geoffrey Joyner, Sotheby & Co. (Can.) Ltd., Tor., Ont., 1975, P. 147
"Graham Noble Norwell, 1901-1967" by Gerald Shebib, Ottawa, 1970

NORWELL, John Craigie

b. 1903

Born at Elie, Fife, Scotland, he began painting at the age of six but turned to other interests until he was over fifty. Influenced by his mother, a botanist and illustrator, who painted in oils and water colours, he is also influenced by the work of his brother Graham although John is self-taught. He admires as well, the work of Tom Thomson and Cornelius Krieghoff. Working in oils he paints landscapes in a decorative realistic style. Some of his work has been on display on the Sparks Street Mall, Ottawa, and at various other locations. He held a solo show of twenty-one paintings at the Bromley Square Apartments, Carling Avenue, Ottawa, where his work was well received. His subjects for that show were taken from the coast of Nova Scotia; from rural Quebec including Wakefield, Ste. Agathe, Gracefield, Montebello and scenes from the coast of California and Maine, U.S.A. For many years he was employed by the firm of Hiram Walker and later with an importer of wines. He has also been active for many years as a swimming instructor. He lives in Ottawa with his wife.

Reference
Visit with artist at his home
Viewing his one-man show in Ottawa in 1977

NOSEWORTHY, George

b. (c) 1930

After spending seventeen years as art director of a Madison Avenue educational publishing house, he was so impressed with a summer visit to Newfoundland where his father was born, that he decided to stay. In 1966 he moved to Conception Bay in order to paint. Noseworthy also teaches art and music to hundreds of local

NOSEWORTHY, George (Cont'd)

children in an effective and informal manner that has aroused quite a bit of interest among educators including Lloyd Dennis co-author of Ontario's Hall-Dennis report. Noseworthy has also discovered impressive talent including a boy who has sold enough of his paintings to finance part of his university education. He is also responsible for the founding of Newfoundland's first fisherman's museum containing over seven hundred artifacts some dating over two hundred years. Since his move to Hibb's Cove he has completed over two hundred and twenty oil paintings, forty-three of which are about the annual seal hunt, and thirty-two of these hang in St. John's new city hall. To paint these canvases he took to the ice floes to record what might be the end of an era for this industry.

References
> *St. John's Evening Telegram*, Nfld., Sept. 6, 1968 "Art Display to Benefit Hospital Fund"
> *St. John's News*, Nfld., Dec. 5, 1969 "Preserving the Traditions of our Fishermen"
> Ibid, June 5, 1970 "Artist George Noseworthy Depicts the Seal Hunt"
> *Time*, July 13, 1970 "The Pied Piper of Hibb's Cove"
> *Toronto Daily Star*, Ont., Apr. 1, 1972 "The Pied Piper Painter of Conception Bay" by Claire Hoy

NOTTEBROCK, Pat

A painter of thoroughbred horses, he was born on a farm in the Barrhead area, eighty miles north of Edmonton, Alberta. As a child, he also lived on farms in Edmonton and in Saskatchewan. He worked at tracks and minor rodeos, sketching the horses he worked with. Captain Stanley Harrison, ranch owner Fort Qu'Appelle, impressed with the boy's sketches, hired him to work on the ranch so that he could aid his art education. At the age of seventeen Nottebrock received his first commission from Russ Graul of Montreal. Since about 1959 he has covered the racing circuit, painting many of North America's top racing horses including those owned by Jack Stafford (Stafford Foods) and E.P. Taylor (Canadian business magnate). Nottebrock intends to paint other subjects as well.

Reference
> Clipping from periodical – "Horse Painter" by Ken Francis

NOVAK, Yozef
b. (c) 1940

Born in Yugoslavia, a cartoonist and draughtsman he took up abstract art in 1957. In 1964 Wallack's Art Gallery, Ottawa, presented an exhibition of his abstract paintings and collages.

Reference
> *The Ottawa Journal*, March 17, 1964 "Abstract Art Exhibit At Wallack's Gallery" by W.Q. Ketchum

NOWAKIWSKA, Halyna

Born in the Ukraine where she received her art education. She came to Canada and since 1949 has lived in Toronto. Working chiefly in oils on masonite she has created big colourful paintings which have been well received. They include such scenes as "Song of Our Days" which depicts three young persons with shaggy hair and short skirts huddling over a guitar, or another painting "Old Song" of days in the past. Mrs. Nowakiwska uses her oils lavishly and in street scenes embeds rough bits of newsprint into her work to give added effect to her painting. A solo show of her work was held at the W. & W. Galleries, Toronto, in the fall of 1966.

Reference
Globe & Mail, Tor., Ont., Oct. 31, 1966 "Nowakiwska bestrides old, new worlds"

NUDDS, Ralph Arnold James
b. 1921

A sculptor, he was born in Blenheim, Ontario and moved to Hamilton, his current residence, in 1923. He studied on his own and under his father and brothers, also lithographers and painters. In 1946 he began welding by making wrought iron furniture. In 1965 he started sculpting in bronze and steel. The Sobot Gallery presented his small scale figures in two shows: October, 1967 and October, 1968 when *The Globe and Mail* noted, "His flowing follow-through of line and a cross-hatching punctuation of surfaces make many of the pieces strong."

References
The Globe & Mail, Tor., Ont., Oct. 7, 1967 "Sobot Gallery"
Ibid, "Glimpses into two artists' solitary worlds"
NGC Info. Form rec'd May 22, 1968

NUDDS, Wallace Albert John
b. 1919

Born in Blenheim, Ontario, a painter, sculptor and cartoonist he studied under John Martin at the Dundas Valley School of Art. Hundreds of his cartoons have been published and his sculptures shown in several galleries. He has exhibited his work at the Sobot Gallery, Tor. (1968); Main Gallery, Hamilton (1970 two-man); Gallery Reos Saltfleet Township (1970, three one-man shows); Beckett Gallery, Hamilton (1970); Tom Thomson Gallery, Owen Sound (1970).

References
NGC Info. Form

NUGENT, John Cullen
b. 1921

Born in Montreal, P.Q., he was raised in Lumsden, Saskatchewan, and studied at St. John's University, Collegeville, Minnesota, then served his apprenticeship under

NUGENT, John Cullen (Cont'd)

Donald Humphrey at St. Cloud, Minnesota, in sculpture and silversmith work. For many years he has produced candles of good quality for churches and individuals. For instance in 1948 he sold two tons of candles and in 1957 ten tons. At first he just supplied individuals and stores in Western Canada then finally centres throughout Canada. In 1960 he received a Canada Council Grant and built a studio and foundry in the form of a unique cone shape. There he casts his work in bronze or other metals using the lost-wax process. He prepared two aluminum alloy life-sized bird sculptures of the whooping crane for the small courtyard outside the main entrance of the Regina airport building. The sculptures were commissioned by the Department Of Transport and made from models prepared by the Saskatchewan Museum of Natural History. In 1964 he created a memorial near Welby, Saskatchewan to commemorate the site of a warehouse and commercial centre for the North West Company built in 1785. Viewing his work M.H. for the *Journal of Royal Architectural Inst. of Canada* noted, " . . . Mr. Nugent has caught something of the essence of hope; his work sits on the landscape in nobility and repose with the ageless quality of a Henry Moore figure on a Scottish Moor." In 1968 he completed a statue of Louis Riel on the legislative grounds of the Regina parliament buildings. In 1975 he was awarded a commission by the federal government's fine arts program for a sculpture to be placed in front of the Grain Commission Building in downtown Winnipeg. The sculpture is 48 feet long, 24 feet wide and eight feet high and is of painted steel. An associate professor and chairman of the visual arts department of the University of Regina, Nugent has held several solo shows of his work including one at the Norman Mackenzie Art Gallery in 1970 where his sculptures in plastic, steel and bronze were on view as a requirement for a new staff member of the visual arts department of the university. Subsequently he held a joint showing in 1973 at the Norman Mackenzie Gallery with painter Ted Godwin. Lives at Lumsden, Saskatchewan.

References

Canadian Art, Summer, 1955, Vol. 12, No. 4 "The Arts in Saskatchewan Today" by R.H. Hubbard, P. 155

Western Producer, April 25, 1957 photos and story by R.H. Macdonald

The Arts in Canada, Ed. Malcolm Ross "Handicrafts" by A.T. Galt Durnford P. 158

Regina Leader-Post, Sask., Apr. 3, 1961 "Artist launching rare operation" by Donna Dilschneider

Star-Phoenix, Saskatoon, Sask., Apr. 8, 1961 "Replica of Whooping Crane" (photo and story)

Weekend Magazine, 1961 Photos by Bruce Moss

Prairie Farmer, Winnipeg, Man., May 17, 1961

Journal of Royal Architectural Inst. of Canada, January, 1964 "Features"

Time (Can. Edition), tl., Oct. 13, 1967 "Saskatchewan – The Spirit or the Man?"

News-Chronicle, Port Arthur, Ont., Apr. 29, 1969 (Column not identified.)

Maclean's Magazine, Tor., Ont., May, 1969 "One sculptor's racy revenge with an embarrassingly real Riel"

Milestone Mail, Sask., Oct. 11, 1969 "Round and About"

Regina Leader Post, Sask., Nov. 26, 1970 "Plastic, steel, bronze show" by Ruth Warick

Winnipeg Free Press, Man., June 14, 1975 "Sask. Artist To Create Wpg. Sculpture"

NGC Info. Form undated

NULITIS, Arnolds

b. 1896

A Latvian by birth, Nulitis came to Canada in 1951 and settled in Toronto. He had graduated from the Academy of Arts, Riga, Latvia, having studied under Professors Purvitis, Tillbergs, and Tone. Since 1953 he has been a member of the Colour and Form Society and since 1954 has served as member and Vice-President of the Canadian Latvian Artists' Society. Nulitis has exhibited his paintings in Latvia (1932-43), Germany (1948-9), Holland (1948), Paris (1949), and Canada since 1952.

Reference

NGC Info. form rec'd Sept. 26, 1956

NUTT, Elizabeth Styring

1870-1946

Born on the Isle of Man, following the death of her father, her mother and family of five moved to Sheffield, England, where both parents had originally come from. There Elizabeth attended a private school in the city and then entered the Sheffield School of Art where she studied under J.T. Cook, Henry Archer and others. At the school her fellow students Arthur Lismer, F.H. Varley, Hubert V. Fanshawe and William S. Broadhead were later to make a name for themselves in the history of Canadian art. Next she studied at Newlyn, England under Stanhope Forbes and then in Paris, France, at the Sorbonne (on a scholarship) and in Florence, Italy travelling with her mother to study there under Professor Simi. Returning to Sheffield she taught at the Firshill Branch Evening Art School and also spent some years writing for the Hamsworth publications mainly on art. In 1914 she completed her Art Masters Diploma awarded by the University of Sheffield and also became a Fellow of the National Society of Art Masters for her thesis on teaching of colour which was published in serial form. Some of her articles were produced in the *Book of Knowledge, The School Mistress* and she wrote a book entitled *Significance: or Flower Drawing with the Children*. In her own painting she exhibited with the Royal Academy, the Sheffield Society of Artists and the Paris Salon. She rose to prominence as an art teacher in various schools associated with the Sheffield School of Art which included the Pupil Teacher's Centre, The Training College and the University of Sheffield. In Canada Arthur Lismer had decided to leave his post as principal of the Victoria School of Art and Design in Halifax and recommended that Elizabeth Nutt be chosen as she was an ideal person of spirit and one who was very able. In 1919 she was appointed Principal of the Victoria School of Art and Design. She set out to create a new interest in fine art and toured the province during the first years of her principalship and succeeded in her task to a great degree. She also built up a wide collection of books at the School. In 1925 she was able to change the name of the School to the Nova Scotia College of Art. She became a member of the Nova Scotia Society of Artists in 1922, and exhibited her fine paintings with the Royal Canadian Academy (A.R.C.A. 1929) and in solo shows at the Nova Scotia College of Art as in 1931 when the writer for the Halifax *Mail* noted " . . . attention must certainly be drawn to the simply arresting paintings of the quaint English cottages in picturing which Miss Nutt, herself an English woman, wields her brush with such vigor and vitality that they take the visitor

NUTT, Elizabeth Styring (Cont'd)

captive, and lead him to linger long before them, recalling all that he has ever read about the picturesque and individual beauty of the little old cottages of old England." The following year tribute to her as a teacher of 'rare ability' who inspired her pupils with an enthusiasm to paint ships, fishing fleets, the sea and coast of Nova Scotia, was made by Albert H. Robson in his *Canadian Landscape Painters*. By 1936 she was advocating art appreciation courses for Canadian Schools and such courses were eventually adopted. She initiated interest in the granting of scholarships by each of the counties of Nova Scotia and through her efforts the Educational Council of the provincial Department of Education sponsored drawing classes at the College for teachers of the city schools; special Saturday morning classes in art for children were inaugurated in 1931; free classes in occupational therapy (small handcrafts) were given to service personnel during 1940-42 as well as a general increase in art activity for the public. In 1943, in failing health, she decided to resign her post at the College and to return to Sheffield where she died in 1946. She is represented in the collections of the National Gallery of Canada, Dalhousie University, Halifax and elsewhere.

Reference

"Significance" or Flower Drawing with the Children by Elizabeth Styring Nutt, J.W. Northend Ltd., West St., Sheffield, 1916 (reprinted 1921)
The Chronicle, Halifax, N.S., Dec. 5th, 1921 "Art's Place In The Community" (address given by Miss Nutt at Truro, N.S.)
Times, Moncton, N.B., Feb. 6, 1925 "Halifax Lady Gives Splendid Lecture On Canadian Art"
Whig-Standard, Kingston, Ont., April 11, 1929 "Art in Canada" by Elizabeth S. Nutt
Mail, Halifax, N.S., Oct. 15, 1931 "A Collection Of Paintings Of 'Quality' " (exhibition of paintings by E.S. Nutt at N.S. College of Art)
Star, Halifax, Oct. 19, 1931 "Will Continue Fine Exhibit Of Paintings"
Canadian Landscape Painters by A.H. Robson, Ryerson, Tor., 1932, P. 170, 172
The Gazette, Mtl., P.Q., Mar. 24, 1936 "Nova Scotian Art Making Progress" (address given by Miss Nutt to Maritime Women's Club of Montreal)
Ibid, Mar. 25, 1936 "Training In Art Need In Schools" (address given by Miss Nutt to Women's Art Society, Mtl.)
A Century of Canadian Art (catalogue) 1938, Tate Gallery, Lond. Eng., P. 26
The Montreal Standard, P.Q., Feb. 18, 1939 "Canadian Art and Artists – Miss Elizabeth S. Nutt, A.R.C.A." by Richard H. Haviland
Chronicle, Halifax, N.S., May 11, 1943 "Art College Principal For 24 Years Retires"
Mail, Halifax, N.S., May 11, 1943 "Art College Head Resigns"
Star, Halifax, N.S., May 12, 1943 "Noted Teacher Retires"
Canadian Art, Vol. 3, No. 1, 1945 "Art In Nova Scotia" by Leroy Zwicker
The Gazette, Mtl., P.Q. April 13, 1946 "Elizabeth Styring Nutt Succumbs in England"
Canadian Art, Its Origin and Development by William Colgate, Ryerson, Tor., 1943 (reprint paper. 1967), P. 142, 167, 173, 223
National Gallery of Canada Catalogue, Vol. 3 by R.H. Hubbard, NGC, Ott., 1960, P. 237
Canadian Painting in the Thirties by Charles C. Hill, NGC, Ott., 1975, P. 97
NGC Info. Form rec'd May 19, 1927

NYILASI, Tibor

b. (c) 1936

Born in Hungary, he studied drawing with Erno Dalos in the city of Dorog. Following the Hungarian uprising in 1956 he arrived in Canada in 1957. He settled in

NYILASI, Tibor (Cont'd)

Brantford and then spent almost two years in the local sanatorium recovering from tuberculosis. He then attended the Ontario College of Art for five years, graduating in 1964 with a medal as top student in fine arts. He has since taught applied anatomy for the Central Secondary School, Hamilton, and has exhibited his oils, water colours, temperas and pencil sketches at the Glenhyrst Art Exhibition (1963) and Gallery Yonge of the W & W Galleries, Toronto (1967). He also did display work, some of it for Expo pavilions and donated a mural, now on display in a Palmerston hospital, to the Ontario Department of Health in gratitude for his recovery. An accomplished musician he sings and plays the mandolin and performed with a Hungarian ensemble at Expo '67.

References

Brantford Expositor, Ont., Dec. 13, 1963 "Hungary Refugee Won TB Bout, Opens Glenhyrst Art Exhibition"
Globe & Mail, Tor., Ont., Aug. 5, 1967 "W & W Galleries"
Hamilton Spectator, Ont., Oct. 10, 1969 "No skullduggery here!" by Christine Cox

OAKLEY, Fred

He is among the artists commissioned by The Niagara Company to produce a series of paintings depicting rural Canada. His work includes illustrations for children's books, magazines, book covers, commercial posters, billboards, and newspaper advertisements. His paintings hang in the Hockey Hall of Fame, Greenwin Enterprises, Canadian Breweries, and other corporate headquarters.

Reference

Biographical information published by The Niagara Company

OBERGFELL, Richard
19-- -1971

Born into an artists' family in Germany, he studied painting for seven years at the State Academy of Art in Stuttgart and later taught there. In 1956 he emigrated to Canada, settling in Cranbrook, B.C., where he painted houses for a living until an auto accident forced him to turn to Fine Art in which he had been so thoroughly trained. In 1962 he moved to Vancouver, where he taught art for the Surrey and Langley night schools, as well as the Port Kells Art Group and the Fraser Valley Art Society. At the time of his death he was working on a school text (200 pages of text with over 400 illustrations) for the teaching of painting and drawing. His work has been displayed in the K.O.O.L. office, Cranbrook (1970) and the Centennial Arts Centre, New Westminster (1972).

References

Daily Townsman, Cranbrook, B.C., June 30, 1970 "Art Workshop Here"
New Westminster Columbian, B.C., April 17, 1971 "Surrey artist 'reactivates' artistic instinct" by Peter Maarsman
Ibid, Mar. 18, 1972 "Kollwitz, Obergfell on Show"

OBERNE, Marjorie Borden

An Ottawa painter she was first taught by Pegi Nicol McLeod. She then studied at the Art Association of Montreal, the Art Students' League of New York, the Chelsea Polytechnic of London, England, the Académie de la Grande Chaumière in Paris, and at the Wiener Kunstakademie, Vienna Austria. She also received encouragement for her work from the late Eric Brown, director of the National Gallery of Canada. In the years 1934-6 she worked with Dr. Marius Barbeau of the National Museum of Canada illustrating his books, as well as exhibiting her own landscapes and portraits at the National Gallery and the Ottawa Art Association. In 1937 she married and moved to Florida to raise a family. During this period of her life she became interested in teaching creative art to small children, working with Bertha Cowan of the Chicago Art Institute, Arthur Lismer of the Art Association of Montreal, Mrs. John Alford of the Rhode Island School of Design, and the University of Miami. After her return to Ottawa, she worked at Fairbairn Studio as a freelance commercial artist and returned to portrait drawing and painting.

Reference
The Ottawa Citizen (date unknown) "Ottawa Artist Has Given Pictures Quality of Corporeal Life" by Carl Weiselberger

O'BRIEN, Hazel

Born in Alberta, she attended art schools in Chicago and Los Angeles. Since 1961 she has been the head artist for the Horseman's Hall of Fame, Calgary, making models, murals, busts, sketches, and displays of western history for the museum.

Reference
Calgary Herald, Alberta, June 13, 1970 "Around the Town" by Suzanne Zwarun

O'BRIEN, J. Leonard
b. 1895

A New Brunswick legislator (1925-30 Legislative Assembly; 1940-45 House of Commons, Ottawa; 1958-65 Lieutenant-Governor of N.B.), he paints scenes of the lumbering industry he knew in his earlier years and other subjects seen during his travels to the Barbados, Ireland and England first captured on film and then transferred to canvas. A 1966 private showing at the Owens Museum of Fine Arts, Mount Allison University exhibited sixty-two pieces of his work.

References
Tribune-Post, Sackville, N.B., Oct. 6, 1966 "O'Brien Art Work Wins Praise Here"
Who's Who In Canada (1958-59 and on), Ed. by B.M. Greene, Assoc. Ed. G.W. Stratton

O'BRIEN, Lucius Richard
1832-1899

Born at Shanty Bay on Lake Simcoe, Ontario, the second son of Lt. Col. Edward George O'Brien, an army officer retired on half-pay (had also served as a British Naval Officer) who settled on a large tract of land on the shores of Lake Simcoe. Lucius was educated at Upper Canada College, Toronto, and later entered an architect's office where he learned surveying and drafting and finally studied and practised civil engineering. Few researchers have elaborated on what he did as an engineer. We are told however that he had a natural artistic talent and painted for years as a hobby until 1872 when, at the age of forty he turned to full-time painting. A self-taught artist he painted scenery in Ontario and Quebec and later journeyed through the wilderness of Western Canada and was one of the early Canadian painters to reveal the beauties of the Rocky and Selkirk Mountains of British Columbia. Later a western tour was backed by the Canadian Pacific Railway who sent him across Canada on a special train to stop at his will to select the best scenery possible. During his career he did small genre scenes in water colours as well and also did some portraits. One of his more frequently reproduced canvases "Sunrise on the Saguenay" a most magnificent painting owned by the National Gallery of Canada (R.C.A. diploma collection) has a striking likeness to the work of the American painter Albert Bierstadt as in Bierstadt's "Western Landscape" reproduced in Ian Bennett's *A History of American Painting* and other such artists as Martin Johnson Heade whose work also appears in this book. O'Brien worked mainly in water colours. He became a member of the Ontario Society of Artists in 1872 and was its vice-president from 1873 to 1880. He had a studio and home on College Street, Toronto where early meetings of the Society were held. The Art Gallery of Ontario has a medium-sized water colour which he did of his College Avenue home. He also became a charter member of the Royal Canadian Academy in 1880 and was the society's first president remaining in that office by election for the next ten years. During this period he worked closely with the Governors-General Dufferin and Lorne and performed his duties we are told with tact and discretion. His good education and middle upper class family background probably made him an ideal link with the influential of that day. O'Brien became art editor for *Picturesque Canada* and was himself a contributor to this two volume publication which had over 500 engravings on wood after the original work by the artists involved. This publication was released in 1882. In 1886 an exhibition of Canadian paintings was sent to the Colonial and Indian Exhibition at South Kensington, England, in which no less than fifteen pictures were done by O'Brien. His work was praised by a Mr. J.E. Hodgson, R.A., who described him as a "considerable and accomplished artist" and whose water colours were "impressive and would bear comparison with the works of the chosen professors of the art in London." Today O'Brien's work shows us what Canada looked like towards the turn of the century. At Sotheby's auction in 1968 the sum of twenty-three hundred dollars was paid for a water colour of an Indian encampment by a lake with Indians paddling ashore in two canoes (10" x 18½") and at another sale by Sotheby's in 1973 an O'Brien water colour of a forest scene with Indian sold for eleven hundred dollars (26-1/4 x 18-1/4). His oil on board, and oil on canvas paintings are not so common as his water colours but for further details see Sotheby's *Canadian Art At Auction 1968-1975* pages 147-149 available in bookstores. O'Brien died (aged 67) in Toronto where he had his studio and he was buried in St. Thomas Churchyard, Shanty Bay the settlement where he was born. In his later

O'BRIEN, Lucius Richard (Cont'd)

years he sketched in the Muskoka lakes district. He was married twice: in 1860 to Margaret St. John of Orillia; in 1888 to Katherine Brough of London, Ontario. E.F.B. Johnston writing almost fifteen years after his death recalled him as follows, "Preferring water colour as a medium, he devoted his talents to the simple and beautiful phases of nature. The lake district of Muskoka was for many years a favourite resort of O'Brien. The smooth surface of the small stretches of water with their changing and delicate colour framed in the dark green of the fir and pine and lit up by the tender sky, appealed to him with a strange fascination. His work is for the eye seeking rest and beauty, ... " In 1943 William Colgate described O'Brien's water colour style as "limpid and flowing" and him as an expert in his craft while in the same breath noted that he was lacking in imagination and invention in his passion to record nature exactly as he saw her being a former engineer viewing with the eye of a topographical artist. His work can be seen in the following collections: British Columbia Provincial Archives, Vic., B.C.; John Ross Robertson Coll. of Tor. Pub. Lib., Ont.; Mr. & Mrs. Jules Loeb, Tor., Ont.; Ontario Govt. Coll. at Dept Pub. Works Bldg., Tor.; Art Gallery of Ontario, Tor.; Agnes Etherington Art Gallery, Kingston, Ont.; National Gallery of Canada, Ottawa; Public Archives of Canada, Ottawa; New Brunswick Museum, Saint John, N.B.; Windsor Castle, England.

References

Picturesque Canada; the country as it was and is (2 Vols.), Ed. Geo. Monro Grant, Tor., 1882

Universal Cyclopaedia & Atlas, Vol. 8, Ed-in-Chief Chas Kendall Adams Revision Editor, Rossiter Johnson, D. Appleton & Co., NYC, 1902, P. 633

Canada And Its Provinces, Vol. 12 "Painting" by E.F.B. Johnston, 1914, P. 605

The Fine Arts In Canada by Newton MacTavish, MacMillan, Tor., 1925 (reprint by Coles, Tor., 1973), P. 24, 25

Canadian Landscape Painters, by A.H. Robson, Ryerson, Tor., 1932, P. 70-72

Canadian Art, Its Origin and Development by Wm. Colgate, Ryerson, Tor., 1943 (1967) P. 32-33

Encyclopedia of Canada, V. 5, Ed. W. Stewart Wallace, Univ. Assoc. of Can., Tor., Ont., 1948, P. 37

Canadian Water Colour Painting by Paul Duval, Burns & MacEachern, Tor., 1954, Plate 14

The Nat. Gal. of Can. Catalogue, Vol. 3, Can. Sch. by R.H. Hubbard, NGC, Ottawa, 1960, P. 237-239, 405 (Sunrise On The Saguenay)

Encyclopedia Canadiana, Vol. 7, Grolier, 1962, P. 420

The Development Of Canadian Art by R.H. Hubbard, NGC, Ottawa, 1967, P. 67, 68

The MacMillan Dictionary of Canadian Biography Edited by W. Stewart Wallace, MacMillan, Tor., 1963, P. 556

Painting in Canada/a history by J. Russell Harper, Univ. Tor. Press, 1966, P. 174, 176-7, 193, 194, 196-7, 201, 208 (ills. 174, 175, 178)

Great Canadian Painting/A Century of Art by Elizabeth Kilbourn, Frank Newfeld, Text by Ken Lefolii/Research by Wm. Kilbourn, Marjorie Harris, Sandra Scott, P. 33

Agnes Etherington Art Centre, Queen's University Permanent Collection, 1968 by Frances K. Smith, Kingston, No. 103

Early Painters and Engravers in Canada by J. Russell Harper, Univ. Tor. Pr., Tor., 1970, P. 239

Art Gallery of Ontario, the Canadian collection by Helen Pepall Bradfield, McGraw-Hill, Tor., P. 339-342

A Concise History of Canadian Painting by Dennis Reid, Oxford, Univ. Pr., Tor., 1973, P. 71, 85-8, 90, 95, 105, 107 (ill. 87, 88)

The Canadian Art Auction Record, Vol. V, 1973 compiled by H.C. Campbell, Chief Librarian, Tor. Pub. Lib., B. Amtmann Inc., Mtl., 1974, P. 50

O'BRIEN, Lucius Richard (Cont'd)

Canadian Art At Auction, 1968-1975 by Geoffrey Joyner, Sotheby & Co. (Can.), Tor., Ont., 1975, P. 147-149
The Ontario Community Collects/a survey of Canadian painting from 1766 to the present by William C. Forsey, Art Gal. of Ont., Tor., 1976, P. 142-3
Newspapers
The Windsor Daily Star, Ont., Sept. 3, 1949 "Anniversary of R.C.A.'s First President" by David Mawr
Examiner, Barrie, Ont., May 14, 1966 "Looking Back — Noted Water-Colorist Born At Shanty Bay" by Helen V. Cox

---

O'BRIEN, Michael David Joseph
b. 1948
Born in Ottawa, Ontario, he was raised in the Canadian Arctic the son of David and Elaine O'Brien. A self-taught artist he began drawing in 1970 and in 1971 exhibited his ink drawings at The Robertson Galleries, Ottawa. He also sculpts in sandstone. Lives in Manotick, Ontario.

References
The Ottawa Citizen, Ont., Nov. 23, 1971 "Delicate pen drawings depict natural things" by Jenny Bergin
NGC Info. Form dated Nov. 23, 1971

O'BRIEN, Paddy Gunn (Mrs.)
b. 1929
Born in Surrey, England, she stayed in Canada from 1940 to 1945 then returned to England. She studied at the Hammersmith School of Art, London (1946-47) and at the University of Reading, Berkshire (Fine Art Dept. — 1947-51). She emigrated to Canada to stay in 1951. She joined the staff of the London Public Art Museum, Ontario, in 1952, as assistant curator. During the period 1955-56 she studied at Académie de la Section D'or, Paris, France under Jean Souverbie. Returning to Canada she continued as assistant curator at the London Art Gallery and then became curator. A painter of portraits and landscapes she has been influenced by the work of painters Cézanne, the Surrealists and Canadian, Jack Chambers. She has exhibited with the Ontario Society of Artists, the Royal Canadian Academy, the Canadian National Exhibition and the Winnipeg Biennial. Viewing her solo show at the Nancy Poole Studio in London, Ontario, in 1971, Lenore Crawford noted her canvas "Monument to an Ontario Evening" as follows, "The oil on canvas is typically Western Ontario in its landscape, character studies of people and that well-known landmark of so many places, a figure of a soldier in First World War uniform atop a pedestal which on one side states it is a memorial to those who died in that war and one another states it is a memorial to the dead of the Second World War . . . . Along the bottom and right, are eight pictures in brown or slate color, divided by greenish bands, that go back into the days of the First World War and even earlier. Like tintypes come alive are the character studies, given just enough vitality to make them believable as pictures of real people and yet static enough to

O'BRIEN, Paddy Gunn (Mrs.) (Cont'd)

be reproductions of pictures rather than portrait-from-life studies. Paddy O'Brien has mastered this subtlety clearly in this painting which achieves a deceptive simplicity in its excellent composition and evokes atmosphere and mood while telling a vivid story . . . . The painting has both strength and refinement and a definite individuality pervades the whole canvas. The success story is followed easily for the past couple of years in the exhibit of 13 paintings. In addition are six drawings absolutely top-drawer in their meticulous technique and the way they catch so completely the mood or character of the persons portrayed." The painting "Monument to an Ontario Evening" was purchased by Dr. Clare Bice for the London Public Art Gallery. Paddy Gunn O'Brien has received a number of prizes for her paintings including the Curry Award at the O.S.A., 1969; the Seagram Trophy for Best Set Design, 1963 and others. She has written a number of articles on art and artists and given lectures and painting demonstrations. She lives in London, Ontario. Member of the O.S.A. and C.A.R.

References

London Evening Free Press, Ont., Apr. 26, 1958 "Color On Canvas — Paddy Gunn O'Brien — Artist or Curator?" by Lenore Crawford
Kingston Whig Standard, Ont., Aug. 15, 1958 "Art Work Exhibition Being Held"
London Evening Free Press, Ont., June 14, 1961 "500 at Artists' Chowder Party Cover London Workshop's Deficit" by Lenore Crawford (P.G. O'Brien and Selwyn Dewdney make quick sketches to raise money for Artists' Workshop of London)
Ibid, Dec. 24, 1970 "Guarantee of permanent public place for works of city artists advocated" by Paddy Gunn O'Brien
Ibid, Feb. 10, 1971 "London artist's opening night exhibit nets purchase for gallery collection" by Lenore Crawford (reproduction of "Monument to an Ontario Evening")
Document from artist Feb. 10, 1976

OBROTZA, Lydia

A Winnipeg artist and the daughter of Mr. and Mrs. Nick Obrotza, she graduated from the University of Manitoba in interior design then went to Rome in 1964 where she studied painting at the Accademia di Belli Arti di Roma and under Luigi Montanarini. She exhibited some of her paintings at the 17th annual art show of Via Margutta, a centre for tourists in Italy. No recent information.

Reference

Winnipeg Free Press, Man., June 9, 1965 "Local Artist Exhibits In Italy"

OCHS, Peter Paul

b. 1931

Born in Endruhnen, Tilsit, Lithuania of German origin, he did his first paintings and drawings in 1949 and took his Senior Matric at high school in Neuwied, Rhineland in 1952 majoring in art, languages and history. He served as an apprentice cabinetmaker. Then at the age of twenty-one he emigrated to Canada (1952) and found it difficult to earn a living at his art so he became an axeman in a lumber camp on Vancouver Island. He did his first sculpture in 1953 after his experience as a woodsman. Then in 1954 he studied at the Vancouver School of Art under J.A.S. MacDonald and in 1956 exhibited his first wood sculptures at the B.C. Outdoor Sculpture Show at U.B.C. He then studied in Europe at the Académie de la Grande Chaumière under O. Zadkine and at the State Academy (Landesschule für Bildende Künste) in Hamburg, Germany under Hans Ruwoldt. In 1958 he founded "The Group of Four" in Vancouver to present geometric abstraction in the visual arts. Over the years Ochs has acquired extensive technical knowledge beginning with his apprenticeship in cabinet-making and later his study of welding, drafting, furniture design, electrical science, machine shop and forging at the Vancouver Vocational Institute. He took a teaching position in Summerland-Okanagan Valley from 1959 to 1964 where he taught Machine Shop, Drafting, Furniture-making, Boat-building and Electrical Science and in the evenings taught painting (1959-60). In 1964 he transferred to the Vancouver High School where he taught art (1964-65) but found at that time that the students were uninterested in this subject so somewhat discouraged Ochs accepted an offer to work as a designing draftsman with a machinery plant. He even worked as a machine operator in a furniture factory in Vancouver, a surveyor and instrument-man for MacMillan & Bloedel, a boat-builder for Spencer Boats in Vancouver and a draftsman for S.F. Products Limited also of Vancouver. He made a comparative study of materials and tools and wrote a handbook for teaching wood sculpture, and a survey of 15th and 16th Century German art (Dürer, Riemenschneider). In 1966 he received a Canada Council Grant to study methods of carving and preserving wood-sculpture, and to take study trips to Northern B.C., Eastern Canada and Europe. It was with this grant that he completed restoration projects of Indian works of art in the Tsimishian area near Hazelton, B.C., and did a series of tests on finishing materials, carving methods and carving tools. He made a photographic study of masterworks of Indian wood carving of Tsimishian and Haida tribes. In his own sculpture he has worked extensively with wood and has been much influenced by the wood carving of the West Coast Indians. His sculpture ranges from small-sized pieces to monumental works in cedar, juniper and imported woods. He is not confined to wood alone but has done pieces in iron, cast stone and concrete while continuing to exhibit his drawings and paintings. Viewing his work in 1965 Belinda MacLeod of *The Vancouver Province* noted "The works are non-objective but done over a fairly long period of time. This, and the fact that Ochs uses different woods – oak, cherry, apricot, cedar – means that there is considerable variety in the show .... The soft stringiness of cedar forces the simplest shapes. Ochs, whose latest works are like abstract totems, thinks this must have been one of the main reasons why the Indians produced this art form. Ochs usually darkens cedar by burning and then waxing, or by rubbing in sunflower seed oil. The craftsmanship throughout the show seems impeccable and the smaller sculptures are a delight to handle." His group shows include U.B.C. (1956); B.C. Centennial Show, Burnaby, B.C. (1958); Bau-Xi Art Gallery (1965) and exhibitions in Calgary, Edmonton, Winnipeg, Toronto, Georgetown, St. Catharines, Quebec City and Seattle. His solo shows include: Okanagan Regional Library, Kelowna, B.C. (1960); The Little Gallery, New Westminster, B.C. (1965, 1966); Avelles Gallery, Van. (1970); New Westminster Public Library, B.C. (1971). He has instructed at the Okanagan Summer

OCHS, Peter (Cont'd)

School of Arts (1971, –). He completed a commission for a large concrete sculpture for the courtyard of The Victoria Museum, Victoria, B.C. During 1967 Ochs was a display designer for the Vancouver Centennial Museum. He lives in Vancouver with his wife Monika and their two sons Eric and Vincent. He is a member of the B.C. Society of Artists (1965), The Federation of Canadian Artists (1966) and the now disbanded Northwest Institute of Sculpture (1958).

References
The Penticton Herald, B.C., Oct. 20, 1959 "B.C. Sculptor Holding Exhibition at Sum'land" by Freda Storey
The Province, Van., B.C., July 3, 1965 "Peter Ochs exhibit mostly wood sculpture" by Belinda MacLeod
The Vancouver Sun, July 6, 1965 "One-Man Show – Wood Sculpture Restful, Easy" by David Watmough
The Vancouver Province, Aug., 1965 "B.C. showing – Art variety pays dividends" by Belinda MacLeod
New Westminster Columbian, New Westminster, B.C., Dec. 7, 1965 "Father's carvings shared by family" by Mildred Jeffery
The Sun, Van., B.C., Oct. 3, 1966 "Wood Sculptures Show Strength" by David Watmough
Der Courier, Winnipeg, Man., 7 July, 1966 "German-Canadian Artist furthered"
The Vancouver Sun, B.C., Jan. 12, 1967 "Totem Restoration" (criticism by Ochs of a restoration project of an Indian village)
Kamloops Daily Sentinel, B.C., Mar. 23, 1968 "Sculptor Of Indian Art" (photo and caption which discusses how Ochs is influenced by B.C. Indian art)
Arts Council Of New Westminster release, April 19, 1971 (re: Ochs' show at New Westminster Public Library)
New Westminster Columbian, B.C., May 14, 1971 "Varied fare at galleries" (re: New Westminster Pub. Lib. show)
NGC Info. Form rec'd 1966

O'CONNOR, Harry

1892-1963

Born in Ottawa, Ontario, he began serious study while attending high school and was apprenticed to a cabinetmaker. He became interested in woodcarving and received much encouragement from Dr. Marius Barbeau. He studied under Henri Lefebvre at the Technical School in Hull, Quebec and found his work and conversation invaluable in his development. He studied antiques gaining a wide store of knowledge and experience in European carving. He taught woodcarving at various times in Ottawa and worked independently on religious carvings, plaques, and furniture. He was employed by the Old Curiosity Shop in Ottawa for twenty-five years. He is represented in the Bytown Museum (The Historical Society of Ottawa). He died in Ottawa at the age of seventy-one.

Reference
Document and letter from artist

ODDY, Allan Colman

b. 1923

Born in Eriksdale, Manitoba, he studied under L.L. Fitzgerald at the Winnipeg School of Art and J. Alfsen and H. Parker at the Ontario College of Art. Member of the Contemporary Artists of Hamilton (1959); exhibited work at the Art Gallery of Windsor; Art Gallery of Hamilton, Westdale Gallery, Hamilton (1961), and Ericksens Second Floor Gallery, Hamilton (1963). Taught in Windsor and Hamilton and is represented in private collections in Toronto, Windsor, Winnipeg and Hamilton. Proprietor of the Alan Gallery, Hamilton.

Reference
NGC Info. Form dated January, 1963

ODJIG, Daphne (Mrs. Chester Beavon)

An Odawa Indian, she was born and raised on the Wikwemikong Indian Reserve of Manitoulin Island one hundred and eighty miles north west of Toronto. She spent eight years in Westminister, B.C. and in Port Arthur before moving to Manitoba in 1963. Since then she has lived on the Koostatak Reserve in Northern Manitoba, runs a native art shop in Winnipeg, and is deeply involved with the Manitoba Indian Brotherhood and The New Warehouse Gallery owned and operated exclusively by native people to show their art work. In her own work she uses pastels, acrylics, pen and ink, and collages to create vivid prints of Indian folklore as well as murals and illustrations for children's books. She produced a seven by ten foot mural for the Pequis Indian School, Winnipeg. Her work has also appeared on Christmas cards. She has illustrated *10 Little Legends for Little People* (Ginn & Co.) and Dr. H.T. Swarz' *Tales from The Smoke House*. Her paintings have been seen in numerous exhibitions including the 1970 Canadian Pavilion at Osaka, Japan's World Fair; a 1971 touring collection in France, Belgium and Canada; 1967 Port Arthur and Vancouver; Place Bonaventure, Mtl.; the State University at Minot, North Dakota; Selkirk, Man., 1968; University of Brandon, 1969; the International Peace Garden; and the Winnipeg Canoe Club, 1969. She is represented in the following collections: Dept. Indian Affairs, Winnipeg and Ottawa; University of Brandon, Man.; Centennial Commission; Manitoba Indian Brotherhood; Manitoba Legislative Bldg.; Dept. Mines and Natural Resources, Man. (Conservation Ed. Section); Calgary Allied Arts Centre and elsewhere. In 1971 her "Thunderbird Woman" appeared on the cover of the Spring, 1971 issue of Tawow. She has been a member of the B.C. Federation of Artists and is on the board of the Manitoba Arts Foundation Folk School.

References
    The Brandon Sun, Man., Nov. 13, 1968 "Odjig show rates raves" by Kaye Rowe
    Winnipeg Free Press, Man., Nov. 12, 1968 "Daphne Odjig's Works Showing in Brandon" by Lillian McCullagh
    Selkirk Enterprise, Man., Dec. 11, 1968 "Art Showing Held In Selkirk"
    Winnipeg Tribune, Man., Nov. 28, 1968 "She Paints Indian Legends" by Eva Wiseman
    Winnipeg Free Press, Man., Feb. 22, 1969 "Artist Daphne Odjig Uses Peanut Shells and String" by Janice McAndless

ODJIG, Daphne (Mrs. Chester Beavon) (Cont'd)

The St. Vital Lance, Man., Mar. 6, 1969 "Talented Odawa Indian Displays Paintings"
Indian Record, Winnipeg, Man., Feb./Mar. 1969 "She Paints Native Legends" by Eva Wiseman
Little Current Manitoulin Expositor, Ont., Apr. 10, 1969 "Manitoulin Reserve Home of Artist Odjig"
Yorkton Enterprise, Sask., June 10, 1970 "Art Centre Notes" by Ethel Castleden
Winnipeg Tribune, Man., Feb. 18, 1971 "Indian Artist Completes Mural"
Winnipeg Free Press, Man., Oct. 30, 1971 "New Leisure" by Sandra Johnson
Winnipeg Tribune, Man., Dec. 14, 1971 "Indian artist 'born with paint brush' in her hand" by Mary Bletcher
Brantford Expositor, Ont., Jan. 19, 1972 "Schools not essential – Canadian native artist"
The Ottawa Journal, Ont., Jan. 4, 1975 (CP Winnipeg) "Haven for native artists" by Steve Kerstetter
see also
I am an Indian by Kent Gooderham, J.M. Dent, Tor., 1969 (co-illustrator Daphne Odjig)

O'DONNELL, Daphne Lee

Born in Quebec City, she has lived in Montreal since the age of nineteen. She attended the Ecole des Beaux Arts and has exhibited her tiny water colours, serigraphs, and drawings at the Pennell Gallery, Montreal (1971).

References
Globe & Mail, Toronto, Sept. 28, 1961 "Color, movement beyond dimension"
See also Fine Arts Dept., Vancouver Public Library

O'DONNELL, Paul
b. (c) 1940

A lifetime resident of Aylmer, Quebec, this Woodroffe High School English teacher, spends his free time making copper and bronze welded figures. He has exhibited his work at the craftsmen's market on the National Arts Centre terrace, Ottawa and in a 1971 show in Aylmer.

Reference
The Ottawa Citizen, Ont. July 31, 1971 "A blaze of creativity" by Don Butler

---

OESTERLE, Leonhard
b. 1915

Born in Bietigheim, Germany, he became interested in drawing about the age of six and at 18 saw his first modern art and about that time decided to become an artist. During the War he was imprisoned in concentration camps for eight years but managed to escape to Switzerland in 1943. There he was interned in a refugee camp until the end of the war. He studied under Fritz Wotruba in 1945 then entered the

Kunst Gewerbe Schule in Zurich (1945-46); studied with Otto Mueller in Zurich (1946-49) and Hans Aeschbacker, Zurich (1949). Oesterle held his first one-man show at Chichio Haller Gallery, Zurich (1949) and in 1950 he exhibited six small bronzes in a show which also included lithographs by Braque, Matisse, and Picasso in the State Gallery in Stuttgart, Germany. He participated in major group shows in Switzerland and Germany between 1947 and 1950. From 1952 to 1956 he confined his exhibitions to group shows in Germany with the exception of a five-man show of Swabian Painters and Sculptors in the Palette Gallery in Zurich. He married in 1952. After completing a sculpture for a children's playground in Berlin in 1955 he decided to come to Canada and arrived here in 1956. His wife and children followed him later. He held his first one-man show in Canada at the Hart House Gallery in 1957 and subsequent shows there in 1964 and 1969. In his work Oesterle has been influenced considerably by his former teacher Wotruba also Aristide Mailoll, Henri Matisse, Henry Moore, archaic Greek art, Egyptian and particularly African sculpture. He has done mainly figurative work, modelling in clay, wax or plaster to be then cast in bronze. He originally started working in stone and recently has returned to carving in stone and wood and is happiest with stone. He has done constructions in aluminum, plexiglas, steel, composition materials, fibreglass and epoxy. These constructions gave him a greater awareness of design and the demands of pure form. He has always tried to combine the demands of form and content in an inseparable unity where one element cannot exist without the other. Viewing his showing at the Wells Gallery, Ottawa in 1965 Carl Weiselberger noted, "That Leonard Oesterle came from Germany to Canada not long ago can be recognized at least from one of his sculptures, his sitting girl in bronze. Her slim, long-necked figure, even the elegant pose she strikes is the spiritual heritage of Lehmbruck, the famous German sculptor, who a few decades ago shocked the bougeois but is now considered a modern classic. But Oesterle is not an imitator. Nearly all the bronzes on view show his sense of form and texture. And gallery-goers, who have become a little tired of found objects from sewer pipes to faucets and clock wheels 'assembled' for abstract sculptures or figurative fun, will enjoy the sight of Oesterle's delicate Teenager, Girl with Slit Skirt or Male Torso." Oesterle taught sculpture in his own studio, then in 1963 became an instructor at the Ontario College of Art where he continues to teach. His commissions in Canada include: Bronze Figure Group (8 ft. high) for Col. McLaughlin Collegiate, Oshawa (1963); sculptural work at St. Augustin Seminary in Scarborough (Crucifix in bronze with overall height of 14 ft.; statue of St. Augustin, 6½ ft.; statue of St. John the Evangelist, 6½ ft; statue of Madonna, 3 ft; statue of The Good Shepherd, 3 ft. h.); carved altar for St. Regis College, Willowdale (1965); large outdoor sculpture, and 60 ft. mural in hammered copper for the Central Laboratories, Dept. of Health of Ontario (1966); sculpture for Erindale College, Univ. Tor.; and sculpture for the Canada Trust Bldg., London, Ontario. His solo shows also include: Gallery Moos, Tor. (1960); Roberts Gallery, Tor. (1963); Gallery House Sol. Georgetown, Ont. (1963); Waddington Galleries, Mtl., P.Q. (1965); Erindale College, Cooksville, Ontario with painter Joan Willsher (1968); Centennial Gallery, Oakville, Ontario with painter Joan Willsher (1969). He has participated in numerous group shows including the Biennial of Christian Art, Salzburg, Austria (1964); Arts Of The Americas, Carnegie Endowment International Center, NYC (1965). Member; Royal Canadian Academy (ARCA 1963, RCA 1967); Sculptors' Society of Canada (1958); Ontario

OESTERLE, Leonhard (Cont'd)

Society of Artists (1963). He is represented in the following public collections: London Public Library and Art Museum, Ont.,; Kitchener-Waterloo Art Gallery, Ont.; and private collections of Samuel and Ayala Zacks; Joseph H. Hirshhorn and Egidius Streiff (Zurich) and many others. Lives in Toronto.

References
Globe & Mail, Tor., Ont., Oct. 5, 1957 "Exhibition of Sculpture In Hart House Quad"
The Toronto Telegram, Tor., Ont., Nov. 19, 1960 "The Critics Are Kept Hopping" by Paul Duval
Globe & Mail, Tor., Ont., Nov. 19, 1960 "Oesterle Exhibits Bronzes"
Kitchener-Waterloo Record, Ont., Feb. 10, 1962 "Art Views – Sculptor To Work In Welding" by Gerald Parker
The London Free Press, Ont., Jan. 12, 1963 "Art Acquisitions"
The Brantford Expositor, Ont., Feb. 16, 1963 "Twenty Glenhyrst Exhibitors Make Toronto Headquarters" by Shirley T. Popham
Georgetown Herald, Ont., Sept. 5, 1963 "Oesterle Sculptures Viewed at House Sol"
The Gazette, Mtl., P.Q., April 1, 1965 "Expression In Two Styles"
Globe & Mail, Tor., Ont., April 14, 1965 "Ever-Strengthening New Woman Is Theme of Sculptor's Works" by Kay Kritzwiser
The Ottawa Citizen, Ont., July 20, 1965 "Smaller art exhibition features three artists" by Carl Weiselberger
Globe & Mail, Tor., Ont., April 5, 1969 "Dunkelman Gallery"
Oakville Daily Journal Record, Ont., Dec. 14, 1968 "Exhibits At The Gallery Complement Each Other"
Globe & Mail, April 29, 1972 "Five Sculptors"
Canadian Artists In Exhibition 1972-73, Roundstone Council for The Arts, Toronto, 1974, P. 161
NGC Info. Forms July 20, 1967, July 7, 1958
Canadian Art, Vol. 20, No. 6 P. 319-20 "Art Reviews – Leonard Oesterle at the Roberts Gallery, Toronto" by Joyce Zemans

OGILVIE, Jessie Aird
b. 1908

Born in London, England, of Canadian parents, she moved to Montreal in 1928 and has since lived in Saraguay, Quebec. She studied under Fritz Brantner and Gooderidge Roberts and Marion Scott at the Montreal Museum of Fine Arts Art School. She is also a member of the Montreal Museum of Fine Arts.

Reference
NGC Info. Form rec'd July 19, 1951

OGILVIE, Willa Margaret
b. 1933

Born in Montreal, P.Q., she studied at the School of Art and Design, Montreal Museum of Fine Arts where she received an honour diploma. She also studied with Gustav Singier at the Académie Ranson, Paris. A member of "Studio 9" in Montreal

OGILVIE, Willa Margaret (Cont'd)

made up of former students of the M.M.F.A. she exhibited with this group during the years 1952-4. Living at Saraguay, P.Q. in 1954.

Reference
NGC Info. Form received April, 1954

OGILVIE, William Abernethy
b. 1901

Born at Stutterheim, Cape Province, South Africa, the son of Walter and Bertha (Frachét) Ogilvie, he attended public school at Stutterheim (1910-14) then Queen's College, Queenstown, Cape Province (1915-20) where he graduated with his Senior Matriculation. He took art training with Erich Mayer at Johannesburg (1921-24). He came to Canada in September of 1925 and settled for a time in Toronto then went to New York City where he studied at the Art Students' League (1928-30) under Kimon Nicoliades. He visited South Africa in 1931 and painted a number of scenes which were later exhibited in important group shows. He worked for a short time as a commercial artist in New York gaining valuable experience for future use. He returned to Toronto at the time of the Depression. In 1932 he teamed up with Charles Comfort and Harold Ayres. They opened an office in Toronto and accepted a variety of commissions from portraiture to advertising layout, architectural decoration to magazine illustration and their firm survived because of the collective diversity of the partners. During the summers each of them had time to develop his own art. Ogilvie did a number of figure studies which he continued to do throughout his career. Jerrold Morris in his book *The Nude in Canadian Painting* draws to the reader's attention influences like the arabesque in Art Nouveau and the geometry of abstract art which he sees in the artist's nude studies. In 1936 Ogilvie was commissioned by the Massey Foundation to do murals for the Chapel of Hart House, University of Toronto. Viewing the completed work, critic Graham McInnes writing in *Saturday Night* noted, "Taking his inspiration partly from the Primitive Italian altar pieces, partly from the formal aspects of the Canadian landscape, and fusing them with his own delicate imaginative quality, Mr. Ogilvie has produced a work whose easy rhythmic flow, and soft cool tones, combine to give an atmosphere of contemplative and austere spirituality. This reaches its height in the main panel on the south wall, in which a refreshingly new treatment of the Madonna and Child motif makes a central group of exquisite charm." A further description was given by Josephine Hambleton in *The Ottawa Citizen* as follows, "Two white doves flutter joyously about the Madonna of the mural. The mother inclines her head tenderly over her solemn Child. He sits on her knee, back straight, hands clutching a white trillium and he stares before him, as though he perceived all the crimes and all the wars throughout history. A bank of white trilliums stretches behind Jesus and Mary, and before them, kneel a Canadian family, the man, clean-shaven, the woman, holding a white trillium, and their little girl. The beasts pay the Redeemer homage too, a shy, proud deer and her speckled fawn and the Heavenly Hosts are men and women of our own age and clime, lifted by religious exaltation from their round of pleasure and of pain, of charity and of crime, of temptation and of repentence, into the dwelling-place of God." Shortly after its completion the Hart House mural was the subject of articles in *Saturday Night*, Bertram Brooker's *Year Book of The Art* (1936), and *The Studio* (No. 533, 1937). While Ogilvie was working in conjunction with the two other artists he continued with his own painting exhibiting with the Canadian Society of Painters in Water Colour (member, 1934) and the Canadian Group of Painters (Founding Member, 1933). A.H. Robson in his book *Canadian Landscape Painters* (1932) noted Ogilvie's work as having "Subtlety and refinement in colour and a delightful sense of design" but noted that the artist's attentions were on his figure painting more than his landscapes. But Ogilvie has always been able to include both figures and landscapes in much of his work and a popular example of this can be found in his numerous war paintings. The opportunity to teach at the School of Art at the Art Association of Montreal brought his partnership with Comfort and Ayres to an end. Comfort went to the Ontario College of Art to teach mural painting, but we are not told what path Ayres followed. At the Art Association (1938-41) Ogilvie gave lectures, taught life drawing, also painting and composition and also assumed the additional responsibilities as Director of the School during his last two years in Montreal. He joined the Canadian Army in 1940 and after basic training was employed as a service artist at CMHQ, London, England, then he was commissioned in 1942 as an Official War Artist. He became senior army artist overseas with a final promotion to Major later on in the war. He painted a variety of scenes in the United Kingdom including AA defences on the Thames estuary, Forestry Corps camps, and invasion training in Scotland. Then he was dispatched to the battle zones in Sicily and Italy and in North-West Europe. Viewing his sketches of the Falaise Gap in France, Josephine Hambleton writing in *The Ottawa Citizen* noted, "Pen and ink lines indicated contours, water-colour washes, the shadows. They conveyed the feeling war had drawn all life to an irrevocable close. The fears, the hopes they had felt a few moments before, the fatigue they had borne, and courage they had shown, could never matter again to the dead soldiers . . . these sketches are in every line, in every tone, alive and horrifying, because their creator made them while he himself was deafened by explosions, blinding gun-fire, and spent days among the dead, days battle robbed of dawn and twilight." Ogilvie was awarded the M.B.E. (Military) for his service as a war artist. His war paintings are deposited in the collection of the Canadian War Museum, Ottawa. After discharge from the Army he returned to teaching and painting at the Banff School of Fine Art (summer, 1946); Ontario College of Art (1947-57); Queen's University School of Fine Art (summer, 1947); Mount Allison University (summer, 1958). He received a Canadian Government Overseas Royal Society Fellowship to study in Italy (1957-58). About this time he joined a geophysical expedition from the University of Toronto during International Geophysical Year, to witness the scientists measure and map the Salmon Glacier on the border of B.C. and Alaska. Ogilvie sketched and painted the huge icefield, the mountains, the peculiar rock formations and the colourful flora in the area then returned to his studio in Toronto. In September of that same year these paintings were exhibited at the Hart House art gallery coinciding with the assembly of the International Union of Geodesy and Geophysics held at the University of Toronto. He continued to exhibit with the Canadian Society of Painters in Water Colour and the Canadian Group of Painters. He made return trips to

OGILVIE, William Abernethy (Cont'd)

South Africa, Mexico, and in Canada he recorded his impressions of Georgian Bay and areas of Southern Ontario. He was commissioned to design a window to commemorate Hart House's 50th Anniversary and the window was dedicated to Vincent Massey. Good reproduction of Ogilvie's paintings can be found in Elizabeth Kilbourn's *Great Canadian Painting* (1966 P. 47) and Paul Duval's *Four Decades* (1972, P. 130). Since 1960 he has been special lecturer in Historical Techniques of Painting at the University of Toronto. His one-man shows include the following: Picture Loan Society, Toronto (annually 1934-66); Gainsborough Galleries, Johannesburg, South Africa (1954); Hart House, U. of T. (1957, 1962); Adler Fielding Gallery, Johannesburg (1963); Victoria College, U. of T. (1964); Wells Gallery, Ottawa (1966, 1967); Fleet Gallery, Winnipeg, Man. (1966); Roberts Gallery, Tor. (1967, 1969, 1971, –). Over the years he has exhibited in many group shows national and international and the very first exhibition of the Canadian Group of Painters in Atlantic City, N.J. (1933); South Dominions (1936); Tate Gallery, Lond. Eng. (1938); World's Fair (1939); Brussels, War Art (1944); NGC, Ottawa, War Art (1945-46); Rio de Janiero (1946); U.N.E.S.C.O. (1946); The Fourth Biennial Exhibition of Canadian Art (1961). Paul Duval notes in his *Four Decades* that Ogilvie holds a significant place in the writing of the history of mid-century Canadian art for his work in water colours. He is represented in the following collections: Edmonton Art Gallery, Alta.; Art Gallery of Winnipeg, Man.; Sarnia Art Gallery, Ont.; London Public Library and Art Museum, Ont.; Art Gallery of Hamilton, Ont.; Art Gallery of Ontario, Tor.; Hart House, Univ. Tor.; National Gallery of Canada, Ott.; Canadian War Museums, Ott. and in many private collections. He lives in Palgrave (Albion Hills) Ontario with his wife Sheelah.

References

Canadian Landscape Painters by A.H. Robson, Ryerson, Tor., 1932, P. 179

A Century of Canadian Art, Tate Gallery, Lond. Eng., 1938, P. 26

Exhibition of Canadian Art, New York World's Fair, 1939, P. 14

Canadian Art, Vol. 2, No. 4, Apr-May, 1945, "Exhibition of Canadian War Art" by Donald W. Buchanan

The Canadian Army At War, The Canadians In Britain, 1939-44, No. 1, King's Printer, Ottawa, 1945.

Ibid, From Pachino to Ortona, 1943, No. 2, 1946, King's Printer, Ottawa

Ibid, Canada's Battle In Normandy, No. 3, 1946, King's Printer, Ottawa

The Canadian Army, 1939-1945 by Colonel C.P. Stacey, King's Printer, Ottawa, 1948, page opposite title page, P. 207

The Growth of Canadian Painting by Donald W. Buchanan, Collins, Tor., P. 57-60

Canadian Art, Vol. 8, No. 2 "Will Ogilvie – Disciple of Fine Line" by Andrew Bell, P. 50-54

Canadian Art by Graham McInnes, MacMillan, Tor., 1950, P. 80, 83, 84

Canadian Drawings and Prints by Paul Duval, Burns & MacEachern, Tor., 1952, 9th page of text, plate 68

Canadian Water Colour Painting by Paul Duval, Burns & MacEachern, Tor., 1954, 19th page of text, Plate 38, 64

The Arts in Canada, Ed. Malcolm Ross, MacMillan, Tor., 1958, P. 29

Canadian Art, Spring, 1958, P. 122

A Painter's Country by A.Y. Jackson, Clarke-Irwin, Tor., 1958, P. 75, 138

Nat. Gal. of Can. Catalogue, Vol. 3 by R.H. Hubbard, NGC, Ott., 1960, 240

The Development of Canadian Art by R.H. Hubbard, NGC, Ott., 1963, P. 111, 112

Great Canadian Painting, A Century of Art by Elizabeth Kilbourn, Frank Newfeld; Text, Ken Lefolii, Weekend Magazine & M&S, P. 47

Painting in Canada/A History by J. Russell Harper, Univ. Tor. Press, Tor., 1966, P. 335, 336, 337

Canadian Water Colours, Drawings and Prints, 1966, NGC, Ott., P. 158, 159
Canada At War by Leslie F. Hannon, M&S, 1968, P. 92
Check List of The War Collections by R.F. Wodehouse, NGC, 1968, P. 136-146
Vincent Massey Bequest, The Canadian Paintings, NGC, 1968, P. 37, 56
The Hart House Collection of Canadian Paintings by Jeremy Adamson, Univ. Tor. Press, 1969, P. 50, 102
Art Gallery of Ontario, The Canadian Collection by Helen Pepall Bradfield, McGraw-Hill, Tor., P. 343-345
Gift from the Douglas M. Duncan Collection & the Milne-Duncan Bequest, NGC, Ott., 1971, P. 95, 117
The Nude in Canadian Painting by Jerrold Morris, New Press, Tor., 1972, P. 13, 56
Charles Fraser Comfort/Fifty Years, Winnipeg Art Gallery, Man., 1973, No. 37
Four Decades, The Canadian Group of Painters and their contemporaries, 1930-1970 by Paul Duval, Clarke, Irwin, 1972, P. 76, 77, 81, 128, 130
Creative Canada, A Biographical dictionary of twentieth-century and performing artists, Vol. Two, Ref. Div. McPherson Lib., Univ. Victoria, B.C./Univ. Tor. Press, 1972, P. 208-209
A Concise History of Canadian Painting by Dennis Reid, Oxford Univ. Press, Tor., 1973, P. 171, 180, 203
The Canadian Art Auction Record Vol. 5, 1973 compiled by H.C. Campbell, Chief Librarian, Toronto Public Libraries, Bernard Amtmann Inc., Mtl., 1974, P. 50
Canadian Artists And Airmen, 1940-45 by Jerrold Morris, Morris Gallery, Tor., 1975, P. 144
Canadian Painting in the Thirties by Charles C. Hill, NGC, Ott., 1975, P. 40, 74, 91
Canadian Art At Auction, 1968-1975 Ed. by Geoffrey Joyner, Sotheby & Co. (Can.) Ltd., Tor., Ont., 1975, P. 149, 150
Fifty Years, The Canadian Society of Painters in Water Colour, 1925-75, Katharine Jordan, Art Gallery of Ontario, Tor., 1975, P. 31
Periodicals, Newspapers & additional catalogues
Saturday Night, Tor., Ont., Sept. 16, 1936 "Mural In Hart House Chapel" by G. Campbell McInnes
The Gazette, Mtl., P.Q., Oct. 12, 1940 "Will Ogilvie Named Director of School"
Canada's Weekly, Lon., England, Mar. 20, 1942 (Forces Exhibition at National Portrait Gallery)
The Gazette, Mtl., P.Q., May 28, 1942 "Lt. W. Ogilvie; Montreal, Exhibits His Art at Overseas Forces' Show"
Ibid, May 30, 1942 "Lieut. Will Ogilvie Was Instructor Here"
The Toronto Star, Tor., Ont., Feb. 5, 1944 (reproductions of Ogilvie's Sicily paintings with captions)
The Toronto Telegram, Ont., Feb. 5, 1944 "Wartime Scenes Painted"
Canadian War Artists, Palais Des Beaux-Arts, 10 Rue Royale, Bruxelles, Belgium, 18 Nov. – 5 Dec., 1944
The Ottawa Citizen, Ont. Apr. 17, 1948 "A War Artist With Canada's Army" by Josephine Hambleton
London Free Press, Ont., May 1, 1948 "Ogilvie Picture Captures Wealth Of Human Drama" by Irene Taylor
Community and Recreation, Christmas, 1948, "Mural Decoration by the Canadian artist Will Ogilvie"
Catalogue of Paintings by Will Ogilvie, Gainsborough Galleries, 25 May - 7 June, 1954
Rand Daily Mail, South Africa, May, 1954 "Exhibition Of Paintings By Will Ogilvie"
The Globe Magazine, Sept. 7, 1957 "An Artist Travels With the Ice Experts" by David Jensen
Globe & Mail, Tor., Ont., Jan. 25, 1958 "Will Ogilvie Art Is Masterful"
Ibid, Dec. 5, 1959 "Ogilvie Watercolors"
Ibid, Nov. 26, 1960 "Sensibility Plus Sense In Ogilvie" by Colin Sabiston
Leader-Post, Regina, Jan. 31, 1961 "Second event display"
Banner, Orangeville, Ont., May 18, 1961 "Art in the Animal Form By Will Ogilvie, MBE, Orangeville Club Talk" by Mrs. Carson Patterson
The Toronto Telegram, Ont., Feb. 2, 1963 "Watercolor Shows Please" by Paul Duval

OGILVIE, William Abernethy (Cont'd)

The Ottawa Journal, Ont., May 7, 1966 "Wells Gallery — Ogilvie Canvases Make Fine Showing" by W.Q. Ketchum
The Winnipeg Tribune, Man., Sept. 12, 1966 "Will Ogilvie here for show"
Globe & Mail, Tor., Ont., Nov. 18, 1967 "Will Ogilvie fashions colorful ink with the North" by Paul Russell
The Toronto Telegram, Ont., "Will Ogilvie exhibition at Roberts Gallery" by Bernadette Andrews
Guelph Mercury, Ont., Nov. 20, 1970 "Scenes By Canadian Artists On Cansave Christmas Cards"
Globe & Mail, Tor., Ont., Nov. 20, 1971 (show at Roberts Gallery, Tor.)
NGC Info. Forms rec'd 1931, 1942, 1946, 1959, 1966, 1967

OGILVY, Carol Cole

Born in Rossland, B.C. she grew up in New Liskeard, Ontario and attended art classes for four years at the Central Technical School, Toronto. Working from a studio built by her father and brother she became known for her painting. She married a mining engineer who was employed in a vital industry during the war and moved from place to place in Ontario. Later she taught high school art in Stouffville, Ontario (1957-65) and in 1966 moved to Roxboro, Quebec. She has exhibited her flower studies done in water colours and pastels in Stewart Hall, Macdonald College, Ste. Anne de Bellevue, Quebec (1968) and at her home in Roxboro, Quebec (1969).

References
Pointe Claire Lakeshore News & Chronicle, Que. Nov. 28, 1968 "N.S. artist exhibits at Macdonald" by Helen K. Legge
Ibid, Oct. 23, 1969 "Carol Cole Ogilvy exhibition to open in Roxboro Monday"
Ibid, Oct. 30, 1969 "Work of Roxboro artist on exhibition till Sunday" by Helen K. Legge

O'HARA, Pat (Mrs. Richard Schneider)

A Vancouver artist who creates poster-maps now sold in stores and city scenes in acrylics exhibited in Jordan's Interiors, Park Royal North Mall (1970), Exposition Art Gallery (Groot-Horst & Associates Ltd. Van., 1972) and elsewhere in Vancouver. She teaches kindergarten at Simon Fraser Elementary School.

Reference
The Province, Van., B.C., June 20, 1970 "Poster-maps on the town"

OHASHI, William Ken

b. 1934

Born in Canada of Japanese descent he received his Bachelor of Fine Arts from the University of Saskatchewan at the Regina Campus (1952-56) then studied sculp-

OHASHI, William Ken (Cont'd)

ture at Goldsmith's College, London, England (1955). In his sculpture he has worked with metal, ceramics, stone and mainly wood including birch, willow, cherry, walnut, olive and maple. He strives for simplicity and has recently ventured into the abstract. He avoids sharp angles and lines so that the feelings of tension and anxiety are not incorporated in his work. He has completed several mural commissions in Regina and Saskatoon. A teacher of English and business fundamentals for adult education classes in Regina he devotes his free time to sculpture. Plays the guitar and enjoys working on his art to music. A former art supervisor for the Moose Jaw Public School Board.

References
> The Continental Times (?) 8 Sept., 1967 "Wood Sculptor Expresses Himself Through Work"
> Leader-Post, Regina, Sask., 26 Aug., 1967 "Artist finds wood good medium for communicating his thoughts" by Kathie Leier

OHE, Katie von der
b. 1937

Born in Peers, Alberta, she became interested in art around the age of eleven and later studied at the Southern Alberta College of Art (1954-59) where she received her B.F.A., then she took a course in Child Education at the Montreal Museum School of Design and Fine Arts (1959) after which she studied sculpture for a year at the Sculpture Centre, New York City. She served her apprenticeship at the Ceramic Arts company in Calgary. In her sculpture she has been influenced by the styles of Henry Moore, Lynn Chadwick, Ossip Zadkine and Joan Miro and has produced work in wood, stone, concrete, wax, bronze, clay and mosaics. She is known for her structural compositions and was described by Clement Greenberg as " . . . one of those rarest of all artists in North America, a good abstract sculptor, doing tight and beautifully sensed little monoliths in terra cotta . . . . " She has done figurative sculpture as well. A graphic artist also she is known for her silk screens, lino cuts, woodcuts and has worked as well in water colours. She has taught at the Alberta College of Art and the Calgary Allied Arts Council in child art also adult classes in designing, ceramics, mosaics, graphic art, sculpture and painting. She is represented in the Calgary Allied Arts Council; Sculpture Centre, NYC; and the Southern Alberta College of Art. A member of the Alberta Society of Artists she lives in Calgary, Alberta.

References
> Document from artist, 1961
> Canadian Art, Vol. 20, No. 2, "Clement Greenberg's View of Art On The Prairies" by C.G., P. 106

O'HENLY, John Donald

b. 1923

Born in Toronto, Ontario, he was educated at the Danforth Technical School, and the Ontario College of Art, Toronto under John Alfsen, Rowley Murphy, Will Ogilvie, and N. Hornyansky. He graduated with his A.O.C.A. in 1947. He has resided in London, Ontario, since 1954 and has taught art at the H.B. Beal Technical School there. His prints, collages, paintings, and drawings were exhibited at the London Public Library and Art Museum, Ontario (1960) and at Canada House Gallery, London, Eng. (1972) in a show featuring ten Canadian printmakers. This exhibition was also displayed in Sheffield, Harrogate, and Leeds art galleries. Represented in the London Public Library and Art Museum and other collections.

References

NGC Info. Form rec'd 1954

London Evening Free Press, Ont., Sept. 5, 1960 " 'Sensitive' art exhibit on display" by Lenore Crawford

Canadian High Commission, London, England, Cultural Affairs Press Release "From London to London", 1972

OILLE, Ethel Lucille (Mrs. Kenneth McNeill Wells)

b. 1912

Born in Toronto, Ontario, the daughter of Dr. and Mrs. John Allen Oille she attended public and private schools in Toronto and then the Ontario College of Art where she studied sculpture under Emanuel Hahn. Subsequently she took further studies at the Royal College of Art, London, England, and returned to Canada. She exhibited her sculpture in a number of Canadian exhibitions including the Ontario Society of Artists (1933). She also developed her technique in woodcuts, wood engraving and scratchboard illustrations. In 1937 she married journalist Kenneth McNeill Wells and they lived for a while in a cabin in the backwoods of Ontario, spent a year in Orillia before settling in Medonte Township where they took the timbers from a run down pioneer home and built a dwelling of their own on a site not far away from the original pioneer location and named the completed house *The Owl Pen*. They bought chickens, ducks, goats and bees and settled down to country life. When war broke out her husband went overseas while Lucille kept their farm going and learned a lot about the care of chickens, ducks, bees, also gardening, building dams, shingling and ditch digging. After the war her husband returned to the farm and they began their life together once more. Her husband wrote about their experiences first in *The Toronto Telegram* in a series of articles, then in book form illustrated by Lucille under the titles *The Owl Pen* (1947), *By Moonstone Creek* (1949), *Up Medonte Way* (1951) and *By Jumping Cat Bridge* (1956). Then they bought an 18 foot cruiser they named *The Moonstruck* and took a 5,500 mile voyage from their Georgian Bay area home southwards to the Gulf of Mexico exploring the history, legends and mystery of the Mississippi through tornadoes, flood, and collision with a Coast Guard Station moored to a riverbank, and other misadventures then finally returned home. From their collective experiences after cruising an estimated 50,000 miles in five years came a series of six books by her husband on boating, one of them *The Moonstruck Two*

OILLE, Ethel Lucille (Mrs. Kenneth McNeill Wells) (Cont'd)

(1964) was illustrated by Lucille. Later came other books like *The Owl Pen Reader* (1969). Lucille Oille has produced some of the finest woodcuts, wood engravings and scratchboard illustrations in Canada and the books by her husband make very enjoyable reading.

References

The Owl Pen by Kenneth McNeil Wells, J.M. Dent & Sons (Can.) Ltd., Tor., 1947
By Moonstone Creek by Kenneth McN. Wells, J.M. Dent & Sons (Can.), 1949
Up Medonte Way by Kenneth McN. Wells, J.M. Dent & Sons (Can.) Ltd., Tor., 1951
In Pastures Green by Peter McArthur, Ed. by Kenneth McN. Wells, J.M. Dent & Sons Tor., 1948
By Jumping Cat Bridge by Kenneth McN. Wells, Heinemann, Lond. Tor., 1956
The Moonstruck Two by Kenneth McN. Wells, M & S., Tor., 1964
The Owl Pen Reader by Kenneth McN. Wells, Doubleday (Can.), Tor. 1947, 1949, 1951, 1969
Oxford Companion to Canadian History and Literature by Norah Story, Oxford Univ. Press, Tor., 1967, P. 825, 826
NGC Info. dated 1933

OKEY, Ronald N.

b. 1921

Born in Northampton, England, his early promise as an artist earned him a scholarship to the Northampton School of Art. He emigrated to Canada in 1949, living in Toronto and Colorado Springs, Colo. until 1954. In 1957 he began studying fine art and was elected to the Ontario Institute of Painters in 1963. Working with palette knife and brush, he spends his summers on the coast of Mass., U.S.A., where he finds as subjects the old harbours and fishing boats of New England. He has had three one-man shows on the West Coast of British Columbia, one of which was presented by the Harrison Galleries of Vancouver (1970).

Reference

Harrison Galleries, Vancouver, information sheet for show, Sept. 25, 1970

OLDFIELD, Clifford Thomas

b. 1923

Born in Montreal, P.Q., he attended classes at the Federation of Canadian Artists, studied under Anne Savage, and at the Montreal Museum of Fine Arts (1937). He also took lessons from Ernst Neumann and attended the Valentine School of Commercial Art for three years. He was working as a truck tank manager for a large Montreal company in 1961 and spending the remainder of his time painting in oils. Was living at Terrasse Vaudreuil, Ile Perrot, P.Q. in 1961.

Reference

NGC Info. Form rec'd Mar. 22, 1961

OLDRICH, Bob

b. 1920

Born in Ostrava, Czechoslovakia, he emigrated to Canada in 1951, settling first in Halifax, and later in Toronto and Calgary. For a time in Toronto he and his wife Dot began designing and making enamelled copper jewellery, ashtrays and small dishes also designs for furniture, sculpture and original block printed or silk screened patterns. During his free time he did paintings and reproduced several of them by silk screen on duck linen including "Musicians", an Eskimo scene and others. He has taught for the art department of the Provincial Institute of Technology and Art in Calgary, instructing in crafts and industrial design. Oldrich deals mostly now in architectural art work and industrial design, working primarily in steel, vitreous enamel, concrete, charcoal, oil, and silk screen fabrics. He received the National Industrial Design Award in 1959 and two design awards for fountain monuments in the 1964 Montreal competition. In 1963 he also secured first prize in enamels at the Canadian Ceramics Biennial. Several of his productions may be seen in Lethbridge, Alta.; the Irrigation Monument; the entrance doors to St. Andrew's Church; the window for Buchanan Chapel "Betonglas". He has also carved a mural for the Alberta Wheat Pool Building in Calgary; created a welded steel and enamel sculpture (sixty feet high) for Jasper House apartment bldg., Edmonton; and assembled a mosaic for the sacristy of Holy Trinity Church, Calgary.

References
> *Globe & Mail*, Tor., Ont., Nov. 11, 1958 "Silk Screen on Linen for Wall Decoration" by Barbara Whalen
> Document from artist, Jan. 23, 1961
> *Lethbridge Herald*, Alta., Dec. 9, 1963 "Monument Artist Former Instructor"
> NGC Info. Form rec'd Feb. 10, 1966

OLNEY, George(s) L.

A self-taught painter in oils, he lives in Danville, Quebec. He has three times exhibited his work in the Public Library of Asbestos, P.Q. (1967-8-9) and once at the Centre d'art du Domaine Howard, Sherbrooke. He has used the pseudonym "Jorge" on his paintings.

References
> News Clipping, Asbestos, P.Q., Dec. 1, 1965 "Elles envahissent maintenant les Commissions scolaires"
> *Le Citoyen*, Asbestos, P.Q., April 16, 1968 "Exposition de Peintures de Georges Olney"
> Ibid, May 14, 1968 "George Olney expose à Sherbrooke"
> *La Tribune*, Sherbrooke, P.Q., May 25, 1968 "Un peintre autodidacte expose"
> *Le Citoyen*, Asbestos, P.Q., Feb. 6, 1969 "Au Vernissage du Peintre Olney" (photo and caption)
> Ibid, Feb. 18, 1969 "La Maternelle A L'Exposition de Peintures" (photo and caption)

OLSANSKY, Klement

Czechoslovakian by birth, he emigrated to the United States and studied under Willington Reynolds at the Art Institute of Chicago. Then he studied at the Na-

OLSANSKY, Klement (Cont'd)

tional Academy of Painting in Prague, returned to Chicago, then moved to Canada, working as a professor of art for the University of Toronto. In 1945 he moved to Montreal and established his own studio. Known as a portrait painter he has painted other subjects as well, including some fine seascapes.

References
   Halifax Chronicle-Herald, N.S., May 15, 1957 "Another Seascape On The Canvas" by J. Keith Young
   Montreal N.D.G. Monitor, P.Q., Dec. 13, 1963 "Famous portrait painter has Loyola exhibition"
   Le Petit Journal, Mtl., P.Q., week of April 18, 1965 "Qu'est-ce qu'une eau-forte?" text by Yolande Rivard

OLSEN, Andreas V.

Originally from Copenhagen, he spent his early years sailing. He came to Canada in 1941 and served with the Canadian Engineers overseas during WW II. He now lives in Saint John, N.B. His exhibitions include Saint John's Union Station (1967); the Atlantic National Exhibition (1967) where he took a first prize; the Corby Library Art Gallery, Belleville (1970); Beaverbrook Art Gallery, Fredericton; the Travelling Maritime Art Exhibition and galleries in Montreal and Ontario. He does seascapes, abstracts and other subjects.

References
   Telegraph-Journal, Saint John, N.B., Oct. 30, 1967 "Oil Paintings to be Displayed"
   The Intelligencer, Belleville, Ont., Sept. 22, 1970 "Maritime Artist's Work to be Shown at Library"
   Ibid, Sept. 29, 1970 "Maritime Artist's Exhibition Shown at Library Art Gallery" by Susan Korah

ONAMI, Roy

One of his portraits was exhibited in the Pinecrest Arts and Crafts Club Exhibition in June 1958 in Pembroke, Ontario.

Reference
   Pembroke Observer, Ont., June 4, 1958 "Art Club Plans Local Exhibition"

ONDAATJE, Kim (Betty Jane Kimbark Jones Ondaatje)
b. 1928

Born in Toronto, Ontario, her father, a Toronto printer and lithographer, prized a fine collection of 19th Century etchings, engravings and paintings. She attended

ONDAATJE, Kim (Betty Kimbark Jones Ondaatje) (Cont'd)

Havergal College, Toronto and following her graduation took one year at the Ontario College of Art then transferred to the Fine Arts Department at McGill University in 1949. There she was expelled from studio classes in an argument with her art teacher and so completed a B.A. degree in Honours English and psychology in 1952, winning prizes for executive ability, short story writing and a fellowship to Queen's University. During this time, she also edited the McGill student literary magazine *Forge* and a young writers' issue of the prestigious *Northern Review*. Moving to Queen's on her scholarship she received her M.A. in English. She spent the next five years teaching English at the Universities of Queen's, Waterloo Lutheran, and Sherbrooke. In 1966 she renewed her art activity and while living in London, Ontario, she began producing the "Hill Series" of paintings relating her attraction for the silence of the Canadian forests and lakes. From 1967 to 1971 she also worked on her series referred to as "The House on Picadilly Street" in which she shows her concern with the trend of modern homes and their impersonal dehumanized interiors. These paintings were done in acrylic using the hard edge style (sixteen paintings; seven serigraphs). She was assisted by the Canada Council in producing serigraph versions of some of these paintings. Next came her "Factory" series, acrylic and acrylic-tape collages in 1970 forming an ultra-large size series of canvases showing her concern for the damage to the environment by industrial activity using several Canadian plants as her models. She has done several other series as well. Viewing her work in 1972 Lenore Crawford of *The London Free Press* noted, "The two series — interiors and factory — have a relationship which can be appreciated if the interiors are looked at first. The artist invites the viewer to go into a room, or a part of one and feel, smell and hear as well as see it. There is a cuckoo clock to hear, a stove giving off odors, but most of all there is the paint that for long stretches is cool and smooth to the imaginary touch and then suddenly warm, when yellow splashes away the white-into grey, or dark blue erases the calm. The artist steps aside. All that remains is the viewer and what he sees, smells, hears, feels. All, that is, except the viewer's realization that actually he has been led into a series of experiences by an artist who knows how to use painting or screenprinting techniques as though they were the extension of a sensitive, exquisitely-balanced emotional instinct and intellect. Similarly the viewer is asked to experience the factory series. The only logical judgment of the paintings is to relate one's personal experience, I think. What I felt was overwhelming fright — the total non-existence of human being in an environment they had created. The factories, trains, trucks, even late-model cars were alone in grand glory, with the elements of sky, landscape and distance as their only enemies. They had eradicated mankind in a far greater victory than nature ever had been able to win over man, because man in disdain for nature had killed off everything he needed for survival." Her solo shows include: MacIntosh Memorial Gallery, Univ. Western Ontario (1969); Jerrold Morris Gallery, Tor. (1969); Merton Gallery, Tor. (retrospective, 1971); Robt. McLaughlin Gallery, Oshawa (1972). Her other shows include O.S.A. 97th Annual (1969); two-man show, London Pub. Lib. & Art Museum, Lond., Ont. (1969); Spring Show, Mtl. Museum of Fine Arts (1970); 30th Annual Western Ontario Exhibition, Lond. (1970); Glenhyrst Arts Council (open juried show, 1970); Agnes Etherington Art Centre, Kingston, Ont. (open juried show, 1970); Art Gallery of Ontario, Realisms Series (1970); three-man show "Graphics 72" at Art Gallery of Brant, Brantford,

ONDAATJE, Kim (Betty Kimbark Jones Ondaatje) (Cont'd)

Ont.; circulating show for London Public Lib. & Art Museum, Ont. (1972); and elsewhere. Her awards include: Canada Council short term grants (1969, 1970); merit awards from Agnes Etherington Art Centre (open juried shows, 1969, 1970); Purchase Award, Society of Canadian Artists (open juried, 3rd show, 1970); Glenhyrst Medical Purchase Award (1970); Purchase Award, South Western Ontario Show, Brantford Art Gallery (1970); Hon. Mention for a silk screen at the International Print Exhibition, Seattle, Wash. (1971); 1st Prize, purchase award for serigraph "The Bedroom" by Glenhyrst Arts Council (open jury show, 1971). She is represented in the following collections: Confederation Art Gallery, Charlottetown, P.E.I.; Glenhyrst Arts Council of Brantford, Ont.; London Public Lib. & Art Museum, Ont.; Montreal Museum of Fine Arts; Northern & Central Gas Corp., Tor.; Ontario Inst. for Studies in Education, Tor.; Owens Art Gallery, Sackville, N.B.; Seattle Art Museum, Wash.; Univ. of Western Ontario, Lond.; Windsor Public Art Gallery, Ont. and in a number of private collections. Her dealer: Nancy Poole Gallery London and Toronto, Ontario. Married D.G. Jones, poet and professor of English Literature at the University of Sherbrooke (married 1950-63). Married Michael Ondaatje, writer, film-maker, poet. Lives in London, Ont.

References

London Free Press, Ont., April 12, 1969 "Paintings for viewer to walk into" by Lenore Crawford

The Toronto Telegram, Ont., July 10, 1969 "This solo show an oasis" by Bernadette Andrews

Toronto Daily Star, Ont., July 26, 1969 "A debut exhibition with a unique air" by Barrie Hale

London Evening Free Press, Ont., Nov. 6, 1969 "Artist told of award on opening night" by Lenore Crawford

Globe & Mail, Tor., Ont., Jan. 9, 1971 "Merton Gallery"

The Toronto Telegram, Ont., Jan. 13, 1971 "Kim Ondaatje is hung up on factories" by Elizabeth Dingman

Chatham News, Ont., Feb. 8, 1971 "Artist" (photo and caption)

NGC Info. Form and letter from artist Mar. 2, 1971

London Free Press, Ont., Mar. 27, 1971 "Ondaatje art wins award"

La Presse, Mtl., P.Q., June 5, 1971 "Aussi, cette semaine"

"Profile – Kim Ondaatje" by Pat Fleisher, 1971

London Free Press, Ont., Jan. 11, 1972 "Ondaatje's paintings scary" by Lenore Crawford

Kingston Whig Standard, Ont., Mar. 24, 1972 "Painter from London winner of top prize at annual jury show"

Kingston Whig Standard, Ont., Apr. 8, 1972 "Current exhibition challenges the viewer" by Barry Thorne

Brantford Expositor, Ont., Apr. 8, 1972 "Gallery opens acquisition-exhibition" by Maureen Peterson

Exhibition booklet for the circulating show organized by the London Public Library and Art Museum, 1972

O'NEIL, Bruce William

b. 1942

Born in Winnipeg, he studied under I.H. Kerr, Stanford Perrot, Stanford Blougett, Marion Nicoll, Ronald Spickett and others at the Alberta College of Art. In 1963

O'NEIL, Bruce William (Cont'd)

he received honourable mention in painting from the Alberta College of Art and the visual arts scholarship the same year. In 1964 he received a tuition scholarship to the Instituto Allende in San Miguel Allende, Mexico. He now lives in Calgary and has shown his work in the Loyola Bonsecours Gallery, Montreal (1968). He has been known for his hard-edge acrylics.

References
NGC Info. Form dated May 25, 1964
The Calgary Herald, Calgary, Alta., Oct. 9, 1965 "Tech Instructor's Exhibition Provides Diversified Display"
The Gazette, Mtl., P.Q., June 1, 1968 "Well-Balanced O'Neill Works, Interesting Fortin Collection" by Richard Jones

O'NEILL, Helen (Mrs.)

A Kirkland Lake, Ontario, artist she is known for her landscapes which she has exhibited at the Northern Ontario Natural Gas Company's travelling exhibition and who has also shown with the Northern Ontario Art Association's exhibitions.

Reference
Kirkland Lake Northern News, Ont., Apr. 16, 1958 "Kirkland Paintings Will Tour Canada"

ONGMAN, Mrs. Marlene
b. (c) 1933

Mother of seven and a self-taught painter, Mrs. Ongman has exhibited her work in Prince George, B.C. in 1964 and 1969 (at the Inn of the North). She is also responsible for the creation of the original Tartan Brewing labels. She is represented in collections in Scotland, New York, South America, San Francisco and Vancouver.

References
Prince George Citizen, B.C., April 16, 1964 "Advice from a painter: buy to suit your taste"
Prince George Progress, B.C., Sept. 20, 1969 "Mother of 7 – she's an artist" by Max Le Breton

ONLEY, Toni
b. 1928

Born in Douglas, Isle of Man, England, the son of James and Florence (Lord) Onley. His father was an English actor. Toni attended St. Mary's primary school and Ingleby Secondary School, Isle of Man, then studied under a local landscape water colourist John Nicholson and at the Douglas School of Fine Arts (1942-46).

He came to Canada in 1948 and settled for a time at Brantford, Ontario. He took further study at the Doon School of Fine Art in 1951 under Carl Schaefer. In his early work Onley was influenced by British painters John Cotman and Peter De-Wint and did traditional landscapes. He married Brantford art critic and amateur painter Mary Burrows in 1950 and they had two daughters Jennifer (b. 1951) and Lynn (b. 1954). He worked at a variety of jobs in order to support his family. Exhibiting in the Western Ontario Annual show of artists under 27 he won an award in 1955. He exhibited as well with the Royal Canadian Academy, The Canadian Society of Painters in Water Colours and his work attracted the attention of art critics. Following the death of his wife Mary, Onley moved with his children to Penticton, B.C., where his parents had retired. There he conducted classes for children Saturday mornings and taught adults nights at Penticton High School. He worked as a surveyor, draftsman, commercial artist and continued with his own painting when time permitted. In 1957 he won a scholarship offered by the Institute Allende, San Miguel de Allende, Mexico, where he took his two daughters. During this period he studied mural painting and fresco and vinylite mediums and was very much influenced by his American (Yugoslavian born) teacher, James Pinto whose abstract impressionistic paintings set Onley on a new direction of non-objective work. He stayed in Mexico three years but returned to Canada to hold exhibitions at the Coste House (Calgary, 1958), Vancouver Art Gallery (1958), New Design Gallery, Van. (1959). By then he was experimenting with collage paintings usually of irregularly shaped pieces of painted paper or canvas pasted to a backing or canvas. Three of his collages were reproduced in Abraham Rogatnick's article on him for *Canadian Art* (Mar./Apr. 1962). In his collage work he did a Polar series numbered from one to beyond forty. These works on large canvases in cool colours of blue, black, grey, green, etc., drew favourable comments from critics and his Polar # 1 won the $2,000 Royal Canadian Academy Zacks Award given to an artist at the society's annual exhibition. With this award Onley studied in London, England, while the award-winning painting was presented to the Tate Gallery having been selected by Sir John Rothenstein (Director of the Tate) as the painting he would like to have for his gallery from the 1963 RCA showing. During this period he studied etching and began to produce work in this medium as an extension of his painting. He had married Gloria Knight in 1961 and in 1967 their son James Anthony was born. In 1961 he completed a 300 sq.ft. mural for the Queen Elizabeth Playhouse in Vancouver and was also one of seven artists chosen to represent Canada at the Paris Biennial. In the years that followed he returned to objective basic shapes from nature giving full play to design with delicate colouring. Although a prolific artist he has been a careful craftsman whether working with paintings large or small, or with serigraphs, etchings and drawings. His silkscreen prints and drawings have received high praise and his paintings, articulate, simple, and subtle in colouring have been discussed by most of the leading critics and historians of the day. Flying has been a hobby which has enabled him to travel to various centres to conduct classes and a variety of other activities. Many of his pencil sketches have been done from the air. Marguerite Pinney made this note of them: "Lovingly executed, these pencil drawings are sketched while piloting his plane over the coast, mountains and valleys of B.C. Sure and delicate, they are a delightful and vital addition to a comprehensive and articulate exhibition." Joan Lowndes also described his drawings as, " . . . fantastic little pencil drawings, eight

ONLEY, Toni (Cont'd)

inches by six, that are the jewels of the show. They are so even in quality they might be compared to beautifully matched pearls. Onley presents nature in an undisturbed prepollution era, heavy with the stillness of primeval times. The lonely rocks send their reflections into the lake." His awards include: Scholarship, Instituto Allende 1957; Canada Council Grant 1961, 1963; Jessie Dow Award at Montreal Spring Show, 1960; one of seven artists to show at Paris Biennial, 1961; Spring Purchase Award (MMFA), 1962; Canadian Biennials exhibitor 1959, 1961, 1963, 1965, 1968; Sam & Ayola Zacks Award, RCA Annual, 1963; Canada Council Senior Fellowship, 1964. He has been living in Vancouver with his family where he is a teacher in the Department of Fine Arts at the University of British Columbia. His one-man shows are as follows: Okanagan Regional Lib., Kelowna, B.C. (1957); Coste House Gallery, Alta. (1958); Vancouver Art Gal. (1958); New Design Gal., Van. (1959, 1962, 1964, 1966, 1968); Dorothy Cameron Gal., Tor. (1960, 1961, 1962, 1964); Blue Barn Gal., Ott. (1961, 1967); The Point Gal., Victoria, B.C. (1961); Otto Seligman Gal., Seattle, Wash. (1962); Gal. Camille Hébert, Mtl. (1963); Pandora's Box Gal., Vic., B.C. (1966); Topham Brown Art Gal., Vernon, B.C. (1967); Western Circuit, B.C. & Alta. (1966-67); Douglas Gal., Van. (1967); Owens Gal., Mt. Allison Univ., Sackville, N.B. (1967); Dalhousie Univ. Art Gal., Hal., N.S. (1967); Confederation Centre Art Gal., Charl., PEI (1968); Agnes Etherington Art Centre, Queen's Univ., Kingston, Ont. (1968); Albert White Gal., Tor. (1968); Gal. Pascal, Tor. (1968, 1970); Art Gal. of Greater Victoria, B.C. (1968); Griffith Galleries, Van. (1968); Bau-Xi Gal., Van., B.C. (1968, 1969, 1971); Simon Fraser Univ., Burnaby, B.C. (1969); Fleet Gallery, Winn., (1969, 1971); Prince Albert Pub. Lib., Prince Albert, Sask. (1969); Graphic Gal., San Francisco, Calif. (1969); New Westminster Pub. Lib., B.C. (1970); Allied Art Centre, Brandon, Man. (1970); Art College Gal., Alta. College of Art, Cal., Alta. (1971); Godart-Lefort Gal., Mtl. (1971) and numerous important national and international group shows (see *Creative Canada* for listing, P. 237). Onley is represented in the following collections: Van. Art Gal., B.C.; Univ. B.C. (Brock Hall Col.); Art Gal. Greater Vict.; Simon Fraser Univ., Burnaby, B.C.; Winnipeg Art Gal., Man.; Lond. Pub. Lib. & Art Museum, Ont.; Willistead Gal., Windsor, Ont.; York Univ., Tor.; Art Gal. of Ont., Tor.; Agnes Etherington Art Centre, Queen's Univ., Kingst., Ont.; NGC, Ott.; Musée d'Art Contemp., Mtl.; Sir Geo. Williams Univ., Mtl.; Mtl. Museum of Fine Arts, P.Q.; C.I.L., Mtl.; Confederation Centre, Charlottetown, PEI; Memorial Univ., St. John's Nfld.; Seattle Museum of Fine Arts, Wash.; Museum of Modern Art, NYC; Tate Gal. Lond., Eng., and the private collections of Mr. & Mrs. Sam Zacks (Tor.); Mr. & Mrs. Percy Waxer (Tor.); Dr. Theodore Heinrich (Tor.); Joseph Hirshhorn (NYC); John David Eaton (Tor.); Paul Arthur (Tor.); J.G. McConnell (Mtl.) and many others. Member: A.R.C.A. (1964); B.C. Soc. of Artists; C.S.P.W.C.; C.G.P.

References
The Canadian Architect, Vol. 6, No. 4, April, 1961 "Art — Toni Onley"
The Star Weekly, Dec. 9, 1961 "Canadians Worth Knowing"
Catalogues — Fourth (1961), Fifth (1963), Sixth (1965), Seventh (1968) Biennials of Canadian Painting
Canadian Art, Mar./Apr., 1962, P. 146 "Toni Onley" by Abraham Rogatnick
Maclean's Magazine, Vol. 76, No. 3, Feb. 9, 1963 "A Vancouver Englishman Wins a Place in the Tate Gallery" P. 45

Canadian Art, Mar./Apr., 1963 "Art Reviews – Toni Onley at the Dorothy Cameron Gallery, Toronto" by George Wallace

Sir George Williams Univ. Collection of Art, 1967, P. 147

Painting In Canada/A History by J. Russell Harper, Univ. Tor. Pr., 1966, P. 409

Painting In Canada by Barry Lord, Catalogue Expo 67, Mtl., 1967, No. 25

Agnes Etherington Art Centre (Queen's Univ.) Permanent Collection, 1968, by Frances K Smith, No. 104

Art Gallery of Ontario, the Canadian collection by Helen Pepall Bradfield, McGraw-Hill, Tor., P. 346

Canadian Art Today ed. Wm. Townsend, Studio International, Lond., Eng. (ill)

The Canada Council Collection, A travelling exhibition of the National Gallery of Canada, Ottawa, 1969, No. 31

Artscanada, February, 1970, Exhibition reviews, "Toni Onley, Bau-Xi Gallery, Vancouver, November, 1969" by Marguerite Pinney

Ibid, February-March, 1971 "In the Galleries, Toronto", by Gary Michael Dault (Onley at Gallery Pascal)

Creative Canada, Volume One, McPherson Lib., Univ. Victoria, B.C., 1971, P. 236, 237

Contemporary Canadian Art (catalogue for show in Africa) 1962 (NGC, Ottawa).

Four Decades, The Canadian Group of Painters by Paul Duval, Clarke, Irwin, Tor., 1972

Ten Years of Painting 1962-72, Bau-Xi Gallery Ltd., Van., B.C.

Canadian Artists In Exhibition 1972-73, Roundstone, Tor., 1974, P. 162

The History of Painting in Canada, Toward A People's Art by Barry Lord, NC Press, Tor., 1974, P. 207

Images for a Canadian Heritage, Canadian Native Prints, Van., B.C., P. 3 (1192 Burrard St., Van.)

A Concise History of Canadian Painting by Dennis Reid, Oxford, Tor., 1973, P. 279

Who's Who In American Art, 1976, Ed. by Jacques Cattell Press, Bowker, NYC, P. 421

NGC Info. Forms, 1957, 1964; Document from artist, 1961

Additional references (Newspaper & Periodical)

The Vancouver Sun, Oct. 15, 1955 "Youngsters 'See' the Wind And Paint It on Canvas" (Toni Onley and his classes) by M. Francis

Courier, Kelowna, B.C., Feb. 7, 1957 "Exhibit of water colors by Toni Onley different from anything seen here before"

Herald, Pent., B.C., Oct. 24, 1957 "Coveted Award To Local Artist" (Institute Allende scholarship to Onley)

The Vancouver Province, B.C., Dec. 4, 1959 "Realm of Art – Onley's Oil-collage work well handled" by The Critic

Ibid, June 4, 1960 "In the Realm of Art" by The Critic (Onley explains his contact with American abstractionists and their influence on his work)

Victoria Daily Times, B.C., Jan. 21, 1961 "Art In Review – Vancouver Abstractionist Creates Fine 'Collages' " by Arthur Corry

Galt Evening Reporter, Ont., Mar. 2, 1961 "Toni Onley Is Winning Acclaim As An Artist"

Herald, Penticton, B.C., May 8, 1961 "Toni Onley to Represent Canada at Paris"

Ibid, Dec. 2, 1961 "Onley Show Gives Rare View of Artistic Growth" by Kay Havergal

The Vancouver Sun, B.C., Feb. 27, 1962 "Interpret It Yourself, Says Onley"

Ibid, Mar. 3, 1962 "Visitors Shocked, Jolted At New Playhouse Theatre"

Ibid, Sept. 21, 1962 "Around The Galleries – One-Man Show Of Collages On" by Flora Kyle

The Toronto Telegram, Ont., Jan. 12, 1963 "Onley Wins Top Honor"

The London Free Press, Ont., Jan. 26, 1963 "Looking At Art – Find Emphasis on Abstracts at RCA Exhibit; Onley Canvas Captures Top Award of $2,000" by Lenore Crawford (photo of Polar No. 1)

Brantford Expositor, Ont., July 19, 1963 "Former City Artist Gets N.Y. Showing"

Globe & Mail, Ont., Sept. 6, 1963 "Tate Acquires Two Paintings By Canadians"

The Vancouver Sun, Nov. 3, 1964 "Trivia, Too – Toni Onley At His Best In Etchings" by David Watmough

The Gazette, Mtl., P.Q., Sept. 4, 1965 "Art – Sometimes Less Is More" by Rea Montbizon

Victoria Daily Times, B.C., Nov. 15, 1965 "Paintings by Onley an unforgettable experience" by Skelton

Victoria Colonist, B.C., Nov. 26, 1965 "At the Gallery – Onley Water Colors Better at University" by Ina D.D. Uhthoff

Victoria Daily Times, B.C., Apr. 16, 1966 "Bare rocks conjure up tense drama" by Robin Skelton

Nelson Daily News, B.C., May 31, 1966 "Acrylic painting taught at NDU"

The Ottawa Citizen, Ont., Sept. 10, 1966 "Vancouver artist calls show 'Inner Landscape' " by C.W.

Vernon News, B.C., Mar. 30, 1967 "Toni Onley's work today and yesterday"

Vancouver Province, B.C., Oct. 13, 1967 "Onley – impact without bigness" by Joan Lowndes

The Montreal Star, P.Q., Dec. 5, 1967 "The art scene – Onley's calm poetry" by Robert Ayre

The Vancouver Sun, B.C., Sept. 20, 1968 "It's Toni's Day – His private, stubborn consistency wins praise" by Ann Rosenberg

Vancouver Province, B.C., Sept. 20, 1968 article on the occasion of his partial retrospective at the Art Gallery of Greater Victoria and print show at Bau-Xi Gallery by Joan Lowndes

Victoria Daily Times, B.C., Sept. 21, 1968 "From The Gallery – Partial Retrospective Honors Onley"

Ibid, Sept. 21, 1968 (about the retrospective at AGGV) by Ted Lindberg

Victoria Colonist, B.C., Sept. 23, 1968 "At the Gallery – Favorite Artist Modifies Style" by Ina D.D. Uhthoff

The Vancouver Sun, B.C., Feb. 24, 1969 "Working Sketches Shown by . . . " by Charlotte Townsend

Ibid, Nov. 12, 1969 "Flyer Toni Onley Takes Off in New Direction" by Charlotte Townsend

Ibid, Apr. 16, 1969 "Second Look at Fine Artist" by Charlotte Townsend

Winnipeg Free Press, Man., May 15, 1969 "A Review By John W. Graham – Onley Landscape Calm, Mystical"

Vancouver Province, B.C., Nov. 13, 1969 "Art and Artists – Onley stretched in second show" by Joan Lowndes

Calgary Albertan, Alta., Feb. 13, 1971 (article on Onley's work with praise) by Helen McLean

Edmonton Journal, Alta., Apr. 8, 1971 "Ordinary objects are enhanced in Onley show"

Winnipeg Free Press, Man., May 22, 1971 "A Review By John W. Graham – B.C. Artist Featured"

Vancouver Province, B.C., Oct. 29, 1971 "Art – Impeccably polite, that's Toni Onley" by Richard Simmins

The Vancouver Sun, B.C., Oct. 29, 1971 "Power sustained in Onley's works" by Joan Lowndes

London Evening Free Press, Ont., Mar. 20, 1972 "Poole Studio show continues through March 29 – Art exhibit combines color, message" by Lenore Crawford

---

OONARK, Jesse (Seekanik)

b. 1906

An Eskimo artist from the area west of Baker Lake, Keewatin, N.W.T., Oonark spent her earlier years as a hunter's wife, designing and making ornate leather clothing. Canadian Wildlife Service biologist Andrew MacPherson was impressed with her work and encouraged her to draw with pencil and paper. She has been drawing since 1959. Within a year, her drawings were being listed in the annual Cape Dorset print catalogue. Her pen drawings, crayons, needlework hangings, and clothing all preserve and record the customs and cultural history of the Es-

OONARK, Jesse (Seekanik) (Cont'd)

kimo. Oonark's work is widely known and has often been exhibited at the National Arts Centre, Ottawa; Winnipeg Art Gallery (1970); Innuit Gallery of Eskimo Art, Toronto (1970 and 1971); Robertson Galleries, Ottawa (1971) and travelling exhibition displayed at the Metropolitan Museum, NYC. The National Museum of Man in Ottawa has also purchased ninety of her drawings.

References
> National Museums of Canada Press Release (1970?) "Two Artists from the Northwest Territories"
> *The Winnipeg Tribune*, Man., Aug. 29, 1970 "Eskimo art: unmistakably their own"
> *The Winnipeg Free Press*, Man., Sept. 5, 1970 (photo and caption)
> *The Winnipeg Tribune*, Man., April 5, 1971 "Her dreams on cloth" (photo and caption)
> *The Gazette*, Mtl., P.Q., Apr. 10, 1971 "Jesse Oonark – a genuine natural artist" by Michael White
> *The Montreal Star*, P.Q., Apr. 15, 1971 "Jesse Oonark's art serenely symbolic" by Terry Kirkman and Judy Heviz
> *Le Droit*, Ottawa, Ont., May 15, 1971 "Oonark et Paneloo montrent des oeuvres vigoureuses et fort personnelles"

OOSTERHOFF, William Frederic Karel
b. 1895

Born in Delft, Holland, he attended the art academy in Amsterdam where he studied modelling and sculpture under Fortuin, Oorschot and Gadefroy. He emigrated to Canada in 1925 and for a time settled in Waterloo before moving to Hamilton. He worked on the Arch of Triumph in Niagara, the mausoleum in Kitchener, Ontario, the bas-relief on the Royal Ontario Museum, the Sunnybrook Hospital in Toronto, and the Arts and Sciences Building of McMaster University, Hamilton, Ontario. He succeeded Cleophas Soucy as National Stone Carver of Canada in 1949 a position he filled until his retirement in 1962 when he was succeeded by Eleanor Milne. During his term as National Stone Carver he applied his knowledge of heraldry and Canadian history and was the moving spirit behind scores of beautiful stone carvings of crests, busts and other sculptures for the decoration of the Houses of Parliament.

References
> NGC Info. Form May, 1931
> *The Ottawa Citizen*, Ont., May 12, 1950 "Half-Forgotten Faces Stare Stonily From Hill" by Austin F. Cross
> Ibid, Mar. 27, 1951 "Parliamentary Carver 'Spudding' Artist at 12" by Kay Rex
> Ibid, Dec. 1, 1959 "Sculptor Carving Prototype Models of Coat of Arms" by Jack Best
> *The Ottawa Journal,* Ont., Nov. 28, 1959 "Puts New Life in Coat of Arms" by Jack Best
> *Le Droit*, Ottawa, Ont., Mar. 4, 1961 "La nuit au parlement, les sculpteurs sont à l'oeuvre" par Jean Charpentier
> *Toronto Star Weekly*, Ont., Apr. 28, 1962 "Canadians Worth Knowing"
> NGC Info. Form Aug. 18, 1965

OOSTERMAN, Pierre

Born in Holland, he was commissioned to create two of his large abstract multi-coloured upholstery fabric wall-hangings for Dupont of Canada's V.I.P. Lounge at Expo '67 with one mural telling the story of the manufacture of nylon and the other the use of nylon yarn in the textile industry. One of his creations hangs in the main lobby of La France Textiles, Limited, Woodstock, Ontario, where he is a purchasing agent. He has done a number of murals for large industries and businesses throughout Canada and the United States. He makes his textiles in stages; first designing the work with oil crayons on paper, next the fabrics are dyed to the desired colours and cut to shape, and finally the fabrics are glued onto a special fabric backing to complete the mural.

References
  Woodstock-Ingersoll Sentinel Review, Ont., Feb. 4, 1967 "Making the Expo Scene" by Peter Krien
  Ibid, Mar. 4, 1967 "Local Murals on Display before Expo Exposure"

OPPENHEIMER, Joseph
1876-1966

Born in Würtzburg, Bavaria, a fourth generation painter, he left school at the age of sixteen when it was realized that he was more interested in drawing than completing his regular school lessons. His parents sent him to Munich to study art. Following his courses in Germany he took further study in Rome. By 1898 at the age of twenty-two, he was in London, England, and two years later in New York City. After stops on his way home he returned to Germany where he worked as an artist until 1933. During this period he became influenced by the Sezessionen movement (a group of German artists who seceded from the academic bodies and exhibiting societies to pursue impressionism; from these artists a further group broke away to become the Expressionists). Robert Ayre felt his work lay in style between Impressionism and Expressionism since his work has the qualities of both. Oppenheimer painted in Paris, Amsterdam, Hiddensee on the Baltic Sea, Venice on the Adriatic, also Copenhagen, and Sando in Norway and many other places. His subjects included figures, floral arrangements, landscapes and a variety of other things as well as portraits. In 1933 he moved to London, England, where he made his home for the next fifteen years. There he became known for his portraits and was a member of the Royal Society of Portrait Painters. Those who sat for him during his career included Harold Macmillan, Yehudi Menuhin, Albert Einstein, Otto Klemperer, Leonid Pasternak, Herman Struck, Earl of Athlone, Lord Bessborough and Camillien Houde. He also painted members of his own family including his mother and his daughter (Canadian artist and portraitist, Mrs. Eva Prager). Oppenheimer first came to Montreal in 1948 and for the next seventeen years until his death he maintained a home both in Montreal and London. He was active right up until the age of ninety when he was still painting scenes in rural Quebec. Four years after his death an exhibition of 150 of his water colours and drawings was held at the Montreal Museum of Fine Arts during February and

OPPENHEIMER, Joseph (Cont'd)

March of 1970. The catalogue and exhibition was organized by Leo Rosshandler, Deputy Director of the Museum. Viewing this show Robert Ayre noted, "This show is not a retrospective, and none of the formal oils are presented, but a few of the drawings – even those that come from the painter's childhood – reveal his accomplishment in portraiture. Of course the drawing of Bismarck he made when he was a boy of 13 is not here – it was given to the Chancellor – but the exhibition includes the exquisite drawings he made of his parents when he was 15, a water color of his mother, 50 years later, a sensitive drawing of Einstein dated 1931 and a portrait of his daughter in 1937. They were all done with love and superb draughtsmanship. Oppenheimer's scrupulous attention to detail, as a student in his teens, is also to be seen in the drawings of the castle at Würtzburg. Though he was to break away into vigorous freedom of expression, he had the fundamental discipline of academic training, and he was always in command of his gesture, however spontaneous." Those contributing to the success of the exhibition by loaning paintings from their collections included Mrs. Fanny Oppenheimer (widow of the artist), Eva and Vincent Prager, Dr. H. Magder and Dr. H. Krohn.

References
    The Gazette, Mtl., P.Q., Aug. 26, 1961 "Art – Portrait By Oppenheimer"
    The Montreal Star, P.Q., July 13, 1961 "Famed Painter, 85 Finds Art Can Pay" by Paul Pross
    Ibid, Feb. 28, 1970 "Flower Power" by Robert Ayre
    The Gazette, Mtl., P.Q., Feb. 28, 1970 "Drawings by Oppenheimer outshine main exhibition"
    Joseph Oppenheimer, Watercolors and Drawings by Leo Rosshandler (Deputy Director, Montreal Museum of Fine Arts)Feb. 17-Mar. 17 1970 (catalogue)

ORBELIANI, Mary (Mrs.)

b. 1873

Formerly a Russian princess by her marriage to Prince Alexis Orbeliani in 1905, she was educated in Leningrad by artists Volkoff, Repin, and Krachkovsky. In 1921 she fled Russia and entered Yugoslavia as a refugee and made her living by teaching French and Art. Later she followed her son to Belgium after the death of her husband in 1952. In both countries she exhibited her transparent water colours. In 1954, once again following her son, she came to Canada and settled at the Scenic Valley Home in Penticton, B.C. In 1957 she attended art courses at the Banff School of Fine Arts. In 1969 she exhibited her paintings at Peebles Motor Inn, Nelson, B.C.

References
    The Edmonton Journal, Alta., July 16, 1969 "Russian princess, now 96, is thankful for language and artistic abilities"
    Nelson Daily News, B.C., June 7, 1969 "Soft Colors Set Theme for Orbeliani Exhibition" by Paul Carbray

ORENSTEIN, Henry

b. 1918

He studied at the Central Technical School, Toronto, and the Ontario College of Art as well as at the Art Students' League of New York under Mary Stepnberg. Member of the Canadian Society of Graphic Art (1949). Residing in Toronto in 1950.

Reference
NGC Info. Form rec'd June 13, 1950

ORENSTEIN, Leo

He held an exhibition of his water colours at the Picture Loan Society in 1946 which included scenes at night, portraits, interiors and other subjects.

Reference
The Toronto Telegram, Ont., Jan. 13, 1946 "Orenstein's One-Man Show"

ORENSTEIN, Oscar

Born in Toronto he studied art at the Ontario College of Art, the American Artists' School, NYC, and elsewhere. He also worked as an artist and set designer with the Canadian Army. Living in Timmins, Ontario, where he is proprietor of the Northern Art Gallery Little Gallery, he was formerly located at Schumacher under the name Porcupine Art Gallery. Orenstein has exhibited his work in New York City, Montreal and Toronto.

References
Timmins Press, Ont., Jan. 7, 1971 "Moves his Art Gallery to Timmins"
Ibid, Dec. 11, 1969 "Proposes Painting Record Of The Historic Porcupine" by Marcel Lamarche

---

ORLOFF, Gregory

He illustrated elementary school science textbooks. One such work is *Through the Seasons: Science for Modern Living*, Longmans, Green & Company: Toronto, 1957.

ORTON, Ann

An Ottawa resident, she studied at the Ontario College of Art specializing in enamelling work in her third year. After graduating in 1961 she lived in Toronto for a year-and-a-half before moving to Ottawa. She works with about two hundred varieties of enamels creating small to medium sized pieces which she usually mounts on wood. Describing her subjects Valerie Knowles noted, "Ann's work has several

ORTON, Ann (Cont'd)

sources of inspiration, one being her three small children. Their pony-tailed profiles and eager faces figure frequently in her designs. 'But often', she says 'it's just their feelings and mine . . . . ' When not using her children or incidents from daily life as sources of inspiration, Ann may draw upon ideas culled from poems, songs and even dreams. Several of her more ambitious pieces derive their inspiration from these sources. Occasionally, however, the chance discovery of an interesting object will give rise to a particular piece of work." When not working on her enamels she conducts art classes for children. Her own work has been exhibited at the Pollock Gallery, Tor.; Wells Gallery, Ottawa; The Merton Gallery, Tor. (1975) and in the annual Ottawa I.O.D.E. show where she was awarded a first prize in 1970.

Reference
   The Ottawa Citizen, Ont., Aug. 7, 1971 "Enamelling – ancient craft still a challenge" (story-photos) by Valerie Knowles

OSBORNE, Dennis Henry
b. 1919

Born in Portsmouth, England, he spent three and a half years as a prisoner of war in Italy and Germany. An art student before the war he resumed his art studies with a grant from the London County Council. He studied at the Camberwell School of Arts and Crafts for four years under Sir William Coldstream, Victor Pasmore, John Minton and G. Monnington and received an Intermediate Certificate in Arts and Crafts and the National Diploma in Design (1950). He studied as well at the Heatherley School of Art, London. He exhibited at the Royal Academy, the New English Art Club, Artists International, and "Young Contemporaries." In 1952 he emigrated to Canada, settling in St. Catharines, Ontario. He has conducted evening art classes at St. Catharines Collegiate and at Smithville High School and courses in portraiture and landscape for the Lakehead Area Art Association (1959). His work has been exhibited at the Ontario Society of Artists shows; the Montreal Museum of Fine Arts; the Hamilton Art Gallery and the Winnipeg Art Exhibition. His "Three Peasants" was chosen for showing at the 20th Biennial International Water Color Exhibition at the Brooklyn Art Museum and was also exhibited in the 1958 Canadian Society of Painters in Water Colour show in Toronto. His ten-foot mural of a central scene of Welland which decorates the waiting room of the Sundy-Macmillan Chiropractic Clinic, Welland, was completed in 1959. He received a purchase award from the Hamilton Art Gallery, Ontario in 1957. Husband of artist Jean Osborne. Member of the Colour & Form Society (1956, Pres. 1957).

References
   NGC Info. Form rec'd June 6, 1957
   St. Catharines Standard, Ont., Nov. 18, 1958 "Local Artist's Work Selected for Exhibition at International Show"
   Fort William Times-Journal, Ont., Jan. 13, 1959 "Art Assoc. Plans Winter Course in Painting"
   Welland-Port Colbourne Tribune, Ont., Jan. 24, 1959 "Mural Adds Cultural Touch To New Chiropractic Clinic"

OSBORNE, Jean

b. 1926

Born in the County of Antrim, Northern Ireland, she studied at the Camberwell School of Arts and Crafts, London, England, on a four year grant awarded her by the Ministry of Education. She studied under Sir W. Coldstream, Victor Pasmore, Claude Rogers, W. Monnington and others, graduating in 1951 with a National Diploma in Design and an Intermediate Certificate in Arts and Crafts. In 1953 she emigrated to Canada, settling in St. Catharines, Ontario. Her work has been exhibited by the London Group, the New English Art Club, "Young Contemporaries" and the Belfast Museum. In Canada she has exhibited at the Hamilton Art Gallery annual shows, with the Ontario Society of Artists and the Colour & Form Society. In October of 1957 she participated in a three-man show at the Hamilton Art Gallery in which her husband Dennis also took part and in 1958 they held a two-man show at the Thielban Gallery, London, Ontario. Member of the Colour & Form Society (1955).

Reference
NGC Info. Form rec'd July, 1958

OSBORNE, John

A Richmond, B.C. painter, he studied in Europe and has taught art in the Mediterranean, North Africa, and Canada for many years. He settled in Richmond in 1961. He has taught the Delta Sketching Club, exhibited his paintings at the art shop in the Richmond Square Mall (1965), and is well-known as a local artist.

Reference
Richmond Review, B.C., July 28, 1965 "Canadian Artists Visit Richmond"

OSBORNE, L.F. (Ossie)

An aircraft engineer by profession, he became so interested in pottery that he gave up his job and moved to California to study with Marguerite Wildenhain in 1956. In 1960 he moved to Victoria, where he and his wife Mary opened the Osborne Pottery Studio. Here he creates, sells, and teaches pottery. His work has been exhibited in Brussels, Paris, Florence. In 1959 he received the Grand Award for earthenware pottery at the Canadian national ceramic exhibition and he is represented in the permanent collection of the Vancouver Art Gallery, B.C. He has also sent pieces to B.C. House in San Francisco.

Reference
Van. Island Events, Victoria, B.C., June 1962 "The Osborne Pottery Studio"

OSBORNE, Mary

She studied pottery at the University of British Columbia and in 1960 moved to Victoria where she and her potter husband "Ossie" set up a studio. In the display room Mary has her wheel and visitors may be lucky enough to catch her at work. The Osbornes mix their own clay. This clay is obtained from the Bazan Bay brickworks and is then mixed with high-fire clay from Saskatchewan and a fire clay from Sumas, B.C. giving them a tough durable body of material with which to work. First the Bazan clay is dried and crushed, then put into a barrel for mixing with the high fire clays, churned by an electric beater, forced through a screen, and allowed to settle after which the water is then siphoned off and the thickened clay put into vats in the sun until firm. The clay is then wedged and stored in plastic bags until needed. Mrs. Osborne's work has been exhibited widely with that of her husband.

Reference
  Van. Island Events, Victoria, B.C., June, 1962 "The Osborne Pottery Studio"

OSBORNE, M.S.

A University of Toronto professor who sketched architectural drawings of buildings in the Greater Toronto area which were published in a local magazine series.

Reference
  Clipping from a magazine dated June 14, 1958 "City's Treasures"

OSBORNE, Rosalynde Fuller

A resident of Hamilton, Ontario, she studied under J.S. Gordon at the Hamilton School of Art; Stanhope Forbes, R.A. at Newlyn, England; the New York School of Fine and Applied Design and with Felicie Waldo Howell, A.N.A., NYC. A member of the Women's Art Association (1924) she made and operated marionettes as well as painted in water colours. She also exhibited and lectured on her collection of dolls, marionettes, and puppets.

References
  The Montreal Standard, P.Q., April 18, 1942, article by Robert Ayre
  NGC Info. Form rec'd Feb. 26, 19--

OSCAR, Art

A Brandon, Manitoba, artist who took teacher training at Brandon College of Fine Arts at the University of Manitoba. After graduation in 1967 he has worked

OSCAR, Art (Cont'd)

as an art supervisor for the Brandon school system, grades five through nine. He paints with acrylics, creates collage paintings and also does sculpture. In 1969 he exhibited at Brandon University, and was noted by Kaye Rowe of *The Brandon Sun* as follows: "His acrylic paintings reveal astonishing imagination, a Gothic touch but done with wit rather than a sense of horror. Even his titles have literary touches; the large canvas of greens, blacks and off-whites draw the eye to a mesh see-through cage behind which a vocalizing female face demands release. His skill in miniaturizing gives these faces, although slightly larger than a hen's egg, some measure of identity and detail."

References
> *The Brandon Sun*, Man., Mar. 6, 1969 "Instructor show work"
> Ibid, Mar. 13, 1969 "Oscar art show offers promise of big future" by Kaye Rowe

OSET, Robert

A painter of landscapes, seascapes, still life and portraits, he has exhibited his work at Notre Dame College School, Welland, Ontario.

References
> *Welland-Port Colborne Tribune*, Ont., May 8, 1967 "Art Exhibit At Notre Dame Set For May 21"
> Ibid, May 19, 1967 "Art Display At Notre Dame School" (photo and caption)

OSGOOD, Ross Reverdy
1867-1946

Born in Oxford County, the son of the late Horatio and Annie (Williams) Osgood, he lived in St. Thomas for about sixty-six years of his life and also in Durham County and London, Ontario for other periods. A painter in oils and water colours he did portraits, figure studies, landscapes, seascapes, religious subjects and still lifes. He is represented in the collection of the Art Gallery of Ontario by several oils and water colours. He served with the Engineers in the Canadian Overseas Expeditionary Force during the First World War (1916-19). He painted the portrait of Sir John A. Macdonald which has been on display in the Ontario Parliament Buildings for many years under the title of "Old Union Jack." Osgood died in St. Thomas at the age of seventy-nine. His paintings appear to have been signed R.R. Osgood(e) according to findings on his work in the AGO collection.

References
> *The St. Thomas Times Journal*, Ont., July 17, 1946 "R.R. Osgood, Talented Artist Dies; He painted Famous 'Old Union Jack.'"
> *Early Painters and Engravers In Canada* by J. Russell Harper, Univ. Tor. Pr. 1970, P. 241 (more detailed Info.)

OSGOOD, Ross Reverdy (Con't)

Art Gallery of Ontario, the Canadian Collection by Helen Pepall Bradfield, McGraw-Hill Co. of Can. Ltd., Tor., 1970, P. 347
Attestation Paper for Canadian Over-Seas Expeditionary Force dated 27th July, 1916, London, Ontario
Certificate of Medical Examination
Discharge Certificate dated May 19, 1919

OSINCZUK, Michael
b. (c) 1890

Born in the western Ukraine, a Byzantine style mural painter, he was educated at the Academy of Art at Krakow (Poland) and graduated in 1914. Following WW II, during which time he was forced to work in German labour camps, he lived in a Displaced Persons camp before going to New York in 1947. He spent a year in Toronto (1949) decorating Holy Eucharist and St. Josaphat churches. In Europe he had decorated fourteen churches including St. George at Lwow. He is considered one of the originators of modernistic Ukrainian church art. Lives in NYC.

Reference
The Evening Telegram, Tor., Ont., Jan. 29, 1949 "DP Paints Toronto Church In True Byzantine Style"

OSTED, Hans

Born in Denmark from a background of artists he came to Canada with his family in 1954 and they settled in Winnipeg. He earned his living as a house painter and through this occupation became familiar with homes in various districts of the city, especially the older areas. He delights in depicting scenes from the city's poorer districts where he finds more colour, character and history in subjects such as a deserted house. His work has been categorized as "magic realism" and has become increasingly popular over the years. His exhibits and awards include: First Jury Art Show, Red River Exhibition (3rd Prize, 1964), Second Jury Art Show (major amateur award, 1965), Third Jury Art Show (1st hon. mention, 1966); Saskatoon Art Salon (1st Prize, 1966), Saskatoon Exhibition (1st Prize, 1969). He has also exhibited with the Manitoba Society of Artists. In 1969 Osted received a Canada Council Bursary to allow him time from his regular work to visit various Canadian art galleries and museums in Eastern Canada and to allow him time to paint. A solo show of his work was held at the Hovmand Galleries, Winnipeg around 1969.

References
Winnipeg Tribune, Man., April 6, 1968 "Winnipeg artist wins $3,500 council award"
Winnipeg Free Press, Man., Apr. 20, 1968 "Local Artist Wins $3,500 Study Grant"
Ibid, Sept. 7, 1968 "Music & Arts — Local Artist Receives Recognition With Grant" by Carmen-Litta Magnus
Catalogue — Hovmand Galleries "Recent Work By Hans Osted"

OSTIGUY, Maryel

b. (c) 1932

An instinctive painter she exhibited about twenty-five pictures at La Boutique, Montreal, in a robust and sure style which included still lifes, landscapes and wood-cuts. At that time she was only seventeen.

References
La Presse, Mtl., P.Q., Nov. 19, 1949 "La peinture instinctive"
Ibid, Nov. 19, 1949 ("Maryel Ostiguy à la Boutique" – photo and caption)

OTIS, Serge

b. 1938

He studied at the University of Sherbrooke; did drawing, decorating and television announcing for a year at Matane. Studied at the Ecole des Beaux-Arts, Mtl. (1959-62); travelled in Canada and the United States (1962-64) and visited Mexico (1965-66). He has been known more recently as a sculptor but he won the first prize in the Salon de Jeune Peinture, Mtl. in 1962. He has exhibited his work at the following: University of Montreal (1964); at the Cultural Centre of Longueuil (1967); Galerie du Siècle, Mtl. (1967); Galerie au Tandem, Mlt. (1967). In 1968 he participated in the show Sculpteurs du Quebec at the Museum of Contemporary Art, Montreal and in 1969 at the Experimental Gallery of that same museum. He has also participated in Expo '67 and did a sculpture and mural for the "Homme dans la Cité" Pavilion there, also he was one of the working animators for the symposium on sculpture at the Youth Pavilion. Michael White of *The Montreal Star* noted his work during his 1969 one-man show "Spirals Unlimited" at the Museum of Contemporary Arts as follows, "He explained that he moved from static flowers to making spiralling flowers and soon the petals dropped off and the purer form of the spiral became the main element of his experiences . . . . He made the spirals at the Quebec Steel workshops."

References
News Clipping – Mtl., P.Q., Aug. 2, 1967 "Les Arts – Un happening de policiers" by Marcel Huguet
La Presse, Mtl., P.Q. Aug. 2, 1969 "Invitation à jouer"
The Montreal Star, P.Q., July 16, 1969 "Montreal sculptor exhibits collection of spiralling steel" by Michael White
Matane La Voix Gaspesienne, P.Q., Aug. 7, 1969 "Serge Otis expose à Montréal"
L'Art Au Quebec Depuis 1940 par Guy Robert, La Presse, Mtl., P.Q., 1973, P. 272, 273

OTTO, Guttorn

b. 1919

Born near Lodz, Poland of German parents, his father was a Lutheran minister, a painter and musician and taught these arts to his sons. Otto studied cello for three years at the Conservatory in Lodz. Then in 1936 he entered the Academy of Fine Arts in Warsaw and studied under Professor Bordjuk. He was conscripted into the German army and spent the war on the Eastern Front where he was wounded.

OTTO, Guttorn (Cont'd)

Following the war he returned to painting and was elected a member of the West German Professional Society of Creative Artists. In 1952 he came to Canada and settled in Toronto. He has taught art at a Bloomington school, at Beaverton and in Toronto. In 1963 one of his paintings was chosen for the Canadian Imperial Bank of Commerce calendar. He has painted in Northern Ontario, Quebec and Manitoba. He has shown his work at Eaton's Toronto (1963, 1970), Eaton's Winnipeg (1964, 1970) and at The Gallery of The Golden Key, Vancouver (1970). Primarily a marine and landscape artist he has also done excellent florals, murals and portraits.

References

Tribune, Stouffville, Ont., Feb. 21, 1963 "Local Man's Art At Eaton's College Street Store"
Examiner, Barrie, Ont., Oct. 12, 1963 "A Noted Artist, Is To Address Local Art Club"
Packet & Times, Orillia, Ont., Jan. 30, 1964 "He'll Paint For The Public"
Examiner, Peterborough, Ont., Aug. 15, 1964 "Artist Must Have Desire To Create Bond Among Humans" by Nick Yunge-Bateman
Winnipeg Free Press, Man., Nov. 23, 1964 article by Ray Sinclair
Ship-Shore News, January, 1967 (photo of Christmas card designed for the Upper Lakes Shipping Ltd. with caption)
Packet & Times, Orillia, Ont., June 24, 1967 "It's A 'Paint-Out' " (photo of Orillia Artist's Guild member/Guild under direction of Otto)
Dunville Chronicle, Ont., Feb. 12, 1970 "Toronto Artist to hold Workshop"
The Toronto Telegram, Ont., May 30, 1970 "Art Removed as Spadina protest"
The Toronto Star, Ont., May 29, 1970 "Dennison returns art to 'insulted' painter" (Otto was opposed to the Spadina Expressway)

OUCHI, Eugene

b. 1943

Born in British Columbia, he attended the Alberta College of Art where he studied under John Esler. A printmaker, he spent 1968-69 in Toronto printing with Jo Rothfels. In 1969 he exhibited with the Society of Canadian Painter-Etchers and Engravers and took the Hornyansky Award at the show. In 1970 he presented work at the Northwest Printmakers 41st International in Seattle and Gallery 1640 in Montreal when Shirley Raphael for *The Gazette* noted, "He uses the white of the paper in embossed strips or shapes, with touches of color in just the right places . . . . The fact that he has kept the exhibit small is refreshing. I've been to many shows where the walls are covered with work . . . Ouchi, on the other hand, believes in saying more by showing less. In his current show . . . he succeeds admirably." Ouchi also had a showing of his work at Gallery Pascal, Toronto, in 1972.

References

The Gazette, Mtl., P.Q., Nov. 14, 1970 "Newcomer's Prints Show Promise" by Shirley Raphael

OUDENDAG, Egbert

b. 1914

Born in Raalte, Holland, his father was a member of a Dutch provincial Parliament and his mother an author, encouraged him in his art. He decided to become an

OUDENDAG, Egbert (Cont'd)

artist at the age of six and at fifteen sold his first painting. During his school years he was an outstanding gymnast, runner and speed skater. He later worked as a military riding instructor at the Dutch Riding Academy. He became a sailor on a freighter plying the North and Baltic Seas. During the war when the Nazis occupied Holland he was suspected of being an underground agent and escaped execution by pretending to be insane. For a time he worked in a stained glass factory and painted landscapes in his free time. His first solo show after the war was a complete sell out. Self-taught in his painting up to his thirties he became a student of famous portraitist Hans Van Meegeren in Amsterdam and studied under him for several years. Van Meegeren who had become wealthy from portrait commissions was reputed to have wanted to obtain revenge from some of his critics by perpetrating a two million dollar hoax in the painting style of the old masters, especially Vermeer, then aging the canvases with a special technique he himself developed. He succeeded with these paintings so well that he sold eight of them but when the truth was revealed the courts and the public took the fakes at face value and Van Meegeren was imprisoned in 1947 but had only served six weeks of his term when he died of a heart attack. After the trial Oudendag, having been a student of Van Meegeren, was discriminated against by museum and gallery officials so he sailed for Canada with his wife Ria and their infant son (they now have two sons, Peter and Paul). Well trained in painting under Van Meegeren and with his own natural ability Oudendag found his feet in his new home. He has developed a simplified style where he uses long and big brush strokes and leaves them virtually unchanged. In his work he has concentrated on life-size portraits and large landscapes working very fast by leaving out all unnecessary detail. He produces about one hundred or more paintings a year. After fourteen years as resident in Ontario, mainly at Dundas, he moved to British Columbia where he converted an old cafe in White Rock into a studio. Basically he was a portrait and figure painter but he has now become known for his landscapes, seascapes and still lifes. He works always from life when doing his paintings. He has exhibited at the following places: Burlington Library, Ont. (1958); Glenhyrst Gardens, Brantford, Ont. (1958); Aberfoyle, Ont. (1960); Fraser Galleries, White Rock, B.C. (1968); Jack Hambleton Galleries, Kelowna, B.C. (1969); Gordon Galleries, Prince George, B.C. (1970) also has shown in the United States at Camelback Galleries, Phoenix, Ariz. and the Zantman Galleries, Carmel, Calif. He is represented in a number of American galleries including the Brooklyn Museum.

References
>Globe & Mail*, Toronto, Ont., Sept. 7, 1949 "Dutch Hoaxer's Pupil Nearly Broke" by Carey Wieber
Ibid, Sept. 16, 1949 (photo and caption)
Examiner, Barrie, Ont., Feb. 16, 1950 "The Barrie Art Club"
Globe & Mail, Jan. 21, 1958 "Learned Portrait Art From Famous Forger"
The Hamilton Spectator, Ont., Jan. 21, 1958 "Dutch Painter Shows Work"
Expositor, Brantford, Ont., April 2, 1958 "Oudendag Exhibit Opening Monday"
Ibid, April 11, 1958 (photo and caption)
Ibid, April 18, 1958 (photo and caption)
The Calgary Herald, Alta., Sept. 29, 1960 "Artist Claims Bias"
The Ottawa Citizen, Ont., Nov. 5, 1960 "Galleries Won't Exhibit His Work"
Vancouver Sun, B.C., Aug. 14, 1964 "Mr. Oudendag Curious Chap With A Brush" by Nels Hamilton

OUDENDAG, Egbert (Cont'd)

The Hamilton Spectator, Ont., Aug. 26, 1965 "West is best – for artist" by Vicki Innes
The Upper Islander, Campbell River, B.C., July 26, 1967 "Big Rock Boat-house 'sends' artist; prawns take back-seat to painting"
Canadian Saturday Night, Toronto, Ont., Jan. 1968 "From out of the west"
White Rock Sun, B.C., Jan. 23, 1969 "Outstanding artist finds White Rock ideal locale" by Margaret Lang
Ibid, June 26, 1969 "Artist commissioned for Stevens portrait"
Kelowna Courier, B.C., July 3, 1969
Ibid, July 10, 1969 "Vancouver Artist Exhibits Here Favors 'The Way It Is' Style"
Ibid, July 14, 1969 "Vancouver Artist Advises Students"
White Rock Sun, B.C., Oct. 30, 1969 "Artist fulfilled childhood ambition" by Laura Lukyn
Prince George Citizen, B.C., Feb. 17, 1970 "Outstanding B.C. artist exhibits work in city" by Bev. Christenson
Prince George Progress, B.C., Feb. 18, 1970 "Dutch-born artist says he paints for himself" by J. Jeff Jones

---

OUELLET, Angémil
b. (c) 1936

From Jonquière-Kénogami, he is a self-taught painter who has done many other things. At the age of thirteen he was a lumberjack, at twenty-eight a prospector and later was a head of a mining company. In 1968 he exhibited his paintings which included nudes, still lifes, landscapes and some surrealistic and impressionistic canvases at Chicoutimi, P.Q.

References

Progrès-Dimanche, Chicoutimi, P.Q., Dec. 1, 1968 "Une trentaine de toiles d'Angémil Ouellet seront exposées en décembre"
Le Soleil, Québec, P.Q., Dec. 14, 1968 "Le peintre Angémil Ouellet accomplit du 'bon boulot' "
Progrès-Dimanche, Chicoutimi, P.Q., Dec. 15, 1968 "Réussite Complète" (photo and caption)

OUELLETTE, Alain

Born in St. Pascal, P.Q., he studied under Roger Larivière. A resident of Ottawa he exhibited there at O.E. Larivière in 1962.

Reference

The Ottawa Citizen, Ont., Nov. 2, 1963 "Entertainment – Promising Painter" Page 4

OWEN, Frederick Howard
b. 1934

Born in Jasper, Alta., he graduated from the Alberta College of Art, Calgary, where he studied under Mrs. Nicoll and Ken Strudy, then took graduate work in

OWEN, Frederick Howard (Cont'd)

ceramics at the University of British Columbia and the University of Alberta, working with Louis Archambault, Wilma Baker and John Reeve, also glaze research work at the Vancouver School of Art under Sybil Laubental. He then worked for two years for the Edmonton Recreation Department; the Recreation and Cultural Branch of the Alberta Provincial Government teaching design, metalwork, and enamel. He has also been set designer and graphic artist for CBXT, Edmonton; taught ceramics at the University of Alberta extension department for four years. From 1968-69 he worked in Ontario for the Elliot Lake Centre for Continuing Education, co-ordinating the arts programs, and in 1970 he moved to Douglas College, New Westminster, B.C., where he is instructor in fine arts. He has worked in traditional ceramics, ceramic sculpture, and experimented with permanently soft clay and clay fabrics. He has exhibited at Studio 60 Gallery (1960), Focus Gallery, Edmonton (1961), Edmonton Art Gallery (1962) and the Public Library, Sault Ste. Marie, Ont. (1970), the University of Alberta (1972) when Ted Kemp noted, "I was impressed by the tactile impressions he gets under smooth glazes, and by the accidents that are much too happy to be quite accidental. I liked especially a little box with an abacus top, and a rectangular receptacle whose lid is an aggressive face to be lifted off by its nose. The gallery displays Fred Owen's work in an appropriate setting, neither antiseptic nor contrived, having ravished an ancient barn for the purpose. Were it not for the subject matter, I'd be inclined to call this small but impressive exhibition a jewel. In fact, I am so inclined, and it is a jewel." Some of his work is in the collection of the Royal Ontario Museum, Tor. (1970). A member of the Canadian Federation of Artists, the Alberta Society for Education Through Art; The Canadian Association for Education Through Art; Studio 60 (which he founded as a student), the X-57 at the Alberta College of Art. While a student he received the T. Eaton Award, the Alberta Drafting Award, the Leon & Thea Koerner Grant, Edmonton Gyro Club Grant (1961) and the Vancouver Sun Scholarship (1961) from the University of British Columbia.

References
NGC Info. Form rec'd Feb. 7, 1962
Elliot Lake Standard, Ont., June 19, 1969 "Royal Ontario Museum Selects Works of Fred Owen"
The Sault Ste. Marie Star, Ont., May 9, 1970 "Talented Artist Shows Ceramics At Sault Library" by Gladys Hornby
Espanola Standard, Ont., Oct. 7, 1970 "Former Resident in New Experiment"
Ladner Optimist, B.C., Sept. 16, 1970 "Master potter to show how, when college opens"
Edmonton Journal, Alta., March 17, 1972 "Let's face it, this is art!" by Ted Kemp

OWEN, Violet (Mrs. Peter Owen)

b. 1930

Born in Edmonton, Alberta, she studied at the Ontario College of Art in Toronto under George Pepper, Jack Nichols, J.W.G. Macdonald and Will Ogilvie and graduated in 1963 then at the Vancouver School of Art under Lionel Thomas, Peter Aspell and Gordon Smith. Her subjects are often portraits and figures described by Virgil Hammock of *The Edmonton Journal* as follows, "There is an Igres-like quality to her drawings . . . . It is by no means as precise in detail as the French

OWEN, Violet (Mrs. Peter Owen) (Cont'd)

master, but like his drawings, we are drawn to the vortex of the work by the finished quality of faces while the remainder is left with only a hint. She has no fear of leaving great areas of large drawings totally blank, yet these blank areas take on an importance they could never have if they were filled with a great deal of meaningless detail." She is a member of the Alberta Society of Artists (1959; Exec. Member 1962-63; Chairman, Edmonton Br., 1964). Her work has been shown at the Centennial Library, Edmonton; the New Brunswick Museum, Saint John; Halifax; and St. John's, Nfld. (as part of the Atlantic Provinces Art Circuit in 1971). Charter member of the Focus Gallery, Edmonton. She lives in Edmonton.

References
> *Jewish News*, Oct. 17, 1963 "Life-Size Oil Painting of Edmonton Cantor for Alta. Art Show"
> *Edmonton Journal*, Alta., May 22, 1964 "Artists' Group Stresses Quality" by Dorothy Barnhouse
> Ibid, May 9, 1969 "Two local artists make impression" by Virgil Hammock
> *Evening Times Globe*, Saint John, N.B., Aug. 12, 1971 "Two Art Exhibits Featured At Museum"
> NGC Info. Form rec'd Aug. 27, 1963

OXBOROUGH, Dorothy Marie (Mrs. H.A. Johnson)
b. 1922

Born in Calgary, Alberta, she grew up in Banff where her father, also an artist, encouraged her in her art. Not far from Banff she visited the Stoney, Cree and Blackfeet Indians who were to become the subjects of her portraits, especially the small children. She studied anatomy at the Vancouver School of Art and at the Institute of Technology and Art, Calgary (1938-41). She married H.A. Johnson, an employee of the Indian affairs and northern development department. As her husband's work took him to various cities they moved from Banff in 1955 to Ottawa (1955-57), Halifax (1957-67) and back to Ottawa in 1967. A realistic painter she has done many portraits and started sketching with pencil and charcoal, then switched to pastels. She also studied oil painting at Fisher Park High School, Ottawa and in the 1970's was reported studying advanced life drawing and working with ceramics at night school. For over twenty-five years she has been known for her portraits of Indian children and adults but was recently commissioned to do thirty Eskimo children and is particularly fascinated by the difference between the facial structure of the Indians and Eskimos. While in Halifax she painted pastel portraits of inshore fishermen. Most of her Nova Scotia work was sold in that province. In addition, she has done portraits of other ethnic groups and numerous commissions for child and adult portraits, animal portraits (principally dogs), still life works. She is represented in the Government of Nova Scotia collection and in the Banff Luxton Museum and in many private collections. Many of her works have been lithographed for use as framing prints, calendars, hasti-notes and other purposes. She is a member of the Nova Scotia Society of Artists (Treas. 1964-65, Sec. 1966-67). She has taken part in numerous art society and municipal shows including the Maritime Art Exhibition Travelling Exhibit sponsored by the Beaverbrook Gallery and has won many awards for her work. Her pictures and reproductions may be

OXBOROUGH, Dorothy Marie (Mrs. H.A. Johnson) (Cont'd)

purchased in various galleries across Canada including Victoria, B.C.; Calgary and Banff Alberta, in Ottawa at the Snow Goose and elsewhere. Living in Ottawa in 1970. She has been interviewed on T.V. and radio many times. Mother of two sons.

References

The Ottawa Journal, Ont., clipping prior to 1958 "Ottawa Artist Finds Best Subjects Among Roly-Poly Blackfeet, Crees" by Ken Parks
The Ottawa Citizen, Ont., Feb. 12, 1970 "Artist with a difference – Native people her subjects" by Eleanor Dunn
Peterborough Examiner, Ont., Mar. 4, 1970 "Portrait Painter Prefers Indian and Eskimo Faces"
Document from artist, 1961
NGC Info. Form 1967 or later.

OZARD, Elmore

b. 1914

Born in Victoria, B.C., he studied at the Vancouver School of Art (1932-36), the University of Washington (B.A., 1947), the University of London, Institute of Education (1956), Slade School of Art (1956), and travelled through Italy, France, and Spain in 1955. A painter and graphic artist, specializing in water colours and serigraphs, he has been influenced in his early work by Paul Nash and later by John Marin. An Associate Professor of Art Education he is also Head of Art Education at the College of Education in the University of British Columbia. He is a member of the B.C. Society of Artists, the Federation of Canadian Artists (former president) and Research Director of the Canadian Society for Education through Art. He is represented in the collections of the Seattle Art Museum and the Heney Gallery in Seattle; the Vancouver Art Gallery and the Art Gallery of Victoria, B.C. Living in Vancouver in 1961.

Reference

Document from artist, November, 1961

OZERDEM, Ulker

Born in Turkey, she attended the Erenkoy Lycee for girls then the State Academy of Fine Arts in Istanbul graduating in 1952 and specializing in a high sculpture course. She also studied at the Art School of The Brooklyn Museum in New York (1953-54) where she won the Fulbright Scholarship. Mainly a sculptor she is particularly interested in wood carving and copper works with relief enamel paint decoration. In her sculpture she prefers to work in a simplified and subjective mode. She held a one-woman show at the Unitarian House, Fredericton, N.B. of eighteen wood carvings. A section of this show was devoted to children by themselves and the other part of her work to children with their parents. She also displayed black and white sketches of Fredericton's older houses, parks and street scenes. She has

OZERDEM, Ulker (Cont'd)

participated in the State Painting and Sculpture Exhibitions in Turkey and World Women's Club, Paris, France.

Reference
   Fredericton Gleaner, N.B., April 14, 1969 "Unique Exhibition By Local Artist"

PACEY, Mary Elizabeth (née Mary Carson)
b. 1915

Born in Ottawa, Ontario, she was educated there at Broadview Public School and Nepean High School then at the University of Toronto (B.A. 1939). Her art training began at the age of ten and she studied at the Ottawa Art Association from 1926 to 1934 and at the Art Gallery of Toronto under Carl Schaefer. After living in several centres with her husband Desmond Pacey, they moved in 1944 to Fredericton, N.B., where Dr. Pacey took up his duties as Head of the English Department at the University of New Brunswick and later Dean of Graduate studies. There she resumed her art studies in 1952 at the University of New Brunswick Summer School and subsequently under Alfred Pinsky, and winters with Lucy Jarvis and Marjorie Donaldson at the U.N.B. Art Centre. A landscape painter mainly (has also studied sculpture) her solo shows include those at the John Thurson Clark Memorial Bldg., Fred., N.B. (1957); Univ. N.B. Art Centre, Fred. N.B. (1963); Bishop's University, Lennoxville, Que (1966); Univ. N.B. Art Centre, Fred., N.B. (1970, 1971). A member of the Fredericton Society of Artists (Vice-Pres. 1957-58, Exec. 1958-59, Pres. 1959-60) she has been represented in travelling exhibitions of the Maritime Art Association and has also exhibited with the Canadian Society of Painters in Water Colour. The Paceys have seven children.

References
   Fredericton Daily Gleaner, N.B., Sept. 16, 1957 "Painting, Drawing Exhibition Sept. 17-27"
   Ibid, Sept. 26, 1957 "Painting Exhibition On Display in City"
   Ibid, Nov. 1, 1963 "Watercolor Show By Mary Pacey Opens Here Nov. 7"
   Ibid, Oct. 19, 1966 "City Artist To Bishops"
   Evening Times Globe, Saint John, N.B., Oct. 24, 1970 "Fredericton Artist To Exhibit"
   Maritime Artists, Volume 1 compiled by Mary W. Hashey, MAA, Fred., N.B., 1967, P. 61

PACHECO, Tim
b. 1948

An Oakville, Ontario, artist who attended the Oakville Technical High School where he studied art. He has worked in pastels, water colours and oils. Has painted scenes with matadors, sailboats and Greek temples for local restaurants and stores in downtown Oakville. Was planning further study at the Ontario College of Art and travel to Paris.

Reference
   Daily Journal-Record, Oakville, Ont., July 6, 1966 "Greatness His Aim – Little Formal Training for Tim But His Paintings Already Known"

PACHTER, Charles

b. 1942

Born in Toronto, Ontario, the son of Harry and Sara Pachter, he attended the University of Toronto and while still an undergraduate he took a trip to France and enrolled in the Sorbonne where he received a diploma from the Faculty of Letters (E.S.P.P.P.F.E.). He then returned to Canada to resume his studies at the University of Toronto and graduated with his B.A. in Art and Archeology in 1964. From there he went to the Cranbrooke Academy of Art, Bloomfield Hills, Michigan, U.S.A., spending two years doing lithography under the instruction of master printmakers and graduated with a M.F.A. diploma (1964-66). While studying there he received a Canada Council Student Bursary (1965) and in his final year was awarded a Cranbrooke Academy Scholarship (1966). It was there that he worked with a group of artist-lithographers who employed a number of improvisations including the making of paper from cotton and linen rag. On his return to Toronto he brought back 3,000 of these subtly-coloured rag paper sheets on which he would do his work. He spent a year looking for a suitable press before setting up his first studio in an old carriage shop on Shaw Street (he had other studios since then). Described as a perfectionist, Pachter creates his unique prints by applying 600 pounds pressure from his flat bed press. He exerts considerable physical effort to achieve this pressure on his stone (Bavarian Limestone) which has his original work on its surface. His hand-made paper sometimes includes such ingredients as human hair, ragged blue jeans or other items. Often he makes each print different as he himself explains, "I take an entire edition of twenty prints and modulate each image with paint, transparent overlays, hand-inking, scratching through the surface, drawing on the print while it is still wet — thus moving a step further into the area of pure painting." Sometimes he cuts up these prints to make a new work by placing the pieces side by side or in some new arrangement. In doing this he also explains, "I have released the printed image from its stencilled prison to create new relationships. This image has been 'liberated.' " Pachter was assistant director of the International Exhibition of Contemporary Sculpture at Expo '67; was consultant to the Ontario Educational T.V. network (1968-69, 72); visiting Assistant Professor at the University of Calgary (1969-70). He did a series of prints on Western Canada also on the Metro Toronto streetcar and the highly controversial "Monarchs Of The North" for which he not only produced prints but paintings and drawings as well. This last series questions the ties of Canada with the British monarchy in that Pachter seems to ask what are the values of such ties when the monarchy, so removed, (with the exception of visiting members of the Royal family periodically) make their home in another country. But Pachter has his critics of such work which include the society known as "Monarchy Canada" who feel the artist is merely examining superficialities against important constitutional advantages and so that question continues to be a lively one for this nation. Since Pachter started making prints he has produced suites of prints for Canadian poets. These suites include the following: *The Circle Game* by Margaret Atwood (8 poems & lithos, Edition of 15, 1964); *Small Stones* by Wook Kyung Choi (6 poems, 6 colour woodcuts, 1 etching, Edit. of 15, 1964); *Kaleidoscopes: Baroque* by Margaret Atwood (6 colour wooducts, Edit. of 20, 1965); *Talismans for Children* by Margaret Atwood (4 poems and colour lithos, Edit. of 10, 1965); *For Turned is the Day*, (7 prayers, 7 lithos, Ed. of 18, 1965); *Expeditions* by Margaret Atwood (8 poems & lithos, 15 handwritten copies, 1966); *Speeches for Doctor Frankenstein* by Margaret Atwood (ten poems & colour wood and lino cuts & silkscreens, 1966);

1457

PACHTER, Charles (Cont'd)

Morning Song, Children's Book (15 colour silkscreens and woodcuts, 15 copies, 1966); *Notebook Pages* by John Newlove (8 poems & lithographs, 15 copies, 1966); *A Black Plastic Button* & *And a Yellow Yoyo* by Alden Nowlan (6 poems and lithographs, Ed. of 15, 1968); *Wiggle to the Laundromat* by Dennis Lee (Children's poems, 12 photolithographs, Ed. of 50, New Press, 1969). He has also done cover illustrations and artwork for McClelland and Stewart, House of Anansi, Canadian Forum Magazine, CBC Graphics, Doubleday, Art Gallery of Ontario poster (72) and TV and film work as follows: Streetcars (summer '72 with Eidos Film Productions of Toronto); Charles Pachter; Printmaker (1968 META, Tor. '68); *4 Artists* (Film by Rex Bromfield, CBC '71) and he has also appeared on CBC's radio programme "Ideas" (Nov. '72) under the topic "Art and Technology." He has also been interviewed on TV (CFTO Tor., Chan. 19) and other networks. His one-man shows include: Pollock Gallery, Tor. (1964); Gallery Pascal, Tor. (1968, 1970); Canadian Art Gal., Calg. Alta (1970); Isaacs Gal., Tor. (1972); Trent Univ., Peterb., Ont. (1969); Victoria College, U. of T. (1969); N. Gallery, Philadelphia (1969); McGill Univ., Mtl. (1968); his own gallery, Shaw St., Tor. (1973); Algonquin College, Ott. (1973, 75); McMaster Univ. Art Gal., Hamilton, Ont. (1974). He has participated in many important group shows including Color Prints of the Americas, Invitational at New Jersey State Museum (1970); Canada at Tokyo International Print Biennale (1972); 23rd Annual Exhibit of Contemporary Canadian Art at the Art Gallery of Hamilton (1972); Expo' GRAFF, Lausanne, Switzerland (1970); Canadian Cultural Centre, Paris (1972) and the Canadian Society of Graphic Art; Canadian Printmakers Showcase; Society of Painters Etchers and Engravers (1969, 71, 71). He is represented in the following collections: Univ. B.C., Van.; Univ. Alberta, Edmonton; Univ. of Calgary, Alta.; Atkinson College at York Univ., Tor.; Art Gal. of Ont., Tor; Univ. Tor.; Granite Club, Tor.; Trent Univ., Peterb.; National Archives, Ott.; Musée d'Art Contemporain, Mtl.; McGill Univ., Mtl.; Sir Geo. Williams Univ., Mtl.; Owens Gallery, Mt. Allison Univ. Sack., N.B. and in the foreign collections of: Library of Congress, Wash., U.S.A., Pforzheimer Library, NYC and in private collections in Switzerland, Sweden, England, France, Argentina, U.S.A. and various centres in Canada.

References
> *The Toronto Star*, Ont., April, 1968 Art – Poetic work of Charles Pachter" by Gail Dexter
> *Globe & Mail*, Tor., Mar. 23, 1968 "Pachter's colors spring from an old carriage repair shop"
> *The Toronto Telegram*, Ont., Mar. 23, 1968 "Art – Now let's press for an atelier" by Bernadette Andrews
> Ibid, Feb. 1, 1969 "Weekend/The Good Life"
> *Calgary Albertan*, Alta., Mar. 22, 1969 "On display" (photo and caption)
> *Calgary Herald*, Alta., Dec. 5, 1969 "Arts and Music – There's A Satirical Streak In A Pachter Print" by Allan Connery
> *Calgary Albertan*, Alta., Feb. 21, 1970 "Pachter lays city's whole western thing right on the line" by Wendy Woodford
> *Calgary Herald*, Alta., Feb. 26, 1970 "Charlie Pachter's Art Works 'High Calibre, Highly Decorative' " by David Thompson
> Catalogue "ESP" (An exhibition organized and circulated by the Extension Services of the National Gallery of Canada) the work of Charles Pachter and John K. Esler (1969-1970)
> *Toronto Daily Star*, Ont., Apr. 5, 1972 "Artist discovers the streetcar" Merike Weiler
> *Globe & Mail*, Tor., Ont., Apr. 14, 1972 "Art – Street car theme of Pachter's Show" by Kay Kritzwiser
> *The Toronto Star*, Ont., June 22, 1973 "Toronto artist depicts the Queen in unusual ways"
> Ibid, June 25, 1973 "Pop art satire: Queen used as subject" by Sol Littman

PACHTER, Charles (Cont'd)

The Toronto Sun, Ont., June 22, 1973 (photo of Pachter with his painting of the Queen)
The Toronto Star, Ont., June 25, 1973 "Artist's home open for show"
The Canadian Forum, Tor., Ont., January, 1974 "Interviews with Canadian Artists: Joyce Zemans interviews Charles Pachter"
The Hamilton Spectator, Ont., Mar. 16, 1974 "Artviews – Artist tackles Canadian identity problem" by Tully Kikauka
The Toronto Sun, Ont., June 11, 1974 "Where it's art"
The Ottawa Journal, Ont., Feb. 1, 1975 "Art news and views" by W.Q. Ketchum
The Toronto Sun, Ont. Feb. 5, 1975 "Charles Pachter: Man versus myth" by Gloria McDade
The Ottawa Citizen, Ont., Feb. 15, 1975 "Two monarchs in a landscape" by Kathleen Walker
NGC Info. Form, Dec. 1, 1972

PACKARD, Peggy Walton

b. 1914

Born in Victoria, B.C., she studied singing in New York for five years and has sung the soprano role in Handel's Messiah and starred in operettas. She felt singing was too confining with all her other interests so she entered the Philadelphia Institute of Fine Arts where she studied sculpture with Paul Manship (b. 1890) and after six years there returned to Canada. She also studied painting summers under Fred Amess, Jack Shadbolt, Gordon Smith and Molly Bobak. Although she seldom submits work to art exhibits she is well known locally for her individual showing of portraits and sculptures at the T. Eaton Company, Hudson's Bay Company and fairs where she has given demonstrations of rapid portraits in pastels. She has received honourable mentions for her sculpture in Seattle and Victoria and has won some first prizes in shows in Vancouver. She is also deft with carpentry, plastering and masonry and over a period of twelve years converted an old Victoria carriage house built in 1853, into a home and studio.

Reference
Free Press Weekly/Prairie Farmer, Winnipeg, Man., June 24, 1959 "For Peggy Walton Packard – Artistry has many facets" by Aves Walton
NGC Info. Form rec'd May 29, 1962

PAGÉ, Lewis

b. 1931

Born in Quebec City, he studied sculpture at L'Ecole Technique de Québec and the Ecole des Beaux-Arts, Quebec. During a showing of his work at the Roberts Gallery in 1967 the *Globe & Mail* reviewer noted his work as follows, "Lewis Page . . . works in welded steel like many of his contemporaries, but his small, often representational scale is his own. Page works like a naturalist with a magnifying glass. His 'Underwater Current' is like a ripple, but with a potential for a tidal crash. 'Convergence' has the sweep of birds downward in flight and something of their drive. Page likes to do animals and he gets a grace and vitality into them . . . . " After working in wood, stone and bronze for several years he began his monu-

PAGÉ, Lewis (Cont'd)

mental sculptures. His work has been exhibited at Galerie Zanettin, Quebec (1964-65); Confrontation 66-67, Mtl. (1966-67); Roberts Gallery, Tor. (1967) and was represented at the World's Fair in Osaka, Japan. He uses found objects in his sculpture like gear wheels and links of chain. Described as one of the few Quebec sculptors to reconcile abstract and figurative expression.

References

Le Soleil, Que., P.Q., Oct. 17, 1964 "Brillante 'première' du sculpteur Lewis Pagé"
La Voix de Shawinigan, P.Q., Dec. 1, 1965 "Au Centre D'Art De Shawinigan – Exposition d'une envergure exceptionnelle"
Le Soleil, Que., P.Q., May 21, 1966 "Lewis Pagé, sculpteur" par Claude Daigneault
Globe & Mail, Tor., Ont., Apr. 29, 1967 "Roberts Gallery"
Montreal-Matin, Mtl., P.Q., Sept. 20, 1969 "La 'famille' à Osaka"
Le Soleil, Que., P.Q., Oct. 25, 1969 "Lewis Pagé: moment III" par Claude Daigneault
Ibid, Nov. 16, 1972 (photo of Pagé's work)
Ibid, Feb. 24, 1973 "Un sculpteur qui fait de la sculpture (!) et des peintres de solitudes et de microbes" par Claude Daigneault
L'Art Au Quebec, Depuis 1940 par Guy Robert, P. 242, 289, La Presse, Mtl., 1973

PAGE, Merrily

A Sault Ste. Marie, Ontario, artist who has painted portraits, personal images, fantasies and landscapes. Described as a superbly perceptive modern impressionist she has done work in oil pastels.

Reference

Sault Ste. Marie Star, Nov. 14, 19-- (photo of her work with article)

PAGE, Patricia Kathleen (Mrs. W. Arthur Irwin)
b. 1916

Born in Swanage, Dorset, England, the daughter of L.F. and Rose L. (Whitehouse) Page, she came to Canada in 1919 and settled in Red Deer, Alta. She attended primary schools in Canada and England and St. Hilda's School for Girls in Calgary. She worked as a sales clerk, radio actress, historical researcher, script writer and became widely known for her poems. In 1942 she was co-editor for the Preview; regional editor in B.C. for the *Northern Review* and script writer for the National Film Board of Canada (1946-50). She married William Arthur Irwin in 1950. Her husband served as Canadian High Commissioner to Australia where she lived, also in United States, Brazil, Mexico and Guatemala (1953-64). She won a number of awards for her poetry including the Governor General's literary award for *The metal and the flower* (1954). She has written a novel, short stories, and numerous poems (see *Creative Canada* for details). A painter and graphic artist, she held her first solo show in Canada at the Picture Loan Society, Tor. (1960); and subsequent solo shows including the Art Gallery of Greater Victoria (1965) and shows

PAGE, Patricia Kathleen (Mrs. W. Arthur Irwin) (Cont'd)

abroad, and in a number of group shows including those organized by the National Gallery of Canada. She lives in Victoria with her husband W. Arthur Irwin, retired publisher of the *Victoria Daily Times*. For further information see *A Dic. Can. Artists, Vol. 2* P. 514-15.

References
> *Creative Canada, Volume One* compiled by the Reference Div., McPherson Library, Univ. Victoria, Univ. Tor. Press, 1971, P. 239
> *Calgary Albertan*, Alta., Mar. 10, 1972 "Poetess coming"
> *Leader-Post*, Sask., Dec. 5, 1973 "Victoria poetess, artist speaks at lecture series" by Jean Scott
> *Charlottetown Guardian*, P.E.I. Mar. 9, 1974 "Poetry Reading Set For Centre"
> *Telegraph-Journal*, Saint John, N.B., Mar. 6, 1974 "To Present Reading At Fredericton"

PAGE, Paul

A Toronto, Ontario, artist who was assistant curator for two years at the London Public Library and Art Gallery. He has done work in film, sculpture, topographical art and favours representational art for his own work. He has given courses in basic painting including a course at All Peoples Art Centre, Sault Ste. Marie.

Reference
> *Sault Ste. Marie Star* (clipping, no date)

PAGE, Peter

A creative jeweller who has exhibited his contemporary work in Montreal at the Marlborough Godard Gallery in 1973.

Reference
> Notice from Malborough Godard Gallery, Mtl. with photo of Page's work

PAGE, Robin
b. (c) 1933

Born in Vancouver Island, he grew up in Sooke, the son of an illustrator and later animator for the Disney Studios in California. Robin studied two years at the Vancouver School of Art but could not find what he was searching for in the courses he followed. He abandoned formal study and while still in Vancouver met a Scot named Jock Hearn and became much influenced by Hearn's Zen philosophy. He made his way to Paris about 1960 where he took a room in the "Beat Hotel" run by Madame Rashau and kept himself going by playing his guitar in

PAGE, Robin (Cont'd)

cafes while continuing to paint "hard edge" work. It was while he was doing this type of painting that he suddenly realized he was missing the real world of seasons, smells, street traffic and the vitality of living in the famous European city. He turned from geometric abstracts to what has now developed into a personal humourous version of surrealism. He went to England in 1961 where he lived in London and elsewhere, experimenting with conceptual art. He married Carol in 1964 (had known her since 1961) and in 1965 abandoned his own art to teach as an instructor at the Leeds College of Art. In 1970 he gave up his teaching job and took a trip to West Germany where he bunked with a friend George Brecht and began his art again. His most prolific period dates from 1970. In Germany he was well received with a one-man show in Cologne where his humour became known not only in galleries but through television. He returned to Canada with Carol in December of 1974. A photo of Page appeared in *Weekend Magazine* which showed him sitting on a stool with a paper bag over his head beside an empty canvas. This was an invitation for the readers to draw or paint him as they thought he would look without the paper bag, the prize being an original signed drawing done by himself to the three artists whose portraits he found most interesting. An article also appeared in this same issue about Page. Over 3,000 entries were mailed to Page's B.C. representative, Galerie Allen, Vancouver and were later exhibited (April, 1975). The competition results were published in the May 19, 1975 issue of *Weekend*. Page has made appearances at art schools and elsewhere to discuss art. A very talented artist.

References
> *Weekend Magazine*, Vol. 25, No. 6 Feb. 8, 1975 "I Am A Unique Idiot – Putting fun back into art" photos by Gar Lunney and article by Marq de Villiers
> *The Vancouver Sun*, B.C., April 7, 1975 "Unveiling a brain beneath the bag" by Susan Mertens
> *Weekend Magazine*, Vol. 25, No. 20, May 17, 1975 "Art in a Brown Paper Bag" by Marq de Villiers (shows winners of competition to paint Page's portrait)

PAGÉ, Rodolphe

b. (c) 1906

A Quebec artist who was an aviator first and started flying about 1927. With an aeroplane designed and built by himself and with a passenger William Ricci he completed a 2,000 mile tour of the Province of Quebec in order to stress the safety of flying. Most of the spots he landed at were pastures and all he had to guide himself with was a road map and a pocket compass. At Trois Pistoles for instance they made a rough landing in which the propellor was damaged. After putting the propellor together again with special glue and extra thick rubber bands and careful adjustment for balance the two men continued their journey. For a time he had a flying school at Chicoutimi and later became a bush pilot. He took up painting and chose many of his subjects while flying. During a showing of his work in 1963 at the Windsor Hotel in Montreal Edward Harper writing in *The Gazette* described his work as follows, "There is one (painting) of Frobisher Bay. There is one of an old house, Victorian – gabled and ginger-breaded. There are

PAGÉ, Rodolphe (Cont'd)

others of lonely harbors in bush areas, of forest clearings bursting with color in the spring, of rivers and mountains and timberlands, all glowing with color. And there are some small, decorative pieces. They all have this in common: they are Northern Quebec, Northern Canada, as seen from the air." At the time of this exhibition Pagé was 57. No recent information.

Reference

   The Gazette, Monday, May 6, 1963 "Out Of The North – A Pilot-Painter" by Roy Kervin (Gazette Aviation Editor) and Edward Harper

PAGET, James (Jim)
b. 1943

Born in Port Perry, Ontario, he studied at the Ontario College of Art under John Alfsen and others graduating with honours then continuing his studies in art at the University of Guelph. Some of his work includes ideas based on Old and New Testaments and Judo-Christian mythologies. Many of his paintings include trees and rocks selected from the surrounding country where he lives. He has exhibited his work at Victoria College (Tor.), Durham College (Oshawa) the Robert McLaughlin Gallery (Oshawa, 1972) and the Whitby Arts "Station" Gallery, Whitby, Ontario (1975). His favourite artists include Rembrandt, Titian and Michelangelo and his former teacher the late John Alfsen has influenced him most of all. Paget has taught art classes at the McLaughlin Gallery; Senior Citizen's Centre, Oshawa and The Whitby Arts Incorporated Centre. Some of these classes have included instruction in a variety of media and subjects including lectures and seminars on aesthetics as well as art history sessions aided by films and slides. He takes his students on painting and sketching trips also tours through galleries. He lives in a small cabin at Ashburn near Claremont, Ontario, just north of Toronto.

References

   Oshawa Times, Ont., Mar. 13, 1972 "Area Artist's Works Displayed At Gallery" by Linda Fox

   Ibid, Jan. 10, 1973 "Paget Appointed Artist For Whitby Art Inc."

   Ibid, April 10, 1975 "One-Man Exhibit" (photo of one of his paintings)

PAGET, John

A Scarborough, Ontario, artist who studied painting first at school in Oakville then won a scholarship to attend night school at the Ontario College of Art. Following his study he free-lanced in the field of commercial art until the Second World War then continued painting as a hobby in 1945. He won the Arthur Award for his painting "Northern Lake" at the York-Scarboro Art Guild show in 1965 which took place at the Canadiana Motor Hotel on the Macdonald-Cartier Freeway. The father of James Paget, Ashburn artist he works as an assistant accountant.

PAGET, John (Cont'd)

Reference

Scarborough Mirror, Don Mills, Ont., Wednesday, May 19, 1965 "Art – Guild president wins show's top award"

PAGET, Mrs. Maude (née Lumb)
(c) 1873-1967

Born in England, she came to Canada early in life and lived most of her years in Victoria, B.C. During an early part of her career however she studied commercial art and was artist for the Hudson's Bay Company in Winnipeg and later Spencer's department store, now T. Eaton Company. Her husband died in 1913 and by 1920 she was living in Victoria, B.C., where she became known for her miniatures. As a miniaturist she executed commissions from Canada and the United States until eye strain forced her to turn to portrait and landscape work. She exhibited twice in jury shows at the Art Gallery of Greater Victoria. In later years she moved from traditional style to modern. She died in a nursing home in Victoria at the age of ninety-three and was survived by a sister Mrs. G. Keddie of Victoria and a brother Conway Lumb of Cartwright, Manitoba.

References

Victoria Colonist, Vict., B.C., Sept. 30, 1967 "Miniatures Were Her Forte"
Victoria Times, Vict., B.C., Sept. 29, 1967 "Well Known Artist Dead at 93"

PAGINTON, George Alfred
b. 1904

Born in Swindon, England, he came to Canada in 1911 settling for a time in Valentia, Ontario, before moving to Toronto. He studied at the Ontario College of Art under J.W. Beatty, Frederick Haines and Frederick Challener. He joined the staff of *The Toronto Star* and was sent on assignments to various parts of Canada to make illustrations for articles. In 1957 for instance he was dispatched to Iroquois, Ontario, to paint scenes of the old town before it was levelled to make way for the St. Lawrence Seaway. On this assignment he painted seven oil paintings of significant views of the old town before 143 of the old dwellings were moved to the new location and the remaining 100 homes demolished. The paintings were used as illustrations for the story of the moving of the town appearing in *The Star Weekly* by Harold Hilliard under the title "Ahead of the Flood." The paintings were later donated by the artist to the relocated town for hanging in the new city hall. In 1965 Paginton won first prize in the 1965 Price Fine Art Awards competition open to commerical artists across Canada. His winning canvas "Floating Logs" was painted at the Fraser River, B.C., when Paginton was on the coverage of the British Columbia Centennial celebrations for his paper.

PAGINTON, George Alfred (Cont'd)

References
Star Weekly Magazine, Ont., Mar. 23, 1957 "Ahead Of The Flood" by Harold Hilliard, P. 22-23
The Toronto Star, Ont., Mar. 19, 1957 "To Give Iroquois Star Artist's Paintings"
The Gazette, Mtl., P.Q., May 31, 1965 "Sunday Painters Awarded $2,500"
Applied Graphics, Don Mills, Ont., June, 1965 "Price Bros. 'Fine Arts Awards' "
Nat. Gal. of Can. Info. Form received 13 July, 1942

PAGNUELO, Françoise

1918-1957

Born in Westmount, P.Q., she studied under Mère Ste-Marthe de Béthanie of the Soeurs de la Congrégation de Notre-Dame; at St. Paul's Academy; School of the Montreal Museum of Fine Arts; The Adam Sheriff Scott School of Art, and summer classes in Georgeville, P.Q. In all, she studied under Edwin Holgate, Lilias Torrence Newton, T.R. MacDonald, Harold Beament and Adam Sheriff Scott. During a viewing of her work in 1952 a writer for the *Sherbrooke Daily Record* noted, "The young artist specializes in landscapes and portraits, does not believe in copying, but paints all her canvases from life. She has a good eye for color and her work has a fresh, appealing quality, modern enough yet not at all startling. She has a number of attractive floral arrangements, some excellent scenes of small fishing villages, a New England farm, Monday morning in a Canadian Village, and several other striking studies." During her career she exhibited her work at the following places: Art Association of Montreal (1941); Henry Morgan Co., Mtl. (1943); Palais Montcalm, Quebec, P.Q. (1946); Amis de l'Art, Mtl. (1947); Amis de L'Art, Saint-Hyacinthe, P.Q. (1949); Atelier à Sainte-Adèle en haut (1949); Cercle Universitaire, Mtl. (1950); Spring Show, Mtl. Museum of Fine Arts (1951); Granby, P.Q. (1951); Club Social, Sherbrooke, P.Q. (1952); Chateau Murray, La Malbaie (1952); Chateau Frontenac, Quebec, P.Q. (1952); Peintres Montrealais, Chalet de la Montagne, Mtl. (1952); Silver Room, Ritz Carlton Hotel, Mtl. (1953, 54, 55, 56); Independent Art Assoc. (1956); 13 peintres féminins Ile Sainte-Hélène, P.Q. (1956). She died at the young age of thirty-nine. Lived in Westmount, P.Q.

References
The Gazette, Mtl., P.Q., May 10, 1941 "Three Young Artists Are Displaying Work"
Ibid, Dec. 4, 1943 "Françoise Pagnuelo Holds 'One Man' Show — Paintings of City and Laurentians on View in Gallery At Morgan's"
Le Canada, Mtl., P.Q., Jan. 9, 1950 "F. Pagnuelo, une artiste du plein-air"
La Presse, Mtl. P.Q., Jan. 11, 1950 "Dans le pays d'en haut" (photo of one of her landscapes and caption)
Sherbrooke Daily Record, P.Q., April 29, 1952 "Paintings Are Displayed At Social Club"
Sherbrooke Tribune, P.Q., April 29, 1952 "Les peintures de Françoise Pagnuelo" (photo of artist with her paintings)
La Presse, Mtl., P.Q., April 11, 1953 "F. Pagnuelo et trois autres paysagistes"
The Gazette, Mtl., P.Q., April 11, 1953 "Art — Variety in Paintings By Françoise Pagnuelo"
NGC Info. Form rec'd 25 June, 1940
Info. sent to NGC Aug. 30, 1965

PAISLEY, Ruth

A Toronto, Ontario, artist who exhibited in 1963 at the Sobot Gallery a number of canvases of abstract work in the mixed media of oils and enamel. Describing her work a reviewer for the *Globe and Mail* noted, "Miss Paisley accomplishes through use of symbols, through the limitations of abstract art, what would be impossible for her to do in representative form. With extraordinary skill, she paints in the same way that Henry Miller and Walt Whitman dared to write."

References
Globe & Mail, Ont., Oct. 5, 1963 "Daring Debut For Gallery In Toronto"

PAJUNEN, Reino

A Lakehead, Ontario, area artist originally from Saskatchewan who creates sculptures from milk cans, hub caps, reflector lights and other scraps of discarded metal. He also constructs other objects from moose horn as well as carving in wood and cowhorn. His subjects include animals which are whimsical and realistic. One of his creations for instance was a tin can cowboy astride his horse. His work has been shown at the Prince Arthur Hotel in Lakehead (1969). He lives in Nolalu just west of Lakehead, and is a member of the Lakehead Area Craft Association.

References
Port Arthur News-Chronicle, Ont., Oct. 31, 1969 "Artist Uses Metal Scraps"
Fort William Times Journal, Ont., Oct. 31, 1969 "Throw Away Sculpture" (found objects scuplture)

PALARDY, Joseph Jean Albert
b. 1905

Born at Fitchburg, Mass., U.S.A., of French Canadian parents he came to Canada with his parents in 1908 and lived in Chicoutimi for three years. He received his education in a seminary then attended the Ecole des Beaux-Arts, Montreal for nearly two years then studied several months in the Saguenay under Jan Van Empel, an American painter of Dutch origin. In the years that followed he spent a good part of his time in rural Quebec searching for his subjects. A painter mainly of landscapes and figures he exhibited once with the Royal Canadian Academy in Toronto and with his wife Jori Smith at the Art Association of Montreal in 1930. He was living in Montreal by 1930 and later became a film director. He met his wife Marjorie Smith at the time he was attending the Ecole des Beaux-Arts.

References
La Tribune, Sherbrooke, P.Q., 17 May, 1930 "Les Jeunes – Marjorie Smith et Jean Palardy" par Léon Jalder
The Canadian Forum, July, 1937 "Contemporary Canadian Artists" by G. Campbell McInnes
Loretteville La Voix du Peuple, Montmagny, P.Q., 6 Mar., 1964 "Louisbourg remeublé par un Canadien-Français"
NGC Info. Form July 11, 1930

PALCHINSKI, John
b. 1940

Born at Cudworth, Saskatchewan, he studied at the Alberta College of Art under John K. Esler, Ron Spickett and Illingworth Kerr (1962-66) and won a scholarship of tuition to San Miguel de Allende, Mexico (1966-67) then returned to Canada and took extended study in graphics at the Alberta College of Art (1968-69); silk screen and lithography at summer workshop conducted by Andrew Stasik at the University of Calgary and photography workshop at Ryerson Polytechnical Institute, Toronto (1971). He received awards for graphics at the Saskatoon Exhibition (1965); Purchase Award at the Sixth Annual Calgary Graphics; Purchase Award, Students' Union S.A.I.T. for painting and received a scholarship from the Province of Alberta (1966, 1967) and a Canada Council Short Term Grant (1970). Viewing his prints in 1972 a *Globe & Mail* writer noted, "Palchinski's serigraphs are shot through with humor, for his amoeba shapes have a Miro tendency to take on human characteristics. Ribbons of color, clearly separated, increase the activity. Serigraphs like 'What Goes Up Must Come Down' and 'A Time to Remember' have a comic strip capacity to eliminate all but the necessary information. Palchinski pokes ritual techniques in the eye with his 'News from General Purpose.' He suspends cutout images in pliofilm bags from clothes pegs, offers numbered patterns, and it all adds up to bold primary results which are a lot of fun. Good. Why can't prints be fun?" Palchinski has exhibited in a number of group shows including the Society of Canadian Painter-Etchers and Engravers 52nd Annual (1968); 9th, 10th Annual Calgary Graphics (1969, 1970); Environment '69, '70; All Alberta '69, '70; Boston Printmakers 22nd Annual (1970) and solo shows at the Alberta College of Art, Graphics (1966); Glenbow-Alberta Art Gallery (1970) and two-man shows at the Alberta College of Art (1967); Gallery 1640, Montreal with John K. Esler – prints (1971). He is represented in the collections of the Montreal Museum of Fine Arts; Alberta College of Art, Calgary; Western Geophysical Company of Canada, Calgary; Imperial Oil, Edmonton; Alberta Provincial Government Arts & Crafts Div.; University of Calgary. Lives in Toronto.

References

Calgary Herald, Alta., May 23, 1970 "Warm, Pleasing Impression – Prints by Calgary Artist on Display at Glenbow"
Globe & Mail, Ont., Jan. 29, 1972 "New Prints"
Toronto Daily Star, Ont., Aug. 11, 1972 "Art – Young artists get wall space beside masters" by Wayne Edmonstone
The Montreal Star, Mtl., P.Q., Aug. 19, 1972 "Grass roots and graphics"
Info. in artist's file NGC Lib.

PALCHINSKI, Sylvia Scott
b. 1946

Born in Regina, Sask., she studied at the Alberta College of Art and received her diploma (A.C.A.) in 1968 then attended the Instituto Allende, Mexico for a year returning to Canada in 1967. She moved from Calgary to Toronto in 1970 and to England where she has worked and studied. Her centre of interest recently is the development of works of art using the cloud as her subject in various forms including pencil and ink sketches, mixed media panels and sculptures. She held a solo show at the Glenbow Art Gallery, Calgary, in 1970. In 1973 a reviewer in the

PALCHINSKI, Sylvia Scott (Cont'd)

Globe & Mail noted her work during a group show at the Aggregation Gallery, Toronto, as follows, "Sylvia Palchinski's work tends to dominate the exhibition by its very nature — shiny stuffed plastic shapes or white cloud forms which proliferate on wall and floor. But her ideas are as deeply rooted in the environment as is the work of her fellow exhibitors. Miss Palchinski came from the prairies where clouds were inescapably valid landscapes. Her Cloud series, either stuffed forms or captured with lighthearted imagination in box constructions, have an original stamp. When she came to Toronto the impact of pollution and the forces which caused it affected her. It's present in a particularly good piece, Black Sun Rising, where she charts the whole dismal business of push buttons, factories and smoke rising through dollar signs to blot out our sun." She has exhibited at the Aggregation Gallery several times since that exhibition. She is represented in the Canadian Art Archives of the Vancouver Art Gallery and the Canada Council Art Bank. One of her mixed media panels appeared on the cover of Artscanada (Feb./Mar. 1973) which number contained her letter from London, England. She has participated in a number of exhibitions including the Canadian Guild of Crafts (C.N.E. Tor. 1969-70); Environment '69, '70; The Twelfth Winnipeg Show (WAG); Group Show, Gallery 93, Ottawa (1970-71); Canadian Printmakers' Showcase (Carleton Univ., Ott., 1971); Burnaby Print Show (1971); Image Bank Post Card Show (Van. B.C., 1971); Survey of Canadian Art Now (Van. Art Gal., 1972) and others. She has been an Alberta Councillor for the Canadian Craftsman's Council and held various teaching positions both elementary and university. Her awards include: Alberta Drafting and Blueprint Co. (1966); Albertacraft Scholarship (1966-68); Outstanding Entry Award, Canadian Guild of Crafts, C.N.E. (1969); Canada Council Grant, Short Term (1971). Her commissions include: Design for neon marquee, Glenbow Art Gallery, Calgary, Alta. (1969); Fabric construction for foyer of Western Geophysical Bldg., Cal., Alta. (1970). Lives in Toronto.

References
   Calgary Herald, Alta., Apr. 27, 1970 "Cloud Exhibits Now On Display"
   Globe & Mail, Tor., Ont., 26 May, 1973 "Earth/Water/Sky"
   Artscanada, Feb./Mar., 1972 "Sixth Burnaby Print Show" by Joan Lowndes
   Ibid, Feb./Mar. 1973 "a letter" from Sylvia Palchinski, P. 34-38

PALEY, Rachel

Born in Tel-Aviv, she is an Ottawa artist who exhibited fifty works at the Ottawa Little Theatre.

Reference
   Le Droit, Ottawa, Ont., June 30, 1972 "Le peintre d'Ottawa Rachel Paley" (photo of her canvas "Earth Man and Space" and caption)

PALFREEMAN, Elizabeth Patricia Mary

b. 1929

Born at Braintree, Essex, England, she studied at the Middlesex Technical College and School of Art under Charles Archer (painting) and Huxley Jones (sculpture) and received the Ministry of Education Intermediate Arts and Crafts Certificate, next she attended the Royal College of Art, London, where she studied sculpture under Frank Dobson, Leon Underwood, John Skeaping and E. Folkard and graduated with her Associate of the Royal College of Art and also received the National Diploma in Design. She travelled for a short period in France and Italy. She came to Canada in 1954 and by the following year exhibited her work at the Spring Show of the Montreal Museum of Fine Arts (1955) and again two years later (1957). Covering a range from abstract to realism she has worked in a variety of materials including stone, reinforced concrete for which she first makes a clay original then a plaster mould of the original and filling the mould with a strong concrete called cement fondu (reinforced with wire mesh, fibre glass and steel rods). The plaster mould is then broken away from the cement and the sculpture cleaned with a stiff brush. With this technique she can achieve many effects in the cement from very smooth to very rough surfaces. In wood she particularly likes working with a whole log so that she can get the full effect of the grain. She has exhibited her work at the Montreal Museum of Fine Arts, the University of Montreal, St. Helen's Island and in Quebec City. She was awarded a sculpture prize at the Montreal Museum of Fine Arts Spring Show (1956) and a tuition scholarship to the Institute Allende, Mexico (1956) but was unable to go there because of limited finances at that time. She has taught art at the D'Arcy McGee High School, Mtl. (1955-56); was advisor on art lessons for thirteen schools of the Catholic School Commission (1956-58); taught sculpture at the Snowdon Y.H.A. (1958-61) and has been teaching sculpture since 1955 at the Montreal Museum School of Art (1955-   ). She exhibited her work at the Dorval Cultural Centre (1971). Living in Montreal (1971). Member: Lakeshore Artists' Association (1957) and Studio 9, Mtl. (1954).

References

Lachine Messenger, P.Q., Nov. 3, 1971 "Sculpture Exhibition at Dorval Cultural Centre"
Information sheet November, 1963
NGC Info. Form rec'd 27 June, 1957
Canadian Water Colours, Drawings and Prints, 1966, No. 39, NGC

PALKO, Helga Maria

b. 1928

Born in Linz, Austria, daughter of Herbert and Eleonore Jandaurek. Her father was an archaeologist and author of books on that subject and a civil engineer for the City of Linz. After graduating from secondary school in Linz she attended the University of Vienna and the Academy of Fine Arts for five years receiving a diploma in painting (1948-53) and her Austrian Teacher's Secondary School Certificate for art, drawing, art appreciation and needlework. She taught at Erstes Bundesreal Gymnasium fuer Maedchen in Linz. She came to Canada in 1954 to Saskatoon where she met Michael Palko whom she had known in Austria. They were married and settled in Regina. Her husband was doing studies in public health at Berkeley University, California. Helga studied at the California College of Arts and Crafts in Oakland, in metal, jewellery, and enamel work. She participated in the Fifth Annual Exhibition at the Richmond Art Centre, Richmond, California and the California State Fair at Sacramento. Returning to Canada in 1956 the Palkos settled in Lumsden, Saskatchewan. Helga gave courses and special workshops in jewellery and enamel work for the Saskatchewan Arts Board (1963). She completed three architectural commissions in Saskatchewan: a mural for St. Mark's Church, Lumsden (1958); enamelled mural for the Provincial Office Building at North Battleford (1959) and later a mural of enamel on steel at the University of Saskatchewan (1967). The Palkos settled in Ottawa in 1960 where Helga continued her work with jewellery, paper mobiles, enamel work and teaching fine crafts. Her work has been known internationally for many years and as early as 1958 when two of her rings were exhibited at the Brussels World's Fair in 1958. She entered her work in the following major competition shows: First National Fine Crafts Exhibition, NGC, Ottawa (1957); First National Competitive Exhibition of Wood Carving and Metal Work, Saint John, N.B. (1957, rec'd 1st Prize for metal work); Third, Fourth, Seventh Winnipeg Shows (1957, 1958, 1961); Tenth Annual Exhibition of Saskatchewan Arts Board (1959); Twenty-ninth Annual Exhibition, VAG (1960); 21st Ceramic National, Iverson Museum of Art, Syracuse (1961) and circuit show in all major U.S. centres (1961-62); Canadian Handicraft Guild Show, Mtl. (First Prize for Enamel, 1963); Canadian National Exhibition, Tor. (Special Prize for Enamel, 1963); "Jewellery '63" (International Exhibit at State Univ. College, Plattsburgh, NY); "Canada Design '67" Dept. Industry (Award of Excellence, 1966); Canadian Fine Craft, NGC (1966-67); Crafts Dimension Canada, ROM (1969); International Jewellery Competition, Prix de la Ville de Genève (Hon. Mention, 1971) and exhibited in the following invitational and Purchase shows: Saskatchewan Arts Board Annual Purchase (1958); Canadian Exhibition Commission for shows in Berlin and Italy (1964); Canadian Religious Art Today, Regis College, Tor. (1966); Expo '67 Canadian Pavilion (1967); Dept. Trade & Commerce for shows overseas (1967); "Hemisfair '68", San Antonio, Texas (1968); Canadian Museum for Contemporary Fine Crafts, Charlottetown, PEI, Purchase Award (1968); External Affairs Protocol Division purchased her work for presentations (1969); Can. Exhibition Commission Show of Fine Crafts at the new Y.M.C.A. Ottawa (1970); Crafts Festival Canada, NAC, Ott. (1971), N.C.D.C. Show (1974); "Metal 4" four-man show at Crafts Gallery, Tor. (1974); World Crafts Conference (Workshop 1974) also WCC Conference and International Crafts Symposium at Sheridan College, Brampton, Ont. (1974); Invitational travelling jewellery show "Body Art" in Sask. and Alta. (1975); staff exhibitions at Algonquin College (1974-76); International Festival of Enamel, Laguna Beach, Calif., U.S.A. (1976). In 1971 she received her letter of standing from the Ontario Department of Education for teaching Art in secondary schools and has conducted courses for the Ottawa Collegiate Inst. Board; Ottawa Y.W.C.A.; Algonquin College, Ottawa; trained craftsmen and set up jewellery production under contract with the West Baffin Eskimo Co-Op., Cape Dorset, NWT (1971); part-time teaching for jewellery and enamel, Algonquin College, Dept. of Visual & Creative Arts and Dept. of Continuing Education (1971-72); trained an Eskimo apprentice in metal work and continued with the Cape Dorset project (1972). With her extensive teaching experience at Algonquin College and elsewhere she is the Teaching Master and

PALKO, Helga Maria (Cont'd)

Co-ordinator of Fine Crafts Program at Algonquin; was second instructor and tour leader on a study trip to Europe with jewellery students of the Nova Scotia College of Art and Design (1975), was visiting artist to the College in 1974. Mother of three she lives in Ottawa with her husband where she continues to produce a wide variety of pieces including bowls, vases, jewellery and other items. She is owner and proprietor of The Sunflower Studio Shop at Spencerville, Ontario, where she also has a studio (1969-76).

References
    Leader-Post, Regina, Sask., Nov. 16, 1957 "Lumsden woman's artistry unique in western Canada" by L.M. Kilmister
    The Ottawa Journal, Dec. 15, 1962 "Art in Ottawa – Two Enamellists Artist-Craftsmen" by Florian
    The Ottawa Citizen, Ont., July 14, 1967 "Mobile swings in royal air" by Betty Swimmings
    NGC Info. Forms 1958, 1965
    Catalogue Canadian Fine Crafts, Can. Pavilion, Expo '67, P. 40
    Catalogue, Canadian Fine Crafts, 1966-67, NGC (various sections)
    Curriculum Vitae 1976

PALL, Jean

A painter of Hungarian descent who lived for a period in Paris. He came to Canada in 1951 first in Toronto for a short time then operated boutiques in Vancouver, Sherbrooke (P.Q.), Montreal and settled in Saint-Jerome in 1966 where he opened a gallery. In his painting his techniques have varied from turn of the century impressionism to 1930's surrealism to modified pointillist-impressionist. He has taught painting in Montreal.

Reference
    St. Jerome L'Echo du Nord, P.Q., Aug. 27, 1969 "Pall: Le peintre dans la vitrine"

PALMER, Frank (Herbert Franklin Palmer)
b. 1921

Born in Calgary, Alberta, son of George Henry and Grace (Barager) Palmer, he attended Rideau Park School and Western Canada High School in Calgary. During the 2nd World War he served in the R.C.A.F. and when possible he attended art classes in his spare time at Vancouver, Toronto (OCA) and Calgary. After the war he attended the Art Centre School in Los Angeles on a D.V.A. grant then was employed by Cleland-Kent Engraving Company, Vancouver (1945-48); was a freelance artist in Calgary (1949-58); joined the staff of the Alberta College of Art (Prov. I.T.A.) as an instructor in commercial and fine arts (1958-). He established his reputation as a fine water colourist early in his career and won the Jessie Dow Award for work in this medium in 1954 also exhibited with the California Water Color Society in 1955. Later he became better known for his fine art work in

PALMER, Frank (Herbert Franklin Palmer) (Cont'd)

other painting mediums. Over the years he has been influenced by Marin, Feininger, Carl Morris and Morris Graves. He exhibited his work as a member of the Alberta Society of Artists (Elec. 1949, Loc. Chairman 1960); Canadian Society of Painters in Water Colour (Elec. 1954, 2nd Vice-Pres. 1962); Royal Canadian Academy (Assoc. 1959, Academician 1966) and his work was chosen for showing in the 2nd, 3rd, 4th, 5th, 6th Biennials of Canadian Painting where his larger paintings had more exposure to a wider audience. His work was also shown during the important exhibit, Fifty Years, The Canadian Society of Painters in Water Colour at the Art Gallery of Ontario in 1975. Represented in the collections of the University of Calgary, Alta.; Calgary Allied Arts Centre, Alta.; London Public Library and Art Museum, Ont.; Art Gallery of Ontario, Tor.; Imperial Oil Collection, Tor.; McMaster Univ., Hamilton, Ont.; National Gallery of Canada, Ottawa (RCA Coll.); Department of External Affairs, Ott; Metropolitan Life Ins. Co., Ott.; Beaverbrook Art Gal., Fred., N.B.; Univ. of New Brunswick, Fred., N.B. He lives in Calgary, Alta.

References

Canadian Water Colour Painting by Paul Duval, Burns & MacEachern, Tor., 1954

The Arts in Canada, Ed. Malcolm Ross, Painting by Robert Ayre, MacMillan, Tor., 1958, P. 30

90th Annual RCA Exhibition, 1970 (see diploma collection)

Art Gallery of Ontario, the Canadian collection by Helen Pepall Bradfield, McGraw-Hill, P. 348

Creative Canada, McPherson Lib., Univ. of Victoria/Univ. Tor. Press, 1972, P. 211, 212

Fifty Years, The Canadian Society of Painters in Water Colour, 1925-1975 by Katharine Jordan, Art. Gal. Ont., Tor., P. 31

Second Canadian Biennial Catalogue, NGC, 1957, No. 24, 61

Third Canadian Biennial Catalogue, NGC, 1959, No. 83

Fourth Canadian Biennial Catalogue, NGC, 1961, No. 65

Fifth Canadian Biennial Catalogue, NGC, 1963, No. 54

Sixth Canadian Biennial Catalogue, NGC, 1965, No. 80

Canadian Art, Vol. 20, No. 2, 1963 "Clement Greenberg's View of Art On The Prairies" by C.G., P. 100

PALMER, Herbert Sidney (Sydney)

1881-1970

Born in Toronto, Ontario, he studied at the Central Ontario School of Art and Design, Toronto, under Frederick S. Challoner and J.W. Beatty. He worked for a lithography firm and sang in the Mendelssohn Choir. Afterwards he became a full-time painter with his studio in the rear of his home on St. Clements Avenue, Toronto. A.H. Robson writing in his book *Canadian Landscape Painters* in 1932 noted Palmer as follows, "Herbert S. Palmer established his reputation as a painter of cattle and sheep in the familiar settings of an Ontario background . . . . There is in all Palmer's work a precision and accuracy of drawing, pleasing and bright colour, and a sympathetic rendering of the Ontario landscape. He has sketched in many parts of the Province, and his cattle pictures reveal, in their landscape settings, something of the real character of the district. His work is deservedly well known and popular." For years he exhibited at the T. Eaton Company Fine Art Gallery on College Street (held 25 consecutive shows at Eaton's also held showings in the branch store in Montreal). When he was twenty-three he first exhibited with the Ontario Society of Artists and five years later was elected a member (1909); the following year he became a founding member of the Arts & Letters Club, Toronto. Here men interested in the arts mixed their diverse talents in a wide variety of activities from theatre to gardening. Although Palmer loved singing he spent more and more of his time painting and working at various tasks of the art societies. By 1915 he was elected an Associate Royal Canadian Academician (RCA 1934) and in 1919 became Vice-President and Treasurer of the Ontario Society of Artists. For fifteen years (1926-1941) he was curator of the Fine Art Department of the Canadian National Exhibition, Toronto and as a result acquired an almost encyclopaedic knowledge on Canadian artists. During a 1941 showing of his work at Eaton's a reviewer for the *Globe & Mail* made these comments, " . . . Palmer's December exhibition at Eaton's, now something of an art institution includes one of the best landscapes he has done. It is a Gatineau scene and came home not long ago after its journey with the National Gallery exhibition which toured the Dominions. Mr. Palmer's recent work was done near Wilberforce in Haliburton. Subdued but rich color — more blue and violet and green — and interesting strength of contour as in the big Gatineau canvas, make some of the pieces in this exhibition the handsomest he has shown." Palmer was a prolific painter and travelled widely in Canada to seek out his subjects but found many of his subjects in Ontario. Sotheby & Company auctioned forty-one of his paintings between 1968 and 1975 which ranged in size from 8½" x 10½" to 20-1/4" x 25-1/4". Many of his sketches were painted on panels, his larger paintings on canvas and canvas board. The highest price paid for a Palmer painting out of this group was $550 (oil on canvas board 10½ x 13-1/4 "Country Farm, Autumn") in October of 1973. This however does not mean that every painting that size by Palmer would fetch that price. It depends on the amount of work, success of the artist in portraying his subject, the desirability of the painting to the public, and the condition of the painting. In 1960 Herbert Palmer was awarded the first Baxter Art Foundation Award for his years of devoted effort to the work of the Ontario Society of Artists, The Royal Canadian Academy and other professional groups. Palmer died in 1970 at the age of ninety in a Metro Toronto nursing home and was survived by a nephew Dr. J.G. Palmer. He is represented in the collections of the Nutana Collegiate Inst., Sask., Alta.; Sarnia Public Library, Sarnia, Ont.; North Toronto Collegiate Inst., Tor.; Hart House, Univ. Tor.; Art Gal. Ont., Tor.; Nat. Gal. Canada, Ottawa, and elsewhere.

References
Books and Catalogues
Canada & Its Provinces, Vol. 12 "Painting" by E.F.B. Johnston, 1914, P. 625
Canadian Landscape Painters by A.H. Robson, Ryerson, Tor., 1932, P. 162, 163
A Century of Canadian Art, NGC, Tate Gallery, Lond., Eng., 1938, P. 26
The Fine Arts In Canada by Newton MacTavish, Macmillan, Tor., 1925, Coles, 1973, see ill. between 144 and 145
The Story of The Club by Augustus Bridle, Arts & Letters Club, Tor., 1945
Painting In Canada (catalogue) January, March, 1946, Albany Inst. of History and Art, P. 33
National Gallery of Canada Catalogue, Vol. 3 by R.H. Hubbard, P. 240-241, 405
Painting in Canada, A History by J. Russell Harper, Univ. Tor. Press, P. 319
Check List of The War Collections by R.F. Wodehouse, NGC, 1968, P. 48

PALMER, Herbert Sidney (Sydney) (Cont'd)

The Hart House Collection of Canadian Paintings by Jeremy Adamson, Univ. Tor. Pr., 1969, P. 103

Art Gallery of Ontario, The Canadian Collection by Helen Pepall Bradfield, McGraw-Hill, Tor., 1970, P. 349-351

Canadian Art At Auction, 1968-1975, Ed. by Geoffrey Joyner, Sotheby, Tor., 1975, P. 150-151

newspapers

Saturday Night, Tor., Ont., Dec. 21, 1923 (photo of mural Palmer painted for main entrance to Temple Bldg., Tor.)

Star Weekly, Tor., Ont., Sept. 15, 1928 "Business of Art Is Creative, Not Reproductive, Palmer Declares" (controversy over a left hand plow Palmer painted into his picture 'Fall Plowing')

The Toronto Telegram, Ont., Dec. 7, 1938 "At The Galleries – Palmer Holds 17th Show At Fine Art Galleries"

The Gazette, Mtl., P.Q., Dec. 29, 1939 (photo of his "The Mill At Barrow Bay" shown at RCA show, Mtl., Dec., 1939)

Globe & Mail, Tor., Ont., Dec. 9, 1939 "Palmer's 1939 show at Eaton's, Tor.)

Ibid, Dec. 13, 1941 (show at Eaton's)

The Telegram, Tor., Ont., Dec. 20, 1947 "At The Galleries – Herbert Palmer's Show Has Definite Appeal"

Press Release, April 28, 1960 Baxter Art Foundation "Baxter Annual Art Awards and Art Scholarships Foundation"

Globe & Mail, Tor., Ont., April 30, 1960 "Art and Artists by Pearl McCarthy – Fellowship Choice Unanimous"

Toronto Daily Star, Ont., May 11, 1960 "Baxter Art Award To Herbert Palmer"

Ibid, Nov. 30, 1970 "Herbert Palmer, 90, landscape painter" (Obituaries)

NGC Info. Form 1920, 1933, 1946

PALMER, Jacqueline (Cajun)

Born in Northern Ontario she has been painting and drawing since her early childhood and moved to Windsor where she opened her own studio and did portraits in water colours and taught children's classes in her spare time. She held an exhibition of her work at the Brantford Public Library while studying art in Brantford. She has also done sculpture from a type of grey paste which dries to a hard shiny metal-like finish. She was planning further study in Europe and if not able to reach there had thoughts of moving to Toronto.

Reference
Brantford Expositor, Ont., June 16, 1969 "Artists Not Understood" by Brenda Cheevers

---

PALMER, Dr. John A.

Originally from Meaford, Ontario, on the shores of Georgian Bay, the son of the late Mr. & Mrs. John Palmer, his interest in art stemmed from his high school days in Meaford when the local high school was presented with several paintings of the late Fred Haines. Palmer was known for his talents in music and played the trombone and won many awards at the Grey County Music Festival and played for the

PALMER, Dr. John A. (Cont'd)

Meaford Citizen's Band. While an intern at the Toronto General Hospital he attended painting classes nights at the Toronto Central Technical School. After graduation from medicine Dr. Palmer practised in Milton, Ontario, where over the years, several leading Toronto artists gathered on weekends. There Dr. Palmer met Ernie Dalton who helped him considerably in his artistic development. In 1952 Dr. Palmer returned to the Toronto General Hospital and several years later became staff surgeon, consultant at Princess Margaret Hospital and medical adviser to the Toronto Argonauts. About 1969 he met painter Lawrence Nickle who invited him on trips to the Canadian wilds and later both men were joined on trips to Algonquin Park and Georgian Bay by artists Mike Cleary and Jim Shortt. Palmer has travelled on snow shoes and by canoe to reach his subjects. He exhibited jointly with Nickle and Cleary and held his first one-man show of fifty landscapes at the Framing Gallery, Toronto, in February of 1973. During the first week of the exhibition thirty paintings were sold. His work is rated as superior to many of the professional artists exhibiting today and Palmer looks to the time when the normal span of surgical practice may give way to a second full-time career. He loves his work as a surgeon even though it tends at times to be hectic, otherwise he would become a fulltime painter.

References
> *Toronto Daily Star,* Ont., Feb. 14, 1973 "Pennington's People — Surgeon as artist wins high praise" by Bob Pennington
> *Owen Sound Sun Times*, Ont., Feb. 23, 1973 "Former Meaford resident holds art show" by Kay Gower

PALMER, Neville

He exhibited his sculpture and drawings at Gallery House Sol, Georgetown, Ontario, in 1969.

Reference
> Exhibition notice from Gallery House Sol, Georgetown, Ont., Sept. 6, 1969

PALMER, Samuel
active 1834-1845

Said to be originally from London, England. There was another English painter Samuel Palmer (1805-81) who produced visionary landscapes and later etchings influenced by Blake's Virgil woodcuts. This Palmer was active in Saint John, N.B., where he did portraits large and miniature. He travelled in the U.S. but was back in Canada at Montreal and Quebec City (1844-45). He managed his affairs rather poorly and was often in debt despite the fact that he was reputedly a fashionable Quebec painter.

PALMER, Samuel (Cont'd)

References
  Painting in Canada/A History by J. Russell Harper, Univ. Tor. Press, 1966, P. 117 (see references)
  Early Painters and Engravers in Canada by J. Russell Harper, Univ. Tor. Press, Tor., 1970, P. 242
  Christie's, Montreal, April 16, 1969 Sale 1, Cat. No. 85 (portrait of Mrs. Daniel Wilkie painted c. 1843)
  Second Annual Review of The National Gallery of Canada, Ottawa, 1969-1970 Canadian Paintings, Sculpture and Decorative Arts Gifts: Paintings, Palmer, Samuel, portrait of Mrs. Daniel Wilkie & Portrait of the Reverend Daniel Wilkie, P. 71

PALM-JOST, Mrs. Ottillie (née Palm)
1876-1961

One of Hamilton's (Ontario) early artists who worked with John S. Gordon and was an illustrator on the Hamilton *Herald*. She became somewhat of a celebrity when she was the first woman in that city to own and drive a car. She did a mural for St. Paul's Lutheran Church in Hamilton. In 1911 she went to Europe where she married a German sculptor Joseph Jost and lived quietly outside Munich through the two world wars. She returned to Hamilton in 1950 and was thinking of resettling in Canada but returned to Germany and died there at the age of 85. She had one daughter who lived with her in Germany and four nephews and a niece in Canada.

Reference
  The Hamilton Spectator, Mar. 29, 1961 "1st Woman Driver Here, Artist Dies In Germany"

PALOVICK, Dick

A Thunder Bay artist who exhibited eighty pieces of art including etchings, paintings and sculpture under the title "Industrial Edge" an exhibition reflecting the impressions made on him by the huge paper mill machinery he had formerly operated. This exhibition was held at the Agora Room and Gallery of Lakehead University, Thunder Bay, Ontario. This work was also shown in London, Ontario.

References
  Thunder Bay News-Chronicle, Ont., May 23, 1970 (photo of Palovick and his work with caption)
  Thunder Bay Times Journal, Ont., May 25, 1970 (photo of Palovick and his work with caption)

PALUMBO, Jacques Gaëtan
b. 1939

Born in Philippeville, Algeria, he received his degree in philosophy (1959); studied at the Ecole des Beaux-Arts, Algiers (1959-60); Centre Claude Bernard where he received his diploma in drawing and plastic arts (1960-64); teacher's certificate,

PALUMBO, Jacques Gaëtan (Cont'd)

France (1964-65). He has exhibited in group shows in Algiers and Paris. He came to Canada in 1965 and settled in Montreal where he became an illustrator (1965-68) then professor of graphic and plastic arts at the Graphic Arts Institute of Montreal (1968) and professor of plastic arts and illustration at CEGEP Ahuntsic, Montreal (1970). Viewing his work in 1975 at Galerie Gilles Gheerbrant, Montreal, Henry Lehmann and Georges Bogardi of *The Montreal Star* noted, "Geometry and color are the bases of Palumbo's visual 'languages.' We see the working out of Palumbo's visual statements from conceptual schemes to printouts to ink and pencil drawings to a suite of silk-screen prints to a series of watercolors. But one is also struck by the sensuality of these seemingly mechanical works. This is especially true of the beautiful series of watercolors in which columns and blocks of color vary in proportion, frequency, and hue. The Open System series and Red series initially appear harder, more brittle. However, as one looks at them a very personal sensibility begins to emerge. The artist's refined choices, his rapport with the printouts generated by cleverly chosen rules is expressed in subtle tensions, rhythms of movement and a dialectic between openness and density . . . . " He is represented in the collections of the Canada Council Art Bank, Museum at Sao Paulo, Brazil; St. Lawrence University, Canton, N.Y.; Sidney Sabine Vitus University, Nurnberg, Germany and elsewhere also private collections of A. Parent (Mtl.); Barbara Ensor (Ottawa); Dr. & Mrs. Barakov (Mtl.) and Susan Lee Cox-Wright (Fort Worth, Texas), others. He has exhibited his work at Club-des-quatre-vents, Paris (1965); Salon d'ernée Bretagne, France (1966-71); Le Musée d'art contemporain, Mtl. (1974). Lives in Montreal with his wife Suzanne and daughter Sophie (b. 1970).

References
The Montreal Star, Mtl., P.Q., Feb. 5, 1975 "Gallery roundup – Palumbo's art combines geometry, color" by Henry Lehmann and Georges Bogardi
L'Art Au Quebec Depuis 1940 par Guy Robert, La Presse, Mtl., 1973, P. 157, 159
NGC Info. Form, 11 March, 1971, 18 January, 1973
Plureil '71 Exposition Musée de Quebec (Professional artists Society of Quebec) P. 26, 27

PAN, Marta

b. (c) 1923

Born in Budapest, Hungary, she became interested in sculpting at an early age. She went to Paris where she focused her attention on abstract art and became known for her "floating sculptures" in Holland, Japan and the United States and has done research into the use of plexiglass. She designed several backdrops for ballets and also costumes for theatre plays. She held a show of her larger productions (audiovisual) and five small pieces of plexiglass sculpture at the Musée d'art contemporain, Montreal, and also took part in a round table discussion there on aesthetics in the urban milieu. She works with her husband architect André Wogensky.

Reference
La Presse, Mtl., P.Q., June 2, 1973 "Arts Plastiques – La petite déesse Pan" par Gilles Toupin

PANABAKER, Frank Shirley
b. 1904

Born in Hespeler, Ontario, the youngest of three sons of David Norman and Sarah Elizabeth (Anderson) Panabaker. He received his early education in Hespeler. His father, originally of Pennsylvania Dutch stock, was born on a farm near Hespeler and worked at the R. Forbes Woolen Mills where he later became manager. Frank also worked there as a boy while attending school, then he was given the opportunity by his father to attend art classes of F. McGillvray and Elizabeth Knowles who had established a school at Hespeler in an old Mennonite church no longer used for worship. His father had always wanted to paint himself but never found the time and was happy to give the opportunity to his children. Frank however was the only son interested in painting. Another gift when he was twelve, was to own his first gun for hunting. Hunting became a diversion he followed for the rest of his life and reflected in many of his colourful duck hunting scenes. Musically inclined he sang in the church choir and for a year played the pipe organ in the church where his father was choir leader. Following his graduation from Galt Collegiate he went to Toronto to study drawing and painting for two years at the Ontario College of Art. He continued his education at Valparaiso University, Indiana where he took psychology, art appreciation, English literature, singing and pipe organ. Then he continued painting and drawing studies at the Grand Central School of Art (c. 1926) where he took classes from Waymen Adams (portraiture), George Pierce Ennis (water colours) and Arshile Gorky (drawing). He became a member of the Salmagundi Club and the Allied Artists of America. Returning to Canada he held his first solo show in 1926 at the Preston Springs Hotel, Kitchener, where he exhibited scenes from the Kawartha Lakes, Northern Ontario and scenes from in and around Hespeler. With money from the sales of that show he was able to marry Katherine Marks. The first picture sold brought money to pay for the marriage licence and the wedding ring. Over the years Katherine has accompanied him on most of his sketching trips including their first trip to Banff in 1929 when they bought two horses for twenty-five dollars each, rented a cabin which they used as their headquarters, bought supplies for the trip and went off to paint at various locations along the mountain trails including Moraine Lake. He did a sketch of Moraine Lake then and afterwards did a larger canvas of the lake when they got back to their rented shack in Banff. The painting which he had considerable technical difficulty in doing was accepted for showing at the National Academy of Design in New York and was purchased by a father for his daughter. She had to choose between the painting and a new car. In 1930 Panabaker was awarded the Jessie Dow Prize for landscape painting at the Spring Exhibition of the Montreal Art Association. In 1931 he held two exhibitions in Toronto, one at Hart House, the other at the Fine Art Galleries. Viewing his work at this time Augustus Bridle declared him a landscape painter of genius with a great future. In 1932 more praise for the young artist came from A.H. Robson in his *Canadian Landscape Painters* as follows, " . . . brilliant and colourful painter with great versatility and his work is rapidly rising in popular esteem." Other exhibitions followed at various places like T. Eaton's College Street Gallery also Simpsons and W. Scott & Sons, Mtl. (1933) and elsewhere including a show in 1934 in the Birks Building, Hamilton. This exhibition was visited by the mother of the President of the United States, Mrs. Delano Roosevelt who bought a seascape for her son F.D.R. and the painting was hung in the White House. Mrs. Roosevelt at that exhibition also saw the painting of Dr. Locke's Clinic at Williamsburg not far from where Katherine grew up so they chatted about the world famous Doctor and whether or not he treated infantile paralysis. In 1939 a sizeable article on Panabaker in the *Bridle & Golfer* by William Colgate described him as a venturesome, wholesome, zestful, skilful, fine colourist and a technically brilliant painter. In 1942 he was elected an Associate of the Royal Canadian Academy. In 1948 his canvas entitled "V-J Night, Ancaster" was acquired by The Art Gallery of Hamilton as a gift of an unknown benefactor. By the mid forties and early fifties Panabaker was sketching with Fred Haines and Fred Brigden in all kinds of weather. They had their humourous moments and once while with Fred Brigden at Eugenia Falls they were left alone by the hotel keeper who took his family to another village for the evening. Alone to manage the hotel and to cook their meals Frank being the younger of the two, put the steaks on the stove and inadvertently slipped into a day dream of being a famous chef (he had borrowed the chef's uniform to cook the meal). Viewing himself in the kitchen window with the chef's hat at a 'rakish angle' he imagined that if he were a famous chef he might serve meals to all kinds of prominent people like movie stars, even Sarah Churchill who might congratulate him for his cooking and when he mentioned to her that he also painted she would look at his pictures and then cable her father Sir Winston about the man who cooked and painted divinely. Her father would return a cable saying he would like to have this man accompany him to the Riviera where they would paint and do some cooking. His daydream was shattered when he discovered that his image in the window was turning bluish and smoky from the badly burned steaks and when he heard Fred Brigden's cries that the place was on fire (or so he thought). Panabaker's book *Reflected Lights* was published by Ryerson Press in 1957 and received the annual Literary Award of the Toronto Women's Canadian Club (1958). It has 24 illustrations of his own paintings in it (12 in colour) and 17 chapters covering his youth, travels and anecdotal stories like the one about his daydream of being a chef entitled "Self-expression". The chapter titles are as follows: "The Emergency", "The Kite", "The Favour", "The Evangelist", "The Upheaval", "The Law", "Greenhorns in the Rockies", "Self-expression", "The Exhibition", "Easy Money" (about the stock market), "The Duck Hunt", "The Disappointment", "Fred Brigden", "Mt. Assiniboine", "Nassau", "Georgian Bay" and "Nova Scotia". In 1958 he was commissioned by the St. Lawrence Development Commission to paint five views of the rapids near Cornwall. The paintings were destined for display at Upper Canada Village. In 1959 he was appointed Trustee of the National Gallery of Canada (was trustee until 1966). He completed a mural of the farmers' market for one of the committee rooms of the Hamilton City Hall (c. 1962). He was commissioned in 1963 by *The Hamilton Spectator* to produce six colourful scenes of Hamilton for reproduction on a calendar. These calendars were sold for one dollar each and were obtainable from the *Spectator* or from the paper's offices in that region. For many years his paintings have been reproduced on Christmas cards for Coutts' "Painters of Canada Series." In 1964 he was elected to the Board of Governors of the Art Gallery of Hamilton. During his career he has painted in many regions of Canada including Beaver Valley, Georgian Bay, Haliburton and elsewhere in Ontario, also in Nassau in the Bahama Islands. He completes about 75 to 100 paintings a year and probably has done over 4,000 paintings up to 1976. Not many of his paintings pass through auction houses. From Sotheby's for instance, six are listed over a period of six years averaging only one a year. He is represented in the following

PANABAKER, Frank Shirley (Cont'd)

collections: London Public Library and Art Museum, Ont.; Art Gallery of Ontario, Tor.; Agnes Etherington Art Centre, Kingston, Ont.; Chesley District High School, Ont.; Charles G. Fraser Public School, Tor., Ont.; Morrisburg Public Library, Ont.; Town Hall Council Chambers Hespeler, Ont.; Club House Burlington Golf & Country Club, Ont. and many other schools, corporations and private collections. He lives in Ancaster, Ontario with his wife Katherine. They have one daughter Frances.

References

Canadian Landscape Painters by A.H. Robson, Ryerson, Tor., 1932, P. 170
Canadian Art, Its Origin and Development by William Colgate, Ryerson, Tor., 1943, P. 177 (Ryerson Paperbacks, 1943)
Reflected Lights by Frank Panabaker, Ryerson, Tor., 1957 (159 pages)
Agnes Etherington Art Centre, Queen's University at Kingston (catalogue of paintings) by Frances K. Smith, No. 105
Who's Who In Canada, 1966-68, International Press Ltd., Tor., P. 837
The Canadian Art Auction Record Vol. 5, 1973 compiled by H.C. Campbell, Chief Lib. Toronto Pub. Libraries, Amtmann Inc., Mtl., 1974, P. 51
Centennial Exhibition of Canadian Paintings, Bd. of Education for City of Tor., P. 9
Canadian Art At Auction, 1968-1975, Edited by Geoffrey Joyner, Sotheby & Co., Tor., Ont., 1975, P. 151
Who's Who In American Art, 1976, Ed. by Jaques Cattell Press, R.R. Bowker Co., NYC, P. 426
NGC Info. Forms Rec'd June 13, 1930; July 17, 1945; July 30, 1946
Newspapers and periodicals
Daily Globe, Tor., Ont., Oct. 25, 1926 "Hespeler Man's Art Attracts Attention"
Saturday Night, Tor., May 9, 1931 (show at The Fine Art Gal., Tor.)
The Toronto Star, Ont., May 9, 1931 "Hespeler Painter Landscape Genius" by Augustus Bridle
The Globe, Tor., Ont., Oct. 24, 1931 "Art and Artists"
Mail & Empire, Tor., Ont., Nov. 14, 1933 "Panabaker's Exhibit Is Rich In Variety" by Pearl McCarthy
La Presse, Mtl., P.Q., Jan. 11, 1936 "Frank Panabaker" (Les Galeries Eaton)
Saturday Night, Tor., Ont., Dec. 5, 1936 (at Simpson Gallery)
Ibid, Apr. 24, 1937 "World Of Art" by G. Campbell McInnes (at Eaton Galleries, Tor.)
The Toronto Star, Ont., Nov. 22, 1938 "Cheery Work Shown By Hamilton Artist" by A. Bridle
Globe & Mail, Tor., Ont., Nov. 28, 1938 "Art and Artists" by Pearl McCarthy (at Simpson Gallery)
Bridle & Golfer, Tor., June, 1939 "Mystery of Light and Air" by William Colgate
The Hamilton Spectator, June 22, 1949 "Work By Panabaker – New Gift To Art Gallery Shows Festive Ancaster" by Eric Williams (the painting "V-J Night In Ancaster" presented to AGH)
The Toronto Star, Ont., Dec. 16, 1950 (at Eaton's, Tor.)
Galt Reporter, Ont., 29 Nov., 1955 "Former Hespeler Artist To Paint Rapids' Picture" (painting of Long Sault Rapids near Cornwall)
The Hamilton Spectator, Ont., Feb. 4, 1956 "Saturday Art Notes" by Mary Mason (general information about the artist)
Ibid, Sept. 4, 1957 (photo of two paintings by artist presented to Sir Cullum Welch Lord Mayor of London, Eng.)
Ibid, Sept. 28, 1957 " 'Reflected Lights' – Panabaker As Author Writes Own Story In Colorful Book" by Kingsley Brown
London Free Press, Ont., Oct. 12, 1957 "Color On Canvas" by Lenore Crawford
Cornwall Standard-Freeholder, Ont., Feb. 1, 1958 "Paintings By Noted Artists Preserve Familiar Landmarks"
The Hamilton Spectator, Ont., July 5, 1958 "Art And Reflections" by Ian Vorres (mention of Panabaker's thoughts of writing another book)

PANABAKER, Frank Shirley (Cont'd)

The Ottawa Citizen, Ont., Oct. 28, 1959 (CP) "National Gallery Trustee Named By Mrs. Fairclough"

The Montreal Star, P.Q., Oct. 29, 1959 "F.S. Panabaker Named National Gallery Trustee" (Mt. Star Bureau release)

Enterprise, Chesley, Ont., Mar. 3, 1960 "H.S. Painting Honors Late Mr. Darcy Vance" (Chesley District High School receives a Panabaker painting)

Galt Evening Reporter, Ont., Oct. 12, 1960 "Galt Artists Display Exciting Painting" (guest exhibitor F. Panabaker)

Globe & Mail, Tor., Ont., May 16, 1961 "Artist Finds Own Work Forged"

Toronto Daily Star, Ont., May 16, 1961 (finds forgery of his work in florist shop near his home)

Leader, Morrisburg, Ont., Sept. 1, 1961 "Panabaker Painting Donated To Library" (to Morrisburg Pub. Library)

The Hamilton Spectator, Ont., Nov. 12, 1963 "City Scenes Feature Spec Calendar – Work of Noted Artist 'Shows Off' Hamilton"

Evening Reporter, Galt, Ont., Feb. 5, 1964 "Prominent Artist Paints Local Landscape Scene" (Hespeler Council Chambers)

The Hamilton Spectator, Ont., Feb. 25, 1964 "Art Gallery Board Named" (Panabaker elected to Board of Governors of AGH)

Ibid, Mar. 5, 1970 "New Burlington clubhouse – Panabaker paints original" by Jim Donnelly (painting for Hamilton Golf Club)

PANELOO
b. 1935

Born near Clyde River, north coast of Baffin Island, she settled in Arctic Bay with her husband Kaminerk and her six children. Drawing on her imagination which has been inspired by the animal world, she has portrayed in her sculpture the mystical and the supernatural animals of legend. Her work has been exhibited at the Robertson Galleries, Ottawa.

Reference
Exhibition circular with biography, Robertson Galleries, 162 Laurier Ave. W. Ottawa (c. 1971)

PANGNARK
b. (c) 1920

From Eskimo Point, Northwest Territories, he is known for his modern sculpture with economy of line or abstract appearance which sometimes gives the impression of being carved from a block shaped stone usually with vertical portions of the block showing as part of the design. There are two illustrations of his carvings in George Swinton's *Sculpture Of The Eskimo*. Some of his work was shown at the exhibit "Two Artists of the Northwest Territories" at the National Arts Centre in Ottawa (1970) and circulated afterwards across Canada. The exhibition was organized by Barbara Tyler of the National Museum of Man in co-operation with the Canadian Arctic Producers to honour the Centennial of the Northwest Territories. Pangnark has exhibited at other two-man shows.

PANGNARK (Cont'd)

References
Sculpture Of The Eskimo by George Swinton, McClelland & Stewart, Tor., 1972, P. 20, 37
newspapers
Kitimat Northern Sentinel, B.C., May 27, 1970 "Art of NWT Crosses Canada"
Winnipeg Tribune, Man., Aug. 27, 1970 "Pongnark's art" (as spelled) photo and caption
Grand Falls Advertiser, Nfld., May 25, 1970 "Two artists from the Northwest Territories"
Clinton News, Record, Ont., May 28, 1970 "Two Artists From The Northwest Territories
will be seen in an exhibition"
Sherbrooke La Tribune, P.Q., Feb. 18, 1974 "Les oeuvres de deux artistes esquimaux à la
Galerie d'art" (showing at University of Sherbrooke)

PANKO, William
1892-1948

Born at Tulukow, Austria, son of Ivan and Barbara (Sawchuk) Panko, he completed
elementary school in his home town and at the age of nineteen came to Canada as
a farm labourer in 1911. He continued farming and in 1920 began working as a
miner in the Drumheller coal mines during the winters. In 1937 he contracted
tuberculosis of the hip and entered the Baker Memorial Sanatorium in Calgary.
About 1945 during his convalescence he took up painting and became a gifted
primitive under the encouragement of artist and therapist Marion Nicoll who taught
him to mix water colours. At the time of his discharge from hospital he had completed enough paintings to arrange a one-man show of his work with A.F. Key,
Director of the Allied Arts Council and of the Coste House, Calgary, in 1947. It
was during this show that three people involved in the field of Canadian art purchased some of his work, Paul Duval, Kathleen Daly and Clifford Robinson. Others
also acquired his work including Maxwell Bates, Janet Mitchell, George Swinton,
Norah McCullough and A.F. Key who wrote of Panko as follows, "Each painting
represented an experience. He had been sent to Harrison Hot Springs in British
Columbia for treatment, therefore the series of mountains and fishing scenes.
For the most part his work told stories of his life in Drumheller valley – stories
of his diminutive home and his rich garden along the Rosebud Creek or stories
of mining operations. These pictorial tales were always told simply, with good
humour and with good taste." He completed about thirty paintings before his
death at the age of fifty-six. All his known works, with two or three exceptions,
were purchased by artists or others associated with the fine arts. An exhibition
"Folk Painters of the Canadian West" was organized by the National Gallery of
Canada in 1959 and a catalogue published for the occasion which included a
listing of fourteen of Panko's works and illustrations of three of his paintings and
one of a blockprint. Four of his paintings were sold by Sotheby & Company between 1968 and 1972 (gouache, water colour, two mixed g & wc). He is represented in the National Gallery of Canada and the McCord Museum of McGill University.

References
The News, Medicine Hat, Alta., Oct. 22, 1947 " 'Primitive' Arts Calgary Display"
The Albertan, Calgary, Alta., Nov. 25, 1947 "Artists Buy Miner's Work"
The Herald, Calgary, Alta., Apr. 17, 1948 "Miner Artist Dies in Edmonton"
Folk Painters of the Canadian West, NGC, 1959
Painting in Canada/A History by J. Russell Harper, Univ. Tor. Press, Tor., 1966, P. 338,
350, 427

PANKO, William (Cont'd)

Creative Canada compiled by Ref. Div., McPherson Lib., Univ. of Victoria/Univ. Tor. Pr., 1971, P. 240
Canadian Art At Auction, 1968-1975, Ed. Geoffrey Joyner, Sotheby & Co. (Can.) Ltd., Tor., Ont., 1975, P. 152
Canadian Art, Vol. 5, No. 4, 1948 "Coast To Coast In Art" P. 200 (ill. with caption)

PANNETON, Louis Philippe
b. 1906

Born in Trois Rivières, P.Q., he was self-taught in drawing and painting and took six months instruction in charcoal sketching under Mr. Graham and Mr. St. Charles at the Monument National, Montreal. From the age of eight he had expressed his wishes to become a portrait painter but financial difficulties during hard times forced him to go to work early after receiving his basic schooling. He became a commercial artist and in 1938 married. At the outbreak of World War Two he joined the reserve artillery but was turned down for active service in 1941. He returned to his art and began painting portraits seriously with the encouragement of his wife. He exhibited his paintings at the Montreal Art Association Spring Show (1942); New York Grand Central Art Exhibition (1942) and the Royal Canadian Academy of Art's 67th Annual Exhibition (1946). He completed his portraits usually in six sittings but on occasion was able to do a likeness in three. Was living in Montreal in 1948 with his wife and daughter.

References
Globe & Mail, Tor., Ont., Nov. 23, 1946 "Boyish Dream of Artist Fulfilled at Academy"
The Toronto Telegram, Ont., Nov. 28, 1946 "Only 2 years on portraits one accepted"
NGC Info. Form rec'd Aug. 22, 1945

PANNETON, Louise (née De Cotret)

Born in Trois Rivières, she drew as a child and studied with the Ursuline nuns. She began serious painting around 1952. She took instruction from Geraldine Bourbeau (5 yrs.), Leon Bellefleur and Jordi Bonet (2 yrs.). Interested in abstract art she exhibited her work in various group shows and in 1962 at the Gallery Zanettin, Quebec City, with artists Denise Heon, Jacques Jourdain, Raymond Lasnier and Jacqueline Savary. At the exhibition the *Quebec Chronicle Telegraph* reviewer described her paintings as light and gay with movement and rhythm expressed in carefully conceived forms and lines and noted, "While the colors used are pale-soft greens, yellows, oranges and blues − they are sufficiently intense to allow her to play with contrasts, playing one color against the other." She also exhibited with Raymond Lasnier and Harvey Rivard and wrote on Lasnier's work following his death in 1968. She went to France with her husband, a doctor on specialization studies, and there she took drawing at the Julian Academy, Paris, and painting, drawing, and theatre set designing at Lyon. She studied ceramics with Pauline Labreque (Canada) and tapestry with Pierre Daquin. She took a tapestry course at the University of Quebec and visited tapestry workshops in Lisbon and in Algeria.

PANNETON, Louise (née De Cotret) (Cont'd)

She had done mostly painting until 1967 then moved into tapestry for which she is better known today. Her hangings range in size from big mural-like works to smaller ones. She kept to traditional texture and bright colours until 1973 then began to add bits of wool which are looped or hanging free from the surface of the work. From North Africa she brought back unusual wools and colours which show genuine audacity, with colours more subtle and subdued in the more three dimensional works which have surprising majesty of panoplies or trophies. In addition to wool she now uses string and cord or rope. Her titles are imaginative a few of which are: "The Bedouin", "Bitter Earth", "Navajo", "The White Dove" and so on (these titles are in French). At times she also uses bits of metallic threads or pieces of aluminum and fibreglass. Viewing her work in 1971 *The Montreal Star* writer noted, "She is a weaver prepared to experiment and among the 16 works in this show she utilizes several materials not often associated with the field. Sometimes her ideas work quite well. Her use of black and white plexiglass rectangles in 'Toccata', by far the best hanging in the exhibition, forms an effective contrast with the same colors in the hooking, with its clearly-defined zones and irregular outline. Similarly, her inclusion of hanging plexiglass tubes and blocks in her ceiling suspended work achieves a chandelier-like impression; the plastic forms acting as light catchers that emphasize the framed hooked elipsoidal tapestry." Her solo shows include: Grenier des Artistes, Grand Piles (1967); Centre culturel de Shawinigan (1967); Galerie Jacques Lacroix, Chicoutimi (1968); Galerie du Vieux, Trois Rivières (1970); Caisse populaire de Victoriaville (1970); Centre d'Art de Cowansville (1970); Galerie l'Apogée, Saint-Sauveur-des-Monts (1971) (1973); Les Gens de mon Pays Galerie, Que. City (1972). She is represented in the following collections: La Presse, Mtl. (entry hall); Town Hall, Trois Rivières; Ministry of Intergovernmental Affairs, Quebec City; Musée de Quebec and elsewhere. She is a member of the Société des Artistes professionnels. Lives in Trois Rivières where she directs the tapestry course given by the University of Quebec.

References

Culture Vivante, Ministère des Affaires Culturelles du Quebec, June 1971, No. 21, P. 46

Canadian Artists in Exhibition, 1972-73, Roundstone Press, Tor., 1974, P. 166

L'Art Au Quebec Depuis 1940 par Guy Robert, La Presse, Mtl., 1973, P. 170, 351

Le guide des artisans créateurs du Québec par Jean-Pierre Payette, La Presse, Mtl., 1974, P. 159

newspapers and other

Le Soleil, P.Q., Nov., 1962 "Les peintres de Trois-Rivières exposent dans la Vieille Capitale" par Paule France Dufaux

Action Catholique, 3 Nov., 1962 "Peintres Trifluviens À La Galerie Zanettin" par Nicole Blouin

Chronicle Telegraph, Quebec, P.Q., Nov. 1962 "Five Young PQ Artists In Joint Showing Here" by F.J.P.

L'Echo Du Nord, 10 Nov., 1971 "Tapisseries de Louise Panneton à l'Apogée"

Le Soleil, Que., P.Q., 25 Nov., 1972 "Louise Panneton de la peinture à la tapisserie" par Claude Daigneault

L'Information médicale et paramédicale, Mtl., P.Q., Dec. 4, 1973 "Les tapisseries de Madame Louise Panneton à la Galerie l'Apogée" par Paul Dumas

Le Nouvelliste, Trois Rivières, P.Q., 26 July, 1975 "Louise Panneton à l'affût des forces de la nature" par René Lord

Commentaires Sur L'Oeuvre De Raymond Lasnier par Louise Panneton

PANT, Sheila

Born in Lucknow, India, she attended Isobella Thoburn College and later Lucknow University where she received her B.A. and M.A. in English literature then her B. Ed in Delhi. She became known for her batiks and exhibited her work in New Delhi in 1967. She came to Canada in 1968 with her husband and two young children. After attending the Ontario College of Education she started teaching with the Metropolitan Toronto Separate School Board with plans to specialize in art teaching. Known for her batiks in Canada as well, she imports all her materials and dyes from India. Once she has decided on the main structure of each batik she develops it with two or three colours. Her batiks are basically inspired by a deep study of Mediaeval Hindu art which in turn originated from the work of poets and dramatists. Describing her work, Sherry Cecil of the Oakville *Journal Record*, noted, "Mrs. Pant's work is entirely figurative, inspired by the folk legends and mythology of both her native India and North America. Her attention to detail in the facial expressions and gestures of her subjects makes these myths come alive. In 'Happy Insensibility', for example, the merriment involved in the celebration of spring is evident in a cock of the head and twist of an arm as well as the facial features. Particularly moving is 'Narada – The Blue Sage', an Indian equivalent to the saint of all music. Meditating joyfully, his complete absorption in his music is almost contagious." Mrs. Pant has exhibited her work in Lambton Gallery, Etobicoke, Toronto (1970); Gairlock Gardens, Oakville, Ont. (1975) and is represented in collections in United States and Canada. She has been invited to show her work in Tokyo and New York. Lives in Oakville.

References
  New Toronto Advertiser, Ont., Apr. 16, 1970 "Batiks and Indian myths"
  Etobicoke Guardian, Islington, Ont., Apr. 16, 1970 "Batiks capture Indian mythology"
  Journal Record, Oakville, Ont., May 23, 1975 "Sheila Pant is elevating batik to a true art form" by Sherry Cecil

PANTON, Lawrence Arthur Colley
1894-1954

Born in Egremont, Cheshire, England, the son of Charles W. Panton (an actuary) and Caroline Colley Panton. He received his education at the Lincoln Grammar School and in Sheffield at the Central Secondary School. Coming to Canada in 1911 at the age of seventeen, he settled in Toronto where he worked for a short time as an office assistant with the Grand Trunk Railway. Next he secured a job as bookkeeper with *The Evening Telegram* until the outbreak of World War One. He served in the 4th Division, Signal Company of the army (1916-1919) and on his discharge returned to the *Telegram* for two years (1920-22). He attended evening classes at the Ontario College of Art under C.M. Manly and F.S. Challener. He married Marion Pye in 1920 (they had one son Charles who was killed in action in World War Two). He took classes at the Central Technical School, Toronto, as well. Finally with sufficient training and natural ability in art he joined the firm of Rous and Mann as designer under A.H. Robson. In 1924 he became art teacher at the Central Technical School where he conducted classes until 1926. He was appointed director of art at Western Technical School (1926-1937) then became art director at Northern Vocational School (1937-51) and

PANTON, Lawrence Arthur Colley (Cont'd)

finally principal of the Ontario College of Art, a position he held until his death (1951-54). He took sabbatical leave to study mixed techniques including tempera painting with American artist William C. Palmer. During all this time he was building a career as one of Canada's important painters. His early work was a lyrical simplified realism which included landscapes, figure studies and residential city scenes. He went on to more vigorous stylization in his landscapes with emphasis on rhythmic patterns. In his final years he achieved greater freedom in semi-abstraction as in his scenes of mist-shrouded rocks of Nova Scotia shorelines. These last paintings were more academic in nature and could be thought of as the work of a painter's painter. The *Saturday Night* of 1954 described them as follows, "In later years, Panton built his major pictures slowly, painting thin layer upon layer. By means of glazes, he achieved a rich luminosity of color. Using this technique, he turned increasingly to abstract forms in his last years. On trips to the Atlantic Coast, he was attracted by the shoreline landscape, with its combination of rock, mist and spray, of the permanent and the transient elements. In these complex paintings, there is a strong element of mysticism and a striving to express eternal truths through visual forms." Panton worked in a variety of media including tempera, oil, gouache, and water colour. He was very active with many societies including the Ontario Society of Artists serving on its council and elected juries almost continuously from the thirties to the time of his death (Elected 1925, Pres. 1931-37); Royal Canadian Academy (former Vice-Pres., & Treas., ARCA 1934, RCA 1943); Canadian Group of Painters (1949); Canadian Society of Painters in Water Colour (Charter Member, 1925); Canadian Society of Graphic Arts (one-time secretary); Canadian Society of Painter-Etchers and Engravers (one-time memb.); worked with the Fine Arts Committee of the Canadian National Exhibition and the National Industrial Design Committee; Federation of Canadian Artists (1942, Chairman, Ont. Div., 1945). Represented in the following collections: Winnipeg Art Gallery, Man.; London Public Library and Art Museum, Ont.; Art Gallery of Ontario, Tor.; National Gallery of Canada, Ott.; Owens Museum of Mount Allison University, Sackville, N.B.; National Gallery of South Australia, Adelaide. He wrote and lectured on the History of Art, Art in Everyday Life and on technical aspects of art and taught painting, composition, design and drawing. A memorial exhibition of his work was held under the auspices of the Ontario Society of Artists at the Art Gallery of Toronto (Jan., 1955) and a retrospective show at Hart House, University of Toronto (Jan. 29 to Feb. 16, 1974). Over the years he held one-man shows at the Laing Fine Art Gallery (Feb., 1949); Board Room of McLaren Advertising, Tor. (Sept., 1949). After his death a show of his work was given by the Park Gallery, Toronto. Panton participated in many group shows national and international (see *Creative Canada, Volume Two*).

References

Canadian Landscape Painters by A.H. Robson, Ryerson, Tor., 1932, P. 168, 201, 203
A Century of Canadian Art, 1938, Tate Gallery, Lond., England, NGC, Ott., P. 26
Canadian Art, Vol. 4, No. 3 May, 1947, P. 99, 100-101
Ibid, Vol. 6, No. 3, Spring, 1949, P. 98, 100
Who's Who in Ontario Art, Tor., 1950, Tor., 1950
Canadian Art by Graham McInnes, MacMillan, Tor., 1950, P. 62, 63
The Monthly Letter, Arts & Letters Club of Toronto, December, 1954 (Obituary and tributes to L.A.C. Panton)

PANTON, Lawrence Arthur Colley (Cont'd)

Canadian Paintings In Hart House by J. Russell Harper, Univ. Tor. Press, 1955, P. 57
September Gale by John A.B. McLeish, J.M. Dent & Sons Ltd., Lond., 1956, P. 187
Canadian Drawing And Prints by Paul Duval, Burns & MacEachern, Tor., 1952, Text & Plate 85
Canadian Water Colour Painting by Paul Duval, Burns & MacEachern, Tor., 1954, Text & Plates 52, 76
The National Gallery of Canada Catalogue, Vol. 3 by R.H. Hubbard, NGC/Univ. Tor. Press, 1960, P. 241
Mount Allison University Collection of Canadian Art, Sackville, N.B., 1965, No. 104
Art Gallery of Ontario, The Canadian Collection by Helen Pepall Bradfield, McGraw-Hill, Tor., 1970, P. 351-354
Four Decades, The Canadian Group of Painters and their contemporaries 1930-1970, by Paul Duval, Clarke, Irwin & Co. Ltd., Tor., 1972, P. 119, 121 (ill.)
Creative Canada, Vol. 2, McPherson Library, UBC/Univ. Tor. Press, 1972, P. 213
Canadian Art At Auction, 1968-1975, Edited by Geoffrey Joyner, Sotheby & Co., Tor., 1975, P. 152-3 (44 entries with prices)
Newspapers and other publications
The Globe, Tor. Ont., Mar. 11, 1931 "Honor Received By Young Artist − L.A.C. Panton Is President of Ontario Society of Artists"
Brochure, The Canadian Fine Art Guild Ltd., Canadian Artists "L.A.C. Panton, Pres. O.S.A." (undated, has biographical details, reproduction of a Muskoka painting with critical appreciation of his work)
The Toronto Telegram, Ont., Aug. 19, 1937 (reproduction of Panton's painting "Pomona")
Mayfair, May, 1948 "The Painter's Art In Layman's Language" by L.A.C. Panton (ill. for text by members of O.S.A.)
Evening Telegram, Tor., Ont., Feb. 5, 1949 "Panton at Laing's" (solo show)
The Toronto Star, Ont., Feb. 5, 1949 "L. Panton In Art Spiritual Realist" by Augustus Bridle
Globe & Mail, Tor., Ont. Feb. 19, 1949 "Art and Artists − Show Panton Paintings In Laing Gallery Exhibit" by Pearl McCarthy
Ibid, Sept. 24, 1949 "Art and Artists − New Depth in Painting Revealed by Panton" by Pearl McCarthy
Ibid, Dec. 31, 1949 (note on Panton taking study in the use of mixed techniques and tempera in Canada and the United States)
Ibid, June, 5, 1950 "Art and Artists − Panton Goes to Doon: Hamilton Pictures Here" by Pearl McCarthy (Panton teaches at Doon)
Ibid, Mar. 16, 1951 "Lawrence Panton Named Principal of College of Art"
Enterprise, Willowdale, Ont., May 17, 1951 "Lucid Talk On Modern Art" by Gladys Allison (Panton speaks to Willowdale Group of Artists)
London Free Press, Ont., Aug. 16, 1951 "First Major Acquisition − Gallery Buys Valued Painting"
Timmins Press, Ont., Mar. 28, 1952 "Panton Defends 'Modern' Artist"
Sault Ste. Marie Star, Ont., Mar. 25, 1953 "Art Has Place in Community − L.A. Panton" (lecture sponsored by Atkinson Foundation)
Globe & Mail, Nov. 22, 1954 "Lawrence A.C. Panton − Art College Head Also Designer, Former Teacher" (Obituary)
The Ottawa Citizen, Ont., Nov. 23, 1954 (CP) "Famed Artist L.A.C. Panton Dies At 60"
Globe & Mail, Ont., Dec. 4, 1954 "O.S.A. Features a Panton Memorial" by Pearl McCarthy
Saturday Night, Tor., Ont., Dec. 18, 1954 "L.A.C. Panton: An Explorer In Art − Teacher and Painter for Three Decades Leaves a Rich Legacy" (four reproductions of his work representing four periods with captions)
Globe & Mail, Tor., Ont., Jan. 8, 1955 "Art and Artists − Panton Work Dominates OSA Show" by Pearl McCarthy
Ibid, Feb. 1, 1958 "Art and Artists − Panton Show Proves Worthiness" by Pearl McCarthy (show at Park Gallery, Tor.)
London Evening Free Press, Ont., April 22, 1961 (show of ten of his paintings and silk screens at London Public Art Museum)
The Ottawa Journal, Ont., July 26, 1961 "Panton Oils Adorn Foyer Of City Hall"
NGC Info. Forms Feb. 5, 1927; Jan. 23, 1943; Aug. 1, 1946

PANTON, Paul

b. 1935

Born in Melita, Manitoba, the son of Reginald L. and Emily Fraser Panton. He spent his early years in Fort William and Kakabeka Falls (1937) Ontario, and in New Westminster, B.C., where he started painting at the age of fifteen taking study under Helen Douglas, Joe Plaskett and later took extension courses from the Vancouver School of Art. Returning to Manitoba in 1953 he worked in a variety of jobs over the years and continued to study art under Steve Repa and Margaret Reiley who taught him tie-dye and batik work. He entered the United College, Winnipeg, on a B.A. course then attended Brandon College as a student also working as secretary to the School of Music of that college. He spent the winter of 1966-67 as reviewer and reporter for *The Penticton Herald*. He has worked as designer and layout man in commercial printing having been employed by New Era Publishing and Leech Printing. Known for his landscapes in oils and water colours with bright colours and happy brush strokes, he has also done work in casein, pastel, ink and pencil. In recent years he has produced batiks and tie-dyes. His solo shows include: Brandon University, Man. (1966, 1968, 1972); Simon Fraser University, B.C. (1966); Okanagan Regional Library, Kelowna, B.C. (1968); Community Arts Centre, Penticton, B.C. (1968); Boissevain Collegiate, Man. (1969); residence of Rolf Pederson, Brandon, Man. (1970); Winnipeg Art Gallery, Man. (1972).

References

New Era, Melita, Man., June 23, 1966 "Paul Panton Will Stage Art Exhibit Saturday"
Boissevain Recorder, Man., Apr. 4, 1968 "Panton Exhibition Opening At Brandon"
Brandon Sun, Man., Apr. 15, 1968 "Panton Opens One-Man Show" by Kaye Rowe
Boissevain Recorder, Man., Oct. 31, 1968 "Panton exhibition at Kelowna"
Kelowna Courier, B.C. Oct. 16, 1968 "Prairie Art Show Here"
New Era, Melita, Man., Oct. 24, 1968 "Panton Paintings At Kelowna"
Penticton Herald, B.C., Nov. 7, 1968 "Ex-Resident Holds One-Man Art Show"
New Era, Melita, Man., Feb. 27, 1969 "One Man Show"
Boissevain Recorder, Man., Feb. 13, 1969 "Panton Exhibits In Boissevain"
Penticton Herald, B.C., Nov. 14, 1969 "Artist Panton's Work A Philosophical Product" by P.M. Ritchie
Brandon Sun, Man., Dec. 9, 1970 "Panton showing wins local approval" by Kaye Rowe
Times Journal, Thunder Bay, Ont., Feb. 2, 1971 "Kakabeka Falls – Former Resident Has Exhibition of Paintings"
Winnipeg Free Press, Man., June 19, 1972 "Panton Works To Be Shown At Brandon U"

PAQUET, Guy

Known for his landscapes of Charlevoix region, Quebec, including old Quebec homes especially in winter.

Reference

Le Soleil, P.Q., Nov. 4, 1972 "Expositions Blier et Paquet – La nature d'ici à l'honneur" par Gislain Lebel

PAQUET, Raymond

Born in Quebec City of English speaking Canadian parents, one of his forebearers was the first Church of England Bishop of Quebec. Following his academic school years he attended the Ecole des Beaux-Arts, Quebec. During World War Two he served overseas for two-and-a-half years with the Royal Hamilton Light Infantry. While serving in Holland he met and married a Dutch girl (they have two grown sons). They returned to Canada and in 1951 settled in Toronto where Mr. Paquet worked in the shoe business continuing painting studies with Adrian Dingle. After living in Thornhill for three years he moved to Aurora then returned to Thornhill. He opened a boutique shop in Thornhill at the shopping plaza at 8238 Yonge Street just north of Langstaff School where his own paintings may be seen. He travelled throughout Europe and the American continent to select other items for his shop including artists' supplies. A painter of landscapes, buildings, floral studies, still life and figure studies, he has exhibited his paintings at the Richmond Inn, the Skyline, Aurora, Newmarket and elsewhere.

Reference
Richmond Hill Liberal, Ont., May 29, 1974 "Local Man Realizes Ambition Opens Art Shop In Thornhill" by Margaret Govan

PAQUETTE, Devona (Mrs. Devona Lorraine Paquette McLorn)
b. 1930

Born in Woodstock, Ontario, the daughter of Mr. and Mrs. Lionel Paquette she began painting at the age of ten and competed in fall fairs. She attended the Ontario College of Art (1951-55) where she studied under such noted teachers as Carl Schaeffer, Eric Freifeld, Sydney Watson, John Martin, Jock MacDonald, David Hall-Humpherson, Fred Hagan, John Mattar, Gregor, Tony Urquart and Rowley Murphy. She graduated with honours. She started her career as prop designer for the Stratford Festival (1955); designer for New Studios, T.D.F. Artists, Tor. (1957-60); artist for Spitzer Mills & Bates Agency, Tor. (1961); promotion artist for *The Toronto Telegram* (1961). She established the Paquette Studios in Kitchener where she and her husband Philip settled in 1961 after moving from Toronto. She has given lectures and demonstrations in water colours in southwestern Ontario. She teaches water colours and lectures in Kitchener, Waterloo, Cambridge and Guelph. A versatile artist in a variety of media she completes several commissions a year from her studio. For instance she has done the ancient Japanese technique of fish printing known as Gyotaku. Using rice paper and India ink she transfers the pattern of the fish in effective brown and grey tones. Also she has done work in egg tempera by incorporating ground pigment with raw egg as the binder for the tempera, plus some oil of clove to maintain a pleasant odor. She applies this medium layer upon layer creating a transparent glaze which gives her work depth. Most of her work however is done in water colours. She favours subjects of rural Ontario 'intensely grass roots' depicted with a spontaneous quality of brush stroke accented often with dark strong pen lines. She finds of particular interest historical buildings and genre scenes. She is also known for her fine life-drawing studies in charcoal. A member of the Kitchener Waterloo Society of Artists, Central Ontario Art Association (Vice-Pres., 1970-72) she has exhibited her work with the Society

PAQUETTE, Devona (Mrs. Devona Lorraine Paquette McLorn) (Cont'd)

of Graphic Artists Canadian Tour (1960); Central Ontario Art Association Touring Canadian Library show (1969) and other group shows. She has held the following solo shows: University of Waterloo (1970); Canadian Artists Gallery, Stratford (1971); Laura Sharpe Gallery, Waterloo (1971); Mutual Life, Kitchener (1973); Gallery H, Galt, Ont. (1973). She is represented in the collections of the Hon Robert Stanfield; Dr. Mathews, Pres. Univ. Waterloo; Electrohome Ltd., Kitchener, and many others. Chosen as one of ten artists for the 1973 Cansave Christmas Cards she was also commissioned to produce two drawings for fund raising by the Canadian Arthritic Society. Mother of three she met her husband Philip McLorn at the Ontario College of Art and they were married in 1957. She had travelled and painted in Mexico and Spain.

References
> *Kitchener-Waterloo Record*, Ont., June 24, 1970 "Her Art Is an Explosion . . . and Hers Delves Into Antiquity" by Frances L. Denney (articles on artists Alyce R. Simon and Devona Paquette by Jane Durban and Frances L. Denney)
> *St. Thomas Times-Journal*, Ont., Sept. 17, 1971 "Popular artist to address first fall meeting of WAA"
> *Kingston Whig Standard*, Ont., Jan. 11, 1975 "Boehmer's centennial calendar much-sought miniature gallery" by Susan MacKenzie
> NGC Info. Form Aug. 14, 1973

PAQUETTE, Joy

b. 1922

Born in Ottawa, Ontario, she attended Gloucester Convent and studied painting under Henri Masson for six years and also under André Biéler at Queen's University for one summer. She exhibited her paintings in a small show at the Canadian Repertory Theatre and in the Montreal Spring Exhibition. No recent information.

Reference
> NGC Info. Form rec'd April 13, 1954

PAQUETTE, Suzanne Marie Cecile

b. 1949

Born in Valleyfield, Quebec, a painter who has been living in Nova Scotia where she has exhibited her work at the Anna Leonowens Art Gallery in a group show (1971), two person show (1971) and at St. Mary's University Gallery, Halifax, in a group show (1972) also at the Nova Scotia Festival of the Arts (1973). She received a Canada Council Grant in 1973.

Reference
> Letter filed NGC Lib. dated July 28, 1974

PAQUIN, Marcelle

She exhibited her paintings of a variety of subjects including character, interior and floral studies at the Caisse Populaire St. Esprit on Masson Street, Montreal, in October, 1972.

Reference
Montreal-Matin, P.Q., Oct. 24, 1972 "Femme Peintre" (photo of artist with four of her paintings, and caption)

PAQUIN, Roger
b. 1941

Born in Deschambault, Quebec, he took classical studies at Quebec and Levis (1954-61) then attended the Ecole des Beaux-Arts, Montreal (1961-66) and studied sculpture with Louis Archambault (1963-64) and integrated arts with Charles Daudelin and Marcel Junius. He received his teacher's certificate for plastic arts (1965-66). In his own sculpture he has exhibited at the Youth Pavilion, Expo '67; at the Musée d'Art Contemporain during the 1967 Quebec Competition and again in 1969 when he was chosen Laureat; at Galerie du Siècle, Mtl. (1967, 1969); New Sculpture, Stratford, Ont. (1968). He is represented in the Musée du Quebec and in other collections. He has taught sculpture full and part time. Lives in Montreal.

Reference
NGC Info. Form rec' 26 Mar., 1968

PAQUIN, Yves
b (c) 1950

A Rouyn, P.Q., area artist, son of Mr. & Mrs. Gilbert Paquin, he has done landscape murals for homes in that area.

Reference
Rouyn-Noranda Press, P.Q., Sept. 26, 1968 (photo and caption)

PARADIS, Claude

A Montreal, P.Q. artist who graduated from the Ecole polytechnique and took evening courses at the Ecole des Beaux-Arts, Montreal. He has done collages and large reliefs composed of diverse elements. His collages have a certain narrative significance (bus tickets, illustrations from history and geometric forms like ellipses, arcs and circles repeated, and complicated forms which could have been drawn by a computer). His reliefs consist of parts of objects including functional furniture and small planks. He exhibited his work at Tabaret Hall, University of Ottawa (1967).

PARADIS, Claude (Cont'd)

References

La Presse, Mtl., 15 April, 1967 (article describing his work)

Le Droit, Ottawa, Ont., Sept. 23, 1967 "Claude Paradis, qui êtes-vous?" (show at Univ. Ottawa)

PARADIS, Guy
b. 1930

Born in rural Levis, P.Q., he studied painting at the Ecole des Beaux-Arts, Quebec (1950-55) where he became professor. In his own painting he is known for his landscapes described by Michael Gouthreau as having, " . . . captured the lonely beauty and silence of rural Quebec with a feeling of one who loves what he painted, of one who believes in the words to a song written by composer Gilles Vigneault, "Mon Pays C'est L'Hiver.' " Paradis has painted other subjects but seems to be partial to landscapes as he explains, "I try to capture or suspend a moment in time . . . . The contrast of a dark trunk of a tree against the whiteness of a snow-covered field is the personification of time itself . . . . I love the country . . . being able to capture on canvas the nature and rugged texture of rural Quebec is my ambition, to express myself in simple natural objects like trees or mountains to me is the most important expression possible." His paintings have been exhibited at Montreal, Chicoutimi and other centres including solo shows in Quebec City at Galerie Zanettin (1964, 1969).

References

Le Soleil, P.Q., Oct. 31, 1964 (photo of Paradis with his works)

Chronicle-Telegraph, P.Q., Oct. 31, 1964 "Quiet Brush, Thin Paint Bring A Welcome Relief"

Ibid, Nov. 24, 1969 "Quebec Painter Finds Wintertime Stimulating" by Michael Gouthreau

PARADIS, Frère Jérôme
b. 1902

Born in Charlesbourg, P.Q., he did general teaching at Notre Dame, Mtl. (1928-35) but in 1914 he first began to copy paintings as part of his growing interest in art. In 1935 he enrolled in the Ecole des Beaux-Arts, Montreal, where he studied plastic arts until 1939. He did no painting for about ten years (1947-57). He spent six years in a retreat in the Laurentians then he returned to Notre Dame in 1958. He started a workshop with a dozen serious art pupils in 1959 and after the next five years took only a few pupils (1964-65). From amongst his students came prominent painters like Jean-Paul Mousseau and Claude Vermette. In his own painting he has been very much influenced by Paul Emile Borduas who was a personal friend. Applying his media with a trowel and knife Paradis creates non-figurative canvases which have been described as having formidable power. His solo exhibitions include those at Librairie Menard, Mtl. (1962); Galerie Marthe Fontaine, Joliette (1963); Galerie Legault, St. Jérôme (1964); Galerie Le Crible, Longueuil (1965); Galerie Le Gobelet, Mtl. (1965-66); Galerie Bonsecours, Mtl. (1969) and his works have been included in group shows since 1935 including those at the

PARADIS, Frère Jérôme (Cont'd)

University of Charlottetown (1964); Place Ville Marie, Mtl. (1964-65); Galerie Jolliet, Que. (1965); Galerie de la Place Royale, Mtl. (1967); Hart House, Univ. Tor. (1967) and St. Edward's University, Texas, U.S.A. (1967). His paintings are in many private collections.

References
Photo-Journal, Mtl., P.Q., May 26, 1965 "Le Frère Jérôme – Trente ans sur la ligne de feu" par Jules Béliveau
Le Journal de Montreal, P.Q., 12 Nov., 1965 "Le frère Jérôme expose à la Galerie le Crible"
Montreal Metro-Express, P.Q., Nov. 16, 1965 "Visages de l'Art" par François Beaulieu
Le Journal de Montreal, 17 Nov., 1965 "Le Frère Jérôme à la galerie Le Crible"
Document from artist, 1969

PARAY, Michael
b. 1911

Born in Calgary, Alberta, he received his early education there then went on to study at the Federal School of Commercial Designing and Illustration at Minneapolis (1931) returning to Canada in 1933 to establish a permanent studio in Toronto. He travelled across Canada visiting cities and towns to make his pastel portraits, a tradition he has continued for many years while returning to his Toronto studio where he also carries out portraits on black velvet. He greatly admires the work of American painter Everitt Shinn who started out as a newspaper illustrator then became a member of the famous Eight (The Ash Can School) and later portrait painter. Paray was guest artist at the 83rd annual exhibition at the Armories, Prince Albert, Saskatchewan. Was living in Toronto in 1966.

Reference
Prince Albert Daily Herald, Sask., Aug. 15, 1966 "Ability To Work Before Crowd Requirements For Fair Artist" Lou Demerais

PARÉ, Alphonse

A renowned carver from Rivière-aux-Chiens near Ste. Anne de Beaupré, P.Q., who studied at the Ecole des Beaux-Arts, Quebec, and is known for his wood carvings in churches and public buildings. He did eight figures (20 inches tall) of traders and trappers carved out of butternut for the cocktail lounge of the Queen Elizabeth Hotel in Montreal, also carved a pine panel (14 x 7 ft.) for the grill-room of this same hotel. He has won prizes for his carvings in Quebec Government competitions.

References
L'Action Catholique, Que., P.Q., Jan. 28, 1950 "L'artiste et son oeuvre" (photo of Paré and his carving)
Star Weekly, Mar. 8, 1958 "French-Canadian in All but Name" by Fred McClement
Canadian Art, April, 1958, Vol. 15, No. 2 "Arts and Crafts In The Queen Elizabeth Hotel" by Robert Ayre, P. 101

PARÉ, Anne

b. 1938

Born in Quebec, P.Q., she graduated from the Ecole des Beaux-Arts, Quebec, in 1960, specializing in the making of tapestries although she is also known for her drawings and constructions on wood base. Both in 1963 and 1964 she won third prize in the Quebec provincial art competitions in the decorative arts division. She also took part in the show "Rythmes et Couleurs" at the Quebec Provincial Museum in 1966; showed a tapestry at the Canadian Pavilion at Expo '67; won the national competition "Perspectives 67" with a tapestry. Received grants from the Minister of Cultural Affairs, Quebec (1965) and the Canada Council (1966). She is represented in the permanent collections of the Musée d'Art Contemporain de Montreal; Musée du Québec; Government of Ontario; Confederation Art Gallery and Museum, Charlottetown. She held her first solo show of about twenty wool fabrics at the Zanettin Gallery, Quebec (1961) and subsequent shows at: Galerie Jolliet, Quebec (1968); La Maison des Arts La Sauvegarde (1968); Galerie d'Art de l'Université de Sherbrooke (1968).

References

Le Soleil, P.Q., Nov. 25, 1961 "Succès de la 'première' d'Anne Paré" par Paule France Dufaux

Ibid, 16 Nov., 1968 "Des études graphiques et cinétiques"

Le Messager Saint-Michel, Sherbrooke, Que., Nov. 30, 1968 "Exposition de Michel et Michèle Denis, céramistes de North-Hatley"

Sherbrooke La Tribune, P.Q., Nov. 30, 1968 "A la Galerie d'art – Trois jeunes artisans exposent"

Canadian Fine Crafts (catalogue) Can. Govt. Pavilion, Expo 67, Mtl., P. 40

L'Art Au Quebec Depuis 1940 par Guy Robert, La Presse, Mtl., 1973, P. 18, 150, 348, 350

PARÉ, Clement

b. 1918

Born at Deschambault, P.Q., he received his general education at the La Salle Academy in Trois Rivières, then entered the Ecole des Beaux-Arts, Quebec, where he studied the decorative arts specializing in sculpture. During his course he studied under Sylvia Daoust, Simone Hudon, Omer Parent, Marius Plamondon and Jean Paul Lemieux. He graduated from the Beaux-Arts in 1943 and the following year received his diploma in teaching drawing. He taught evening courses for the Beaux-Arts and children's art courses at Levis (1949); directed a course in biological drawing (1949); taught drawing to pre-med. students (1951); has taught drawing for the Faculty of Science at Laval University and taught modelling and drawing at the Ecole des Beaux-Arts, Quebec, since 1950. In his own sculpture he works in wood, stone and metal but uses mostly stone for public buildings. He often works at the St. Mark quarry where he cuts directly onto the stone. He prefers stone over most other media. Some of his work can be seen in the permanent collection of the Ecole des Beaux-Arts, Quebec and elsewhere as far south as Mexico. He is a member of the Sculptors' Society of Canada (1956, Sec. 1959-62, Pres. 1962 –); Sculptors' Association of Quebec (1962). Living at Ste-Foy, P.Q. in 1958.

PARÉ, Clement (Cont'd)

References
Newspaper clipping (unidentified) article by Y.T.
Biographical sheet from Sculptors' Assoc. of Quebec
NGC Info. Form rec'd July 19, 1958

PARÉ, Paul

Working mainly in sculpture with wood he is influenced by Brancousi, Rodin and ancient Egyptian art. His work has been described as having sensitivity and the feeling of nostalgia, optimism and a love of life and reveals his search for purity. Since 1968 he has shown his work at a number of places in the Province of Quebec including the Palais Montcalm (Quebec City), Maison Routhier and the Art Centre of Percé, the cultural and recreational centre of Rive-Sud (1971). He also participated in the folklore festival at Baie Saint-Paul (1971).

References
L'Evénement, Quebec, P.Q., Mar. 16, 1963 "Son violon d'Ingres"
Le Soleil, Quebec, P.Q., May 21, 1970 "Exposition" (photo of Paré's sculpture with caption)
L'Action, Quebec, P.Q., Oct. 8, 1971 "Rive droite . . . en bref" par Rénald Massicotte

PARENT, Louis Joseph
b. 1908
A highly esteemed Montreal sculptor who graduated from the Ecole des Beaux-Arts, Montreal (1932) and received a Certificate in Ceramic Chemistry, H.E.C., Mtl. (Chemistry 1939-40; Ceramic Clay and Glazes 1941-42; Ceramic Stoneware and Pottery 1942-43). Travelled to the United States where he received his Bachelor of Arts from Alfred University, New York (3 yr. course); Industrial Art studies at The Pennsylvania Museum School of Industrial Art (1935). During those years of study he received bursaries and awards which included: bronze medal from Ecole des Beaux Arts (1929); bursary from the Ministry of Commerce and Industry of Municipal Affairs, Quebec (1939) First Prize for his work at the Pennsylvania Museum School of Industrial Art (1935) and bursaries from The School of Arts and Crafts, Montreal (1941, 42, 43, 44), bursary from Notre-Dame, Indiana (1956). He was chosen as the sculptor to produce work for the 175,000 square feet shrine known as the "Way of the Cross" located on Mount Royal adjoining St. Joseph's Oratory. Each statue is 12 feet high and weighs 15 tons. Working in collaboration with Italian sculptor Hercolo Barbieri, he completed 16 "Stations of the Cross" by 1959. The original plan calls for 40 statues a project which is considered to be unparalleled in the Christian world. Parent has done considerable teaching during his career first for the Montreal School Commission, evenings (1932-35) and at the Ecole du Meuble (1951 —). No recent information. He was living in Montreal in 1959.

PARENT, Louis Joseph (Cont'd)

University of Charlottetown (1964); Place Ville Marie, Mtl. (1964-65); Galerie Jolliet, Que. (1965); Galerie de la Place Royale, Mtl. (1967); Hart House, Univ. Tor. (1967) and St. Edward's University, Texas, U.S.A. (1967). His paintings are in many private collections.

References

The Gazette, Mtl., P.Q., Jan. 10, 1946 "Gigantic Religious Work of Art Planned on Mount Royal Flanks" by Richard Daignault
The Standard, Mtl., P.Q., Mar. 9, 1946 (photo of the artist & work)
La Presse, Mtl., P.Q., Sept. 26, 1959 (photo of Parent's work with caption)
Le Nouvelliste, Trois Rivières, P.Q., Oct. 19, 1959 "Nouvelle série de cours sous la direction du sculpteur Parent, à la Grange-aux-Moines" par Gérard Marchand
Biographical information on file at NGC Library, 1957

PARENT, Louise

b. 1930

Born at St. Jerome, P.Q., she studied art under Alfred Pellan and Stanley Cosgrove at the Ecole des Beaux-Arts, Montreal, P.Q. and won a scholarship from the Société d'Études et de Conférences given by the French Government. She studied painting and child education in art also History of Art. A member of Société d'Etudes et de Conférences (Littérature) she was living in St. Jerome in 1953. No recent information.

Reference

NGC Info. Form rec'd May 26, 1953

PARENT, Michel

A Quebec City artist who was chosen from among a group of ten artists to enliven the exterior walls of three buildings in that city. This project was commissioned by Benson & Hedges and undertaken with the support of the city and the Quebec Provincial Museum. A teacher at the Ecole des Beaux-Arts, Quebec, he is also known for his paintings in which he has been influenced by artists like Kandinsky, Miro and Klee. Parent has exhibited his work a number of times including shows at the Zanettin Gallery, Quebec (1965) and the Quebec Provincial Museum, Quebec (1967). Some of his work shows pure fantasy and includes flowers, suns, houses; other pictures present a harmony of colour and form either geometric or baroque. He also produces works that have a diversity of materials including blocks of wood, and plastic.

References

Chronicle-Telegraph, Quebec, P.Q., Nov. 6, 1965 "Artist Does Not Shock Viewer, But Pleases Him"
Quebec L'Action, P.Q., Nov. 13, 1965 "Michel Parent: peindre pour appréhender le quotidien" par Jean Royer

PARENT, Michel (Cont'd)

Le Soleil, Quebec, P.Q., Nov. 9, 1965 "La peinture de Michel Parent, une expression intellectuelle" par Claude Daigneault
Chronicle-Telegraph, Quebec, P.Q., Dec. 1, 1967 "Students Out In Force At Exhibition Opening" by M.B.F. (to honour their teacher Michel Parent)
Le Soleil, Quebec, P.Q., Dec. 9, 1967 "Michel Parent: peindre, un jeu d'enfant" par Grazia Merler
Ibid, Dec. 9, 1967 "Une oeuvre déterminée par la composition" by G.M.
Quebec L'Action, P.Q., Dec. 16, 1967 "Au musée du Québec L'exposition de Michel Parent: La logique de l'image" par Jean Royer
Le Soleil, Quebec, P.Q., June 29, 1972 "Et les murs changeront de visage . . . "
L'Art Au Quebec Depuis 1940 par Guy Robert, La Presse, Mtl., P.Q., 1973, P. 432

PARENT, Mimi

b. 1924

Born in Montreal, P.Q., the daughter of architect Lucien Parent, she received her education at Sacred Heart Convent then enrolled in architecture at the Ecole des Beaux-Arts, Montreal. She took some courses with Alfred Pellan and found such new and exciting aspects in his teaching and work that she switched her studies to full time painting and etching. She won first prize for engraving from the Beaux-Arts in 1947 and the same year also won the Cézanne Medal awarded by the French Embassy. She became a member of the group Prisme D'Yeux headed by Pellan who opposed the then strict academicism of the Beaux-Arts. She participated in the 1948 exhibition of this group which included Louis Archambault, Leon Bellefleur, Jean Benoit, Jacques de Tonnancour, Albert Dumouchel, Gabriel Filion, Pierre Garneau, Arthur Gladu, Lucien Morin, Alfred Pellan, Jeanne Rheaume, Goodridge Roberts, Roland Truchon and Gordon Webber. She also participated in productions of Les Ateliers d'arts graphiques which included works of French Canadian poets, musicians and artists under the artistic direction of Albert Dumouchel and technical production of Arthur Gladu. She held her first solo show in the autumn of 1947 at the Dominion Gallery and *The Gazette* reviewer made the following comments, "In her drawings of which there are 31, Mimi Parent reveals a firm, expressive line and aptness in the placing of her subject. There are several nudes . . . and a number of portraits, including four of herself, all confidently set down with a minimum of means . . . . The engravings include besides a Madonna and Child, "Le nu au Zeppelin,' showing a reclining woman near a window through which can be seen an airship; two nude models resting, and a young girl seen against a curtained background. Her paintings include some colorful still lifes – fruit and chinaware playing their useful parts – and poppies and peonies have supplied the incentive for rich color, (the reviewer then noted two seascapes, self portraits and went on to note:) Nudes of ample form in gay colored settings also attract her, while greater grace marks 'Deux Japonaises,' which shows young women under parasols. Strong sunlight envelops the figures and incidentals in 'Le petit déjeuner' and 'Trois personnages sous le soleil," while lower tones mark 'Un coin de mon atelier' and 'L'heure du bain.' " May Ebbitt of *The Herald* noted, "Whether they liked it or not, art connoisseurs realized that Mimi Parent had something extraordinary. Anyone of her age, who, after painting for only four years, could produce work so striking in its seeming abandon to inspiration and its daring richness of color

PARENT, Mimi (Cont'd)

would be worth watching in the years ahead. As for Miss Parent, herself, she has the air of a woman who knows what she's doing and where she's going — despite her girlish looks and her volatile conversation." She held a second solo show of 33 drawings in 1948 at the Librairie Tranquille, Montreal, then she left for Paris where she became an important contributor to the Surrealist movement with the production of her creative objects, poetry and paintings, exhibiting her work in international surrealist exhibitions.

References
>The Gazette, Mtl., P.Q., Sept. 27, 1947 "Mimi Parent's Work Has Cheerful Color"
>The Standard, Mtl., P.Q., Sept. 27, 1947 "Girl Artist 23, Scores at One-man Exhibition" by Zoe Bieler
>The Herald, Mtl., P.Q., Oct. 4, 1947 "Young Montreal Artist Creates Sensation Here" by May Ebbitt
>The Citizen, Ottawa, Ont., Oct. 4, 1947 "Montreal Painter Would Rouse Canadian Artists"
>Catalogue-International Surrealist Exhibition, Spring 1961 directed by André Breton; managed by Jose Pierre and Tristan Sauvage (contains biographical material with comments by André Breton and Rodovan Ivsic)
>NGC Info. Form rec'd Oct. 22, 1947
>Canadian Art by Graham McInnes, Macmillan, Tor., 1950, P. 90
>L'Art Au Quebec depuis 1940 par Guy Robert, La Presse, Mtl., P.Q., P. 66, 206, 207, 312

PARENT, Murielle

b. 1945

A Montreal, P.Q., artist who is a graduate of the Ecole des Beaux-Arts of Quebec where she won the Lieutenant-Governor's Medal and first prize in painting. She has been working in acrylics and applying an air brush technique in many of her canvases. In her work she strikes at the established values of our society and political conscience is apparent in her paintings. Reviewing her show at Gallery III in Old Montreal, Catherine Bates of *The Montreal Star* noted, "Sometimes quality shows through best in a small exhibition. Certainly the ten canvases at Gallery III . . . are quite sufficient to mark Murielle Parent as one of the young talents to watch." She held her first major exhibition at the Centre Culturel Canadien in Paris.

References
>Le Devoir, Mtl., P.Q., Feb. 2, 1973 (note in Galerie III show)
>La Presse, Mtl., P.Q., Feb. 17, 1973 "Le retour de l'homme" (Galerie III show)
>The Montreal Star, P.Q., Feb. 24, 1973 "Small successes — Gallery III, Murielle Parent" by Catherine Bates

PARENT, Omer

b. 1907

Born in Quebec, P.Q., he attended the Quebec Beaux-Arts; the National School of Decorative Arts, Paris and the René Vincent Workshop, Paris (1926). He had gone to Paris with his friend Alfred Pellan. Returning to Canada he had a studio in Montreal for a year (1928-29); became head decorator for Henry Morgan Stores, Mtl.

PARENT Omer (Cont'd)

(1929-36); teacher of drawing, decorative art and commercial art (advanced courses) at the Ecole des Beaux-Arts, Que. (1939-49); Director of Studies at the Beaux-Arts, Que. (1949-64) and taught drawing and commercial photography there; was a collaborator in the taking of inventory of works of art for the Province of Quebec (1943-54); professor of drawing for the Faculty of Science at Laval University (1943-47); President of the Committee of Education and the Arts of Quebec Provincial Exhibition (1951); Secretary of the Canadian Conference of the Arts (1958); Assistant Principal, Ecole des Beaux-Arts, Que. (1959). He was appointed Officer of the Order of Canada in 1971. In his own painting he is conscious of relief and colour, painting in a fluid manner, giving the effect of an optical illusion like crumpled paper. He has done considerable work in the "Op" art line beginning with colour bars that produce a visual sensation of movement. In the last few years his works have been three dimensional in nature as in his murals at the Science Pavilion of Laval University (three murals in this Pavilion) he has also done murals for the Chapel de l'Hotel Dieu de Chicoutimi; Faculty of Commerce, Laval University. His paintings have been exhibited at the Musée du Québec (1966) and Galerie Jolliet (1969) in solo show and the following group shows: "Rythmes et couleurs", Musée du Québec (1966); "Cinq Peintres du Québec", Maritime Provinces (1966); "Vingt-cinq ans de libération", Musée du Québec (1967); Centre d'Art, Ile d'Orléans (1967); Orly, France (1967); Festival de Québec (1968); "Sondage" (1968), Musée des Beaux-Arts, Mtl.; Concours de la Province, Que., Musée d'Art contemporain, Mtl. (1969); Osaka, Quebec Pavilion (1970); two-man show with Henry Saxe at Laval University, Que. (1972); "Québec 74" Musée d'Art contemporain, Mtl. (1974). He is represented in the Musée du Québec and Musée d'Art contemporain and in many private collections. He is also represented in The Canada Council Art Bank.

References

Le Soleil, Que., P.Q., Aug. 20, 1966 "La première exposition d'Omer Parent" par Claude Daigneault

L'Evénement, Que., P.Q., Sept. 8, 1966 "Première Exposition de la Saison" (photo and caption)

Panorama de la Peinture Au Québec 1940-1966, Musée d'Art contemporain, Mtl., 1967, P. 38

L'Information médicale et paramédicale, Mtl., P.Q., Nov. 1969 "Omer Parent et les jeux de la couleur" par Paul Dumas

Quebec 74, Musée d'Art contemp. Mtl., 1974 (see Omer Parent)

L'Art Au Québec depuis 1940 par Guy Robert, La Presse, Mtl., 1973, P. 153

NGC Info. Form

PARIS, François

A graphic artist who showed his ink drawings at Galerie de L'Etable (works from the CIL choice); exhibited as well in Montreal at the Square des Arts and the Centre d'Art. He opened his own gallery in Montreal in two rooms of the former study of Sir Georges Etienne Cartier.

PARIS, François (Cont'd)

Reference

Photo-Journal, Mtl., P.Q., June 29, 1966 "L'étude de Cartier devient une galerie" par Michelle Tisseyre (photo of artist with his work)

PARKER, Gretchen
b. (c) 1915

Born in Montreal, P.Q., she studied at the Ecole des Beaux-Arts there then moved into the field of designing women's clothes and in the 1950's lived in various cities in the United States (Kansas City, Minneapolis, and Chicago). She has also travelled to London, England, and Majorca. She is known for her portraits in pastels, water colours and oils, and has done thousands of them. She has been described as having the unique ability to capture amazing likenesses even when portraying children. She was living in Beaconsfield (just outside Montreal) in 1973.

References

Weekly Post, Town of Mount Royal, P.Q., June 1, 1967 "Painting of a Town Resident by Distinguished Former Townite"

The Gazette, Mtl., P.Q., April 18, 1973 "Quebec Women – Artist's world always smiles" by Adrian Waller

PARKER, Harley Walter Blait
b. 1915

Born in Fort William, Ontario, he attended the Ontario College of Art where he studied under Franklin Carmichael and John Alfsen. After graduation he worked for the firm of Cooper and Beatty, designers, also Eaton's and during World War II he served in the camouflage section of the Canadian army. Following the war he attended Black Mountain College in North Carolina where he studied under painter, photographer and typographer Josef Albers who was an important pioneer in experimental design teaching. Returning to Canada he joined the staff of the Ontario College of Art in 1945 where he taught water colour painting for many years and then design. In 1957 he joined the staff of the Royal Ontario Museum where he became display chief for the Division of Art and Archeology. In 1958 with a Canada Council grant he took a two months' tour of Europe to study advanced display techniques in several museums. Returning home he set to work on a programme of modifying various displays, and creating others for the Royal Ontario Museum including the invertebrate paleontology gallery opened in 1967. Parker was also design consultant for Expo '67. Member of the Canadian Society of Graphic Art (1941; Vice-Pres. 1945, Sec. 1954, Pres. 1955-56). Lives in Toronto.

References

Globe & Mail, Tor., Ont., June 14, 1958 "Artist to Study Display Methods"

Barrie Examiner, Barrie, Ont., Apr. 29, 1964 "Design Expert To Speak Here Tomorrow Night"

The Telegram, Tor., Ont., Sat., Jan. 21, 1967 "The McLuhan Of The Museum" by Paul Grescoe

Time Magazine, Tor., Ont., Feb. 3, 1967 "Ontario – Multisensory Museum" P. 16

NGC Info. Forms Rec'd April 20, 1954; Dec. 29, 1955

PARKER, Jessie Cecilia

b. 1891

Born in Courtland, Ontario, she studied under Marion Long in Toronto. In 1912 she moved to Winnipeg, Manitoba, when she married lawyer Benjamin C. Parker. She studied evenings at the University of Manitoba School of Art; under W.J. Phillips; two winters at San Miguel Allende, Mexico; Old Mill Art School, Elizabethtown, N.Y.; the Positano Art School, Italy, also under Elliott O'Hara, Walter Colbrooke and Stanley Turnbull (portrait artist). Influenced by the French Impressionists she works in the media of oil, casein, water colours for her portraits and landscapes. She has also done a limited amount of mosaic work. She took a painting tour of Spain and southern France. During the 1930's and 40's she had a studio in her own home where a group of artists sketched regularly. Her work has been exhibited in Winnipeg and Montreal. She was a member of the Winnipeg Sketch Club for thirty-one years (1924-44; 1953-63) and served as secretary (two years) and was on the council (twelve years). A landscape she did in Mexico was exhibited in the Manitoba Centennial show "150 Years of Art In Manitoba" (1970). Living in Winnipeg in 1970.

References

NGC Info. Forms rec'd Oct. 20, 1958; Mar. 29, 1962
Winnipeg Sketch Club, A Brief History of The Winnipeg Sketch Club by Madeline Perry; research by Lily Hobbs, 1970
150 Years of Art in Manitoba, An exhibition for the Manitoba Centennial 1970, Winnipeg Art Gallery, Winnipeg, Man., 1970, P. 96
Document from artist, 1963

PARKER, Jessie Maretta

b. 1943

Born in Prince Edward Island, the daughter of Rev. James and Mrs. Parker of Windsor, N.S., she was educated in Wolfville and Sackville, N.B. She studied art at Mount Allison University under Alex Colville, Lawren Harris, Jr. and David Silverberg graduating in 1965 with her B.F.A. During her studies she received scholarships, bursaries and awards from Mount Allison University. She spent seven months painting in London, England and travelled widely throughout Europe. She has held solo shows at Windsor (1966); Dartmouth Heritage Museum (1969); Zwicker's Gallery, Halifax (1969); Miners' Museum, Glace Bay (1973); Can. Forces Base, Greenwood (1973) and the Arts & Culture Museum, Lunenburg (1973). Viewing her show at Zwicker's Gallery, Gretchen Pierce in the Halifax *Mail-Star* noted, "Her paintings, drawings and graphics . . . are largely based on the concept of nature. She went through several periods in her work from the realistic to abstract but now they are 'figurative visionaries.' By this she means that if people are not used in her work, then allusions to them, the state of society or the human condition are used. Visionary to her means the interpretation of ideas, and not using things in their normal perspective." She works in a wide variety of media including copal oil glazes; acrylics; oils; enamels, gilt; ink; water colour; monoprints, itaglio; serigraph; and woodcuts. She has won a number of prizes for her work including: an award at the Mount Saint Vincent College International Exhibition, Halifax (1969); First Prize, Contemporary Division at the Valley Art Association 13th Annual

PARKER, Jessie Maretta (Cont'd)

Exhibition, Bridgetown, N.S. (1969). She has been teaching art to grades 10, 11 and 12 at Colonel Gray High School, Charlottetown and also doing free lance photography in 1973.

References
Mail-Star, Halifax, N.S., Jan. 21, 1969 "Art For Art's Sake – Nothing Else Will Do Her" by Gretchen Pierce
Chronicle Herald, Halifax, N.S., Aug. 27, 1969 "Wins Award" (Mount Saint Vincent College Gallery Show)
Wolfville Acadian, N.S. Sept. 26, 1969 "Jessie Parker Wins Top Art Award"
Mail-Star, Halifax, N.S., Oct. 28, 1969 "Windsor Artist To Exhibit"
Acadian, Wolfville, N.S. Nov. 21, 1969 "Windsor Woman's Paintings Displayed At Heritage Museum"
Mail-Star, Halifax, N.S., Nov. 5, 1969 "Painter Gives Messages" by Clyde Horner
Free Press, Dartmouth, N.S., Nov. 5, 1969 "Anger and violence in this art show" by Mona Mitchell Maund
Ibid, Nov. 20, 1969 "Free Press review stirs some controversy"
Chronicle-Herald, Halifax, N.S., July 2, 1973 "One-man art shows by Windsor artist"

PARKER, John Frederick Delisle (Palette)
1884-1962
Born in New York City and arriving in England at the age of nine, he was educated in English schools. His family had moved there when his father was appointed American Consul in Birmingham. The consular jurisdiction included Stratford-on-Avon and his father became active in cultural activity of the community and was even elected president of the Shakespeare Society in Birmingham. Opportunities were afforded young John to attend the theatre and meet well-known actors and Shakespearean scholars, an experience which served him well throughout his life in his cultural pursuits. Later while in London on newspaper work he studied evenings at the Croydon Art School. Next he spent five years in Paris at the Ecole des Beaux-Arts; the Sorbonne; the Académie Julian where he did painting under Professor Jean Paul Laurens, and the Académie Grande Chaumière under Théophile-Alexandre Steinlen. At the Julian he came in contact with a lively group of students that included the gifted artist André Dunoyer de Segonzac later to become known for the transparent qualities he strove for in his paintings. Segonzac and Parker corresponded for years afterwards. He studied painting as well in United States under Robert Henri in New York City also sculpture, and had a studio at 1931 Broadway. In this medium he created the bronze head of British actor Sir Johnston Forbes-Robertson in the role of Shylock and the work became the property of the actor. Parker was active in art circles and exhibited his work with several well-known artists' clubs. His interest in American revolutionary history led to his paintings of events during their struggle for independence and four of his oils were acquired for the Valley Forge Museum of American History. As a keen student and writer of history, a number of his paintings were depictions of people and events of the past. Several of his paintings on Canadian history were used as illustrations for his articles appearing in the *McGill News* between 1931 and 1934. He also wrote, acted in and directed several plays. He travelled widely in Europe,

PARKER, John Frederick Delisle (Palette) (Cont'd)

Manila, Asia, North Africa (went into the desert on camel back with the desert patrol) and the East and West coasts of United States (Florida & California); the West Coast of Canada on lengthy visits as well as across Canada. But for almost a decade he lived in Paris (1926-34) where his fluency in French made it possible for him to participate fully in the rich cultural life of that great city. He painted portraits, colourful street scenes, the Seine and its quays and bridges, old churches and historic mansions. In 1931 his illustrations appeared in a de luxe edition of François Villon's poems to celebrate the 500th anniversary of the poet's birth. Villon had received his Bachelor's and Master's degrees from the Sorbonne in the mid 1400's and was greatly admired for his skill as a poet. He was widely celebrated by the 19th Century romantic writers. The book entitled *Oeuvres de François Villon* was produced in a limited edition of 333 copies and received warm praise by the noted scholar Emile Magne who felt that Parker had adapted himself admirably to his function as illustrator. To produce the illustrations (eight full-page in colour, 34 black and white drawings) Parker studied intensely the records and the history of 15th Century France to make his work historically accurate and blended this information with his fine creative imagination. The Vancouver and Victoria Public Libraries have copies of this book. When he took his trip to North Africa in the 1920's he did many water colours in Tunisia including studies of the French colonial army (Spahis, Senegalese and Foreign Legion) by permission of the French government and produced sixty pictures which were shown in 1931 at the Colonial Exhibition in Paris at the Pavilion of the Overseas Forces of the French Army. He was back in Canada in 1934 this time to live permanently in Vancouver. He accompanied his sister-in-law Mrs. Charles H. Parker and Dorothy Dallas on a visit to Emily Carr's studio on August 27th of that year and on August 30th Emily wrote in her diary how Mr. Parker humourously felt that she could hold her own as a painter anywhere. And she noted how Mr. Parker had left her studio inspired to work at his own painting. As early as 1927 he had advised his sister-in-law to purchase Emily's paintings. A one-man show of his work took place at the Vancouver Art Gallery also in 1937. In 1941 he became a member of the B.C. Society of Artists and in 1946 and 1947 was on the executive. His canvas "The Old Carr House, Victoria" shown in the society's annual show was purchased for the permanent collection of the Vancouver Art Gallery in 1946. From 1941 to 1958 he was a faithful contributor to the B.C. Society of Artists annual showings. Then in 1958 his painting and writing activity was curtailed because of failing health. For 18 years he had contributed a regular art column to *The Vancouver Province* (1940-59) under the pseudonym of "Palette" providing most valuable accounts of West Coast art activity. Throughout those years he continued to paint when time permitted. His early work was signed John Parker, then John F. Parker and after the 1930's, J. Delisle Parker. On the occasion of his 1951 show at The Vancouver Art Gallery, Lawren Harris in the forward for the exhibition folder noted, "He has ever been the one knowledgeable and perceptive writer on art who has always detected, acclaimed and encouraged vital new talent in this province and yet he himself remains almost unknown. It is indeed time that the public became aware of his work for it has creative virtues of rare quality. Delisle Parker is a poet in paint. In addition to this his paintings have an admirable, rich paint quality, are highly organized and embody an imagination and sensitive perception of whatever he paints. Whether it be city scenes, the Fraser Canyon, the Cariboo country or

PARKER, John Frederick Delisle (Palette) (Cont'd)

Indian legends his paintings possess a poet's vision of unusual distinction." Other showings of his work included one at Eaton's in Toronto (1945) and showings of his Tunisian paintings in Vancouver (1943) and a smaller showing for Lord Alexander of Tunis (c. 1946); a group show at the UBC Library and showings in the Studio Shop and the Lambert Studio in Vancouver. Parker died on September 28, 1962 at the age of seventy-eight. Dorothy Dallas of Vancouver (Professor Emeritus of French, UBC) acted as Executor for his estate. Parker is represented in the following collections: Vancouver Art Gallery; University of British Columbia; Officers' Mess, Defence College, Kingston, Ont.; Valley Forge Museum of American History, Valley Forge, P.A.; The City of Odessa, Ukraine and in many private collections in United States, Canada and elsewhere.

References

Letter from Dorothy Dallas with enclosed biographical profile on J. Delisle Parker by Miss Dallas and Mrs. W. Kaye Lamb (Sept. 14, 1974)

McGill News, December, 1931, No. 1 "Carignan-Salières Regiment" (The First Military Organization in Canadian History) by J. Delisle Parker, P. 23-28, 38

Ibid, September, 1932, No. 4 "Karrer Regiment" P. 41-46 by J. Delisle Parker

Ibid, December, 1932, No. 1 "An Artist's Wanderings in Tunisia" by J. Delisle Parker (with illustrations by the author)

Ibid, September, 1933 "Frontenac: Why No Authentic Portrait of Him Exists" by J. Delisle Parker (with two illustrations painted by author)

Ibid, June, 1934 "Jacques Cartier – The Pioneer In North American Exploration" by J. Delisle Parker

Victoria Times, B.C., Mar. 15, 1943 "Artist On Visit Here"

Vancouver Province, B.C., Dec. 6, 1946 (Parker's canvas "The Old Carr House, Victoria" purchased by Van. Art Gal.)

Canadian Art, Spring, 1949 (reproduction of his "Fishing Village")

Vancouver Province (Magazine Section) Sat., Feb. 24, 1951 " 'Palette's' Paintings" by Stella Creese

Ibid, April 3, 1951 "In The Realm Of Art – 'Guest' Reviews Palette's Show" by Hunter Lewis (photo of Parker with his work)

Exhibition folder by Van. Art Gal., April 3 through April 22nd, 1951 with list of 43 paintings and notes on artist by Lawren Harris

The Province, Van., B.C., Aug. 26, 1953 "Palette Exhibit – Paintings Capture Life Of Far-Away Places" by D.O.L.

NGC Info. Form rec'd June 6, 1947

Hundreds and Thousands, The Journals of Emily Carr, Clarke, Irwin & Co. Ltd., Tor./Van., 1966 "Hopes and Doldrums" Aug. 30th 1934-35, P. 144

Oeuvres de François Villon, Illustrées par John Delisle Parker, Paris, J. Bernard, 1931 (316p. ill. – Victoria Public Lib. R 841.2 V759)

PARKER, Lewis

b. (c) 1927

Born in Toronto, Ontario, in school he made cartoons with a fountain pen on the arms of his chums for a nickel a drawing. He became interested in Indians and read books about them. He felt that they deserved more understanding than was generally given them. Later he worked as an apprentice artist for a Toronto firm during the 1940's and received friendly criticism from Bert Grassick who was a political cartoonist for *Maclean's*. Over the years Parker worked at book illustra-

PARKER, Lewis (Cont'd)

tion, commercial art and political cartooning. He has been illustrator and cartoonist for *Maclean's* for a good number of years. During World War II he was staff cartoonist in Holland for the Canadian Army paper *The Maple Leaf*. In recent years he has spent more time with his great interest in depicting the positive aspects of Indian life. In 1968 he was awarded a Canada Council grant to paint the Indians of Mexico and after returning home he received a commission to illustrate Huron Indian life for the reconstructed fort Sainte-Marie Among The Hurons, near Midland, Ontario, a project under the direction of Vernon Mould who commissioned Parker for the illustrations. Parker ended up doing thirty-six paintings for the fort and the project had grown to such proportions that he had to enlist the assistance of an artist partner, Gerald Lazare, in order to complete several of the paintings on time. He also became so obsessed with the accuracy of his work that he made sure every farm implement, ceremonial mask, canoe design and other objects were reproduced as close to the likeness of the original 17th Century details as possible. Much of his information for this project came from Jesuit writings. His ambition is to paint the lives of every Indian nation in North America. Parker has several interests beyond his art including photography, jazz piano and has a large collection of tape-recorded music. He lives in Toronto with his wife Eleanor and their four children.

References
   Maclean's Magazine, January 18, 1958 "In The Editors' Confidence – Some cannibalism among our caricaturists" (photo of MacPherson and Parker drawing each other and the results, also a few notes about each)
   Ibid, February, 1965 No. 78, P. 32 "In The Editors' Confidence" (photo of Parker and mention of him restoring an old dwelling for his home, and biographical notes about himself)
   The Canadian Magazine, May 15, 1971 "The Day Of The Hurons" Paintings by Lewis Parker (with biographical notes about the artist)
   Flame Power by Peter C. Newman, Longmans, Green & Co., Tor., 1959 (drawings by Lewis Parker)
   see also back issues of *Maclean's* for his illustrations and cartoons
   numerous other books

PARKER, William W.

b. (c) 1894

An Edmonton, Alberta, painter who was first a pioneer farmer in the Edmonton district. Then he taught English and composition in schools for over forty years. He also wrote two books of poetry and several novels including *Bush Homestead Girl*. During the 1920's and 30's he was a reporter for *The Edmonton Journal*. He took up serious painting around 1961 and in 1967 exhibited two hundred oil and pastel paintings at St. Martin's Separate School in Edmonton. He won prizes in provincial fairs for his portraits and landscapes. Parker has also conducted classes in painting for beginners at St. Martin's. He has produced as well inlaid bowls, plates, lamps and other craft projects.

References
   The Edmonton Journal, Alta., Sept. 8, 1964 "Ex-Teacher Turns To New Career"
   Ibid, Dec. 18, 1967 "St. Martin's Pupils View Paintings Of Early West"

PARKER, William (Wishdea)
b. (c) 1905

An Ojibway Indian from Woodville, Ontario, who was a woodsman and builder for many years until ill health forced him to retire. He turned to making clay pottery and pipes using the techniques of his ancestors which he had learned as a boy living on the Hiawatha Indian Reserve. Working within the restored fort of Sainte-Marie-Among-The-Hurons near Midland, Ontario, he has been the centre of attraction for thousands of visitors. Over the years he gathered pieces of original pottery from ancient Indian village sites in Ontario and from the curves of these pieces was able to estimate the dimensions of complete units of pottery. The replicas he has produced have been so exact that they have astounded archaeologists and historians alike. Parker ground various types of stone to duplicate the mixture of stone and clay the ancient Indians used. His work bench is a split cedar log and his tools are those awls and scribes of animal bone and deer hooves used in centuries past. Some of the tools are the original ones found at the site of old villages while others have been crafted by him on the spot. His Indian name is Wishdea which means one who works with fire.

References
    Barrie Banner, Ont., Aug. 27, 1969 "Ojibway Indian brings art to Sainte-Marie"
    Woodstock-Ingersoll Sentinel-Review, Ont., Aug. 13, 1969 "Indian pottery gains new life"

PARKINSON, Cathy (née Marguerite Muirhead)

Born in Regina, Saskatchewan, she graduated from the University of Saskatchewan in 1962 with a B.A. in geology (paleontology) then spent a year with the Geological Survey of Canada. She studied for a number of years under Ernest Lindner in Saskatoon then moved to Ottawa about 1964 and in 1968 enrolled at the Ottawa Municipal Art Centre where she studied under artists Victor Tolgesy, Art Price, Madja Van Dam and John Sadler. In 1972 she was appointed a full-time on-the-site liaison officer for the centre. Her other interests include reading, bird watching, music, dancing and yoga. In her home she enjoys a small collection of art works. She has travelled extensively in connection with the visual arts, attending exhibitions and conferences and is a member of the Canadian Conference of the Arts and an associate member of the Canadian Artists' Representation (Ontario Division). Mother of two children she shares many of her own interests with them.

Reference
    The Ottawa Journal, Ont., Oct. 12, 1974 "Faces of Ottawa — Cathy Parkinson" by W.Q. Ketchum

PARKINSON, Patricia Anne (Pat Parkinson)
b. 1938

Born in London, England, the daughter of Nora and Frederick E. Cleary she studied at the Regent Street Polytechnic, London, England (1958-62); Chelsea Art College, London, England (1964) under artists Lawrence Gowing, Norman Blamey, Edward

PARKINSON, Patricia Anne (Pat Parkinson) (Cont'd)

Middleditch and Leon Kossoff and received her National Diploma in Design. She also taught art part-time in a secondary school in London and for a youth club evenings in east London. She married Dr. David K. Parkinson in 1964. They came to Canada with their three children in 1968. Between 1964 and 1971 she put her art aside to care for her children but in 1970 found time for a printmaking course. Her exhibitions include "Young Contemporaries" (juried show), London, Eng. (1961); Bradford City Art Gallery (group show, 1962); Whitechapel Art Gallery (group show, 1963); "Open Studio" (group show, 1971), Edward Johnson Bldg., Tor.; Women's Festival, St. Michael's College, Tor. (1972); Artists' Co-op (opening show), Richmond St., Tor. (1972); Canadian Imperial Bank of Commerce, Bloor St., Tor. (1972); "Open Studio" (group show) Morris Gallery, Tor. (1973), solo show, Metropolitan Central Library, Tor. (summer, 1973). She is a member of the Canadian Artists' Representation (Ontario). Lives in Toronto, Ont.

Reference
NGC Info. Form rec'd June, 1973

PARLANE, William George

b. 1914

Born in Prince George, B.C., at the age of twelve he won First Prize for a map he created in water colours. Although mainly self-taught he attended Saturday morning classes at the Art Gallery of Toronto under J.E.H. MacDonald. As he continued his own art studies he was influenced by Canadian artists Fred Brigden, A.J. Casson and Herbert Palmer. He became a freelance artist and among his projects are designs for Canadian Christmas T.B. Seals, maps for Pierre Berton's *The Mysterious North* (1956) and illustrations for Farley Mowat's *Canada North* (1967). In the early 1970's he began spending more time on his landscape painting mainly in water colours also some acrylics. He has already held three one-man shows at the Gibson House Gallery in Willowdale, Ontario.

References
The Mysterious North by Pierre Berton, McLelland & Stewart, 1956
Canada North by Farley Mowat, McLelland & Stewart, 1967
Evening Times Globe, Saint John, N.B., Nov. 13, 1969 (note on his designs for Christmas seals)
Simcoe Reformer, Ont., Nov. 20, 1969 "In Ontario – Christmas Seals Unique Design"
Digby Courier, N.S., No. 20, 1969 "Christmas Seal Artist"
Document from artist, December, 1976

PARLEY, Kay

She exhibited with the annual all-Saskatchewan art shows sponsored by the Saskatchewan Arts Board. In 1951 A.Y. Jackson, on his way home from the Northwest Territories, purchased her painting "Bonspiel" when he viewed it on exhibit in Regina. Ms. Parley is from Weyburn.

Reference
Leader-Post, Regina, Sask., Dec. 21, 1951 "Weyburn artist sells painting"

PARR

An Eskimo hunter of the Kingnimuit (of Cape Dorset) people who after spending most of his life struggling for survival against the harsh environment of the Arctic settled in the Cape Dorset area. He had great moments in his life too as a successful hunter and Kayakman. No longer capable of hunting because of his age he turned to making drawings and prints based on his lifetime experiences. The Western Baffin Eskimo Co-operative produced thirty-three of his prints between the years 1961 and 1970. Parr was one of the first Eskimo artists to experiment with the technique of etching. Avrom Isaacs, interested in Eskimo art for many years, noted Parr as follows, "Through this project (Cape Dorset Co-op) he was able to spend the last years of his life recreating on paper the most dramatic and meaningful recollections of his past. His drawings depict the earlier days before the Eskimo was completely reliant on the white man. Since it was only natural to draw what was most important to him, almost all of his work depicted the hunt. The drawings teem with caribou, seals, walrus, etc. They are loose, rough drawings in which the action constantly threatens to run off the page . . . They are history and reveal a life style that has already passed." Showings of Parr's work include those at The Art Shop of The Montreal Museum of Fine Arts; The Simon Fraser Univ. Gallery, B.C. and a travelling show organized and circulated by the National Gallery of Canada in cooperation with The Canadian Eskimo Art Committee (1967).

References
> *Canadian Art*, Jan./Feb. 1965 Issue No. 95 "Eskimo Pencil Drawings: A Neglected Art" by Terrence Ryan, P. 30 (Parr ill. on P. 34)
> *Eskimo Graphic Art, 1966*, West Baffin Island Co-op, Cape Dorset/Arctic Prod. Ltd., Ottawa, Nos. 1, 2 & 3
> *Eskimo Prints* by James A. Houston, Barre Publishers, Mass., 1967, P. 88-90
> *Cape Dorset*, exhibition catalogue, show organized and circulated by NGC in cooperation with The Can. Eskimo Art Committee (Prints 37-40)
> *Eskimo Graphic Art, 1969*, Can. Arctic Prod. Ltd., Ottawa, Nos. 19, 20
> *Artscanada*, December 1971/January 1972 "The Eskimo World" (special issue) "Continuities in Eskimo graphic style" by Joan M. Vastokas P. 68 (ill. by Parr on P. 72, 75, 76)
> Exhibition folder, The Art Shop of The Montreal Museum of Fine Arts, text by Avrom Isaacs
> Exhibition sheet, The Simon Fraser Gallery, Simon Fraser Univ. (biographical)
> Notes
> Early Eskimo prints were limited to thirty copies
> Later prints were done in fifty copies then the original device (stone block, stencil or plate) was destroyed

---

PARRIS, Mary (Mrs. J.E.)

b. 1914

Born in Edmonton, Alberta, she had painted for many years but took no formal training until the opening of the art department at the University of Alberta around 1944. She also took extension classes at the Banff School of Fine Arts in 1957 and attended workshops in 1959 and 1960. She did mostly landscapes and some figure and still life studies in water colours before turning to abstract painting in the medium of liquitex (similar to casein). She has taught water colour painting classes at the Edmonton Art Gallery. When viewing her work in 1962 Clement Greenberg referred to her "originality of feeling." A member of the Edmonton Art Club and the Alberta Society of Artists she lives in Edmonton.

PARRIS, Mary (Mrs. J.E.) (Cont'd)

Reference
Document from artist, 1961
Canadian Art, Vol. 20, No. 2, 1962 "Clement Greenberg's View Of Art On The Prairies" by C.G., P. 102

PARSONS, (William) Bruce
b. 1937

Born in Montreal, P.Q., he received his education at Loyola High School for Junior Matriculation (1950-54) and Loyola College for equivalent to Senior Matriculation (1954-56). He then attended Sir George Williams College, Montreal, evenings to study commercial design while working days for Hinde and Dauche Paper Company as artist and designer (1956-57). He continued his art education at the Ontario College of Art, Toronto, in 1957, where he studied painting under J.W.G. Mac-Donald and graphics under F. Hagen, receiving the O'Keefe Scholarship (1958) and the Lieutenant Governor General's (sic) Medal (1961) graduating in Drawing and Painting. He travelled in Europe during 1962 for seven months visiting London, Paris, Madrid, Rome, Florence and he painted and sketched on the Balearic Islands off the coast of Spain in the Mediterranean. In 1962 he was appointed Curator and Co-ordinator of Group Activities for the Regina Public Library and was responsible for organizing the exhibition programme for Regina's civic gallery. During 1963 and 1964 he attended University of Saskatchewan's Emma Lake Workshop and the Regina Campus sessions conducted by Kenneth Noland (1963) and Jules Olitski (1964). Also in 1964 he attended a Western Canada Art Circuit conference in Winnipeg and visited several artists' studios and public galleries. In the same year he was elected representative for Saskatchewan to the Co-ordinating Committee of the Western Canada Art Circuit. In 1966 he was successful in receiving a Canada Council award to enable him to devote full time to painting. His solo shows followed in 1967 at the Bonli Gallery, and at the Regina Public Library where he showed paintings and drawings which Nancy Gelber described as follows, "All drawings and most of the canvases come from his Rose Series painted since 1965. Mr. Parsons' 'flowers' look like clouds or puffs of smoke and their stems resemble hockey sticks, pipes and forwards and backward Ls. Often he's painted more than one rose to a stem. Color schemes which ought to clash, don't. Brown, green, bright blue and pink seems perfectly comfortable beside each other in an orange background. One striking portrait presents an orange rose with a yellow stem floating in a deep purple background. His lines are plain and uncluttered, made strong by the background." He held subsequent shows at the Regina Public Library (1968); Centennial Gallery, Halifax (1970); Galerie III, Place Bonaventure, Mtl. (1973); Canadian Consulate General, NYC (1974) and in the following group shows: The Ohio Invitational Show (1964); Montreal Spring Show (1964); Sixth Biennial Exhibition of Canadian Painting (1965). More recently he has become interested in the production of conceptual art through a variety of things like time sequences in the growth and ripening of fruit with each stage presented in juxtaposition with the other; the ripening and dehydrating action of apples; colour sequences in the ripening of bananas and other areas as in his video tape project on family resemblances found in a small Newfoundland community. Describing

PARSONS, (William) Bruce (Cont'd)

Parsons' work in 1973 Virginia Nixon of *The Gazette* noted, "His method is typical of the conceptual artist, who begins by carrying out a project — usually one involving time and space ranges too broad to permit exhibitions per se — and then presents to the public the written, photographic, videotape, or other records he has made about his project." He is represented in the Canada Council Collection, the Art Bank and a number of other collections. Teacher of painting at the Nova Scotia College of Art and Design, Halifax (1973).

References
> *Edmonton Journal*, Alta., June 8, 1963 "Focus Gallery Show Features City Artist" by Dorothy Barnhouse
> *Regina Leader-Post*, Sask., Sat., June 19, 1965 "Parsons art exhibition has rich use of color"
> *Sixth Biennial Exhibition of Canadian Painting, 1965*, NGC, Ottawa
> *Regina Leader-Post*, Aug. 16, 1966 "Local artists claim awards" (Can. Council grant)
> *The Toronto Telegram*, Tor., Ont., Feb. 7, 1967 "Art" by Barrie Hale
> *Regina Leader-Post*, Sask., Apr. 3, 1967 "Regina artist sells 20 paintings opening night" by Nancy Gelber
> *The Canada Council Collection – A travelling exhibition of the NGC, Ottawa, 1969*
> *Canadian Art Today*, Ed. William Townsend, Studio International, London, Eng., 1970 "Memories of Saskatchewan" by Andrew Hudson, P. 49, 51
> Regina Public Library release, Regina, Sask. 1968
> *Halifax Mail-Star*, N.S., July 4, 1970 "Poetry doesn't balance gallery guest book"
> *The Montreal Star*, P.Q., Dec. 1, 1973 "Gallery III, Bruce Parsons" by Catherine Bates
> *The Gazette*, Mtl., P.Q., Nov. 14, 1973 "When is non-art art? – When it's Conceptual Art(!)" by Virginia Nixon
> Curriculum Vitae, William Bruce Parsons, January, 1966 (see NGC Lib. File)
> NGC Info. Form (c) 1964

PARSONS, Helen Somerton (Mrs. Reginald Shepherd)
b. 1923

Born at St. John's Newfoundland, she studied at the Ontario College of Art in Toronto under John Alfsen, Manley MacDonald, George Pepper and Gustav Hahn and graduated with her A.O.C.A. She returned to Newfoundland in the summer of 1949 with her artist husband Reginald Shepherd to assist in organizing the Newfoundland Academy of Art. A portrait artist she was commissioned to paint historical portraits for the Newfoundland Museum in St. John's. Lives in St. John's.

References
> NGC Info. Forms rec'd July 31, 1950; Nov. 13, 1950; Aug. 15, 1951

PARSONS, Madeleine

She started painting in 1960. A native of Westmount she studied under Dr. Arthur Lismer and his staff at the Montreal Museum of Fine Arts. She has exhibited her paintings and drawings at different galleries holding her first solo show at the Lantern Theatre, Montreal, in October of 1963. Lives in Outremont.

Reference
> *The Montreal Star*, P.Q., Oct. 22, 1963 "Paintings by Parsons on Display at Opening" by Francis Allen

PARSONS, Paul

A Newfoundland painter who studied part-time for five years at the Newfoundland Academy of Art and spent one year in London, England. He operated an art gallery for two years and established a studio in St. John's, Newfoundland while also heading the St. John's School of Art. His solo shows include those in St. John's at the art club of Prince of Wales Collegiate (1967) and at the Arts and Culture Centre (1968).

References
  St. John's Evening Telegram, Nfld., Oct. 26, 1967 "PWC displays art of Paul Parsons"
  Ibid, June 28, 1968 "Art in progress" by Robert Percival

PARSONS, William
b. 1909

Born in Toronto, Ontario, he studied at the Ontario College of Art under G.A. Reid, J.E.H. MacDonald, Arthur Lismer, J.W. Beatty and others and graduated in 1930. He worked in display advertising doing design and art work also for the Canadian National Exhibition (did grandstand backdrop) and has received awards for his designs. As a landscape painter, mainly in oils, he chooses for subjects the rugged countryside of Haliburton, Algonquin Park and Northern Ontario. His paintings have been purchased for the Vincent Price-Sears Roebuck travelling collection. A member of the Newmarket Art Club (1953 — Pres. 1953-54) his paintings have been exhibited at the Studio Showcase, Thorncliffe Park shopping mall (1964) and in various one-man shows and group shows in Toronto and Calgary. A reproduction of his "Beaver Dam" done in Algonquin Park was reproduced in *Canadian Insurance/Agent & Broker* (1972). His work has excellent colour and is done in a lively impasto style. He lives in Newmarket, Ontario.

References
  Era & Express, Newmarket, Ont., Jan. 15, 1959 "Begin Art Instruction For Art Club Members"
  Toronto Leaside Advertiser, Tor., Ont., May 28, 1964 "Thorncliffe Gallery Exhibits"
  Canadian Insurance/Agent & Broker, December, 1972, P. 23
  NGC Info. Form rec'd Sept. 5, 1956

PARTINGTON, Charles Thomas
b. 1916

Born at Maple Creek, Sask., a self taught potter and ceramist he received much encouragement and assistance from Stan Clarke of White Rock, B.C. and Rex Calhoun of North Surrey, B.C. He held a one-man show of pottery at Min Tonge Art Salon, Pender Street, Vancouver, B.C. (1963) and received the purchase award for best ceramics in the Fraser Valley Exhibition (1963, 1966). He was Deputy Convenor for the Fraser Valley Exhibition (Arts and Crafts Div., 1963, 64) and Convenor (1965, 66); Chairman, Ceramics Division, Langley Arts Council (1965,

PARTINGTON, Charles Thomas (Cont'd)

1966); Chairman, Centennial Arts Exhibition of Langley (juried show of painting, pottery and weaving, 1967). Member of the Fraser Valley Pottery Guild (1961) and the Langley Arts Council (1964). Lives in Langley, B.C.

Reference
NGC Info. Form rec'd June 1, 1967

PARTRIDGE, David Gerry

b. 1919

Born in Akron, Ohio, U.S.A. he had a fascination for fossils and the natural structures of plants as a child. From 1928 to 1935 he lived in England where he received his early education. At the age of sixteen he came to Canada. He enrolled as a student at the University of Toronto in 1938 where he studied geology, palaeontology and took art training under Carl Schaefer at Hart House (1940-41). In 1941 he joined the R.C.A.F. where he received his wings and was a flying instructor until the end of the war in 1945 when he became a naturalized Canadian citizen. While in the service he married in 1943 (he and his wife Tibs now have two grown children). He then studied art under Cavin Atkins at summer school in Toronto (1945). He became a teacher at Ridley College, St. Catharines, and during the summers took courses at Queen's University (1946-47) under André Biéler, Carl Schaefer and Will Ogilvie; under William Palmer in 1947 for egg tempera and varnish mediums; under Charles Comfort at his studio in Toronto for oil mediums. In the summer of 1948 he attended the Art Students' League in New York under Harry Sternberg. Then he was awarded a British Council Scholarship to study at the Slade School of Art in London, England (1950-51). Returning to Canada he resumed his teaching job at Ridley College and also taught at St. Catharines Collegiate; founded the St. Catharines Public Library Art Gallery and became its first curator (above activities during 1952-56 period). But in 1956 he retired from full-time teaching and went back to Europe where he studied print-making under William Hayter at Atelier 17 in Paris and also lived and worked in England until 1958. Returning to Canada once more he settled in Ottawa and held a solo show of water colours, oils and engravings at Robertson Galleries in 1959 the same year his work was selected for showing at The Third Biennial Exhibition of Canadian Art. While living in Ottawa he made trips outside to give talks and classes on art to the Northern Ontario communities of Timmins, and Sault Ste. Marie. He also became teacher at the Ottawa Municipal Art Centre. His interest in nail art began just after his return to Canada when he was rebuilding a house in Ottawa. From random nails sticking out a beam he got the idea of using them as an art form and tried some experiments then and there. Earlier he had been influenced by the work of Hungarian born artist Zoltan Kemeny whose reliefs were displayed at Atelier 17 in Paris where Partridge had studied. The reliefs and the cellular like structures in Kemeny's work were particularly fascinating to Partridge. By 1960 Partridge had produced about a dozen of these nail works and in an article for *Canadian Art* entitled "Configurations" he discussed his nail constructions. At that point he had turned to the nail constructions as an interval from his painting and graphic work and explained, "They are, certainly, apart from what might be termed my serious painting, but they have had some effect on it. They have satisfied an urge for complete abstract creation with which I am not content in painting." Some of these works were exhibited with his drawings at Robertson Galleries. But he was still better known for his paintings and prints (one of which was acquired by the NGC in 1962). In 1962 however he won the sculpture prize in the 79th Annual Spring Exhibition of the Montreal Museum of Fine Arts for an entry of wood and nails entitled "Standing Configuration No. 9". By July of 1962 his configurations had caught the interest of *Time Magazine* in an article for the July 27th issue in which his other works were also discussed. Concluding the article *Time* quoted Partridge as saying, "The one common denominator of my works is that they create a unified whole, really out of chaos." In the Autumn of 1962 he returned to London, England where his work became very popular. For the next twelve years he worked in that city holding periodic solo shows at The New Vision Centre (Lond.); New Charing Cross Gal. (Glasgow); University of Sheffield; Leicester University; Hamilton Gal. (Lond); Covent Garden Gal. (Lond); returning to Canada periodically where he continued to show his work and fill commissions like two large murals in the foyer of York University Library in Toronto (two panels of nail art each 12 x 21 ft touching in corner) completed in September of 1970 after six months of work. His dealers in Canada were Galerie Godard Lefort (Mtl.) then Roberts Gallery (Tor.) who displayed his work in solo shows. Back in Canada in 1975 he settled in Toronto where Roberts Gallery became his main dealer. Sol Littman in *The Toronto Star* (1973) had described his work as follows, "With whatever common nails he has on hand, the artist achieves remarkable texture and relief. Gleaming rows of wire-brushed nail heads catch the light to suggest the scales of metallic reptile or some aboriginal city seen from high in the air. You will enjoy this show by a fine artist working with an unusual material." Norah-Jean Perkin in *The Windsor Star* (1975) noted, "Amazingly he does not plan his nail works beforehand, but starts with one nail and lets it grow from there. He builds up mountains and hills with successively higher rows of nails, and descends gradually or sharply into valleys often cut by narrow space or crevasse. The flat heads of the nails and the polished, painted wood backings catch the light and reflect it, emphasizing different parts of the piece depending on where you are standing . . . . Pursuit, a 48-by-36-inch wall-hanging, reminds me of a slithery amoeba, ready to start multiplying any minute. There are so many dips, curves and angles within the body of nails that light is constantly caught and reflected throughout the piece, creating a feeling of movement . . . . Best of all, Partridge has a sense of humor. His Homage to a Common Nail is a 14-inch spike surrounded by thousands of smaller nails. It's a whimsical look at what Partridge, who once concentrated on painting, has been doing full-time for the past 17 years. Yet anyone who would spend that much time hammering nails a fraction of an inch apart, has to be serious." His one-man shows include: St. Catharines Art Gallery (1956, 1959); The Rose & Crown, Fletching Sussex, Eng. (1957); The Robertson Galleries, Ott. (1959, 1960, 1962); The Gallery of Contemporary Art, Tor. (1959); Queen's University, Kingston, Ont. (1961); Here & Now Gal., Tor. (1961); Galerie Agnes Lefort, Mtl. (1962, 1965); Jerrold Morris Internat. Gal., Tor. (1962); The New Vision Centre, Lond., Eng. (1964); Commonwealth Inst. Art Gal., Lond. Eng. (1965); New Charing Cross Gal., Glasgow, Scot. (1965); University of Sheffield, Eng. (1966); Leicester University (1967); Hamilton Galleries, Lond., Eng. (1967);

PARTRIDGE, David Gerry (Cont'd)

Covent Garden Gallery, Lond., Eng. (1970); Art Gallery of Windsor, Wind., Ont. (1975); Mayfair Gallery, Lond. Eng. (1974). See *Creative Canada* for listing of his group shows. He is represented in the following collections and buildings by commissioned works: Nat. Gal. of Canada, Ottawa; Uplands Airport (Dept. of Transp.), Ottawa; External Affairs (Govt. Canada), Ottawa; Art Gal. Ontario, Tor.; Agnes Etherington Art Centre (Queen's Univ.), Kingston; Can. Bank of Commerce, Mtl.; Mtl. Museum of Fine Arts; Oldham Art Gal., Lancs., Eng.; Victoria & Albert Museum, Lond., Eng.; Tate Gal., Lond., Eng.; Leicester Univ., Eng.; Library of Congress, Wash., D.C., U.S.A.; Ohio State Univ., USA; Robt. Mayer, Winnetka, Ill., USA; Gallery of New South Wales, Sydney, Aust.; Nat. Gal. of Malaysia; Museum of Contemp. Art, Santiago, Chile; Commissions: Town House Motel, Ottawa (Nail Head Lounge); Royal Trust Bldg., Ottawa; Hiram Walker-Windsor, Ont.; Arndale Property (Boardroom), Lond., Eng.; Royal Garden Hotel (Ceiling Roof Restaurant) Lond., Eng.; Pillar Holdings, Lond., Eng., David Group (Office Lobby Wall) Loughborough, Eng.; North-West Electricity Board, Blackpool, Lancs., Eng.; Shanklin Hotel, Isle of Wight, U.K. He is a member of: Royal Society of Arts; Royal Canadian Academy (ARCA, 1962); Ont. Soc. of Artists (1962). Lives in Toronto with his wife.

References

Newspapers & Magazines

Review, Niagara Falls, Ont., Feb. 22, 1950 "D. Partridge In 'Modern Art' Talk For Local Artists"

Globe & Mail, Jan. 19, 1954 (Partridge hangs his painting of Ruper St. Market Lond. for show at St. Catharines Art Gallery)

Toronto Daily Star, Ont., Jan. 22, 1959 "Art Review – Atom-Age Artists Show Wild Vision" by Hugh Thomson

Le Droit, Ottawa, Ont., Feb. 13, 1959 "Galeries Robertson – Exposition d'un peintre d'Ottawa"

The Ottawa Citizen, Ont., Feb. 18, 1959 "Experimentation Vital In Rewarding Art Show" by Carl Weiselberger

Le Droit, Ottawa, Ont., Feb. 20, 1959 "Le rideau se lève . . . . David Partridge, d'Ottawa, expose, à une Galerie Robertson tout à fait rénovée des oeuvres qui causeront de la controverse"

The Ottawa Journal, Ont., Feb. 21, 1959 "Artist David Partridge Paintings Pack Appeal" by W.Q. Ketchum

Daily Star, Sault Ste. Marie, Ont., Feb. 22, 1960 "Painter To Give Classes"

Le Droit, Ottawa, Ont., May 25, 1960 "Leçon de peinture sur le mail"

Daily Press, Timmins, June 2, 1960 "Art Instructor To Give Course"

Ibid, Sept. 10, "Will Give Art Course Here"

The Ottawa Journal, Oct. 19, 1960 "Artist Uses Unorthodox Bold Style" (configurations) by W.Q. Ketchum

Toronto Daily Star, Ont., May 13, 1961 (review of show at Here & Now Gallery)

St. Catharines Standard, Ont., Mar. 1, 1962 "Open Invitation – Distinguished Artist Returns To Lecture at Rodman Hall"

Le Nouveau Journal, Mtl., P.Q., Mar. 26, 1962 "David Partridge remporte le prix de sculpture du Salon du Printemps"

The Gazette, Mtl., P.Q., June 2, 1962 "Nail Configurations" by Dorothy Pfeiffer

Ibid, May 8, 1962 "Intriguing Abstracts In Partridge Exhibit" by Carl Weiselberger

The Gazette, Mtl., P.Q., June 2, 1962 "Nail Configurations" by Dorothy Pfeiffer

Time Magazine, July 27, 1962 "The Arts – The Nail Man"

The Ottawa Journal, Ont., Sept. 4, 1962 "Royal Trust Mural – Quarry Waste Becomes Art" by W.Q. Ketchum

The Ottawa Citizen, Ont., Sept. 5, 1962 "Art Returns To Construction" by Carl Weiselberger

Ibid, Apr. 13, 1964 "Famous Tate Gallery buys Canadian's work" by Carl Weiselberger

The Hamilton Spectator, Ont., May 12, 1964 "Nails Make A Name For This Canadian" by Sheila Dunn

St. Catharines Standard, Ont., 23 May, 1964 "Former City Sculptor's Work Chosen"

The Toronto Telegram, May 15, 1965 "Not With A Bang But Gentle Taps" by Sheldon Williams

Montreal Metro Express, Que., 11 May, 1965 "David Partridge: le succès lui est venu sur un lit de clous"

The Ottawa Citizen, Ont., Oct. 19, 1965 London (CP) "Hotel has royal neighbours" by Carol Kennedy (she quotes a London art critic who says Partridge's work is "most striking and successful work of art in the hotel")

The Ottawa Journal, Mar. 16, 1967 London (CP) "Ottawa Artist's Ironmongery on View" by Harold Morrison

Vancouver Province, B.C., 3 July, 1970 London (Southam) "See the nail? Now get the picture?" by Sheila Thomas

St. Catharines Standard, Ont., Nov. 26, 1970 "Former City Teacher Uses Hammer, Nails To Create Art"

The Montreal Star, Que., London (CP) Dec. 1, 1970 " 'Naillies' in big demand" by Iain MacLeod

International Herald Tribune, Oct. 21 - 25th, 1970 "Art in London – Perfecting a New Form: The 'Nailie' " by Max Wykes-Joyce

Le Devoir, Mtl., Que., Dec. 5, 1970 London (CP) "Londres – Le sculpteur qui doit le plus à l'industrie du clou: Partridge"

Penticton Herald, B.C., Dec. 28, 1970 London (CP) "Nail-making Industry Should Appreciate Art" by Iain MacLeod

Corner Brook Western-Star, Nfld., Dec. 1, 1970 London (CP) "Canadian makes nail sculptures"

Lethbridge Herald, Alta., Dec. 16, 1970 London (CP) "Canadian David Partridge greatest beneficiary of industry – Sculptor 'nails' works together to capture fine arts prize"

The Toronto Star, Ont., Oct. 12, 1973 "Nailing down artistic success" by Sol Littman

Globe & Mail, Tor., 13 Oct. 1973 (review by Kay Kritzwiser)

Ibid, Tor., Ont., Apr. 5, 1974 London (CP) "Nail mural artist returning to Canada"

Windsor Star, Ont., June 7, 1975 "Norah-Jean Perkin – Nothing lost for lack of a nail"

Books and catalogues

The Third Biennial Exhibition of Canadian Art, 1959, NGC, Ott., No. 42

Canadian Art, Vol. 17, No. 5, 1960 "Configurations" by David Partridge (photos by Betty Williamson)

The Fourth Biennial Exhibition of Canadian Art, 1961, No. 66

Canadian Art, Vol. 18, No. 2, 1961 "18 Print-Makers" by Elizabeth Kilbourn, P. 108

Ibid, Vol. 19, No. 2 "A Survey of the work of 21 more Canadian artists" P. 148-149

NGC Annual Report 1962-63, Section 5, Purchases, Prints, P. 33

Canadian Sculpture, Expo 67, Editor Natan Karczmar, Introd. by William Withrow, Photos by Bruno Massenet, Graph, Montreal, 1967, Plate 26

Sculpture '67 by Dorothy Cameron, NGC, 1967 "David Partridge" P. 74

Agnes Etherington Art Centre Permanent Collection by Frances K. Smith, Queen's Univ. Kingston, Ont., 1968, No. 106

The Canada Council Collection – A travelling exhibition of the NGC, Ottawa, 1969 Prints, Drawings, Water-Colours and Gouaches

R.C.A. 90th Annual Exhibition 1970, Sculpture #89 (see other years)

Art Gallery of Ontario the Canadian collection by Helen Pepall Bradfield, P. 355

Canadian Art Today Ed. by Wm. Townsend, Studio Internat., Lond., Eng., 1970, P. 102 (York Univ. nail construction)

Creative Canada, Volume One, Ref. Div. McPherson Lib., Univ. Victoria/Univ. Tor. Pr., 1971, P. 242

Canadian Art At Auction 1968-1975 Ed. by Geoffrey Joyner, Fwd. by Paul Duval, Sotheby & Co. (Can.) Ltd., Tor., 1975, P. 153

PARTRIDGE, David Gerry (Cont'd)

Who's Who In American Art, 1976 Ed. by Jaques Cattell Press, R.R. Bowker, NYC, P. 430
Ecole de Montreal par Guy Robert, Mtl., 1964, P. 135
NGC Info. Forms 1947, 1952, 1964
Vie Des Arts, Hiver, 1967 No. 45 "Les Gouttes D'Airain De David Partridge" par Pierre Rouve (good photos in this article as well) P. 52-55

PARTRIDGE, Donald Warren

b. 1900

Born in Cincinnati, Ohio, the son of Rev. Dr. Warren Graham Partridge and Mary Catherine (Payne) Partridge he was educated at the Albany Academy, Albany, N.Y.; United States Naval Academy, Annapolis, Maryland and began his business career in the engineering department of Leblond Machine Tool Co., Cincinnati, Ohio and with Nesbitt-Thompson & Co., Mtl., Que. (1921-25) arriving in Montreal in 1921. He had also received his earliest drawing instruction from his father then studied art at the Winchester School, Pittsburg, Pa. (1905-1911); McGee Art School, Pittsburg, Pa. (1911-13); Roger Deering, Kennebunkport, Maine (1946-47); Wilfred Barnes, Mtl. (1948). He studied as well under Austin Irwin (Monte Carlo); Wallace B. Phillips (Lond. Eng.); Reginald Butt (Kingston, Jamaica); Richard Jack, R.A., R.C.A. who was also a close friend who painted with Mr. Partridge and his wife on the Coast of Maine, the Laurentian Mountains and numerous other localities. He also received encouragement and help from D.I. McLeod (see Vol. 4), A.Y. Jackson (see Vol. 2) and Glen C. Hyatt (of Van., B.C. and Alaska). He held a joint show with his wife Jean (Hughes) Partridge at The Art Shop, Mtl. West (1954) also at Shawmut Inn, Kennebunkport, Maine; Lakeshore Assoc. of Artists, Lake St. Louis, Anglers Club, Lachine (1957); Montreal Museum of Fine Arts Spring Exhibition (1957). Living in Dorval, Quebec in 1968.

References
The Montreal Star, Que., Mar. 24, 1954 "Family Effort Fills Art Shop Exhibition"
NGC Info. Form June 25, 1957
Who's Who in Canada, 1966-68, Eds. Fraser, Barnett, White, Internat. Press Ltd., Tor., Ont., P. 1430

PARTRIDGE, Jean Eleanor (Hughes)

Daughter of the late J.A. and Martha Hughes she married Donald W. Partridge and settled in Montreal. She received instruction in painting from Richard Jack, R.A., R.C.A., and painted with him on the Coast of Maine; Laurentian Mountains and elsewhere (1945-51). Studied as well with D.I. McLeod of Toronto and Mrs. Alma Levinson of Kennebunk, Maine (1920-56) and others. She exhibited her paintings at Shawmut Inn, Kennebunkport Maine; Jury shows of the Lakeshore Association of Artists (1957); with her husband at The Art Shop, Montreal West, and other members of their family. She was living in Dorval in 1968.

PARTRIDGE, Jean Eleanor (Hughes) (Cont'd)

References

NGC Info. Form June 25, 1957 (Donald W. Partridge file)

The Montreal Star, Quebec, Mar. 24, 1954 "Family Effort Fills Art Shop Exhibition"

Who's Who In Canada, 1966-68, Eds. Fraser, Barnet, White, Intern. Press Ltd., Tor., Ont. (see Partridge, Donald Warren P. 1430)

PARZYBOK, Christine Currlin

From San Francisco she came to London, Ontario, where after several group shows exhibited with four other women artists under the title of "Ms." (the other artists were: Rebecca Burke, Kerry Ferris, Jamelie Hassan, and Nelda Oman). Describing her work Lenore Crawford of the *London Evening Free Press* noted, "She puts shells, sea salt crystals or pebbles in porthole-like containers, with glass covers so that the contents can be seen. Or she uses other wooden objects which might have come from a ship. A couple of pieces are free-standing sculpture and the question is whether this will be the major phase in her work in the immediate future." She is represented in the Canada Council Art Bank.

References

London Evening Free Press, Ont., Oct. 26, 1972 " 'Artistic conviction' marks Ms. showing" by Lenore Crawford

PARZYBOK, Stephen M.
b. (c) 1944

A London, Ontario, artist who exhibited his sculptures, drawings, and collages at the Trajectory Gallery in 1974 when Lenore Crawford of the *London Evening Free Press* noted, "He belongs thoroughly to this age of technology, to the extent that he states in an explanation of his work, "I have tried to create an awareness of the human reality contained in the technical object. Culture fears the technical object just as man fears the unknown. I am attempting to build a language in my sculpture which will have a common denominator evident to the art world and the world of technology.' " Crawford continues "All are made beautifully, to turn away any interference by flaws to set the viewer on a direct path to the artist's goal. There is something beyond the reality of technology that can only be called 'spiritual' in the sculptures." Mr. Parzybok is represented in the Canada Council Art Bank.

References

London Evening Free Press, Ont., May 16, 1974 "London artist's works convey world of technology" by Lenore Crawford

PASCAL, Karen Madsen (Mrs.)
b. (c) 1946

Originally a sculptor working in welded steel, she won her first international award in 1968. In 1972 she exhibited at the Eaton's College Street Gallery, Toronto, and

PASCAL, Karen Madsen (Mrs.) (Cont'd)

in the same year won a Brucebo Scholarship For Canadian Artists to study and work on the Swedish Island of Gotland. She took her welding and other sculpting tools with her to continue work in this medium but soon became absorbed in religious art and turned to experimentation with banners. Working with complete freedom in association with a Swedish art school her results were so impressive that she was urged by the Canadian Guild of Artists to hold a solo show. Subsequently she exhibited her banners in many major Canadian centres including the St. Lawrence Centre Theatre Lobby, Toronto (1975) and the Metropolitan United Church, Toronto (1975). Describing her work at the St. Lawrence Centre, Tom Harpur in *The Toronto Star* noted, "Two of the largest hangings, both on biblical themes, are directly over the bars at either end of the lobby. While all of them have their own special appeal, the most arresting banners are those where the specific religious motif is least explicit. The movement, energy and job of the creative design itself speaks for the heart of the matter." She was one of six artists invited to submit designs for the banners for the Great Hall of Hart House at the University of Toronto. In her studio in Montreal she is ably assisted in her work by Heather Kalinowski and Chistina Roberts.

References
> *Globe & Mail*, Tor., Ont. Mar. 10, 1972 "Rejoicing Dancers"
> *The Montreal Star*, Quebec., Feb. 24, 1973 "Canadian Guild of Crafts – Karen Pascal"
> *The Toronto Star*, Ont., April 5, 1975 "An Artist For God" by Tom Harpur (Religion Editor)

PASCALE

A Quebec City artist who studied at the Beaux-Arts of Quebec two years in a day course and then finished her studies evenings. After her marriage she also worked at the Beaux-Arts for a year as a model. Known for her country scenes she works in oils, inks, charcoal, water colours and drawings.

Reference
> *L'Action*, Quebec, P.Q., Aug. 10, 1966 "Une jeune femme peintre réussit à concilier son art et sa vie de famille" par L. Plante

PASCOE, Major Claude

A retired *Toronto Daily Star* writer who won recognition as an artist in the tradition of Vincent Van Gogh. He won first prize for the best submission of the month in the MGM-sponsored Van Gogh painting competition. An international competition, the artists had to base their work on any subject painted by Van Gogh and Pascoe chose still life featuring potatoes.

Reference
> *Toronto Daily Star*, Tor., Ont., Dec. 9, 1957 "Claude Pascoe wins prize for painting"

PASK, Kay (Mrs. Steve Pask)

An artist from Atwater, Saskatchewan, and graduate in fine arts from the University of Saskatchewan she has studied under Milton Achtemichuk of Yorkton and Terry Holbein a former art instructor at the Yorkton Composite School. A teacher of Grade 6 at Gillen School, Esterhazy, Sask., she continues her studies at the University of Saskatchewan during the holiday months. She has exhibited her paintings in oils, acrylics, pastels and water colours at the Yorkton Art Centre, Yorkton, Saskatchewan (1970).

Reference

Esterhazy Miner, Sask., Feb. 4, 1970 "Atwater artist has works hanging at Yorkton"

(de) PASSILLÉ-SYLVESTRE, Micheline (Micheline de Passillé)
b. 1936

Born in Montreal, P.Q., she worked as a lab technician at the University of Montreal (1955) and was interested in some painting and enamel work. She began using old glass and copper left over from a roofing repair job. Then she started working at her home with a kiln. In 1957 she married Yves Sylvestre who had just received his diploma in geology from the University of Montreal. In the autumn of 1958 they left for Quebec City where Yves was doing work on his M.Sc. in Geology. By this time they had been working together and at the close of 1958 held their first exhibition together at the Palais du Commerce de Montréal. In 1959 Yves turned his interest from geology to full-time artisan work. They won a prize from the Montreal Chamber of Commerce (1960) and prizes in the Concours Artistiques de la Province de Québec in 1960 and 1962. With their 1962 prize they travelled in France and Italy. Their work of a varied nature in a variety of techniques is highly regarded for its fine aesthetic value while still remaining functional. Their exhibitions include: Galerie de la Boutique, Quebec City (1960); Galerie des Artisans, Mtl. (1965); Galerie Jean du Sud, Mtl. (1967); Galerie Tournesol, Mtl. (1966 group show); Canadian Fine Crafts, Can. Govt. Pavilion, Expo 67; Galerie Nova et Vetera, Mtl. (1968); Galerie du Vieux Trois-Rivières (1968). They are represented by murals in collections of the late Pope John 23rd (1962); late Rt. Hon. Lester B. Pearson (1961); late Hon. Daniel Johnson (1967); and collections of members of the cabinet of the French Government; Musée du Québec; Quebec House, NYC and elsewhere. Member of the Canadian Handicraft Guild she lives at Sainte-Adèle-en-Haut, Terrebonne, P.Q.

References

Magazine Chatelaine, Décembre, 1963
Magazine Maclean, Août, 1965 "La Guerre À La Pacotille" par Pierre Desrosiers
Le Devoir, Mtl., P.Q., June 26, 1965 "de Passillé-Sylvestre"
Time Magazine, December 23, 1966
Canadian Fine Crafts (catalogue) *Expo 67*
Le Nouvelliste, P.Q., Trois Rivières, P.Q., Nov. 23, 1968 "Exposition des oeuvres de Passillé-Sylvestre"
L'Art Au Québec Depuis 1940 par Guy Robert, La Presse, 1973, P. 362, 363
Le guide des artisans créateurs du Québec par Jean-Pierre Payette, La Presse, 1974, P. 311, 312
NGC Info. Form rec'd July 7, 1967

(de) PASSILLÉ-SYLVESTRE, Yves (Yves Sylvestre)
b. 1932

Born in Montreal, P.Q., he graduated from the University of Montreal in geology and married Micheline de Passillé the same year (1957). Both were interested in fine crafts and soon entered a joint venture of making various attractive items fashioned mainly with enamel on copper. Yves was primarily interested in making objects from metal while his wife Micheline specialized in designing and enamelling the work. In the autumn of 1958 they moved to Quebec City so that Yves could pursue his degree of M.Sc. By the end of that year they had held their first joint exhibition at the Palais du Commerce back in Montreal. In 1959 Yves decided to devote his full time to enamels. The partnership formed by Yves and Micheline has proved rewarding to them including the winning of a prize from the Montreal Chamber of Commerce (1960) and prizes for ceramics in the Concours Artistique de la Province de Québec in 1960 and 1962. With their 1962 prize they travelled in France and Italy and on their return home continued to produce a variety of work using several techniques. They have received praise for the aesthetic and functional value of their works which are to be found in the collections of many prominent people both in Canada and abroad (see Micheline above for details already listed on collectors and exhibitions). Yves is a member of the Canadian Handicraft Guild and lives in Sainte-Adèle-en-Haut, Terrebonne, P.Q., where he shares a workshop with his wife.

References
Magazine Chatelaine, Décembre, 1963
Magazine Maclean, Août, 1965 "La Guerre À La Pacotille" par Pierre Desrosiers
Le Devoir, Mtl., P.Q., June 26, 1965 "de Passilé-Sylvestre"
Time Magazine, December 23, 1966
Canadian Fine Crafts Expo 67 (catalogue)
Le Nouvelliste, P.Q., Trois Rivières, P.Q., Nov. 23, 1968 "Exposition des oeuvres de Passillé-Sylvestre"
L'Art Au Quebec Depuis 1940 par Guy Robert, La Presse, 1973, P. 362, 363
Le guide des artisans créateurs du Quebec par Jean-Pierre Payette, La Presse, 1974
NGC Info. Form rec'd July 7, 1967

PASSMORE, Clara (Mrs. Jim Passmore)

She started painting around 1958 and has spent winter months in Arizona studying at the Arizona School of Art and returning home to Kamloops, B.C., with her husband for the balance of each year. A painter of a variety of subjects including still life, flowers, portraits and landscapes she held a solo show of her work at Woodward's Mall in Kamloops (1968).

References
Kamloops Daily Sentinel, B.C., July 20, 1965 "Colorful Portrait Results From Copied News Picture"
Ibid, June 17, 1968 "Local Artist Shows Pictures"

PATCHING, Helen

She held her first solo show at the Photographic Stores, Sparks Street, Ottawa, in 1945 when she exhibited water colour and oil paintings including flower studies and Gatineau landscapes.

Reference
> *The Ottawa Citizen*, Mar. 21, 1945 "Helen Patching Shows Oils and Water-Colors" by E.W.H.

PATEL, Mahen

Born in Dar-es-salaam, Tanganyika, a painter, sculptor and printmaker he studied in Tanganyika; India; England, and Canada. He has exhibited his work at the Lalitkala Academy, New Delhi (1959); International Exhibition, Tokyo (1961); solo show in Tata, Bombay (1961); Hampstead Artist Council, Lond., Eng. (1965, 1966, 1967); solo show Commonwealth Gal., U.K.; Canadian Society of Graphic Art (1969); Society of Canadian Painters, Etchers & Engravers (1969); three-man show, Medicine Hat Library (1969); solo show, Mona Lisa Art Salon, Calgary (1970); Print Club, Philadelphia (1970); solo show, Florida, USA (1970-71); invitational show, Regina (1971); Canadian Art Galleries, Calgary (1971); Gallerie Fore, Winnipeg. He is represented in private collections in India, England, Canada, U.S.A. and elsewhere.

References
> Biographical sheet, Gallerie Fore, Selkirk Avenue, Winnipeg, Manitoba

PATERSON, Alice (née Alice Pringle)

Born in Hamilton, Ontario, the daughter of Mr. & Mrs. John Pringle she studied in Hamilton under John Sloan Gordon and Hortense Mattice Gordon. A painter for a number of years she has done many sketches of locations in Moosonee and Moose Factory in Northern Ontario especially of buildings like the old Hudson's Bay Company store built in 1871 and demolished in 1959. She also visited the Bay's Rupert House built at the mouth of the Rupert River on the east coast of James Bay, Quebec. During her northern trip she filled her sketch books with many other subjects and also brought back stories of the fascinating people she met there including Indians, Eskimos, pilots, nurses, teachers and the chief factor of Moose Factory and his wife (Mr. & Mrs. J.J. Wood). Living at Bowmanville, Ontario, in 1960.

Reference
> *The Hamilton Spectator*, July 7, 1960 "Goes North on Pilgrimage" by Elsie Carruthers Lunney

PATERSON, Mrs. Gordon

A miniature painter who won six prizes for one of her paintings at various exhibitions. She addressed the University Women's Club, Toronto, in 1938 on the history of miniature painting under the title "Painting in the Little" and showed examples of her own work.

References
>   *Globe & Mail*, Tor., Ont., Nov. 21, 1938 "Painting Miniatures Subject of Address"
>   Ibid, Nov. 22, 1938 "Miniatures Charm Art Connoisseurs"

PATERSON, Robert Allen
b. 1936

Born in Unity, Saskatchewan, son of Mr. & Mrs. George Paterson he was raised in Sudbury, Ontario, where his father worked in the mines, then as city treasurer and later real estate agent. While attending high school he worked summers in a Sudbury printing plant where he learned about lithography. He received his first formal art instruction at the Sudbury Arts and Crafts Club summer school of art. Following his graduation from the Sudbury High School he entered the Ontario College of Art in Toronto in 1954 and there studied under Fred Hagan, Gustav Weisman, Carl Schaefer, Alex Millar, Thomas Bowie and Jock Macdonald covering courses in painting, printmaking, mural work and sculpture (1 Yr 1955-56). While still a student he assisted R. York Wilson with murals for Imperial Oil (1956-57) and the O'Keefe Centre, Tor. (1960) also assisted Sydney H. Watson with murals for Imperial Oil and the Toronto General Hospital. Each summer he taught in Sudbury for two weeks (1956, 1957, 1958). In 1960 he was winner of the Baxter Award given by the Ontario Society of Artists and travelled to Italy, Greece and Egypt. In 1962 he held a one-man show of his work at the Picture Loan Society, Toronto and the following year was elected a member of the Ontario Society of Artists (1963) and the Canadian Society of Painters in Water Colour (1963). His favourite medium has been water colour and next various graphic media. In 1963 he was also recommended by the Art Gallery of Toronto as a printmaking instructor for the West Baffin Eskimo Cooperative. He flew to Baffin Island in the fall of that year and had a small printing press shipped there to carry out the project. In 1964 he continued as supervisor of printmaking at Baker Lake until 1965 and was back under contract in 1973 for three months with the Eskimo Cooperative Association of Povungnituk, Quebec, to teach techniques of making prints from carvings (or transition from three-dimensional carvings to two dimensional drawings) and other work. On one occasion he worked with a class of eighteen Eskimos ranging in age from 17 to 55. While in the north he produced some of his own work including portrait, figure studies and landscapes. He has done extensive teaching at Dundee, Scotland, Ontario College of Art, Printmaking Department Assistant (1966-67); St. Clair College, Chatham; Georgian College Summer School of the Arts, Tor. (1972). His one-man shows include: Creighton Mine, Ont. (1st solo show 1957); Seven Oaks Restaurant, Tor. (1958); Sudbury Public Lib., Ont. (1958); Picture Loan Society, Tor. (1962); Robertson Galleries, Ottawa (1965,

PATERSON, Robert Allen (Cont'd)

1967); Pollock Gallery, Tor. (1967); Barrie Public Library, Ont. (1972). Living in Barrie, Ont. (1972). His dealer in 1972 Nancy Poole's Studio, London and Toronto, Ontario.

References
Sudbury Star, Ont., Sept. 4, 1965 "City Artist Recalls Highlights of Year Spent as Art Instructor With Eskimo"
Ottawa Journal, Ont., Oct. 5, 1965 "Fine Collection Of Arctic Canvases" by W.Q. Ketchum
Ottawa Citizen, Ont., Oct. 7, 1965 "Toronto artist gives lyrical touch to Arctic scene" by Carl Weiselberger
The Toronto Telegram, Ont., Feb. 10, 1967 "Art" by Barrie Hale
Regina Leader Post, Sask., Aug. 6, 1968 "Jo Clarke"
Barrie Examiner, Ont., Aug. 2, 1972 "If They Are Interesting Paterson Paints Them"
Ibid, June 9, 1972 "Toronto Artist To Teach Art Course At Georgian"
NGC Info. Forms 1958, 1965, 1972

PATON, David
b. 1921

Born in Fernie, B.C., he studied at the Farnham School of Art and the Guildford Polytechnic, nights, during his war service in England. Returning to Canada he attended the University of British Columbia and Carleton College, Ottawa, where he graduated with a Bachelor of Journalism (1949) and subsequently took his B.F.A. and M.F.A. degrees from Cranbrook Academy of Art, Bloomfield Hills, Michigan, U.S.A. He attended the Artists' Workshop in Toronto under R. York Wilson, William Winter, Tom Hodgson, Cleeve Horne and Jock Macdonald. In 1957 he exhibited with the Ontario Society of Artists at the Art Gallery of Ontario. He taught painting and drawing at the Artists' Workshop in Toronto and was an instructor in painting at the Central Technical School, also exhibited with United Nations in Canada and the Haddasah Club, Toronto. Held two one-man shows in Toronto before moving to Halifax where he has taught graphics, drawing and painting at the Nova Scotia College of Art and participated in a two-man show (of paintings and drawings) at the Dalhousie Art Gallery with Alex Tissington (1968).

References
Catalogue – Exhibition of Paintings, Drawings, Sculpture by David Paton and Alex Tissington, Dalhousie Art Gallery
NGC Info. Form rec'd July 2, 1958

PATRIC (Mrs. Ruth Patric McPherson)
b. 1897

Born in Winnipeg, Manitoba, she did not start to draw and paint until she was forty. She studied at the Victoria School of Art under Mrs. Ina Uhthoff (part time) and at the Vancouver School of Art (part time) under B.C. Binning, J.L. Shadbolt, C.H. Scott and Fred Amess; became a member of the Federation of Canadian Artists (1945, Executive for B.C. Region 1947-48-49). During an exhibition of her casein

PATRIC (Mrs. Ruth Patric McPherson) (Cont'd)

gouache paintings at The Vancouver Art Gallery (1950) Palette of the Vancouver *Province* noted, "The pictures will appeal to an unusually wide range of gallery goers since her style combines modern tendencies with a considerable decorative charm and easy recognizability of objects depicted . . . . Colour schemes and intriguing distribution of lines and masses vary from the rich band of red in 'Summer Glow, Queen Charlotte Fisheries' to a fine relationship of form and color in the more poetic 'Shadows of the Evening Behind Linton Ways.' " She was living in Vancouver in 1956.

References
Letter to H.O. McCurry, Director NGC, July 12, 1949 (letter signed by Mrs. Ruth Patric McPherson)
The Vancouver Province, B.C., April 1, 1950 "In The Realm Of Art – Waterfront 'Caught' By Vancouver Artist" by Palette
NGC Info. Forms rec'd July 6, 1949; Mar. 19, 1956

PATRICE, Rita

She started painting about 1963 and took courses from Mme. Pauline Clément. She participated in a group show where her portraits of John F. Kennedy and Winston Churchill attracted much attention. Musical as well she plays the accordion and piano.

Reference
La Salle Le Messager, Verdun, P.Q., Oct. 7, 1965 "Rita Patrice – Son talent et ses oeuvres" par LU

PATRY, André (Andy)
b. (c) 1942

Originally from Brownsburg near Lachute, P.Q., the son of Mr. & Mrs. Adélard Patry, he became assistant horseman at the Rocky Mountain Ranch at Blezard Valley, Ontario (knows how to breed, train, develop, raise, ride and care for horses). He ranched and worked as a blacksmith in Quebec for thirteen years before moving to Ontario. He took part in two Calgary Stampedes in 1958 and 1959 where he rode horseback, broncbusted and saddle bronc rode in events winning several classes. A skilled artist of horses, a non drinker or smoker he spends every available cent on his painting supplies. He works in oils and was described by *The Sudbury Star* as having " . . . a great talent for capturing the high spirits of a horse, the beautiful line of a shining flank, the toss of a mane."

Reference
The Watchman, Lachute, P.Q., December 16, 1970 "Former local resident – He shoes horses . . . . trains, paints them" (photos and story compliments of *The Sudbury Star*)

PATSTONE, A.C. (Alfred Cyril)

b. 1908

Born in Bentley, Alberta, the son of an Anglican pioneer missionary, his family moved to the Maritimes in 1917. By the age of fourteen he was experimenting with oil painting, designing and engraving and later became an engraver with Gordon Plummer of Saint John, New Brunswick. In 1929 he joined the firm of Henry Birks & Sons in Hamilton, Ontario, and also attended the Hamilton School of Fine Arts where he studied painting, gemology, design and architecture. In 1937 he won an Award Certificate for a portrait of a fisherman and an Honourable Mention for a seascape at an exhibition in Saint John, New Brunswick. In 1953 Birks & Sons transferred him from Hamilton to Montreal where he continued his painting between overseas assignments as a buyer and design consultant for the firm. It was through his travel that he was afforded opportunities to study the work of European and other artists in art galleries and exhibitions. He has been strongly influenced by American artist Andrew Wyeth and has remained a romantic realistic painter of vanishing Canadian barns, old houses, Western grain elevators including Prairie and Maritime scenes and generally those subjects which interest him in rural areas. In 1963 he was transferred to Edmonton, Alberta as a gemologist and exhibited there his steadily increasing production of paintings. At the age of fifty-five he turned to full time painting producing about seventy pictures a year. In 1973 a solo show of his work was held at Galerie Roslyn in Montreal and proved so successful that he decided to establish a studio in that city. He is dedicated to 'craftsmanship and naturalism' in his work which is proving popular, especially his series of "Vanishing Canadian Barns". Each year he travels across Canada on sketching trips after which he returns to his studio to devote his time to 'painting up' on canvas (with painstaking care for minute detail) numerous sketches made on his travels. He lives in Montreal but has land in New Brunswick overlooking the Saint John River Valley. He has a fondness for snow-shoeing in the countryside of Quebec and is drawn to that province for its beauty.

References
The Montreal Star, P.Q., June 15, 1973 Section B, Lifestyles, "Artist's golden years coming up roses"
Star Weekly, Tor., Ont., Aug. 4, 1973 "Canadians"
Document from artist

PATTERSON, Abe

An expert wood carver from the Pembroke, Ontario, area who made a totem pole for the Pembroke Centennial which opened on the 6th of July, 1958. Patterson took two months to complete the totem carvings on a specially selected pine tree.

Reference
The Ottawa Citizen, Ont., May 17, 1958 (photo of artist at work on totem pole; caption for photo "A Centennial Cut-Up")

PATTERSON, Alice Barron

Born in Brantford, Ontario, she was educated in Germany and Switzerland then returned to Canada and settled in Brantford where she studied painting under Hortense Gordon at the "Y" Art Club. She was President of this club from 1946 to 1949 and also a member of the Easel Club in that city.

Reference
 NGC Info. From rec'd July 19, 1951

PATTERSON, Andrew Dickson
1854-1930

Born in Picton, Ontario, the son of Hon. Christopher Salmon Patterson, Supreme Court of Canada Judge, and Mary (Dickson) Patterson, he moved with his parents to Toronto at an early age. There he attended Upper Canada College and afterwards travelled to London, England, where he studied art at the South Kensington School specializing in portraiture under Sir John Everett Millais. He returned to Canada and established a studio in Toronto (1880) then Ottawa (1891-2) and spent the remaining years in Montreal. He painted portraits of many outstanding people of his day. He did the portrait of Sir John A. Macdonald in 1885 and in 1888 took this painting to Paris where it was photo-engraved by the firm of Goupil Cie. (originators of the photogravure process). An edition of 250 copies was published on Indian paper and a quantity of these were autographed by Macdonald. By 1930, according to Patterson, none of the photo-engravings were obtainable but had become collectors' items. The original painting remained in Patterson's possession until its purchase by Robert Meighen of Montreal and was then bequeathed to his son, Lieut. Colonel Frank Meighen who in turn presented it to the Right Hon. Arthur Meighen who was then living in Toronto. Other sitters for Patterson were: J. Sandfield Macdonald, Sir Geo. W. Ross, Hon. J.B. Plumb, Sir Wm. J. Ritchie, Sir Casimir Gzowski, Sir Chas. Fitzpatrick, Sir Oliver Mowat, Sir Daniel McMillan, Hon. J.B. Snowball, Hon. A.B. McClelan, Hon. E.B. Chandler, Sir Daniel Wilson, Rev. Dr. John McCaul, G.R.R. Cockburn, Archibald MacMurchy, Dr. John Watson, Sir Frank Smith, Sir Wm. P. Howland and Homer Watson (Can. Artist – Portrait in NGC). Remarking on his work in 1914 E.F.B. Johnston noted, "His methods for many years were perhaps a little academic, but he broke away from the scholastic restrictions and subsequently painted some very free and strong examples of portraiture in accord with his own individual interpretations." Patterson also contributed to book illustrations. He was a member of the Ontario Society of Artists (1881); Royal Canadian Academy (ARCA 1882, RCA 1885). He exhibited with the Art Association of Montreal, World's Fairs in Chicago and St. Louis; Pan-American Expn., Buffalo, 1901, where he was awarded a bronze medal. He died in his 77th year. He married Edyth Lalande in 1901. His work is in the following collections: National Gallery of Canada; Agnes Etherington Art Centre, Kingston, Ont.; Art Gallery of Ontario; Ont. Govt. Dept Pub. Works (Leg. Bldgs, Tor.); John Ross Robertson Collection, Tor.

References
 Canadian Men and Women of The Time, Ed. Henry James Morgan, Briggs, Tor., 1912, P. 887

PATTERSON, Andrew Dickson (Cont'd)

Canada and Its Provinces, Vol. XII, "Painting and Sculpture In Canada" by E.F.B. Johnston, P. 629
The Fine Arts In Canada by Newton MacTavish, MacMillan, Tor., 1925, P. 34
The Globe, Tor., Ont., Aug. 1, 1930 "Eminent Painter Dies In Montreal"
The Montreal Star, Mtl., P.Q., Aug. 4, 1930 "Dickson Patterson, R.C.A."
The Times, Picton, Ont., Aug. 7, 1930 "Noted Painter Born in Picton, Died in Montreal" (obituary)
Canadian Art, Its Origin And Development by William Colgate, Ryerson, Tor., 1943 (Paperback, 1967), P. 23
National Gallery of Canada Catalogue, Vol. 3 by R.H. Hubbard, NGC, Ott., 1960, P. 242
The MacMillan Dictionary of Canadian Biography, Ed. W. Stewart Wallace, MacMillan, Tor., 1963, P. 583
Painting in Canada/A History by J. Russell Harper, Univ. Tor. Press, Tor., 1966, P. 176
Agnes Etherington Art Centre, Queen's Univ., Permanent Collection, 1968, by Frances K. Smith, see Cat. No. 175 "Portraits Of Record" near back of book)
Early Painters and Engravers In Canada by J. Russell Harper, Univ. Tor. Press, Tor., 1970, P. 245
Art Gallery of Ontario, The Canadian Collection by Helen Pepall Bradfield, McGraw Hill, Tor., 1970, P. 355
Canadian Art At Auction, 1968-1975, Ed. by Geoffrey Joyner, Sotheby, Tor., Ont., 1975, P. 153
NGC Info. Form (undated)

PATTERSON, Daniel (Dan)
1884-1968

A bachelor farmer of the St. Thomas, Ontario, area who created a piece of folk art by saving 2,000 empty condensed milk cans which he then strung together into a kind of "pop art" work also resembling "a four poster bed" described by Pierre Théberge, Curator of Contemporary Canadian Art, NGC, as follows, "Patterson made his construction for no apparent reason other than that he enjoyed doing it. It is totally abstract and it does not seem to have any kind of symbolic significance. He simply used Carnation Milk cans because they were readily available and he drank the milk because he had no refrigeration. It is both simple and mysterious. His work has the character of a compulsion, totally unreasoned; and it is much more closely related to something like the Watts Towers than . . . naive paintings . . . . " Jean-Paul Morisset, Director of Extension Services of the NGC, suggested the work be entered in The Second Triennial of Naive Art in Bratislava, Czechoslovakia, under the name of "The Construction" and it won second honourable mention in 1969. The work was purchased by the NGC in 1970 from Mrs. W. Earl Anderson, only surviving relative of Dan Patterson (who died in 1968 aged 84) and the work has been on display at the Gallery in Ottawa.

References
Times-Journal, St. Thomas, Ont., Aug. 16, 1968 "Late Elgin Bachelor Farmer May Yet Be International Folk Art Celebrity"
Ibid, Aug. 23, 1968 "Milk Can Art Will be Sent To Czech Show"
News clipping, Jan. 25, 1969 "The bachelor farmer who started tin can art" by Barry Conn Hughes
La Presse, July 19, 1969 "Dan Patterson en Tchécoslovaquie"
Newsletter, NGC, 29 Sept., 1969 "Milk Can Whimsy Wins Award"
The Montreal Star, Oct. 11, 1969 "Posthumous Art Award"
Artscanada, December, 1969 "Patterson's tins in Czechoslovakia" by Pierre Théberge, P. 22, 23 (photos)

PATTERSON, Daniel (Dan) (Cont'd)

The Montreal Star, P.Q., Oct. 11, 1969 "Posthumous Art Award"
Charlottetown Guardian, P.E.I., May 11, 1970 "Only A Bachelor . . . "
Vie Des Arts, Mtl., P.Q., Hiver, 1969-1970 "Arts – Actualities – Expositions"
Third Annual Review of The National Gallery of Canada, 1970-1971, Canadian Painting, Sculpture and Decorative Arts, Acquisitions, P. 71

PATTERSON, Glen
b. 1952

Born in Victoria, B.C., the second of three sons of Dr. and Mrs. T.H. Patterson of Kanata, Ontario, he studied art at the Ottawa High School of Commerce and afterwards attended the Ontario College of Art, Toronto, on a scholarhsip (1970-74) where he took a general course with concentration on sculpture working alongside a college staff artist Royden Rabinowitch with whom he exchanged ideas. Before leaving to study in Toronto he began a large metal sculpture commissioned by the community of Kanata (Kanata-Beaverbrook Community Association, public subscriptions, the Carleton Board of Education and March Township Council) through Bill Ellis, a member of the community association and the main force behind this project. He began work in the summer of 1970 and finally completed the nearly two ton welded steel sculpture entitled "The Watcher." Measuring nine by ten feet, located on a hill in the grounds of the Earl of March Secondary School, the sculpture has proven to be a popular focal point for children and much admired work of art by the residents of the community. After completing his studies at the Ontario College of Art he returned to Ottawa where he established modest living quarters combined with his studio. There he has created some thirty or so modern pieces of sculpture basically derived from geometric designs while also continuing to work on drawing, painting and illustration. Working on a part-time basis for the CBC he has designed sets and coordinated visual presentations for the children's T.V. programme "Pencil Box". He has for some time been art director for the *Canadian Review* but found that this job cut into other areas of his endeavours so much that he relinquished this work. He still contributes illustrations to the magazine. He held a solo show of his sculpture, drawings, paintings and illustrations at the Earl of March High School (c. 1973). He has a developing interest in photography and uses this medium to capture the effects of his work and generally keep a record of the projects he has undertaken including aspects of conceptual art. He has been interested for instance in gardening using various plants and flowers to achieve desired effects. Japanese miniature gardening techniques have interested him considerably and he has done some experiments in this direction. Although being based in Ottawa he may eventually continue his career in western Canada especially his ties with the CBC.

References

The Ottawa Journal, Ont., Nov. 22, 1971 " 'Watcher' watches – 2-ton, 9-foot sculpture overlooks Kanata"
Star Weekly, Tor., Ont., Mar. 4, 1972 "Youth – The teenager who hitched his way to a career in sculpture" by Maureen Johnson
Interviewed artist March 5th, 1977

PATTERSON, Joyce Isobel

b. 1930

Born in London, Ontario, she studied drawing under Patrick Landsley at the Montreal Museum of Fine Arts (1958-59); at the Vancouver School of Art (1959-60); at the University of British Columbia where she graduated with her degree of BFA (1964-68); taking a further course in Art Education at the University of B.C. she studied graphics under R.C. Steele, and design under Penny Gouldstone (1968-71). She has participated in a group show "Deer Lake Printmakers" at Avelles Gallery, Vancouver (1972) and a Vancouver LIP Artists Employment Project (1972, 1973). Her etchings series "Persona" are in private collections as are her "Personae" which are in the City of Vancouver Collection as well as "Renewal", an untitled series and monoprints "Earth days". She has taught part-time at Douglas College, New Westminster (1971) and graphics at the Vancouver Island Summer School of the Arts (1972). A founding member and secretary of the Deer Lake Printmakers Society (1971-72). Living in Vancouver in 1973.

References

NGC Info. Form rec'd 6 Feb., 1973

Perception: Journal B.C. Art Teachers' Association, Vol. 12, No. 2, Spring, 1971 "Experiments in graphic imagery" by Joyce I. Patterson

PATTERSON, Kay (Mrs.)

A graduate of the Ontario College of Art, Toronto, and well known for her paintings, she has done teaching of art at the Thames Theatre, Chatham, Ontario (was co-founder of classes with Mrs. Alice Clarke) as part of the Community Service Courses now offered at St. Clair College of Applied Arts and Technology. She exhibited her own work of oils, water colours and acrylics at the Thames Theatre in a solo show during the autumn of 1970 and subsequently with her daughter Linda in March of 1972. Lives in Chatham, Ontario.

References

Chatham Daily News, Ont., Sept. 25, 1970 "Chatham Artist Honored At Thames Theatre Show"

Ibid, Feb. 26, 1972 "Mother, Daughter Show Opens"

Ibid, Apr. 13, 1972 "Kay Patterson To Teach College Courses In Art"

PATTERSON, Linda

A Chatham, Ontario, artist, she exhibited her sketches and etchings of Chatham buildings at the Thames Theatre, St. Clair College of Applied Arts and Technology with her mother Kay Patterson.

Reference

Chatham News, Ont., Feb. 26, 1972 "Mother, Daughter Show Opens"

PATTERSON, Muriel

Born in Manitoba, she started painting at the age of seventeen, graduated from the Alberta College of Art, Calgary; attended many seminars with professional instructors and took a specialized course at the Banff School of Fine Arts in 1972. She settled in Prince Rupert, B.C., in 1966 and joined the staff at City Hall as a draftswoman and has been teaching art classes and ceramics through the Recreation Commission at the Civic Centre. In her own work she paints scenics, abstracts, portraits and collages in oils, water colours, acrylics, enamels, also does batiks as well as ceramics. Travelling in her station wagon she has camped along the way between Prince Rupert and Fiddler Creek in Jasper National Park, a journey that cuts roughly across the middle of British Columbia. She planned a trip to the Queen Charlotte Islands or the Stewart and Mezziadin Lake areas on the mainland. She was commissioned to do a series for a private collection in Saskatchewan. Muriel Patterson is interested in assisting young people needing background basics in art, architecture or topographical planning, who intend to go on to advanced courses at college or university. In 1971 a showing of her work under the title "Muriel Patterson Retrospective 1948-1971" was held at the Museum Art Gallery, Prince Rupert, when it was noted, "The paintings will please all tastes, with Oliver Lake pencil and ink drawings, harbor oils and grey day watercolors, and gay abstracts in acrylics." A subsequent show of her work was also held at the Museum Art Gallery in 1974. Living in Prince Rupert in 1974.

References
Prince Rupert News, B.C., Oct. 26, 1971 "About 'Them' " by J.W.
Ibid, Nov. 15, 1971 "A great variety seen in exhibition"
Ibid, Feb. 6, 1974 "Local artist finds area exciting" (article with photo of artist beside one of her paintings)

PATTERSON, Nancy-Lou

An assistant professor of fine arts at the University of Waterloo and former art instructor at the University of Seattle, she came to Canada in 1962 with her husband, Dr. E. Palmer Patterson, associate professor of history at the University of Waterloo. Nancy-Lou is known for her own art work which includes stained glass windows, altar and chapel decorations and paintings. She is also known as a practising poet and her poems have appeared in Canadian Forum, Canadian Poetry, Prairie Schooner and the Beloit Poetry Journal. Her commissions include sixteen stained glass windows and decorations in the chapel of the Mennonite Conrad Grebel College, Waterloo; terra cotta altar cross at St. Luke's Church, Winnipeg, and the altar and chapel decoration at St. Monica House, Waterloo. She has painted scenery for the Kitchener-Waterloo Little Theatre and is also curator for the University of Waterloo Gallery of the Theatre of Arts. Mother of six.

References
Globe & Mail, Tor., Ont., Oct. 26, 1964 "History of Mennonites Depicted in Windows"
Galt Evening Reporter, Ont., Oct. 3, 1968 "Annual Art Show Opens Central Church, October 8"

PATTERSON, Naomi

A Prince George, B.C., artist, she did two oil paintings depicting winter and summer in the Fraser Canyon, for the Hotel Simon Fraser's Canyon Room in Prince George.

Reference
Prince George Citizen, B.C., Mar. 13, 1961 "Local Artist" (large photo of artist at work and caption)

PATTISON, Albert Mead
b. (c) 1887

Born in Clarenceville, Quebec, he studied arts and architecture at McGill University and later worked part time as an illustrator for the Montreal *Gazette*. He would only work part time so that he could devote the remainder of his attentions to his paintings which he exhibited at The Montreal Museum of Fine Arts several times. Pattison died at Hudson, Quebec, at the age of 70.

Reference
Le Droit, Ottawa, Ont., Nov. 29, 1957 "Un ex-dessinateur de la 'Gazette' meurt à Hudson"

PATTON, Harold Preston
b. 1929

Born in Calgary, Alberta, he started drawing at the age of six and later attended Saturday Morning Classes at the Vancouver School of Art. At fifteen he won first prize in the Sir Ernest MacMillan exhibition at the Vancouver Art Gallery for an oil painting. He studied evenings at the Vancouver School of Art (1946-50) and also attended the Banff School of Fine Arts (1948) and day classes at the Vancouver School of Art for a short period. He joined the firm of The Parisian, a Vancouver department store, where he worked as manager of advertising and display for five and a half years. In 1954 he was granted leave-of-absence from this firm to travel to Europe. While in England he was hired by a London firm as a travelling art consultant. Returning to Canada in 1955 he went back to work with The Parisian for a time then became a free lance artist in advertising, display, interior design, mural work, portraiture, sculpture and ceramics. Early in his painting career he was influenced by the work of El Greco, early Spanish School and modern trends of various Paris schools. He became interested in television work too doing announcing, commentating, designing and occasionally an advertising model. He had his own weekly T.V. programme "The Lively Arts" a series of commentaries, interviews and discussions on local, national and international cultural activities. He was assistant director of the Calgary Allied Arts Centre for two years (1958-60). He had served on the Centre's Programme and Education Committee and was a member of the National Council for Child Education prior to being appointed to the Arts Centre's staff. At the Centre he organized a Mozart Society, Jazz Workshop, local theatre group, recitals, and with two Calgary musicians Gerald Bales and John Searchfield he organized a Handel-Purcell Festival under the sponsorship of the Centre. He designed and directed a production of Jean Anouilh's "Ring Round

PATTON, Harold Preston (Cont'd)

The Moon" for a local theatre group who won the Visual Presentation Award in the Alberta Provincial Drama Festival; was designer for "Workshop 14". Did designs for productions of "Brigadoon", "Auntie Mame", "Mary Stuart", "Merry Widow", "The Women". He taught several painting classes at the Centre including portraiture, anatomy; also History of Music, Music Appreciation, Art Appreciation and Creative Child Drama. He organized one of the largest Eskimo Exhibitions ever held in Western Canada and was successful in establishing a Record Library in the Allied Arts Centre. In 1962 he became music critic for the Calgary *Herald* and also art critic. He was appointed Canadian director for the Vincent Price Exhibitions in the 1960's and moved to Toronto where he heads a staff of six. A member of the Alberta Society of Artists and the Calgary Film Society, he is represented in a number of private collections. Vincent Price purchased several of his paintings for the Price Collection.

References

Document from artist, 1961

Canadian Art, Vol. 20, No. 2, March/April, 1963 "Clement Greenberg's View of Art on The Prairies" by C.G., P. 96, 97

Victoria Times, B.C., July 23, 1966 "Price Collection Starts Tour In Victoria" by Ab Kent

PAUFLER, Elsa

She came to Canada from Germany in 1952 to join her husband Horst. A painter of subjects which mainly revolve around nature including seascapes she also creates rock figurines which she paints and shapes. The rocks are mainly found in the area of Gabarus where she selects as well, driftwood for her driftwood art. Describing her work Inder Gupta noted, "Elsa paints in oil. Her colors are rich and vibrant. There is a violent gaiety in her seascapes. Her works mainly revolve around nature, as she observes it. There is a set quality about her paintings. They don't show the kind of restlessness as one observes in Paufler's." A member of the Maritime Arts Association and mother of Ralph (a budding artist) and Stephen, she intends to pursue her art career full time after her family is grown and settled.

References

Cape Breton Post, Sydney, N.S., Aug. 7, 1971 " 'Village Art Gallery' " by Francis H. Stevens

Ibid, Aug. 4, 1973 "Village Art Gallery – Gabarus" by Inder Gupta

PAUFLER, Horst

A graduate from the State Academy of Arts (Landes Kunst Schule), Hamburg, Germany, where he studied industrial and advertising design and specialized in typography and calligraphy. He began his professional career in 1949 with the Tempo Advertising Agency in Hof, Bavaria. In 1954 he came to Sydney, Nova Scotia, where he was hired as an artist for CJCB-TV (1954-1961). Then he moved to Toronto, Ontario. He held several responsible positions with various firms in-

PAUFLER, Horst (Cont'd)

cluding Williams and Hill where he played a major role in the production of three award-winning industrial films and several commercials including those for Esso, Quaker and General Foods. From 1965 to 1967 he was chief designer with Worden and Watson Ltd. of Toronto and handled advertising and interior design accounts for IBM, Chrysler Canada and its Rootes Motors Division. In 1967 CJCB-TV made him an attractive offer and he returned to Sydney to become the station's Art Director. In his own painting he is known for his portraits, landscapes, scenes of the sea, old farmhouses, genre scenes of Cape Breton in the media of oils, water colours and pastels. Reviewing his work in 1971 Francis H. Stevens in the *Cape Breton Post* noted, " . . . Paufler is among the relatively few who paint exactly on the spot of the subject of his observation. He explores, finds something that bids him pause and thereupon goes to work on it . . . . In an hour of observation on-the-spot he absorbs the whole life of the scene as the click of a camera shutter cannot . . . . In the meantime, Paufler has advanced to the use of pastels and water colours to convey instantaneous impressions keenly perceived. These are mediums demanding more of skill than does an oil painting which can be worked over and modified in the process of painting it. The pastels and water colours in the Village Gallery are an exciting development of his career. They are noteworthy in conveying atmospheric effects, such as clouds touched by sunlight. They are done spontaneously, sometimes explosively." Paufler has instructed courses for the Sydney Arts Council. In June of 1971 he opened his own gallery the "Village Art Gallery" in Gabarus (south of Louisburg, N.S.) where he settled with his wife Elsa, an artist in her own right, who joined him in Canada after he had established himself. At the gallery he and his wife show their work and the work of other artists. A solo show of his work was held at the James McConnell Memorial Library in Sydney, N.S. in 1970. A member of the Maritime Arts Association.

References
  Cape Breton Highlander, Sydney, N.S., Jan. 15, 1969 "Horst Paufler To Instruct Course"
  Cape Breton Post, Sydney, N.S., Nov. 25, 1970 "An Art Review – Artist's Work Is Bold – Yet Sensitive" by Francis H. Stevens
  Ibid, Nov. 24, 1970 "Exhibition Opens Today"
  Ibid, April 7, 1971 "Group Selects Paufler Design For Letterhead"
  Ibid, Aug. 7, 1971 " 'Village Art Gallery' " by Francis H. Stevens
  Ibid, July 28, 1972 "A Review – Village Art Gallery Offers Aesthetic Rewards" by Frank H. Stevens
  Ibid, Aug. 4, 1973 "Village Art Gallery – Gabarus" by Inder Gupta

PAUL, Awana G. (Mrs.)

Born in Winnipeg, Manitoba, she studied nights in ceramics and sculpture (1948) and in Metz, France under René Gayé in design and ceramics for six months; in Ottawa under Eleanor Milne and Brodie Shearer at the Municipal Art Centre for sculpture (1960-66); under John Hogg in Britain for sculpture and restoration in gold leaf; with Eleanor Milne in gold leaf work at the House of Commons, Ottawa and she took several other courses in ceramics, batik, design and sculpture. She worked on restoration of the Senate Room 256, Parliament Bldgs., Ottawa

PAUL, Awana G. (Mrs.) (Cont'd)

(c. 1962); gold leaf work in the British High Commission Bldg., Ottawa (c. 1963) and restoration work in the House of Commons, Ottawa, assisting Eleanor Milne, National Stone Carver of Canada (1965). She has exhibited her work in the following places: ceramics, Metz, France; ceramics, ceramic sculpture at Dept. Economics & Development, Tor.; Municipal Ceramic Centre group show, Ottawa City Hall; sculpture at Municipal Art Centre, Ottawa City Hall; ceramic sculpture, batik design at the Lennox & Addington School Board, Napanee, Ont.; carvings (slate bas-relief), Hull, Quebec; ceramics, stoneware, sculpture at the Ottawa Valley Crafts Assoc. at Lofthouse, Ottawa. She married Norman Fraser Paul in 1950 and they have one grown son Stephen. She lives in Ottawa but has a studio at Roblin, Ontario, under the name "Pauldale Studio of Arts & Crafts" where she teaches ceramics and other crafts to her students. Member: Ottawa Valley Crafts Assoc.; Potters' Guild; Les Compagnons de l'Art.

Reference
NGC Info. Form rec'd Feb. 5, 1967

PAUL, Gregory Preston

b. 1933

Born in Toronto, Ontario, he studied four years at Northern Vocational School, Toronto, under R. Short, A. Sullivan, P. Gardner, J. Bennett and E. Curry and at the Doon School of Fine Art (at a later date) for two weeks under Yvonne McKague Housser. After graduating from Northern Vocational in 1953 he joined the firm of Landy Advertising. About this time he had one of his paintings accepted for showing in the Royal Canadian Academy annual exhibition, a rare honour for an artist just out of school. After seventeen years in the advertising business he established in 1970 his own studio and art school in King City, just north of Toronto, called The School of Creative Art where batik, pastels, pen and ink, drawing, water colour, acrylic, charcoal, paper mache, block printing and wood carving courses are given. His own paintings were shown in a group show at the Richmond Inn under the sponsorship of the Brush and Palette Gallery (1966). Describing his work in 1971 Kay Kritzwiser noted, "Paul is obsessed by the patterns of colors set up by the wind in the trees. In his small collection of paintings, that movement is explored with the intensity of an Emily Carr painting. The Emily Carr search for that vibrancy in nature has been a challenge in his own painting." He lives in King City just north of Toronto with his wife Joan and their two children Victoria and Doug.

References
Aurora Banner, Ont., Feb. 9, 1966 "Gregory Paul's paintings outstanding in Richmond Hill exhibit"
Ibid, Dec. 16, 1970 "Greg Paul of King City – Gives up 'rat race' to teach and paint" by Ann McWilliam
Globe & Mail, Tor., Ont., July 8, 1971 "Kicking the old treadmill habit" by Kay Kritzwiser
NGC Info. Form rec'd Jan. 15, 1954

PAUL, Louise
19 – - 1961

Born in Fort William, Ontario, she studied at the Ontario College of Art then opened a studio in Toronto specializing in sculpture. She moved to New York City in the late 1930's where she sculpted portrait heads of Helen Hayes, Vincent Price, Elissa Landi and acting Mayor of New York, Newbold Morris, also New York's police commissioner Valentine and others. During World War II she returned to Toronto and devoted much of her time to helping wounded veterans with art lessons at the D.V.A. Occupational Therapy Department at the Christie Street Hospital. One of her former veteran students, badly burned on the hands and face continued his art studies in Paris after the war. In 1958 she gave up sculpture and turned to painting portraits of children at her Bloor Street East studio in Toronto. She died in 1961 at Oakville, Ontario, leaving a brother Ernest Paul of Toronto, an aunt Mrs. Louise Beeman of Oakville and a niece Mrs. Lawrence Nickle of Wawa.

References
>   *Record Star*, Oakville, Ont., Jan. 15, 1959 "Children's Portrait Painter's Work At Public Library"
>   *Toronto Daily Star*, Ont., Jan. 31, 1959 "Put Police Chief's 'Head' In Safe" by Vancy Kasper (portrait head stored in safe between sittings)
>   *The Toronto Telegram*, Ont., Aug. 14, 1961 "Was famed Sculptor"

PAUL, Pijush Kanti
b. (c) 1934

Born in Seremba, Malaya, a painter of village, fishing, farming and mining scenes his work was exhibited in the National Art Gallery of Malaysia and in various art centres throughout Europe and South East Asia. He came to Canada in 1964 and has had showings of his work in Toronto, Stratford, Hamilton and elsewhere and settled in Toronto where he became director of the Colonade Art Gallery. Originally he was a brush painter but switched to finger painting through an accident years ago in Malaysia. While he was working on a landscape the bristles of his brush broke and he had to finish his painting with his fingers. Realizing what a direct communication there was between his mind, vision and fingers in this technique he continued to paint with his fingers. He does both representational and abstract painting using vivid colours like burning orange, rust, bright yellow and blue revealing a certain exotic Oriental influence of his early years combined with a new influence of his North American environment. He exhibited his paintings in 1968 at the Parkview Art Gallery, Niagara Falls and demonstrated to members of the Niagara Falls Kiwanis Club at the Sheraton-Brock Hotel. He lives in Toronto.

References
>   *Niagara Falls Review*, Ont., Oct. 26, 1968 "This artist needs no brushes" by Brian McConnell
>   *Toronto Daily Star*, Ont., Dec. 5, 1969 "Artists put heart into their work" by Lotta Dempsey

PAULS, Mary (née Mary Funk)

Born in Morden, Manitoba, she won scholarships in school for her artwork which eventually enabled her to study at the Winnipeg School of Art for a year under Professor G. Eliasson. She lived with her husband in Winkler where she belonged simultaneously to art clubs in Morden, Winkler and Morris, travelling back and forth to their meetings. Then she moved to Steinbach where she became a member of the Steinbach Art Club. She does pen-and-ink sketches and paints on velvet background, also works with conventional media on canvas. She was commissioned by the Steinbach Hospital Board to paint a hospital mural depicting a Christmas nativity scene on a mural measuring 52 feet by eight feet high. After two months the mural was completed on time. Being an outdoor project Mrs. Pauls used fifteen sheets of plywood measuring 4 by 8 feet each, and painted in the scene with boat enamel which withstands severe weather conditions without losing its colour. One of her paintings depicting her childhood farm experience entitled "Going Visiting" was presented to Queen Elizabeth on her visit to Steinbach in July of 1970. An ambition of Mary Pauls is to paint a series of pictures of the Hutterite colonies. Hutterite customs have fascinated her for years. The mother of four boys she enjoys teaching them the rudiments of drawing and painting.

References
  Carillon News, Steinbach, Man., Dec. 30, 1965 "Housewife's Artwork Attracts Attention"
  Ibid, July 8, 1970 (photo of Mary Pauls with her painting "Going Visiting")

PAULSEN, Ingerid

Born in Norway she studied at the Oslo State School of Crafts in Norway and the Royal Academy of Fine Arts, Copenhagen. She has travelled extensively with her artist husband, Piet Kuiters, and has exhibited in Norway, Denmark, Spain and Morocco. Her paintings vary in size and shape including circular paintings she calls mandalas. She uses a variety of techniques including oil on canvas, acrylic on canvas, collage and aquarelle. In the case of her mandalas she uses round lacquered wood panels. Her work was described by Beth Raugust in the Montreal *Gazette* as follows, " . . . . regardless of medium she usually casts fairy-tale images bursting with brilliant color . . . All of her paintings are happy works although some blend the joyous with the mystical." When she begins her mandalas she doesn't plan beforehand but starts drawing with a pencil and it comes out spontaneously although she has been influenced to some degree by Oriental folklore. She came to Canada with her husband in the spring of 1969 (they have two children). Her paintings were exhibited in 1969 at Place Bonaventure's Better Living Centre, and at the Boutique Soleil, both in Montreal.

References
  The Gazette, Mtl., P.Q., Sept. 23, 1969 "She finds joy in a paintbox" by Beth Raugust
  The Montreal Star, P.Q., Oct. 9, 1969 "Better Living Centre and Galerie Libre – Illusions of space and a feast for the eye" by Catherine Bates

PAULSON, Hannibal
b. 1918

An artist who was an explosives specialist with the Princess Patricia's Canadian Light Infantry in the Second World and Korean wars and retired from the services in 1961. He turned to cartooning in ink and then in a process he calls sculptoon, a combination of cartooning and sculpture which he then photographs for the finished product. His idea is to prepare clay model heads of prominent political figures and a series of clay-model bodies in different postures. He plans to model both Canadian and foreign personalities. He lives in Montreal.

References

The Montreal Star, Mtl., P.Q., Oct. 14, 1972 "Add sculpture to a cartoon and, hey presto – sculptoon!" by Terence Moore

PAUTA
b. 1916

Son of Saila he was born at a small inland camp called Kilaparutua on the Foxe Peninsula of Baffin Island some miles north of Cape Dorset. His father Saila was a great hunter and was renowned for his strength which was evident in his hunting (could kill a walrus with one thrust of his harpoon). While Pauta was still a small boy the family moved to another camp at Nuata where his father worked for the Hudson's Bay Company. As a teenager, Pauta at first carved harpoon heads and other implements in ivory, then later became a carver then graphic artist of subjects to do with camp life and the hunt, including the polar bear, caribou and owls. In 1960, a widower, he settled with his second wife Pitaloosie at Cape Dorset. He had met her at Frobisher Bay while working on the Dew Line. In 1967 he participated in an International Sculpture Symposium in Toronto and his massive limestone bear stands in company with other large works in Toronto's High Park. He lives at Cape Dorset with his wife and their four children. His son Mikiseeti by his former marriage, is also an accomplished carver.

References

Letter of information dated 24 Feb., 1970, from A. Stevenson, Chief, Northern Services Div. Dept of Indian Affairs and Northern Development (copy deposited in NGC Lib. artist's file)

Inunnit, The Art of the Canadian Eskimo by W.T. Larmour, Information Canada, 1968, P. 53

Sculpture of the Eskimo by George Swinton, M&S, Tor., 1972, P. 41, Plate 60; P. 56, Plate 78; P. 186, Plate 461; P. 187 Plates 462-3-4-5-6-7-8

Artscanada, December, 1971; January, 1972, P. 106

Dorset 76 (Cape Dorset Annual Graphics Collection 1976), M.F. Feheley Publishers Ltd., Tor., P. 33, Plate 35; Page 70, 71 (biographical note)

PAVAI, Nicholas

A Montreal, P.Q., artist who painted three murals in the Arctic Exhibit section of the Hill Island duty-free shop, Thousand Islands near the Ivy Lea Bridge. The firm of International Resort Facilities Limited, responsible for the construction of the

PAVAI, Nicholas (Cont'd)

shop hired Tower Company Limited, engineering contractors of Montreal to build the shop. Parvai received many helpful hints from employees of Tower Company who had worked in the Arctic but even before starting his preliminary drawings he spent weeks of research to gain as much information as possible about the Arctic and the Eskimos. All three of the murals are in blues, greens and whites. The first panel (22-1/2 x 12 ft h.) deals with a poetic composition of the Arctic which blends the lives of primitive Eskimos and the scientific invasion of recent decades. The second panel (35 ft x 14 ft h.), the central panel, shows members of a small settlement of Eskimos leaving their skin-covered tents to go seal hunting in kayaks. The third (35 ft x 10 ft h.), depicts the Arctic Winter by four igloos showing through the snow with a background of sky and snow and ice in panoramic blend with the Aurora Borealis adding a haunting light to the sky. Pavai is employed by the Display Department of Eaton's Montreal branch store.

Reference
The Gazette, Mtl., P.Q., June 14, 1960 "Murals Satisfy Experts"

PAVELICK, Ann (Mrs.)

A Saskatoon artist, she taught handicrafts for three years while living in Yorkton. A self-taught painter in oils she paints outdoor scenes in all seasons and also does miniatures of prairie flowers on velvet, bordered by delicate frames. Nancy Russell in the Saskatoon *Star Phoenix* described her work as follows, "Her style is soft and her pictures are gentle. There is a consistent attractiveness to her paintings, mainly because they portray beautiful components of nature and she has mastered her interpretation of these components . . . . Nature is always at rest, her scenes have a serenity about them that is never replaced by the turbulence of a storm or blizzard. Her flowers are constantly in bloom and her log cabins always standing. This constant pleasure is justified, as Mrs. Pavelick sees only joy and satisfaction in her work." Each year she travels to the countryside and also spends much of her time with her husband Lou at their summer home at Candle Lake in Northern Saskatchewan. A solo show of her work was held at the St. Thomas More Gallery in Saskatoon in March of 1975.

Reference
Star Phoenix, Saskatoon, Sask., Mar. 14, 1975 "Accent on art with Nancy Russell – Painting source of joy"

PAWCZUK, Eugene

b. 1946

Born in Germany of Ukrainian origin, he immigrated to Canada with his parents. He studied art at the Central Secondary School in Hamilton and then attended the Ontario College of Art for a brief period. A versatile artist he does sculpture, paint-

PAWCZUK, Eugene (Cont'd)

ing, engraving, and is known for his fine drawings in chalk and pencil. His subjects range from mythological animals to portraits. Reviewing his 1972 show, *The Hamilton Spectator* described him as, " . . . one of the most promising of the young Hamilton area artists" and found his 1971 show revealing, "an impressive display of technical ability and, in many instances, of true insight." He paints in a traditional style and his portraits are executed in oil and water colour in the finest of detail. He feels that portraiture can be as outstanding and innovative as other branches of fine art. His work has been shown in Hamilton at the Petteplace Gallery, the Art Gallery of Hamilton, the Beckett Gallery and in Brantford at the Art Gallery of Brantford. He also participated in a show of Ukrainian art and artifacts at the Hamilton Public Library for the 53rd anniversary of Ukrainian independence. He was awarded a Canada Council grant in 1970 and a grant from the Elizabeth T. Greenshields Foundation in 1972. He lives in Grimsby, Ontario.

References
The Hamilton Spectator, Ont., Jan. 22, 1971 "Ukrainians enrich Canadian culture"
Ibid, April 15, 1972 "Grimsby artist moves in one direction – forward"
Information through the courtesy of Dominion Foundries & Steel Ltd., Hamilton, Ont.

PAWSON, Ruth May
b. 1908

Born in Stratford, Ontario, she moved to Regina, Saskatchewan, at the age of three with her parents. There she was educated and later attended the Regina College of Art (c. 1940) where she studied practical art under Augustus Kenderdine and the History of Art and Art Appreciation under Prof. Gordon Snelgrove graduating with her Associate of Fine Arts degree. Later she attended the Emma Lake Summer School where she did outdoor sketching under Kenderdine (1941-42-46) and summer sessions at the Banff School of Fine Arts under A.Y. Jackson. She became a teacher in elementary schools and also taught a children's Saturday Morning Class for five years at the Regina College of Art. In her own painting she has been striving to capture the feeling of limitless space, freedom, and serenity found in the prairies. While she was teaching at Davin School in Regina in 1952 one of her paintings was selected by a committee of the National Gallery of Canada for reproduction by the silk screen method. The painting, a Saskatchewan harvest scene was done by her along the highway west of Brora, a few miles north of Regina, and was one of sixty works of Canadian landscape painters reproduced under this plan. Viewing her 1975 solo show at the Dunlop Gallery, Regina Central Library, Lora Burke for *The Leader-Post* noted, "For all the care in composition, there is nothing stilted in Ms. Pawson's work. Her brush moves with a lyrical freedom; her palette is as varied as the seasons she commemorates. In some paintings, there is a clarity of the sort more usually associated with watercolor than with oil. It is an effect both observant and accurate. The unfiltered light of the plains produces just such clear-cut lines and pure color. For me at least, the exhibition provided a surprise. I had thought of Ms. Pawson as primarily a landscape artist. But this exhibition includes prairie towns and city streets. They are painted with the same direct appreciation that characterizes the landscapes." She is represented in the permanent collection of the

PAWSON, Ruth May (Cont'd)

Banff School of Fine Arts, the Saskatchewan Arts Board and in collections else-where. Her more recent shows include: Two-woman show at the art gallery, 13th floor of the Saskatchewan Power Corporation in Regina (1970) and the Dunlop Gallery at the Regina Central Library, Regina (1975). She retired from teaching and lives in Regina where she devotes her full time to painting. She was Secretary to the Federation of Canadian Artists, Regina Branch (1951-54).

References
>   *The Leader Post*, Regina, Sask., Nov. 12, 1952 "Reginan's canvas bought by National Art Gallery" (not purchased but only loaned for the purpose of silk screen reproduction)
>   *The Western Producer*, Saskatoon, Sask., Feb. 5, 1953 (photo of painting)
>   *Union Farmer*, Saskatoon, Sask., April, 1957 (reproduction of her study of grain elevators in spring time)
>   *Regina Leader Post*, Sask., June 29, 1970 "Artists' work on display"
>   Ibid, July 10, 1970 "Prairie scenes are portrayed" (photo showing Dorothy Martin and Ruth Pawson with their work)
>   Ibid, May 28, 1975 "At the galleries – Pawson on prairie" by Lora Burke
>   NGC Info. Form rec'd Oct. 13, 1954

PAWULA, Kenneth

A Victoria, B.C., artist who exhibited his paintings at the Victoria Art Gallery. In the work shown he married impressionist-like atmospheres to international style hardedge paintings. Describing his work Glenn Howarth in the *Victoria Times* noted, "Always there is a window of soft sky set inside a hard edged composition of circles, romboids and triangles. It is as though the artist conceived his paintings while looking out from inside a boldly decorated airplane cockpit. With each patch of sky there is no horizon or landscape below. Pawula titles one canvas 8 Miles High . . . the shallow picture space of hard-edge work is broken and color frontality be-comes a skin stretched over an open space behind. Going through Pawula's sky hole the painting gives the illusion of opening out."

Reference
>   *Victoria Times*, B.C., Jan. 29, 1972 "Art – Looking Through Sky Hole" by Glenn Howarth

PAWULA, Mrs. Kenneth

A Victoria, B.C., artist who displayed her jewellery at the Victoria Art Gallery at the same time as her husband exhibited his paintings. Her work included a plaque commissioned to commemorate the retirement of a university president.

Reference
>   *Victoria Times*, B.C., Jan. 29, 1972 "Art – Looking Through Sky Hole" by Glenn Howarth

PAXY, Charles

b. (c) 1916

Born in Hungary, he attended the Ludovica Military Academy at Budapest where he learned in addition to his regular courses the art of wood carving. He left his native Hungary for Germany in 1945 and came to Canada in 1950 settling in Sudbury in 1952. An employee of the International Nickel Company in the ventilation department he created most of his sculptures (over three hundred of them) in a studio 3,200 feet underground. He started his activity as unofficial sculptor for Inco in 1959 and since then has produced the Inco and Falconbridge trophies for competitions within both companies. His style has been described by the *Sudbury Star* as follows, " . . . is closely, almost uncannily, related to his mining subject. The element of the rough hewn is redolent of the mining reality as observed by a man who has been right with the mining scene for 17 years." But Paxy has created a number of other works not related to mining subject matter such as a set of two-inch high chessmen. He prefers to work in wood but has also created sculpture in clay, stone, and plaster. Much of his work however depicts miners, mining scenes, and machinery. He carved for instance the Inco Mine Rescue Trophy in stained basswood. An exhibition of his carvings was held at the Sudbury Museum and Arts Centre in 1969. He has been workshop director for the Sudbury Arts and Crafts Club where he has passed on his knowledge to members of the Sudbury community and has also demonstrated his art to teachers and students attending art workshops at the Sheridan Technical School.

References

Sudbury Star, Ont., Jan. 6, 1968 "Arts, Crafts Club Plans Full Program" (article with photo of Paxy carving)
Ibid, July 23, 1969 "Sculpture Done in Wood"
Ibid, Oct. 14, 1969 "City Wood Sculptor's Work On Display at Arts Centre"
Ibid, Feb. 14, 1972 "Artists Display Wares at School Workshop" (photo of Paxy carving while students watch)

PAYEUR, Michale John

b. 1945

A graduate of the Ontario College of Art he received an Eaton Foundation travelling scholarship and visited art centres in Europe including Italy where he studied avant-garde work in plastic sculpture. From this experience he experimented and then created modern and relatively inexpensive sculptures by moulding plastic. He has also worked on a backdrop for the Scottish World Festival at the C.N.E., Toronto (1972); life size figures for the Ford Theatre at the Ontario Science Centre, Toronto and art displays for the Indian Museum in Ottawa. He has exhibited his work in solo shows in galleries in Toronto including the Shaw-Remington Gallery. He was associated with the Abra Jackson Studios in Brampton who handled works by Jackson Turner, Joseph Flasko, Rick McCarthy and Gary Stark. Was living in Brampton in 1972.

Reference

The Daily Times, Brampton, Ont., Aug. 15, 1972 "Municipal Complex Possibilities – New Sculptor Has High Hope" by Mike Lawson

PAYNE, Anabel

A Fort Frances, Ontario, artist she exhibited her paintings at the Fort Frances Downstairs Art Gallery in the local public library. She has been an active member of the Fort Frances Art Association for many years and has served on the board of the International Art Association. In her painting she works mainly in oils and is interested in a wide variety of subjects. For several years she has volunteered her services to help out a group interested in painting and holding their meetings at the Downstairs Gallery.

Reference
The Daily Bulletin, Fort Frances, Ont., April 7, 1969 "Art News"

PAYNE, David H.

Born in England, the son of a church minister, he was destined to enter the ministry like two of his brothers. He won a scholarship in art and his parents not wishing to waste such an opportunity being of modest means, allowed him to enter the Royal College of Art, South Kensington, London, England, where he studied painting under Sir Alfred East. At the College he won a bronze medal. He came to the prairies, Canada, in 1913. He enlisted in the army at the outbreak of W.W. I. (1914) and went back overseas to the war where he was gassed. While recovering in Kingswood Park Hospital at Tunbridge Wells, Kent, he married a Miss Kirker originally from Belfast, Ireland, who had been on the same boat as him to Canada in 1913. He returned to Canada with his bride and settled in Regina in 1919. He got a job as a letter carrier for the Regina Post Office and in the evenings and holidays devoted his time to painting. After about five years he had enough paintings to hold his first solo show in 1925 under the auspices of the Local Council of Women's art committee in the Regina College. A landscape painter he used a rich and delicate palette to render many scenes of Saskatchewan. He moved to Port Alice on north Vancouver Island in 1936 where he worked for a pulp and paper company. He returned to Regina to visit his son and daughter-in-law, Harold & Mrs. Payne in 1945. An article appearing in the Regina *Leader-Post* about this visit also mentioned his activity on the west coast. It indicated that he had painted among other subjects the Indian villages and totem poles of Vancouver Island.

References
Saturday Night, Tor., June 20, 1925 "Canadian Art Notes"
Unidentified news clipping, Regina, May, 1925 "War Hero, Letter Carrier, Now Artist, D.H. Payne Today Shows Work to City"
Leader-Post, Regina, Sask., May 14, 1945 "Payne tells of coastal art – Western artists take rightful place now"
Saskatchewan: Art and Artists, April 2 – July 31, 1971, Norman Mackenzie Art Gallery/ Regina Public Library Art Gallery P. 41, 53 (ill.)

PAYNE, Mrs. Edward N.

Born in Dunfermline, Scotland, she graduated from the Edinburgh College of Fine Arts. She came to Canada in 1955 and lived in Toronto for two and a half years where she met and married a chemical engineer. They lived for a time in New Brunswick, Nova Scotia, Newfoundland, and Niagara Falls, Ontario. A painter and potter she is known for her figurines in clay of genre subjects like children at play or other subjects such as a colourful clown or a miniature landscape. She has exhibited her works in the art department of Anderson Meldrum and Anderson, Buffalo, N.Y., and some of her clay models are also in Toronto. The mother of five she is a member of the Niagara Craft Association and the Canadian Potters' Guild. Living in Niagara Falls, Ontario, in 1969.

Reference
>   *Niagara Falls Review*, Ont., June 4, 1969 "Work and hobbies can be combined" by Ruby Sibbett Lindsay

PAYNE, Emma Solvason (Mrs. Gordon Payne)

From Hunts Point, Queen's County, N.S. her painting "Fish House Interior" was purchased by the Province of Nova Scotia on the occasion of the 2nd Centennial Visual Arts Exhibition of Nova Scotia Artists held at the Citadel Gallery, Halifax, in 1967. This exhibition went on a five week tour of Nova Scotia following its run at the Citadel Gallery. The wife of Gordon Payne, artist, she has exhibited with him at the "Ten Mile House", Bedford and elsewhere.

References
>   *Mail Star*, Halifax, N.S., May 4, 1963 "Successful Artist Found New Scope In Nova Scotia" (joint show)
>   *Liverpool Advance*, N.S., Dec. 28, 1967 "Queens County Artist Signally Honoured"

PAYNE, Gordon Eastcott
b. 1890

Born in Payne's Mills, Ontario, as a boy he watched his uncle W. St. Thomas-Smith work at his easel. He attended public school and high school in Niagara Falls. At the age of nineteen he entered the Albright Art Gallery, Buffalo, where he studied under Mary Cox for a year. Next he studied at the Ontario College of Art under G.A. Reid, J.W. Beatty, William Cruikshank and Robert Holmes (1910-14). As a youth he was employed as a blacksmith's striker, a carpenter's helper and pressman. When he became an art student he worked as a waiter, theatre usher and drove a horse and cart for a Toronto newspaper. At the time of his graduation, W.W. I broke out and he went overseas as a signals officer and, during W.W. II served as an instructor with the Commonwealth Air Training Scheme. In the summer of 1920 he studied at the Pennsylvania Academy of Art at Chester Springs under a teacher, Garber. He worked as a commercial artist for a number of years and lived for a time in London, Ontario. He produced books of drawings for Upper Canada Col-

PAYNE, Gordon Eastcott (Cont'd)

lege, Ontario Ladies College, Whitby; Ridley College and Appleby School (1928-30). In 1934 he founded an art gallery association and opened a gallery in the basement of the library under the name of the Ingersoll Art Gallery Association which was the only gallery of its kind in Canada serving the smaller cities and towns. He conducted children's classes at the Ingersoll Gallery, 1934-37 and adult education classes at the Ingersoll Gallery and also at Liverpool, N.S.; Doon School of Fine Arts, 1946-50 and opened Toronto's largest private school of art, The Payne School of Fine Art, 1946-58. He retired to Nova Scotia and set up a studio at Hunt's Point, Queens County where he has painted numerous landscapes and seascapes in oils, water colours and also made fine drawings for which he is known. He is influenced to some degree by St. Thomas-Smith, Willard Metcalfe and Winslow Homer. During his solo show at the Ten Mile House, Bedford, N.S., in 1963, the reviewer for the Halifax *Mail-Star* noted, "A master of mood, this is shown in the folksy quality of some of his lobster shacks, the peacefulness depicted in 'Snowy Day at Hunt's Point" and the . . . magnitude of some of his seascapes, while 'Foggy Day, Hunt's Point Wharf' has such depth and character that one can feel the swirling mist and smell the fish. Painting in a realistic style, his treatment of bracken and grasses is particularly effective, while he uses color with imagination and warmth as shown best in 'Beech Woods', sunset views of Hunt's Point and other works." He was on the Exhibition Committee of Western Art League, London, Ontario from 1937-39 and won prizes at the Western Exhibition, London, Ontario, 1939; Hadassah Annual Prize, 1957 and the Purchase Award of the Maritime Art Association in 1960. He has been a contributor to Canadian National Exhibitions and many other group shows at various times. His solo shows also include those at E.J. Coles, Woodstock, Ontario; O.B. Graves Galleries; University of Western Ontario; White Point Lodge, N.S. and elsewhere. He is represented in the Art Gallery of Edmonton, Kitchener-Waterloo Art Gallery, Art Gallery of Ontario and in many private collections. Was actively involved with various art societies which included: Art League of Toronto (1919); Graphic Arts Society (1921); Ontario Society of Artists (1925); Society of Canadian Painter-Etchers and Engravers (1946); Nova Scotia Society of Artists (1959) and the Arts and Letters Club, Toronto. His wife Emma Solvason Payne is a painter in her own right and has exhibited jointly with him.

References

Niagara Falls Review, Ont., Feb. 11, 1935 "Falls Man Is Gallery Head"
Evening Free Press, London, Ont., Dec. 2, 1938 "Gordon Payne O.S.A. Exhibits"
Review, Niagara Falls, Ont., May 22, 1950 "Gordon E. Payne Has School of Art"
Mail-Star, Halifax, N.S., May 4, 1963 "Successful Artist Found New Scope In Nova Scotia"
Books & Catalogues
Appleby School, a sketch-book by Gordon E. Payne, 1930, 5 plates (500 copies)
Ontario Ladies' College, Whitby Drawings by Gordon E. Payne, 1930, 8 plates (300 copies)
Ridley, a sketch-book by Gordon E. Payne, 1930, 7 plates (300 copies)
Upper Canada College, a sketch-book by Gordon E. Payne, 1930, 8 plates (300 copies)
Maritime Artists, Volume 1 compiled by Mary W. Hashey, Maritime Arts Assoc., 1967, P. 62
Art Gallery of Ontario the Canadian Collection by Helen Pepall Bradfield, McGraw-Hill Co. Can., 1970, P. 356
NGC Info. Forms, 1930, 1965
Document from artist 1960

PAYNE, Gordon MacEwan

b. 1933

Born in Ashcroft, B.C., he attended Washington State University majoring in fine arts then attended the College of Education at the University of British Columbia where he received his B. Ed. with a major in fine arts. He taught in B.C. high schools for four years then turned to full-time painting and sculpture in 1965. Viewing his one-man show of paintings at the Bau-Xi Gallery in 1967 Joan Lowndes for the Vancouver *Province* noted, "His color wheels evoke those used by art students and could indeed resemble exercises, were it not for his virtuosity. As it is the boldness of his hues, the precision of his execution, and the swirling centrifugal movement he imparts to the spokes of his wheels, add up to works of genuine impact." Payne's solo shows include those at the Burnaby Gallery, Burnaby, B.C. (1964); The Little Gallery, New Westminister, B.C. (1965); Bau-Xi Gallery, Van., B.C. (1967) and group shows with the Granville Group, Canvas Shack (1963), Pandora's Box, Victoria, B.C. (1967). Living in Vancouver in 1967.

References

Vancouver Province, Van., B.C., June 5, 1965 "This one-man exhibit shows change of style" by Belinda MacLeod
Ibid, Jan. 20, 1967 "Spotlight on Art – A tonic for the eyes in Op art colors" by Joan Lowndes
Victoria Times, Vict., B.C., Mar. 4, 1967 "A voice from the Gallery – Artist Becomes Old Friend If you Take Time to Visit" by Tony Emery
NGC Info. Form rec'd Nov. 19, 1965

PAYNE, Reginald A.

b. 1915

The son of an architect, he was influenced by his father's drawings which kindled his interest in painting. After attending schools in Montreal he was employed by his father's contracting business but he left this work to become a full-time painter. Largely self taught he received guidance from Joseph Guinta, a neighbouring artist in Montreal and has been influenced to some extent by the work of Tom Thomson and the Group of Seven. Working mostly with brush and oil paints and sometimes palette-knife (has also worked in water colours) he sketches his subjects on the spot and later completes a finished painting in his studio. Occasionally he will photograph a scene, but prefers to work from his sketches. His subjects include scenes of the Eastern Townships, Quebec, and Cape Breton Island. He settled in Port Hawkesbury, N.S., with his wife and four children. His solo shows include those at United Church, Knowlton, P.Q. (1963, 1964); Anglican Church Hall, Port Hawkesbury, Cape Breton, N.S. (1969, 1970, 1971); Sheiling Motel, Port Hawkesbury, Cape B., N.S. (1972) and at his home and studio in Port Hawkesbury (1973).

References

Eastern Townships Advertiser, Knowlton, July 8, 1964 "Townships Artist To Repeat Exhibit"
New Glasgow News, N.S., June 24, 1969 "One Man Art Exhibition In Hawkesbury"
Chronicle Herald, Halifax, N.S., June 5, 1970 "Oil Paintings to be displayed"
Sydney Cape Breton Post, N.S. Sept. 23, 1971 "Arts Exhibits" (photo and caption)
Ibid, Aug. 23, 1972 "Exhibit Of Oil Paintings"
Ibid, June 16, 1973 "Local Artist To Show His Works"

PAYTON, Evlyn Beatrice

b. 1920

Born in London, England, the daughter of Lady Eaton she was educated in England, France, Italy and Germany. She studied nights at the Ontario College of Art for oils under Marion Long, Dorothy Austin, William Winter and others and under Mary Schneider for water colours; completed a five year course in acrylics and other media by correspondence with the Famous Artists Studios; studied as well at Toronto's Three Schools and classes at the Art Gallery of Ontario. Photography has also been an integral part of her art and she has participated in exhibitions of the Toronto Camera Club in 1973 and 1975. Because of a serious allergy to cleaning and mixing agents for traditional painting and sculpture media she has worked with casein, polymer and crushed rock to give her painting texture and atmosphere. Viewing her 1970 show at the Albert White Gallery, Kay Kritzwiser in the *Globe & Mail* noted, " . . . her paintings are so strongly in relief they have a sculptural quality. Mrs. Payton works chiefly with gesso on board. Sometimes she glazes her surfaces, building them with as many as 40 glazes to a painting. To get even closer to her denied sculptural bent, Mrs. Payton crushes the rocks of Haliburton and the Muskokas and builds the fragments into her gesso surfaces. When all the summer people have gone from the Muskokas and the only sound at the lake edges are lonely bird calls, you can sometimes hear her ancient chain-gang sound of rock pounding against rock. The finely crushed rock adds to the texture and color of marble to her work. Mrs. Payton has a color sense perceptive enough to get strength in her Muskoka paintings by the very colors she leaves out . . . . Her limited palette suits the Ontario north but it works as well for her paintings of the two old ladies of the French southern village of La Rochelle." Her solo shows include those at: Music Library, Tor. (1967); Agincourt Pub. Library, Tor. (1970); Albert White Gallery, Tor. (1970); Skelton Fine Art Gallery, Collingwood, Ont. (1972); St. Andrew's College, Aurora, Ont. (1972); Heliconian Club, Tor. (1973); Erindale College, Univ. Tor., a retrospective show (1973); group shows include National Society for Painters in Casein (1970, 1971, 1974-75 travel show); Annual shows of the Heliconian Club, Tor. (1970, 1971, –); National Arts Club, N.Y. (1968, 1970); Western Fair Art Exhibition, Lond., Ont. (1970, 1971); Canadian Nature Show (1975-76, touring major cities), and others. The wife of Russell T. Payton, Q.C. and mother of three, she lives in Toronto. Member of the Heliconian Club. She has won awards at the Western Fair Art Exhibition (1970, 1971).

References

Globe & Mail, Tor., Ont., May 20, 1958 "Person to Person – Hospital Patient Busy at Work" by Lotta Dempsey
Ibid, Jan. 10, 1970 "Albert White Gallery" (her first major solo show)
Ibid, Jan. 29, 1972 "After a Fashion" by Zena Cherry (note on solo show at Skelton Fine Art Gal.)
The Toronto Telegram, Ont., Feb. 7, 1970 (solo show at Agincourt Pub. Lib.)
NGC Info. Form rec'd Apr. 17, 1975
Canadian artists in exhibition, 1972-73, Roundstone, Tor., Can., 1974 P. 166

PAZUKAITE, Vanda

b. 1911

Born in Lithuania, she studied there in Panevežys and gained her early art training under J. Zikaras, the well-known sculptor. She attended the College of Art in

PAZUKAITE, Vanda (Cont'd)

Kaunas and graduated in 1940. She took post graduate work at the Vilnius Academy of Art. Between 1945 and 1947 she taught art at the Panevežys High School. She studied piano and in the years after W.W. II became known as a creative painter, teacher, pianist and writer. From 1947 to 1956 she was forced to work in Siberian labour camps. She returned to Lithuania in 1956 and resumed her creative life. She was a member of the Association of Artists in Lithuania and has exhibited her works in the galleries of Warsaw, Prague, Budapest, Leningrad, Moscow and other cities in Eastern Europe. In 1965 she came to Canada and settled in Toronto. In 1966 a showing of her work was held at the Willistead Art Gallery under the auspices of the Gallery and the Lithuanian community of Windsor. In her show was a large collection of work done over the years including drawings, wood and lino-block prints and paintings plus work done in Canada. On viewing the show Kenneth Saltmarche noted, " . . . the collection reflects a good deal of the spirit of a woman who has suffered much but who has also seen and captured much of the beauties of the world around her. There is no question about Vanda Pazukaite's abilities – she reveals them in a surprising variety of styles and manners of expression. For me, her best work is in the field of drawing and block-printing. She is a born designer and has a marked feeling for the dramatic patterns and moods of nature . . . one is given the feeling that the artist has taken a whole new attitude to her work just as she has begun to assume a new and free life in this country. She shows, through her work, a strong inclination to the subject of the sea and shore and in many of her studies of sand dunes one finds the pictures saturated in sunshine and light. These are exceedingly happy pictures. They reflect, for me, a quite remarkable personality." She was living in Toronto in 1966.

References

Windsor Star, Ont., Sept. 17, 1966 " 'Happy' art on show" by Kenneth Saltmarche

Catalogue – copy in artist's file at NGC Library – showing at the Willistead Art Gallery of Windsor, 14 Sept., 1966 Introduction by Kenneth Saltmarche, Director, Willistead Art Gallery of Windsor (biographical notes, photo of artist, 3 ill., listing of 42 works)

PEACHELL, Mrs. Laura

She first began weaving around 1949 and received her instruction from Mary Megs Atwater at the University of British Columbia in a summer course. For a time she lived in Moose Jaw, Saskatchewan, but moved from there to Guelph, Ontario, in 1939, where she has become one of the foremost weavers of that city. There she instructs in weaving at the University of Guelph and also gives lessons to several groups as distant as North Bay and Sault Ste. Marie under the sponsorship of the Ontario Department of Education. Her tapestries hang on the walls of many modern buildings including the Guelph City Hall where her 40 inch by 44 inch tapestry of the Guelph City crest, woven on a vertical loom especially built for the job, hangs in a place of honour. Canadian wool being too rough in texture was replaced by yarn from Copenhagen. The city crest was woven in black, brown, white and three shades of blue. She intertwined the yarn to give the impression of many colours. Active in a number of weaving societies in North America she is a former president of the Ontario Handweavers and Spinners Association and member of

PEACHELL, Mrs. Laura (Cont'd)

the Ontario Craft Foundation, the Canadian Guild of Weavers, Guelph Creative Arts Association, Guelph Craft Guild and the Looming Art Association of California. She has collected many books on weaving from various countries she has visited. Formerly a professional musician herself, her husband is supervisor of music for the Guelph Public School Board.

References

Guelph Mercury, Ont., Dec. 3, 1969 "City Woman Weaves City Crest Tapestry"
Ibid, Sept. 17, 1970 "Weaver Happy To Pass Skills On" by Patti Slawich

PEACOCK, Don

A sculptor and musician living near Port Credit, Ontario, who has completed well over seventy-five works, some of which have been exhibited in the Art Gallery of Ontario, the National Gallery of Canada and galleries in Hamilton and Sarnia. He carves abstract shapes in wood, preferably walnut or mahogany and to get large enough pieces for his work he often laminates several logs together. He has been involved with architecture for many years and has been senior job captain on many of the larger architectural buildings in the Port Credit area. He has been on the executive of the Ontario Society of Artists and chairman of the Professional Artists of Canada. He received his B.A. in music and was a piano teacher at one time. His other interests include building furniture and constructing an aquarium system for raising tropical fish.

Reference

The South Peel Weekly, Port Credit, Ontario, May 21, 1969 "In Port Credit — A Sculptor And Musician Talks About His Work"

PEACOCK, Frances

Born in New Brunswick, she received her early training under Jack Humphrey and Miller Britton and she attended summer school at Mount Allison and Queen's Universities. Since 1970 she has become very active in the St. Catharines area after being busy for many years raising a family and living in six different countries. Her collage "Old Ties" depicting a Welland bridge and ship was selected as Picture of the Month by the Rose City Art Festival Committee in Welland. She is known for her drawings, collages and oils and has exhibited in a three-woman show at Oak Hall, Port Colborne, with Anne Stedneck and Jean Tripp. Her awards include honourable mention and first prize at Niagara District Art Association shows and second prize in the Rose City Art Festival. She has served as director of the St. Catharines Art Association and Pelham representative for the Niagara District Art Association, member of the Port Colborne Cellar Art Studio and the Welland Brush and Palette Club. She lives in Fonthill, Ontario.

References

Welland-Port Colborne Tribune, Port Colborne, Ont., Jan. 9, 1973 " 'Old Ties' Bridge-Ship Scene Picture Of Month"
Ibid, July 4, 1973 "Family — Oak Hall Art Show To Feature Three Area Female Artists"

PEACOCK, Graham

b. 1945

Born in London, England, he studied painting and sculpture at the Goldsmiths School of Art (Univ. Lond.) under Kenneth Martin and William Tucker. He was awarded his Diploma of Art & Design in Painting & Sculpture, B.F.A. Honours (1962-66). Then he travelled to Greece, Turkey and the Middle East. Returning home he set to work on sculpture taking his inspiration in part from the Constructivists. From his sculpture he made drawings and from the drawings a series of paintings. In 1967 he did post-graduate study at Leeds College of Art, Yorkshire, and was awarded a post-graduate diploma in painting. In 1967 he was appointed lecturer at Newport College of Art and Design, England, and in 1968 was awarded an Italian Government Scholarship in Painting and took leave from Newport College to work at The British School in Rome as a visiting artist. He next worked in a private studio in Rome. That summer he lived in New York and travelled throughout Europe visiting academies of fine art and also art collections in London, England, and New York. He accepted an appointment at the Department of Art and Design, The University of Alberta, Edmonton, and then became associate professor at the University. He continued to work on his painting in a private studio in Edmonton. Viewing his 1971 show of paintings 1967-71 at the Lefebvre Gallery, Edmonton, Alasdair Dunlop noted, " . . . in his earliest work, the drawings, one can see very distinct influence from the type of art school training developed by William Scott in England. Again one catches hints on the block forms so beloved of the Ecole de Paris in the persons of Soulages of Poliakoff . . . a period spent in New York must also be seen as a very direct influence on his style. After his arrival in Edmonton his style becomes distinctly less 'painterly' and in its hard edged breaking down of the picture surface, one can perhaps detect the influence of late Mondrian. In his latest work I think one can discern the reintroduction of painterly values. Even before reading the short interview in the brochure for the exhibition, I have felt that the influence of Larry Poons was a decisive factor in Graham Peacock's progression. Further one can see him dealing with the problems of shallow space, trying to solve these problems in a similar way to much of the later work of Matisse. However, he does not have the figurative basis of Matisse and is therefore setting himself a rather more complicated problem. He solves this by constructing a hard edged grid over an indetermined loose area of color which defines space only in as much as it is controlled by the grid. The grid itself provides a window through which one looks at a series of color movements whose planar movements are defined only in terms of the grid structure, and this creates a paradox between the static and the moving or between no color and color." Peacock's solo shows in Canada include: Lefebvre Gallery, Edmonton (1971); Memorial University Art Gallery, St. John's, Nfld. (1971); Alberta College of Art, Cal., Alta. (1972); The Edmonton Art Gallery, Edm., Alta. (1972); touring exhibition "Striations 1971-72" circulated by Memorial University Art Gallery, St. John's, Nfld. (1973). He has participated in many group shows in England, Wales, Italy, United States and in Canada including: Faculty Exhibition, Univ. Alberta Dept. of Art (1969, 1970); Alberta Society of Artists (1971, 1972, –); "All Alberta", Edmonton Art Gallery (1970); "Renaissance 71", Canadian Universities Art Festival, York University, Tor. (1971); "West 71", Edmonton Art Gallery (1971); 12th Annual Calgary Graphics, ACA Gallery, Cal., Alta (1972) and others. He is represented in the following collections: Leeds Educational Authority, Leeds, Yorkshire, Eng.; Newport Art Gallery, Newport, Wales; The British Ambassador,

PEACOCK, Graham (Cont'd)

Rome, Italy; and the private collections of Peter Phillips, Designer, B.B.C-T.V., Cardiff, Wales; Keith Phelpstead, Designer, Newport, Wales; Mrs. Arnold, Tadcaster, Eng.; Roy Slade, Dean of the Cocoran School of Art, Wash., D.C.; Wm. Hnidan of Hnidan-Holubitsky Architects, Edm., Alta.; Colin Burrell, Director of the Lefebvre Gal., Edm.; Edwin Turner, Playwright, Edm.; Mrs. S. Shapiro of Edmonton. He was elected Chairman of the Alberta Society of Artists in 1971.

References

> *Edmonton Journal*, Alta., Apr. 8, 1971 "A welcome change to see an artist in progression" by Alasdair Dunlop
> Catalogue for show at Lefebvre Gallery, "Graham Peacock, Paintings & Drawings 1967-1970" Mar. 28 to Apr. 12, 1971
> Catalogue for show at Memorial Univ., Nfld., May 1 to May 23, 1971
> *Corner Brook Western-Star*, Nfld., June 2, 1973 "Art exhibit to open"
> Catalogue for show at Memorial Univ., Nfld., "Graham Peacock 'Striations' 1971-72" (list of 35 paintings & drawings), February, 1973
> *Calgary Albertan*, Alta., June 5, 1973 "Artists meet" (Peacock elected Pres. of A.S.A.)
> *Artscanada*, December, 1974, Issue Nos. 192/193/194/195, "Reviews" P. 109
> *Canadian artists in exhibition 1972-73*, Roundstone Council, Tor., Ont., 1974, P. 167
> *Canadian artists in exhibition 1974*, Roundstone Council, Tor., Ont., P. 25, 41

PEACOCK, Wilbur K.

An engraver who served overseas in the 4th Battalion, First Division, of the Canadian army and after the war returned to a job of mechanical draughtsman. He exhibited his work with the Society of Canadian Painter-Etchers and Engravers including a scene "Old Log House, Haliburton" reproduced in *The Toronto Telegram* in 1942. He was a member of the C.P.E. and was living in Toronto in 1954.

References

> *The Toronto Telegram*, Ont., April 11, 1942 "Old Log House, Haliburton" (photo of print by Wilbur K. Peacock)

PEARCE, Deborah
b. 1952

A Burlington, Ontario, artist, and daughter of Stuart and Ellen Pearce, she studied art at Nelson High School under naturalist artist Robert Bateman and took further studies at Mount Allison University, Sackville, N.B., where she graduated with her B.F.A. in 1975. Recently she has been working from her own home in Burlington and from a Hamilton studio doing portraits and experimental canvases. In March of 1975 she took a six month sketching trip to Africa with the assistance of a Canada Council grant and some advice from her former teacher Robert Bateman who had taken a world tour in a Landrover and spent two years in Nigeria. Her goal was to record the facial structures of people in each area of the continent but she came up against political and geographical obstacles which restricted her travel to Uganda,

PEARCE, Deborah (Cont'd)

Kenya and Tanzania. On an earlier trip across Canada she had taken an auto mechanics course before setting out. This knowledge stood her in good stead during her African travels. Once however when her van broke down she lived in a village for more than a week but she turned this delay into a positive experience and learned from village women their own method of tie-dying fabric using wax, also spinning, and making a three-day fermented bread on a round outdoor cooking platform. On her return to Canada she did water colour paintings and graphite drawings which she completed from photographs she had taken on her African trip. These works were shown at the Alice Peck Gallery, Burlington, in November, 1975 under the title "Wanawake '75" (Woman '75) and also at Bethune College, York University, Toronto. Prior to her African trip she spent a year teaching children on a Northern Ontario Indian reservation (1969); became a Crossroads Canada volunteer in Nevis, British West Indies (1972); visited Haiti (1972); travelled across Canada in a battered Volvo station wagon camping as she went along from Sydney, N.S., through Fort Walsh, Alta., to Okanagan, B.C. (1974).

References
The Spectator, Hamilton, Ont., Mar. 1, 1975 "Artist Debbie has designs on Africa" by Susan Malcolm
Ibid, 28 Oct., 1975 article by Susan Malcolm about Miss Pearce's African trip
Burlington Gazette, Ont., 7 Nov., 1975 "African adventure: Caught in art at Peck Gallery" by Val Whitefield

PEARCE, Fay (Mrs. Robin Pearce)

She exhibited her oils, gouaches and drawings at the Fine Arts Gallery of the University of British Columbia (1959) and at the Civic Centre at Nelson, B.C. (1959). She has conducted art classes for children at the University of British Columbia and classes at the summer session of the Nelson School of Fine Arts (at L.V. Rogers High School), Nelson, B.C.

References
Exhibition notice Fine Arts Gallery, UBC, March 18 – April 5, 1958
Daily News, Nelson, B.C., Feb. 21, 1959 "More Courses Offered for Arts School July 7 to 31"

PEARCE, Robin

Formerly a staff lecturer with the Arts Council of Great Britain he has worked in films, the B.B.C. and the C.B.C., and has also lectured in art and done administrative art work in East Africa, England and Canada. During his show at the Picture Loan Society, Toronto, in 1957, the *Globe & Mail* noted, "His paintings also run a range from fairly representational to abstract, but always with a lively vitality. Perhaps the best group in this showing is a trio of gay figure studies from East

PEARCE, Robin (Cont'd)

Africa." He became supervisor of arts and crafts at the University of B.C. extension department and has taught jointly with his wife at the Nelson School of Fine Arts, Nelson, B.C.

References
Exhibition notice, Picture Loan Society, Tor., May 10, 1957
Globe & Mail, Tor., Ont., May 4, 1957 "Exhibitors"
Daily News, Nelson, B.C., Feb. 21, 1959 "More Courses Offered for Arts School July 7 to 31"

PEARCEY, Kelvin Ronald
b. 1947

Born in Birmingham, England, he came to Canada at the age of four and attended schools in West Flamborough, and took further visits to England and Montreal. He settled in Toronto where he entered the Ontario College of Art and studied silk screening, graphics, stained-glass, ceramics, weaving and jewelry and graduated after four years of study. He was a member of a group of artists named FunCo involved with the United Nations conference for Human Enivronment held in Stockholm, Sweden.

Reference
Brochure on artist (undated)

PEARL, Sonia (Mrs.)

An Ottawa artist especially known for her fine printmaking and painting. Viewing a group show at Wallack Galleries, Kathleen Walker noted, "Sonia Pearl is the most accomplished etcher of the group. Her haunting landscapes and muted colors are very fine." She has won prizes for her paintings exhibited at the Ottawa Art Association shows. She is a member of the Ottawa Art Association and a member of the Ottawa Municipal Art Centre (Ottawa School of Art).

References
The Ottawa Journal, Ont., Oct. 25, 1966 "Painting Exhibition — Autumn Landscape Tops at Fair Show"
The Ottawa Citizen, Ont., Feb. 22, 1974 "Local etchings provide nice foil for sculptures" by Kathleen Walker

PEARN, Maxwell Clark
b. 1909

Born in Sussex, New Brunswick, Canada, he graduated from Sussex High School in 1925 then attended Mount Allison University, Sackville, N.B. (1925-27); Yale

PEARN, Maxwell Clark (Cont'd)

University School of The Fine Arts, New Haven, Conn., U.S.A. (1928-29). He also studied under Philip L. Hale two months (1931) and Bernard M. Keyes, Boston, Mass. (1931-33), and on the advice of Sir Wyly Grier went to Toronto where he received criticism from Grier and Lawren S. Harris and established a studio during the years 1934-36 and again in 1938. He exhibited his work with the Ontario Society of Artists at the Art Gallery of Toronto (1935-38) and also showed his work with the Hamilton Art Association and New Brunswick artists at the New Brunswick Museum, Saint John (1939). He was living in Sussex, N.B. in 1940.

References
NGC Info. Form rec'd April 17, 1935
Letter to H.O. McCurry, Jan. 4, 1940, from M.C. Pearn, Sussex, N.B.

PEARSE, Edward

Born in Sault Ste. Marie, Ontario, the son of Mr. & Mrs. F.H. Pearse, he attended the Central Public School and the Sault Ste. Marie Collegiate. He studied weekends at the Algoma Art Society school for six years under Carl Schaefer, Jacques de Tonnancour, Alex Miller, Gustav Weisman, Aba Bayefsky, Henri Masson and others (1951-57). He took further study at the Instituto de Allende, Mexico (1958-59). He lived and worked in Niagara Falls for four years (1960-64) before settling in Sault Ste. Marie where he worked as display and advertising artist for a department store (1967-75) and then turned to full-time painting in 1975. In his own art he has worked in a wide variety of media and styles ranging from abstract to almost photographic realism. His subjects include still lifes, nudes, landscapes (especially landscapes of Algoma), collages with combined subject matter and materials. His solo shows include those held at: YMCA, Sault Ste. Marie (1960); Allied Arts Centre, Sault Ste. Marie (1965); Centennial Room, Sault Ste. Marie Public Library (1968, 1975). Viewing his 1975 solo show Linda Richardson of the Sault Ste. Marie *Star* noted, "Like most local artists, Mr. Pearse paints Algoma landscapes. His pastels and watercolors detail the quiet, serene beauty of Northern Ontario forests, while his oils boldly declared the majestic splendor of Lake Superior." A former president of the Algoma Society of Artists, he lives in Sault Ste. Marie, with his wife Jessie.

References
Star, Sault Ste. Marie, Ont., May 28, 1958 "Year's Study – Youthful Artist Going to Mexico"
Globe & Mail, Tor., Ont., June 7, 1958 "Sault Artist Goes to Mexico"
Star, Sault Ste. Marie, Ont., June 8, 1959 "Sault Artist Returns From Mexican Studies"
Ibid, Mar. 25, 1960 "Artist Ed Pearse to Exhibit March 26 and 27"
Ibid, Oct. 30, 1965 "TSO heads arts week"
Ibid, Nov. 3, 1965 "Mrs. Pearse must miss Ed's art show" by Mary Jane Charters
Ibid, Nov. 6, 1965 "Texture experiments, liven Pearse's art" by Nan Rajnovich
Ibid, Nov. 9, 1968 "Ed Pearse one-man show will open November 14" by Louise McLurg
Ibid, Nov. 16, 1968 "Pearse called an artist of substance" by Dr. G.A. Stehr
Ibid, Apr. 7, 1975 "Pearse has one-man show after 6 years" by Jackie Hoffman
Ibid, Apr. 11, 1975 "Artist catches Gros Cap moods" by Linda Richardson

PEARSE, Harold

He taught art on the West Coast then travelled to Montreal and took a course at Sir George Williams University graduating in 1969 with his Master of Art Education. At that time he held a solo show of his work at the University art gallery which was viewed by Michael White as follows, "In his teaching Pearse was involved with sound, making it, playing with it as a means of expression, trying to express its qualities through other mediums. Much of this he explained that he did in the classroom with his students. At Sir George Williams art department Pearse has carried on this research within the painting and graphic disciplines. What has happened is that he has made nice hard-edge show pieces that look conservatively craftsmanlike on the gallery walls. He has become involved in the local and contemporary hard edge style problems of eye-twisting, creating ambiguity as it is called and only in a series of prints is there a hint of the earlier personal and special involvement with sound and rhythm and poetry." White went on to note that he would have liked to have seen further work by Pearse using sound as the subject of multi-media research. Pearse has continued to work on his art using photography as a major factor in his expression. He held showings of his work at the Nova Scotia College of Art and Design (1971, 1972) and is represented in the Canada Council Art Bank, Ottawa.

References
> *The Montreal Star*, P.Q., June 19, 1969 "Art Scene – Hard-edge pieces" by Michael White
> Exhibition folders from the Nova Scotia College of Art (1971, 1972)
> Canadian Council Art Bank listing of artists represented in their collection.

PEARSON, Charles Gordon
b. 1907

Born in Toronto, he graduated in Dentistry from the University of Toronto in 1932 and practised his profession for three years. He became interested in Canadian art through Dr. James McCallum the noted patron of the Group of Seven and Tom Thomson. He visited Georgian Bay to paint in March, 1934 and the following year he married and moved to Go Home Bay in April of 1935 to continue painting full time. By 1936 he was exhibiting his work at the MacDonald Galleries in Toronto and was reviewed by Graham McInnes in *Saturday Night*, during a second solo show a year later, as follows, " . . . he is one of the few conscious and unashamed imitators of the Group of Seven who is at the same time thoroughly sincere. Added to which, he is forging slowly but surely a personal style, while the improvement in his work resulting from a year's living in the North Country is quite astonishing. His color is clearer, his tonal values more coherent, his designs more close-knit; these sketches are well worth a visit."

References
> *Saturday Night*, Tor., Ont., Mar. 21, 1936 "World of Art"
> Ibid, May 29, 1937 (review by Graham McInnes)
> NGC Info. Form rec'd June 20, 1926

PEARSON, Elva

An Edmonton artist, she first attended art classes at the museum and received a scholarship to attend the Southern Alberta Institute of Technology where she took a commercial art course, then moved to Vancouver. She had a showing of her paintings in Edmonton in 1948 at the Museum of Arts when the *Edmonton Journal* noted, "The pictures and sketches now to be seen are in oils, water-colors, charcoal and pencil and reveal a considerable talent in the direction of figure subjects, the conspicuous quality being in character representation; this having been lacking so far among the Edmonton artists. Here it is brought to a high pitch of effectiveness, mainly due to the practice – obvious from the sketches – of the use of the note book on all occasions. Pencil sketches of casual personalities, taken as opportunity offered, show this trait, and the results are estimable."

Reference
> *Edmonton Journal*, Alta., Mar. 22, 1948 "Edmonton Artist Winning Praise" by F.H. Norbury

PEARSON, (Mrs.) Freda (Freda Canellakos)
b. 1902

Born in Ottawa, Ontario, of French-Swiss and Greek parentage, she studied art at the Ottawa Art Club classes in 1925 under Major J.S. Chenay (water colours), Major W. Boss (perspective and architectural drawing); the Ottawa Art Association where she studied landscape painting in tempera and oil painting under Paul Alfred (Meister) and George Pepper, and life and portraiture classes under Franklin Brownell and George Rowles; Ottawa Board of Education life classes under Ernest Fosbery; Grand Central School of Art, New York, where she studied anatomy and the chemistry of colours, evenings, while a student nurse at old St. Luke's Hospital in New Rochelle. Subsequently she studied Journalism at Columbia University. Later she became a member of the French art club Le Caveau where modelling in clay was taught by Louis Leygue who made sculptures for the ballroom of the French Embassy in Ottawa. She is considered to be an authority on old handmade silver and ivory carvings and contributes articles to various publications on these subjects as well as on food and nutrition. She is represented in numerous private collections mainly by portraits and nudes. Presently on the executive of the Cheese and Wine Society she was interviewed on cheese and wine tasting in 1962 by Lorraine Thomson of the programme "VIP." She lives in Ottawa where she continues to paint and write.

References
> Interview with artist, 1977
> Document from artist, 1977

PEARSON, (Mrs.) Joan

A Port Credit, Ontario, artist whose paintings became popular during their showing at the Carling Festival of Arts in 1968. She is a member of the Oakville Arts Society.

Reference
> *Streetsville Review*, Ont., Sept. 11, 1968 "Art exhibit in Oakville"

PEARSON, Leo Earl

b. 1883

Born in Lawrence, Kansas, U.S.A., he studied art teaching methods at the Throop Institute Pasadena, California, where he graduated with his Art Normal Diploma in 1906. He took summer courses at the Los Angeles School of Art and Design, College of Fine Arts at the University of Southern California, and the Art Students' League of Los Angeles (1906-08); Teachers' College, Columbia University, N.Y., where he received his Fine Arts Diploma in 1912; Stanford University, Calif., B.A., 1923 majoring in Fine Arts; summer course at Otis Art Institute, Los Angeles (1927); summer course at Roche Studios, Los Angeles, for commercial art work (1928); summer course in interior decoration and costume design at University of Washington, Seattle (1929); summer course, California School of Arts and Crafts, Oakland, Calif. (1931). Instructed in art at Camrose Normal School, Alberta (1913-1916). He moved to Calgary, Alberta, in 1916 where he became an instructor in drafting and art subjects at the Provincial Institute of Technology and Art and was still a teacher there in 1935 when he completed an information form for the National Gallery of Canada. In his own painting he exhibited his work at a non-jury exhibition at the Art Gallery of Toronto (1943) and held a solo show of thirty water colours in the galleries at the Calgary, Alberta, Exhibition Grounds in 1946 when the Calgary *Albertan* noted his work as follows, "While most of them depict mountain and other Alberta scenes, there are some views along the California coast and a few flower studies. They show superb control of color and wash, and a realization of the value of transparency in this medium. Nearly all are sunny and cheerful in color, and show careful drawing and accurate perspective as well as a strong sense of design in arrangement. Water is expertly portrayed in various moods." Was a member of the Alberta Society of Artists (on council 1931-35); Pres. Calgary Sketch Club in 1932.

References
   Calgary Herald, Alta., Apr. 19, 1943 "Calgary Artist Shows Picture in Toronto" (at Art Gallery of Toronto)
   Albertan, Calgary, Alta., July 11, 1946 "Artist Shows Versatility"
   NGC Info. Form rec'd March, 1935

PÊCHEUX, Serge

He came from France, to Montreal, Canada, in 1954, a self-taught artist who does floral studies, nudes, and other subjects in figurative style on brown roebuck and black velvet.

Reference
   Photo-Journal, Mtl., P.Q., Mar. 15, 1967 "Ne tirez pas sur le chevreuil!" par Marcel Huguet

PECK, Hugh A.

1888-

Born in Montreal, P.Q., he was a member of the Arts Club of Montreal (Pres. 1927) and of the Art Association of Montreal. He exhibited his work at the Montreal Spring Exhibition of 1931.

PECK, Hugh A. (Cont'd)

Reference
NGC Info. Form rec'd May 4 (c. 1930)

PECK, Mrs. Merrill (MERRILL)

A Montreal, P.Q., artist, she held her first solo show at the Handicraft Guild in 1957. She studied at the Montreal Museum of Fine Arts and with Herman Heimlich and attended the Instituto de Allende, Mexico in 1958. Her subjects have included scenery from California, Mexico, the Lower St. Lawrence, Eastern Townships, and the subjects noted by Rea Montbizon as follows, "Merrill, as Mrs. Peck signs her paintings, shows that she has had some sound training and much fun. Merrill has a good eye and a sure hand, setting down with considerable charm and facility for characterization her drawings of some steep Mediterranean shorelines, Alpine settings, or scenes of the Montreal waterfront." She has worked in a variety of mediums and styles.

References
Leader-Mail, Granby, Oct. 11, 1961 "M. Peck holds exhibit in Cowansville"
The Gazette, Mtl., P.Q., Dec. 12, 1964 "Hundred And One Pictures"

PECK, Miriam Louise

b. 1900

Born in New Westminster, B.C., she studied at the Vancouver School of Art and the University of Washington where she received her B.A. and M.A. majoring in art. She became a teacher of art in Vancouver Public Schools and later teacher of art at the College of Education of the University of Manitoba. She did research to improve the standards of original designs. Later she moved to the State of Washington where she attracted the interest of several large manufacturing firms by her experiments with non-inflammable products using glass and metallic materials in weaving where she also strove for more creative effects. Her work was shown at the Vancouver Art Gallery.

References
NGC Info. Form rec'd 1944
Standard-Freeholder, Cornwall, Ont., July 29, 1950 "Canadian Artist Develops Design"

PECK, Robin

b. 1950

Born in Alberta, educated at the Nova Scotia College of Art and Design graduating with M.F.A. in 1975. Exhibited sculpture at the Nova Scotia College of Art and Design in 1972, 1973 and at Mount Saint Vincent University in 1975 in a group

PECK, Robin (Cont'd)

show. Was awarded Canada Council Grants 1972-74. Has participated in various exhibitions in the Maritimes (1972-75).

References
    Exhibition sheet – "From Craft Into Art: Three Dimensional Art In Nova Scotia" by Ron Shuebrook, show held at Mount Saint Vincent University, Halifax, N.S. Aug. 30, 1975

PEDDER, M.E.

Born in Hertfordshire, England, he came to Canada at the age of fourteen. Painting has been his interest from school-days when he designed posters, class pins and painted back-drops for plays in local churches. He settled in Verdun, Quebec, where he continued his interest until 1963 when ill health curtailed his other activities and he began spending more time on his art. He studied the fundamentals of painting for two years. Working out of his home he has produced mainly landscape paintings which have been inspired in some cases by photographs.

Reference
    Verdun Messenger, P.Q., June 5, 1968 "Exhibition"

PEDERSEN, Paul Aleksander
b. 1906
Born in Vadso, Norway, he studied in Tallinn, Estonia under Laikmaa, Kaigorodoff and Deters. He came to Canada in 1950 and settled in Winnipeg where he became a member of the Manitoba Society of Artists in 1955. He was awarded an honourable mention in 1957 for submitting a design for the new Canadian silver dollar.

Reference
    NGC Info. Form

PEDERSEN, Tilde

Born in Denmark where she studied art she came to Canada in 1954 and settled in London, Ontario, where she has exhibited her paintings at the Glen Gallery and at the Richard Crouch Branch Public Library. Her paintings range from representational, abstract to non-objective and she has used flowers as a motif in many of her pictures. Lenore Crawford has mentioned that the artist has a good colour sense and knows how to use paint.

References
    London Evening Free Press, Ont., March 8, 1973 "Work shows art influence of 2 nations" (Denmark and Canada) by Lenore Crawford
    Ibid, Sept. 14, 1973 "Artist shows changing style" by Lenore Crawford

PEDERY-HUNT, Dora de (see also under de PEDERY-HUNT, Dora in Volume 1)
b. 1913

Born in Budapest, Hungary, the daughter of Attila (physicist) and Emilia de Pedery, she lived in Hungary and Germany, 1945-48 before coming to Canada in 1948. She married A.B. Hunt in 1949 (marriage dissolved, 1960). She is known for her fine cast medals and small scale sculpture including heads, figures, plaques and masks but has also done large architectural sculptures and church interiors. She taught art at the Northern Vocational School, Tor. (1949-60) and at the Ontario College of Art. She designed the Canada Council Medal (1961); International Co-operation Year Association Medal (1965); Humanities Research Council Medal (1965); Tom Symons Medal, Univ. Tor. (1966); Canadian Centennial Medal (6,000,000 for school children, 1966); Commissioners Award Medal, N.W.T. (1967); plaque for presentation to Hon. L.B. Pearson upon retirement (1968). Her solo shows include: Laing Galleries, Tor. (1959); Robertson Galleries, Ottawa (1962); Dorothy Cameron Gallery, Tor. (1965); Art Gallery, Memorial Univ., St. John's, Nfld. (1966); The Douglas Gallery, Van. (1966); Wells Gallery, Ott. (1967) and many group shows including the Biennial of Christian Art, Salzburg, Aus. (1964); International Exhibition of Contemporary Medals, The Hague, Neth. (1963), Athens (1966), Paris (1967); International Exhibition of Contemporary Religious Medals, Rome (1963); Canadian Religious Art Today, Regis College, Tor. (1963, 1966); Can. Govt. Pavilion, Art Gallery, Expo '67, Mtl. (1967). Her honours include: Canada Council Award (1958); Ontario Society of Artists Sculpture Award (1963); National Council of Jewish Women, 1st Prize (1966); Purchase Award at Uno-A-Erre/ Arezzo, Italy (1964-66). She is represented in the following collections: Nat. Gal. of Can., Ott.; Art Gallery of Ontario, Tor.; Dept of External Affairs; Royal Cabinet of Medals, Brussels, Bel.; Royal Cabinet of Medals, The Hague, Neth.; Museum of Contemporary Crafts, Charlottetown, P.E.I. She is a full member of the Royal Canadian Academy; Sculptor's Society of Canada (former Pres.); Ontario Society of Artists. Organizer for the first exhibition of contemporary medals in Canada at the Minotaur Gallery, Tor., and as Canadian representative for the Fédération Internationale des Editeurs de Médailles, France, she assembled Canadian exhibits for this society.

References
NGC Info. Form rec'd July, 1967
Recent Miniatures and Medals, Dora De Pedery-Hunt (brochure – Laing Galleries, Tor., 1967)
90th Annual Exhibition, 1970, R.C.A. (catalogue)
Art Gallery of Ontario, The Canadian Collection by Helen Pepall Bradfield 1970, P. 356-58
Creative Canada, Vol. One, McPherson Lib./Univ. Tor. Press 1971, P. 94
Who's Who In American Art, 1976, P. 138

PEDONI, John

Born in Milan, Italy, he studied art in Milan and Rome. He came to Canada in 1952 and for a time was a free lance artist. Then he worked part time at various jobs while he studied nights to qualify as an art teacher. He joined the staff of the Woodbine Junior Heights School in 1960 and became Chairman of the Art Program and also conducted classes in life drawing at Victoria Park, evenings. In

PEDONI, John (Cont'd)

his own painting he exhibited landscapes, still life and other subjects in oils, pastels, water colours, etchings also sculptures at the Lower Hall at Markham Centennial Library, Markham, Ontario (1969) and participated in a four-man show at "The Differance" library at Bathurst and Highway No. 7 just north of Toronto (1969).

References
Markham Economist & Sun, Ont., June 5, 1969 "John Pedoni Exhibits Art"
Ibid, Feb. 6, 1969 "Paintings on display" (at Markham Centennial Library)

PEEL, John R.

He came to Canada in 1856 and entered the trade of marble cutter in the firm of Peel & Powell, 493 Richmond Street, London, Ontario, and had established his own business by 1864. He taught drawing at the Old Mechanics' Institute in that city and gave charcoal drawing lessons to students at the rear of his marble works where his own children attended. From these lessons the Western School of Art was formed in cooperation with the Griffiths brothers in 1870. Two of his children became noted artists, Paul and Mildred. John Peel did work for various buildings and churches in addition to the making of monuments. Paul and Mildred, the most artistically gifted of his five children did much of the carving in the shop for several years. John Peel's marble memorials were rich in ornamentation. It is believed that the Peel marble shop eventually was bought by a Mr. Loveday who knew the family well and who probably worked for John Peel for a number of years. John Peel's home at 238 Richmond Street was moved to Pioneer Village, Fanshawe Lake, near London, Ontario, in 1962, due to the fame of his son Paul.

References
Advertiser, Lond., Ont., Feb. 26, 1927 "Richmond Street House Paul Peel's Birthplace"
Record, Jarvis, Nov. 5, 1959 "Memoirs On Paul Peel by Canon D.J. Cornish"
London Free Press, Mar. 22, 1962 "Artist's Home Set for Move to Fanshawe"
Paul Peel, Memorial Exhibition In The Art Gallery, Lon., Pub. Lib. & Art Mus., Lond., Ont., November, 1970 (see Introduction, first page)
The Globe Magazine, Lond., Ont., Feb. 13, 1971 "His Paintings Were Sold For $5" by Joan Pierson

PEEL, Mildred (Lady Ross)
(c) 1855- (c) 1916

The eldest daughter of John Robert Peel, owner of a granite and monument company and art teacher in London, Ontario. She studied under her father and helped with the various sculptural commissions for her father's monument business along with her brother Paul. She painted portraits in Winnipeg in 1883 and executed a series of portrait busts in sculpture for Normal School, Toronto (c) 1886. She went to Paris (c) 1891 along with her brother Paul where she painted and studied. She was back in Canada by 1907. She married in 1907 former Premier of Ontario, George William Ross who was knighted in 1910. One of her paintings was a portrait of Laura Secord. She had done a sculptured bust of the heroine for the monument

PEEL, Mildred (Lady Ross) (Cont'd)

at Stoney Creek. She used as her painting model, the great-grand niece of Laura, Phoebe Louise Laskey (Mrs. B. Noble) who had been a close friend of Mildred during their school years. This Secord portrait was purchased by the Ontario Government for $500 and hung in the legislature. In 1936 a portrait of her husband, Sir George W. Ross, was discovered under her painting of Laura Secord by X-Ray. Some thought was given to cleaning off the Secord portrait to restore the portrait of a former Premier which was painted either by Mildred Peel herself or by W.A. Sherwood. This idea was abandoned when sisters of Phoebe Laskey (model for Laura Secord) convinced the Ontario Government that the portrait of Sir George had been partially scraped off before the Secord portrait had been started. Mildred exhibited her work with the Art Association of Montreal, the Ontario Society of Artists (elected OSA 1889) and the Royal Canadian Academy. See J. Russell Harper's *Early Painters and Engravers in Canada*. A portrait of Mildred Peel, painted by her brother in 1886 is in the collection of the London Public Library and Art Museum, Ontario.

References

> *Globe*, Tor., Ont., 3 Sept., 1920 (article about Lady Ross bequeathing proceeds of "Waiting for the Bath" to surviving brother and sister)
> *London Free Press*, Ont., 7 July, 1933 (Mildred, eldest daughter of John Robert Peel)
> *The Toronto Star*, Ont., Feb. 24, 1936 "X-Ray Test Reveals Ex-Premier's Portrait Under Laura Secord's"
> *Mail & Empire,* Tor., Ont., Feb. 27, 1936 (CP) "Artist's Friend Original for Painting of Secord — London Sisters Relate Heroine's Descendant Chosen Model"
> *The Gazette*, Mtl., P.Q., Mar. 23, 1936 (CP) "Ontario Will Keep Secord Portrait"
> *Painting In Canada/A History* by J. Russell Harper, Univ. Tor. Press, 1966, P. 204
> *Early Painters and Engravers in Canada* by J. Russell Harper, Univ. Tor. Press, 1970, P. 246-7
> *150 Years of Art In Manitoba*, Winnipeg Art Gallery, Manitoba, 1970, P. 96
> *Paul Peel Memorial Exhibition In The Art Gallery* by Clare Bice, London Public Library & Art Museum, Lond., Ont., November, 1970, No. 17 ("Portrait of my Sister")

PEEL, Paul

1860-1892

Born in London, Ontario, he was the youngest of five children of John Robert Peel a monument maker. His father also taught drawing at the Mechanics' Institute in London and ran his own business known to Londoners as The Peel Monument Works, located at 493 Richmond Street of that city. There he also conducted lessons in a studio just behind his monument works where amongst his students showing outstanding talent were his eldest child Mildred and his youngest, Paul. Both Paul and Mildred later helped out in the business and did much of the fine carving that left the shop. Paul had begun his studies under his father about the age of twelve (c. 1872) but even in school at the age of eight he was constantly drawing cows, horses and other subjects. Then he took studies under a local professional artist, William Lee Judson who had studied in Paris under Bouguereau and Lefebvre. He also studied at the Western School of Art which his father helped found. The Peel family were far from being wealthy and lived in a frame house at 238 Richmond not far from the monument works (the house was moved to Fanshawe

PEEL, Paul (Cont'd)

Pioneer Village at the Fanshawe Dam, London in 1962). Some of the money Paul earned during his study years came from painting decorations on circus wagons. His father realized he was destined for greater things than the monument business, so he gave his son his blessings and sent him to Philadelphia to stay at an uncle's place while he studied at the Pennsylvania Academy of Fine Arts, enrolling in 1877. There the school had newly come under the direction of Thomas Eakins just back from his advanced studies in Europe. Eakins insisted on his students making studies from life whether animal or human, and he himself embodied in his work a fine union of classicism and impressionism. Peel did well there and even worked at the academy as an instructor to help pay for his studies. During the three years at the academy he returned each summer to Canada. In 1880 he completed his course at Philadelphia and for a short period set up a studio in Toronto where he was remembered as a distinguished-looking Bohemian type with a soft velour hat, velvet coat and loose flowing bow tie. His studio was located over the Rice Lewis shop on King Street East across the street from Oliver Coate and Company, auctioneers. In 1880 he went to London, England, where he attended the Royal Academy for a few months and also worked at the British Museum. He moved to Paris in 1881 where he studied for the next five years under such eminent teachers as Lefebvre, Boulanger, Gerôme and Constant. He was a favourite pupil of Gerôme and Constant. He adapted himself to life in Paris and with his facility for languages spoke French well. He was a handsome figure of a man with his sweeping curly brown hair and his neatly trimmed Van Dyke beard. He was nimble and athletic. He took up fencing for recreation and became skilled enough to meet on equal terms with the best of swordsmen in France. Later he met Canadian artists George and Mary Reid in Paris and found them a studio in the Latin Quarter and suggested to Reid that he should study under Benjamin Constant. Peel spent his summers at Calais, in Normandy, and Brittany at Concarneau and Pont-Aven where he met a tall dark Danish girl, Isaure Verdier, a painter of miniatures and an accomplished musician. Paul played the violin fairly well himself so they had similar interests. Isaure's family was well off but Paul had little money. The Verdiers however liked Paul and with his steady progress and industry in his profession, Isaure was given permission to marry him. Their wedding took place in Copenhagen in 1882. They had a son Robert (b.c. 1884) and a daughter Marguerite (b.c. 1886). He adored his children and by 1888 had begun a series of paintings of them which were to receive attention internationally. The most famous was "After the Bath" awarded a third class medal in 1890 by the Société des Artistes Français at its annual Paris Salon. This was a painting of his two children fresh from the tub, one standing and the other sitting before an open fireplace from which a glowing fire reflects its light on their bodies. Sarah Bernhardt made a bid for the painting but it was sold at a higher price to the Hungarian Government and hung in the National Art Gallery of Budapest for about thirty-one years. Inflation of World War One forced the Hungarian National Gallery to sell the work in 1922 to Henry Pocock and James Colerick (Colerick Bros. art dealers) of London, Ontario. Colerick who knew Peel in the early days in Canada had kept an eye on this picture. Pocock had financed the purchase and hung the painting in his home (had a replica made by a London artist John P. Hunt). Having won Honourable Mention in 1889 for his "Que La Vie Est Amère" (The Modest Model), the Bronze Medal in 1890 for "After the Bath", and having his pastel study "The Two Friends" purchased by

PEEL, Paul (Cont'd)

Princess Alexandra of England c. 1890 and other important collectors purchasing his work, he thought the time was right to return to Canada with over sixty of his paintings for an exhibition and auction at Oliver, Coate & Company in Toronto. He visited his family in London as he had done on other occasions and also displayed some of his paintings there. He then went on to Toronto for the exhibit on the 13th and 14th of October, 1890 and the auction on the 15th. Names of the attending patrons read like a Who's Who which included Sir Edmond Walker, G.A. Reid, F.M. Bell-Smith, J.W. Beatty, city politicians and many others. The highest price paid for a painting was $325 for "The Venetian Bather", a nude study of a young girl before a mirror, purchased by W. Wakefield and now in the collection of the National Gallery of Canada, Ottawa. This painting has been one of the most frequently reproduced of Peel's paintings in Canadian art books over the last two decades. The smaller study for this painting is in the collection of the Edmonton Art Gallery. In Toronto where times were financially hard the auction yielded a net receipt for Peel of about $2,000 which was a great disappointment for him. He returned to Paris and continued to paint feverishly for the remainder of his brief life working well into the night on many occasions and when he became exhausted would lie down on a cot in his studio and fall fast asleep. He contracted a lung infection and during a rest one day died in his sleep. His loss not only was deeply felt by his family but by his old teachers Constant and Gerôme. To escape from the associations of the past Isaure took the two children to Chicago where they lived for several years on the sales of her miniature paintings. After ten years they returned to Paris and for a few years lived in Copenhagen, then settled in a lovely old house in Provence in the south of France near Nice. Robert Peel, Paul's son, became an engineer in California and Marguerite his daughter, became an accomplished painter in her own right (she died in 1959 at her home in Laguna Beach, Calif.). While many of the Peel paintings have been given, bequeathed or purchased, to and for public collections, many others have remained in private hands or art dealers' hands. In 1929 for instance Pocock sold "After the Bath ' to C.H. Carlisle, general manager of Goodyear Tire and Rubber Company of Toronto for an undisclosed amount, the picture value being estimated by international art experts at that time to be $50,000. The painting was next purchased by R.S. McLaughlan, auto manufacturer, in 1930. In 1972 it was made a bequest by the McLaughlin estate to the Ontario Government who turned it over to the Art Gallery of Ontario. There are two other paintings by that title, one discovered in Paris in 1936 and brought to Canada and certified authentic by Sir Wyly Grier but declared by Peel's daughter Marguerite to be not the work of her father. A third version was owned by a Frank M. Gray in 1903. There are also two studies, a small and a large one. The small study is owned by a Miss Patricia Brooks-Hammond and the larger one by Mr. & Mrs. Jules Loeb of Toronto. There are also three known versions of its companion picture "Before the Bath". The large finished painting is in the Hospital For Sick Children, Toronto, a smaller one in the collection of Montreal art critic Edgar A. Collard and a third was in Cincinnati in 1926 with its present owner unlisted. A comprehensive study was made by J. Edward Martin. Working out of Ottawa in 1974, he compiled a catalogue which lists 200 of Peel's paintings and their alternate titles, original owners, solo and public exhibitions, bibliography for each painting and detailed general bibliography, present known collectors. Since the completion of Martin's catalogue some of the paintings no

PEEL, Paul (Cont'd)

doubt have changed hands. For example, the "Discovery of Moses", listed by him as owner unknown, was acquired by the National Gallery of Canada. Two copies of this catalogue have been deposited in National Gallery of Canada Library. A memorial exhibition of Peel's work was held at the London Public Library and Art Museum in November, 1970, and a catalogue issued for the occasion which lists 34 works, with 12 reproductions and an introduction by Clare Bice. Recent prices paid for Peel oil paintings include "Girl Feeding Calves, Brittany", 27-1/2" x 40-1/2" — $5,000 in 1970; "The First Lesson", 24" x 31" $3,750 in 1974. Paintings by Paul Peel can be seen in the following public places and galleries: Glenbow-Alberta Inst., Calgary; Edmonton Art Gallery, Alta.; London Public Lib. & Art Museum; Univ. of Western Ontario, Lond.; Art Gallery of Ontario; City of Toronto; Hospital For Sick Children, Ont.; Robt. McLaughlin Gallery, Oshawa; Agnes Etherington Art Centre, Kingston, Ont.; NGC, Ottawa; Montreal Museum of Fine Arts, Mtl.; Beaverbrook Art Gallery, Fred., N.B.; Columbus Gal. of Fine Arts, Columbus, Ohio.

References

Paul Peel: Catalogue Raisonné by J. Edward Martin (Manuscript with select bibliography) April, 1974 (see NGC Library)

Globe, Tor., Ont., 16 Oct., 1890 "Paul Peel's Pictures"

Dictionary of National Biography, Vol. XLIV by Leslie Stephen & Sidney Lee, Smith Elder & Co., 1895, P. 209

Canada: An Encyclopedia, Vol. IV, Edited by Martin Hopkins, Linscott Co., Tor., 1898-1900, P. 404

Canadian Magazine XXXV, No. 1, Tor., May 1910 "Paul Peel and His Art" by Isabel C. Armstrong, P. 49-57

Art In Canada: The Early Painters by Edmund Morris, Tor., 1911, P. 38-40

Canada and Its Provinces, Vol. XII, Glasgow, Brook, Co., 1914 "Painting and Sculpture in Canada" by E.F.B. Johnston, P. 606-607

Bryan's Biographical Dictionary of Painters and Engravers, Vol. IV, Geo. C. Williamson, Bell, 1919, P. 86

Advertiser, London, Ont., Sept. 5, 1922 "Peel Paintings Shown In London" ("The Twins" & "The Dancing Doll" shown at Colericks' Art Store)

news clipping (London, Ont.), Nov., 1922 "Europe's Poverty is Fortune For London" (Colerick negotiates acquisition of "After the Bath")

news clipping (Tor., Ont.) Nov. 1922 "Painting Sold at $2,000 Might Bring $750,000 Now"

Globe, Tor., Ont., Nov. 27, 1922 "Canada To Regain Painting That Made Canadian Famous" ("After the Bath" purchased)

Mail & Empire, Tor., Ont., Nov. 27, 1922 "Famous Painting by Paul Peel Comes to Canada from Hungary"

Toronto Evening Telegram, Ont., Mar. 7, 1923 "Canada's Foremost Artist Got $2,000 For Pictures Now Worth $750,000 — Auctioned His Life's Work For Pittance 30 Years Ago — What Toronto Paid For Life Works of Canada's Great Artist" (list of paintings auctioned, price paid in 1890 and value in 1923)

London Free Press, Ont., Mar. 17, 1923 "Famous Painting Arrives In City — Henry Pocock and James Colerick Get Peel's Picture" ("After the Bath" valued between $50,000 and $100,000)

Saturday Night, Tor., Ont., May 19, 1923 "Exaggeration About Paul Peel"

The Fine Arts In Canada by Newton MacTavish, MacMillan, Tor., 1925, P. 28-30

The London Free Press, Ont., July 31, 1926 "Londoners Get Prized Painting — Colerick Brothers Obtain 'The Wreck' By Paul Peel"

A Portfolio of Canadian Art, Vol. 1 by Frederick R. Jacob, Rous & Mann, Tor., 1926

London Advertiser, Ont., Feb. 26, 1927 "Richmond Street House Paul Peel's Birthplace — Quaint Frame Building Near Horton Street . . . " by E.J. Carthy

PEEL, Paul (Cont'd)

A People's Best by O.J. Stevenson, Musson Co., Tor., 1927, P. 135-140

Globe, Tor., Ont., Aug. 15, 1929 "Paul Peel's 'Harvesters' Goes to Council Chambers"

Toronto Star, Ont., Dec. 21, 1929 "Paul Peel's Masterpiece Famous 'After the Bath' Bought By Toronto Man" (C.H. Carlisle buys painting for $50,000)

Globe, Tor., Ont., Dec. 17th, 1930 "Peel's Masterpiece Is Subject Of Suit" (Colerick sues Pocock for share in sale of 'After the Bath')

Mail & Empire, Tor., Ont., Dec. 17, 1930 "Famous Masterpiece Is Involved In Suit – London Man Claims Share of Profits From 'After the Bath.' "

The Dalhousie Review, October, 1930 "Painting and Sculpture in Canada" by M.O. Hammond, P. 387, 388

Toronto Star, Ont., May 1, 1931 "To Show Peel Paintings Hidden In Widow's Home" (Miss Margaret Browne, friend of Peel family, brings "Jeunesse", "Study for the Dancing Doll", "Good Morning" to Toronto for exhibit at the Robert Simpson Fine Art Galleries)

Ibid, May 1, 1931 "Pictures of the Family of Paul Peel and the Home in France"

Ibid, May 1, 1931 "Three Unknown Gems of the Great Canadian Artist Paul Peel"

London Advertiser, Ont., Oct. 14th, 1931 "Agreement Out of Court Settles Suit Over Painting By Famed London Artist" (Colerick-Pocock suit is settled)

Canadian Landscape Painters by A.H. Robson, Ryerson Press, Tor., 1932, P. 72, 76, 78, 92

The Toronto Star, Ont., July 6, 1933 "Peel Painting Brings Only $4,000 – Believe 'The Orchestra Stalls' Will Remain in London Family" (painting goes from T.P. Loblaw estate to W.R. Newport)

London Free Press, Ont., July 7, 1933 ("The Orchestra Chairs" goes to W.R. Newport)

Canadian Homes & Gardens, September, 1933 "A Famous Painting to Grace a Toronto Hall" ("Before the Bath" owned by Norman Seagram, Tor.)

Toronto Telegram, Ont., Jan. 4, 1936 "Paul Peel Twice Painted Famous 'After the Bath' Canvas Now in Toronto, First Canvas Sold for $20,000 – Regarded as Greatest 'Discovery' Yet Brought to Canada – Sir Wyly Grier Considers Replica Undoubtedly Genuine and in Some Ways Finer Than Original"

Mail & Empire, Tor., Ont., Mar. 5, 1936 "Paul Peel's Daughter Spurns 'After the Bath' Endorsed by Sir Wyly"

The Toronto Star, Ont., Mar. 6, 1936 "Grier Repeats Stand Picture Peel's Work"

Mail & Empire, Tor., Ont., Nov. 14, 1936 "Relates History of Famed Canvas – Marguerite Peel Says She Acted as Model for Noted Father" (three versions of "After the Bath" mentioned)

Toronto Star, Ont., 14 Nov., 1936 "Says Peel Painted 'After Bath' Thrice"

Ibid, 18 Dec., 1936 "Peel Self-Portrait Is Purchased By Kin" (withdrawn by Peel family from auction at $3,500)

Ibid, Dec. 21, 1936 "Paul Peel Picture Was Too Expensive For Queen" by R.E. Knowles (Knowles interviews Marguerite and sister of Paul Peel – Peel speaks French mostly to his children – Queen Alexandra tries to buy "The Toad-Boy" finds it too expensive)

Ars Longa by Newton MacTavish, Ont., Pub. Co., Tor., 1938 P. 145, 146, 156, 201, 227

Toronto Star, Ont., 17 Jan., 1941 "Peel Masterpiece Is 'All Right' Not 'Cracking Up,' Says Expert"

Canadian Art, Its Origin and Development by William Colgate, Ryerson, Tor., 1943 (paperback 1967), P. 38, 77

G.A. Reid by Muriel Miller Miner, Ryerson, Tor., 1946, P. 48

London Free Press, Ont., Sept. 17, 1954 "Displays Self-Portrait Of Famed City Artist, Hope It May Stay Here" (following Paul's death children are taken to USA by mother)

Ibid, Sept. 18, 1954 "Self-Portrait by Paul Peel On Display at Art Gallery"

Ibid, Sept. 25, 1954 "Daughter Reflects Mother's Portrait – Peel Painting Will Be Given to London"

Ibid, Apr. 21, 1959 "Willed by Artist's Daughter – Paul Peel Paintings Bequeathed to Museum"

Ibid, June 6, 1959 "Peel Paintings Come Home" by Lenore Crawford

Record, Jarvis, Ont., Nov. 5, 1959 "Memoirs On Paul Peel By Canon D.J. Cornish" (discusses Peel's early sculpture in London, Ontario)

London Free Press, Ont., Nov. 19, 1959 "Peel Painting Is Presented To Museum"

Nat. Gal. of Can. Catalogue of Paintings & Sculpture, Vol. 3, Can. School by R.H. Hubbard, NGC/Univ. Tor., Ottawa, 1960, P. 243

PEEL, Paul (Cont'd)

London Free Press, Mar. 22, 1962 "Artist's Home Set for Move To Fanshawe"
The Development of Canadian Art by R.H. Hubbard, Queen's Printer, Ottawa, 1963, P. 74-5
London Free Press, Ont., Sept. 21, 1963 "Paul Peel painting – Bequest to City of London of Covent Garden picture still has its mystery but pigments as fresh as new"
Painting in Canada, A History by J. Russell Harper, Univ. Tor. Press, 1966, P. 204, 217, 221, 225
Three Hundred Years of Canadian Art by R.H. Hubbard and J.R. Ostiguy, NGC, Ottawa, 1967, P. 94, 95
Agnes Etherington Art Centre, Permanent Collection (Queen's Univ.) by Frances K. Smith, Kingston, 1968, No. 107
Art Gallery of Ontario, the Canadian collection by Helen Pepall Bradfield, McGraw-Hill, Tor., 1970, P. 358-361
The Mr. And Mrs. Jules Loeb Collection by Pierre Théberge, NGC, Ottawa, 1970, No. 36 (sketch for "After the Bath")
Paul Peel, Memorial Exhibition In The Art Gallery by Clare Bice, London Public Library and Art Museum, Lon., Ont., November, 1970
Early Painters and Engravers In Canada by J. Russell Harper, Univ. Tor. Press, 1970, P. 247
The Globe Magazine, Tor., Ont., Feb. 13, 1971 "His Paintings Were Sold For $5" by Joan Pierson
Globe & Mail, Tor., Ont., 30 June, 1971 "Oil by Peel Sheds Years of Grime" by Kay Kritzwiser
Ibid, 21 June, 1972 "After the Bath: a new pet for AGO" by Kay Kritzwiser
Oshawa Times, Ont., 28 July, 1972 "Former McLaughlin Art Treasure Now at Art Gallery of Ontario"
The Nude in Canadian Painting by Jerrold Morris, New Press, Tor., 1972, P. 7, 39
High Realism in Canada by Paul Duval, Clarke Irwin, Tor., 1974, P. 25, 31
The History of Painting in Canada by Barry Lord, NC Press, Tor., 1974, P. 106
The National Gallery of Canada Seventh Annual Review, 1974-75, Acquisitions – Post-Confederation Painting and Sculpture, P. 102 (purchase of "The Discovery of Moses")
Canadian Art At Auction, 1968-1975, Ed. by Geoffrey Joyner, Sotheby & Co., Tor., Ont., 1975, P. 154
A Concise History of Canadian Painting by Dennis Reid, Oxford Univ. Press, Tor., 1973, P. 96-98, 100, 301
Enjoying Canadian Painting by Patricia Godsell, General Publishing Co. Ltd., Don Mills, Ont., 1976, P. 92, 94, 95

PEHAP, Erich (Eric) Konstantin
b. 1912

Born in Viljandi, Estonia, he studied in the State College of Art and Crafts in Tallinn and later at the Estonian Academy of Fine Arts "Pallas" at Tartu, Estonia where he studied oil painting (1937) and graphic art (1939). He also attended a course in graphic technique at the Graphic Institute in Stockholm, Sweden. For the period 1940-41 he was awarded an Estonian Government Ministry of Education Award. He participated in exhibitions in Estonia, Vienna, Munich, Warsaw, Prague, Stockholm and elsewhere from 1934 on and he held one-man shows in Estonia and Sweden. He has worked as a free lance artist and illustrator in Tallinn and Tartu (1932-1939); taught free hand and line drawing in high school in Tartu (1939-41); was decorator and artistical adviser at the Commercial Centre in Viljandi, Estonia (1941-43) then free lance and commercial artist in Stockholm (1944-49). Coming to Canada in 1949 he settled in Toronto where he has been active with the Estonian Artists' Society (1955); The Colour and Form Society (1952) and The Canadian Society of Graphic Art (1952). He has developed a new

PEHAP, Erich (Eric) Konstantin (Cont'd)

direct graphical method for platemaking and for printing. A one-man show of his selected prints (1932-1972) was held at St. Peter's Exhibition Halls, Mount Pleasant Road, Toronto. Pres. Estonian Soc. of Artists, Tor. (1960).

References
Eric Pehap (exhibition notice) selected prints 1932-1972 opening Oct. 6, 1972, St. Peter's Exhibition Halls, Tor.
Globe & Mail, Tor., Ont., Nov. 28, 1959 "More Fine Prints and Drawings"
NGC Info. Forms 1951, 1961

PELLAN, Alfred (Alfred Pelland)
b. 1906

Born in Quebec City, P.Q., the second son of Alfred Pelland and Maria-Régina Damphousse, brother of Réginald (b. 1905) and Diane (b. 1907). His mother died (c. 1908) leaving his father, a locomotive engineer, to raise the family with the help of a maid. His father took advantage of his off-duty time to be with his children for family walks, games and took them to visit his big locomotive of the Frontenac Express which ran between Quebec and Montreal. This gave Alfred a great source of pride and for a few years he thought his father actually owned his own locomotive. When he was ten he received for Christmas, a working model of a locomotive his father made for him. The model is still his proud possession and rests on a ledge of a playroom of his home. Until the age of thirty-seven he suffered from undetected appendicitis. He was often away from school and when back at his desk would constantly sketch on the margins of his copy book. He did exceptionally well in his art class and not so well in his other subjects which interested him little. Once his father was confined to his home by an illness and bought some art supplies. When he returned to work and laid aside his paints, they were discovered by his son Alfred. It was then that the boy realized painting was what he wanted to do for a living. His first attempts, as related by his biographer Germain Lefebvre, were copies of calendar and magazine pictures which then gave way to his sketching from nature. Travelling to and from his subjects he carried his material on a handcart. At a chosen site strollers and playmates looking over his shoulder and asking questions bothered him so much that he found more interest in working at home on still life subjects experimenting with compositional arrangements. Little of his early work survives. In 1920 he entered the Ecole des Beaux-Arts in Quebec City with the whole-hearted support of his father. He saved his allowances for art materials by taking his lunch breaks at home and walking back and forth to school. He enjoyed the understanding of the school director, Jean Bailleul and was able to choose his teachers and plan his own schedules. He was a serious student and the faculty was so impressed with his hard work that they allowed him possession of a key to the school studios to pursue his studies beyond the hours of regular classes. There were however limited facilities to study works of more modern movements in the form of reproductions. Pellan did well in his studies winning prizes every year and in his final year he won all the prizes given for drawing, painting, sculpture, pen drawing, anatomy and sketching. He was accorded the unusual honour of having one of his paintings "Coin du vieux Quebec"

PELLAN, Alfred (Alfred Pelland) (Cont'd)

purchased by the National Gallery of Canada in 1923 during its showing at the Montreal Spring Exhibition. In 1925 he was awarded the grand prize of a poster competition organized in Quebec by the Kiwanis Frolics Program but the greatest reward for the young student was a Quebec Government painting bursary to study in Paris. A co-winner, Omer Parent received his bursary for study in decorative arts and accompanied him to Paris. Pellan arrived in the city in the early autumn of 1926 and after a few weeks of freedom enrolled in the Ecole supérieure nationale des Beaux-Arts de Paris where he attended his classes faithfully in order to meet the requirements of the bursary. Then he attended the studio of Lucien Simon considered by many to be the best teacher of painting available. Simon recommended Pellan for the school's first prize for painting which he received in 1928. He spent short periods living in the premises of the Canadian pavilion of the cité universitaire and the United States pavilion. But he joined his friends at the Ecole Supérieure and lived in the Montparnasse section of Paris where survival was easy with low rents and inexpensive meals aided by a further spirit of camaraderie often in reciprocation of a kind action of a fellow artist a day or week before. Pellan was drawn into the mainstream of contemporary art, a world apart from the traditionalism of Quebec. In 1935 he attracted attention of critics with his exhibition at the Académie Ranson, particularly the attention of Jacques Lassaigne who noted the ability of Pellan to assimilate the lessons of Picasso and Bonnard and others in fine still lifes while still maintaining his own identity. The same year Pellan won first prize for his "Composition abstraite en rouge et noir" (now titled "Instruments de musique"), in the Salon de L'Art mural de Paris judged by artists such as Robert Delaunay and Ossip Zadkine. Artists exhibiting included Léger and Picasso making this achievement of Pellan an impressive one. He visited Picasso on two occasions and on the second was able to see this famous artist's work in his studio. Picasso expressed an interest in seeing Pellan's paintings but the young Canadian felt he was not ready to have his work seen by such a great artist, and put the matter off until the meeting simply never took place. Pellan preferred to work at the academies of the Grande Chaumière or the Colarossi. Sales of his paintings were not sufficient to live on so he obtained a number of commissions for graphic design and for a period worked for a poster publisher, designed a perfume bottle for Revillon, painted directly onto the fabric of dresses designed by Schiaparelli. Some of his dresses were acquired by Madame Miró when she shopped at the Côte d'Azur. Pellan at times was not able to make enough to get along so he reluctantly asked his father for financial assistance which was willingly given. In 1935 Pellan visited Florence on his motorcycle accompanied by the actor Alain Cuny. In 1936 his father persuaded him to return to Canada and apply for a teaching post at the École des Beaux-Arts de Québec. He consigned all his baggage and materials in Paris in the event that his return to Canada was only a temporary move. An interview was arranged by his father with Joseph Simard, Secretary of the Province, and proof was required of his ability regardless of the success Pellan had achieved in Paris. So Pellan did a few paintings and sculptures. Two of the artists who had sent him to Paris were among those reviewing the applicant, Clarence Gagnon and Horatio Walker. He was afterwards interviewed by Simard. Pellan expressed his great admiration for Braque, Juan Gris, Klee, Léger, Matisse, Miró and Picasso. It was then decided that his work was too modern, too avantgarde and therefore a bad influence on the students. With his father's full under-

 Pages 1569 and 1570 are reversed

pated in several group shows, then with great success in New York City at the Bignou Gallery during April of 1942 where he was lauded by critics including Doris Bain of *Art News* as follows, "After some early training in his home town he went to Paris, became a member of good standing of its school, and remained there till 1940 when he came home with shows and sales all over Europe to his credit. In his middle thirties, he seems to have just hit his top stride in time for his first New York exhibition, because the brightest, gayest, and for our taste the best of his compositions bear the date 1942. Earlier works are in a primitivish vein and there are also some worthy excursions into Surrealism. But the new Pellans are semi-abstractions full of pattern and painted in a Matisse-derived palette. Flat paint is used to indicate still-life objects which seem paper thin but have an odd sort of three dimensional quality full of verve and daring. Pellan can't stand empty space and fills it all up with charming pattern, covering coffee pots, sauce pans, and even lemons with polka dots, using French wall-paper as background for still-lifes full of flowers, fruit, and checked tablecloths. And it is all organized." Despite this good reception in New York, Pellan made no sales due perhaps to a pro-American artist campaign to bring the American public behind the artists of their own country. Braque also made no sales. In 1943 Pellan completed a commission of two murals for the Canadian Legation in Rio de Janeiro depicting Canada West and East. This same year he joined the staff of the Ecole des Beaux-Arts, Montreal, then under the directorship of Charles Maillard an eminent painter but rigid traditionalist in teaching. Pellan's liberal approach to teaching soon brought him in conflict with Maillard and involved the students as well. The situation reached a climax following a lecture at the Montreal Botanical Garden by French painter Fernand Léger who publicly decried academic art. Léger was a close friend of Pellan and stayed at the latter's place during his visit to Montreal. Students attending the lecture from the Beaux-Arts were carried away with the moment and cried "down with Maillard and down with academism." Pellan was blamed and matters went from bad to worse but finally Maillard resigned and was succeeded by Marcel Parizeau, the progressive teacher of architecture from the Ecole de Meuble and friend of Pellan. After only a few weeks Parizeau died suddenly and was in turn succeeded by Roland Charlebois, a miniaturist painter. Pellan continued teaching at the Beaux-Arts until 1952. About the time Pellan joined the staff of the Ecole des Beaux-Arts, Borduas became offended by Pellan's acceptance of such a position which would seem to align him with regular traditional forms of study limiting the freedom of the students to anything other than the prescribed guidelines of the various courses. But Pellan had joined the school to implement his own ideas and made an attempt to explain this to Borduas. He went to Borduas' house to give his position but Borduas had already made up his mind that he had gone over to the traditionalists (some other reasons have been suggested by Germain Lefebvre including rivalry felt by Borduas). From that point on Pellan and Borduas went their separate ways taking with them their respective followings of young artists; Borduas leading the Automatists and Pellan the Prisme d'Yeux. While both movements sought liberation from the traditionalism of Quebec, the Automatistes chose the non-objective path while the Prisme d'Yeux chose a variety of new ways to see the world around them through Surrealism, Cubsim, or in the words of the *Prisme d'Yeux* manifesto drafted by Jacques de Tonnancour in 1948, "We seek a painting liberated from all contingencies of time and place,

standing Pellan quite happily packed his bags and returned to Paris where his abstracts, still lifes and portraits had been well received. In 1937 he visited Greece and spent three weeks on the island of Santorin, travelling with two architects attached to Le Corbusier's studio. The scenery influenced him profoundly, even years later Santorin was the subject of one of his paintings. In 1937 he was unexpectedly surprised by a visit of the Minister of Fine Arts of France and the curator of the Musée de Fontainebleau and their purchase of two of his paintings, one of which now hangs in the Musée de Jeu de Paume (Musée national d'Art Moderne, Paris) and another painting in the Musée de Grenoble. His work continued to attract the interest of critics like H.W. Sendberg a Dutch journalist, during a group exhibition in the Hague (1937-38). By 1939 Pellan was recognized as one of the important painters of the French School which included Dufy, Dali, Fautrier and Picasso, all of whom participated in the 1939 show "Paris Painters of Today" at the Museum of Modern Art in Washington. He also became a painter of the gallery of Jeanne Bucher whose other artists included Braque, Ernst, Kandinsky, Léger, Lurçat, Marcoussis, Picasso, Arp, Giacometti and Lipchitz. World War II brought an end to Pellan's stay in Paris. He gathered together his work (more than 400 paintings and drawings) and personal effects and shipped them home to Quebec. He had to leave his sculpture behind. His return trip was paid for by the Quebec Government who took several of his paintings as payment. He arrived in Quebec City in June, 1940. From his European work he chose 161 pieces for an exhibit, within days of his arrival, at the Musée de la Province de Québec. The same exhibit was shown at the Art Association of Montreal (this exhibit was slightly reduced in size because of the limited space). Robert Ayre on viewing the show for *The Montreal Standard* prophetically remarked, "If Alfred Pellan stays at home, he ought to be a vital influence in Canadian painting. He might have an effect on public taste, but if that is slow in developing, his example and the fact that the Provincial Museum has acquired some of his works may give courage to painters who have been trying to break away from the old established habits." Ayre's favourable appreciation was shared by Maurice Gagnon, Marcel Parizeau and Reynald of *La Presse*. Pellan had been staying with his father since his return from France and now decided to live in Montreal stopping for a few weeks at Philip Surrey's studio until finding a place of his own a block away at 3714 Jeanne Mance Street. In this area, lived many painters as well as actors, poets and musicians. He renewed old friendships with Jean-Charles Harvey, Dr. Dumas and widened his circle of colleagues through Philip Surrey to include Jori Smith, Jean Palardy, John Lyman, Jacques de Tonnancour, Goodridge Roberts and others. He was attracted particularly to the group of artists connected with the Ecole du Meuble who were deep into progressive trends in art led by Paul-Emile Borduas; others like Maurice Gagnon, librarian at the school, and Marcel Parizeau, teacher in architecture became his close friends. He participated in the group show "Première exposition des Independants" along with John Lyman, Goodridge Roberts, Philip Surrey, Eric Goldberg, Louise Gadbois, Louis Muhlstock, Paul-Emile Borduas, Mary Bouchard, Jori Smith and Stanley Cosgrove. In 1941 he spent the summer as guest of Jori Smith and her film director husband Jean Palardy. His first few weeks were spent in complete relaxation and then he painted a number of landscapes and portraits of young girls who visited the Palardys. These paintings he exhibited in his studio in December of that year to the delight of the critics and his patrons. He partici-

from restrictive ideology and conceived without literary, political, philosophical or any other interference which could adulterate expression and compromise its purity." Those signing the *Prisme d'Yeux* manifesto included: Pellan, de Tonnancour, Louis Archambault, Leon Bellefleur, Albert Dumouchel, Gabriel Filion, Pierre Gauvreau, Arthur Gladu, Jean Benoit, Lucien Morin, Mimi Parent, Jeanne Rheaume, Goodridge Roberts, Roland Truchon and Gordon Webber. This was a loose knit group who thrived during the period 1946-50 at the Ecole des Arts graphiques where Albert Dumouchel was teaching printmaking and where three editions of *Les Ateliers d'Art graphique* were conceived. Other attending artists to the Ecole des Arts graphiques included Jean-René Ostiguy, Jean Leonard, Gerard Tremblay, Gilles Henault and Roland Giguère. But the Prisme d'Yeux movement, because of its broad concept did not move forward with the same thrust as the Automatiste group, founded with the manifesto *Refus Global* which sought liberation from prevailing social structures of Quebec. The *Refus global* struck out at the oppressive forces of society and gained front rank status with the intellectual revolutionaries. Pellan's *Prisme d'Yeux* was more of an artistic revolution and for this reason had a comparatively limited appeal. Among Pellan's followers was a most attractive young woman named Madeleine Polisena who attended the Ecole des Beaux-Arts. They met one evening in 1947 during a reception at Jacques de Tonnancour's home and were married on July 23rd, 1949. They moved in 1950 from Pellan's studio on Jeanne Mance Street to the Auteuil house, an old Canadian home on a quiet road along the Mille Illes River near St. Rose East, north of Montreal. There he changed the inside of the house to accommodate a large studio. The walls of the house were painted white to accommodate the many mementos, paintings, and decorations he and Madeleine had gathered together over the years. In 1952 he was awarded a Royal Society of Canada fellowship for research studies in France and arrived in Paris with his wife. Disappointed he found that the Paris he knew twelve years before had vanished. He turned his attentions to his work after finding a studio at 19 bis Avenue Victor-Hugo, Boulogne-sur-Seine. He had also brought a large collection of his paintings from Canada and exhibited them on a number of important occasions, drawing praise from André Breton at a solo show in the Coq Liban, Paris, in 1954. But his most memorable event was his retrospective show at the Musée national d'Art moderne in Paris in February and March of 1955 when articles of praise appeared in a number of French newspapers. His painting "La Chouette" measuring 82" x 66" was purchased by the Museum and is a magnificently intricate surrealistic work with a central nude figure of a woman with an owl-like head, surrounded by symbols of time, love, the night, and a host of other elements, unified by Pellan's subtle use of green and the Jackson Pollock-like calligraphy woven through much of the composition. In November of 1956 Pellan returned to his studio in Ste. Rose, Quebec and the same month an exhibition of his work initiated by Mayor Drapeau was held at the Montreal city hall in the Hall of Honour. Some controversy centered around a few of his paintings in that a councillor tried to have them removed because they depicted women not in keeping with the councillor's Christian standards. But only one picture was actually removed. *The Montreal Star* noted, "It consists of more than 100 works, from drawings about twelve inches by nine to canvases nearly seven feet by six. I thought it rather touching that the artist should include his first picture 'Les Fraises' painted when he was fourteen, and two others from the next year. It is as if he continues to be astonished at himself — 'Look how far I have come!' And this contradicts the impression of arrogance you may sometimes get from Pellan's painting. It isn't arrogance. It's just the virtuoso's delight in the exercise of his powers and the pictorial world he exploits for its own sake, the world of the eye . . . . There are overtones of mystery here, too. Some of the paintings carry a surrealist burden of the portentous. But it isn't the hidden that is the strength of Pellan's art; it is the explicit, in a wealth of inventiveness and fantasy." In 1957 Pellan won first prize in the mural competition for the City Centre Building in Montreal. The contest was country-wide for the mosaic mural, which overlooks the main foyer of the ten storey building, and was laid by Joseph Iliu noted mosaic artist. In 1958 he received a Canada Council fellowship award and set to work on his series of Jardin paintings, six of which were exhibited in a showing at the Denyse Delrue Gallery in April of 1958 when among other reviewers, Dorothy Pfeiffer in *The Gazette* favourably noted, "There was a time when one seldom mentioned Pellan without at the same time thinking of Picasso. But that time is past. Alfred Pellan need kow-tow to no one. He has become his own unique influence and master of amazingly decorative concentration and effect . . . . Certain sections of his enormous canvasses — or murals — are covered with brilliant-hued squiggles of thick paint giving one the impression of having been squeezed from a pastry-tube. While on other sections are affixed shells, beads, jackstraws, sprinkled sand and glass. In some places the paint is so lavish it looks as if it had been mixed with mortar. All the paintings give out a glow, cast a spell, or make one blink with their mysterious light." Perhaps in this series "Jardin bleu" is one of the most beautiful and enchanting canvases measuring 54-1/4 x 73-1/2 feet, in essence a night scene of the most gorgeous blue accented by the tiny white lights of a timeless hamlet. In the sky is the love theme of man and woman arched around a glowing candle set inside a muted moon. This painting is reproduced in Germain Lefebvre's book *Pellan* (P. 103). In 1960 Pellan was honoured by a retrospective exhibition sponsored jointly by the National Gallery of Canada, the Montreal Museum of Fine Arts and the Art Gallery of Toronto (one in a series of shows devoted to senior Canadian artists). Among his other notable mural commissions are: a painting for the Winnipeg Airport (1963); Place des Arts, Mtl., stained glass window (1963); National Library of Canada, two murals, one a tribute to writing of all civilizations and the other on subjects covered by the library's basic book collections (1968). After about 1965 Pellan's awards followed in quick succession through greater appreciation for his achievements in the visual arts. He also made a brilliant contribution to the theatre by design of props, costumes, sets and makeup for the plays *Madeleine et Pierre* by André Audet (1944-45), *La nuit des rois* by Shakespeare put on by Compagnons de Saint-Laurent, Gesu, Mtl. (1946) and a later version by Théâtre du Nouveau Monde, Place des Arts, Mtl. (1968-69) and also designed the curtain maquette for the Montreal Theatre Ballet (1957). While discussion here of Pellan's works would follow along an endless highway, mention should be made of his "Végétaux marins" (1964), a most brilliantly imaginative painting allowing the viewer to peer from the multicoloured seabed to the surface above, the seabed and surface joined by two dark vegetal forms reaching upwards through the translucent blue water lit by daylight and accented by a colourful drifting egg-shaped marine creature. This painting is owned by the Art Collection Society of Kingston (see *Pellan*, P. 133). His solo shows include the following: Académie Ranson, Paris (1935); Galerie

PELLAN, Alfred (Alfred Pelland) (Cont'd)

Jeanne Bucher, Paris (1939); Musée de la Province de Québec (1940); Montreal Museum of Fine Arts (1940); Galerie Bignou, NYC (1942); Galerie Municipal, Que. (1942); Galerie l'Atelier, Ott. (1952); Coq Liban, Paris (1954); Cercle Paul Valéry, Paris (1954); Musée national d'Art moderne, Paris (retrospective, 1955); Hall of Honour, City Hall, Mtl. (retrospective, 1956); Laing Galleries, Tor. (Nov. 1957); Galerie Denyse Delrue, Mtl. (1958, Hommage à Pellan, 1960); Robertson Gal., Ott. (1960); NGC, MMFA, Mus. Que., AGT (retrospective, 1960-61); Roberts Gal. Tor. (1961); Gal. Libre, Mtl. (Présence de Pellan, 1963); Kitchener-Waterloo Art Gallery (1964); Howard Domain, Sherbrooke, P.Q. (1964); Roberts Gal. Tor. (1964); WAG (1968); Musée d'Art Contemporain (Voir Pellan, 1969); Mus. Que., MMFA, NGC (Pellan, 1972-73); Ecole des Arts visuels, Univ. Laval, Que. (Pellan – Costumes et décors de théâtre, 1972); Galerie de Montréal (Décors et costumes, gouaches d'Alfred Pellan, 1972). His awards and distinctions include: Prov. of Quebec Bursary, Paris (1926-30); 1st Prize in poster competition, Kiwanis Frolics Program, Que. (1926); 1st Prize Première Grande Exposition d'Art mural de Paris (1935); represented Canada at Art Inst. of Chicago exhibit of artists from 40 countries (1945); 1st Prize, painting, 65th Annual Spring Show, MMFA (1948); 1st Prize, Quebec Competition (1948); Bursary, Royal Society of Canada for research in France (1952-53); 1st Prize, mural competition, City Centre Bldg., Mtl. (1957); Prof. of Painting at Canadian Art Centre (1958); National prize, painting, Univ. Alta. (1959); Canada Council Medal (1965); Jury member of Quatrième Biennale de Paris (1965); Companion of the Order of Canada (1967); Centenary Medal Canada Confed.; NFB Voir Pellan (1969); Doctorate, honoris causa, philosophy (fine arts), Univ. Ottawa. (1969); RCS (1971); Doctorate, honoris causa, arts, Univ. Laval (1971); Doctorate, honoris causa, law, Sir Geo. Wms. Univ. Mtl. (1971); Prix Philippe Hébert, Soc. Saint-Jean Baptiste (1972); Molson's Prize (1973); Doctorate, honoris causa, Univ. Montreal (1974).

References (token selection)

Painters of Quebec by Marius Barbeau, Ryerson, Tor., 1945, P. 40

Alfred Pellan by Donald W. Buchanan, Soc. for Art Publications/M&S, 1962

The Nat. Gal. of Can. Catalogue, Vol. 3, Can. School, by R.H. Hubbard, NGC, Ott., 1960, P. 244-45

Modern Painting in French Canada by Guy Viau, Dept. Cultural Affairs, Quebec, 1967, P. 42-47

École de Montréal par Guy Robert, Éditions du Centre de Psychologie et de Pédagogie, Mtl., 1964

Creative Canada, Volume Two, Ref. Div. McPherson Lib. Univ. Vict. B.C./Univ. Tor. Pr., 1972, P. 215-217

PELLAN by Germain Lefebvre, M & S, Tor., 1973 (a major work on the artist beautifully written and illustrated)

L'Art Au Québec Depuis 1940 par Guy Robert, La Presse, Mtl., 1973 (see index)

Dossier de Presse Retrospective Alfred Pellan par le Centre de documentation, Musée du Québec, 1973

A Concise History of Canadian Painting by Dennis Reid, Oxford, Tor., 1973 (see index)

Canadian Art at Auction, 1968-1975, Edited by Geoffrey Joyner, Foreword by Paul Duval, Sotheby & Co. (Can.) Ltd., Tor., Ont., 1975, P. 154

Painting in Canada: a history by J. Russell Harper, Univ. Tor. Press, Tor., 1966 (2nd Ed. paper, 1977) see index

NGC Info. Forms, 1946

Newspaper & periodical articles (token)

PELLAN, Alfred (Alfred Pelland) (Cont'd)

The Montreal Standard, Mtl., P.Q., Oct. 12, 1940 "Pellan's Exhibition 'A Painter's World of Shapes, Rhythms' " by Robert Ayre

The Montreal Herald, Mtl., P.Q., Apr. 21, 1942 "Critics Acclaim Montreal Artist – Alfred Pellan's N.Y. Show Wins Wide Approval" by Don Gilbert

Art News, Volume XLI, No. 5, April 15-20, 1942 "Passing Shows – Pellan" by Doris Brian

The Ottawa Citizen, Ont., Feb. 16, 1948 "XX – Alfred Pellan" by Josephine Hambleton

Ibid, June 5, 1948 "Pioneer In A Canadian Art Revolt" by Josephine Hambleton

Mayfair, Tor., Ont., July, 1948 "Quebec's most 'modern' painting is the new storm centre of Canadian Art" by Paul Duval

Journal of the Royal Architectural Institute of Canada, January, 1949 "Alfred Pellan" by Jacques G. De Tonnancour

La Presse, Mlt., P.Q., Nov. 13, 1954 "Alfred Pellan et Robert Blair" par R. de Repentigny

Ibid, Nov. 10, 1956 "Pellan ne cherche pas le confort" par R. de Repentigny

The Gazette, Mtl., P.Q., Apr. 19, 1958 "Pellan Exhibits Exotic 'Gardens' " by Dorothy Pfeiffer

Le Devoir, Mtl., P.Q., Apr. 19, 1958 "Formes et Couleurs – L'Art Des Jardins" par René Chicoine

Photo-Journal, 30 April – 7 May, 1960 "Pellan l'oublié?"

Le Droit, Ottawa, Ont., 29 Oct., 1960 "Pellan à la Galerie – La Peinture de Pellan est poétique, dit Jean Cassou"

The Star Weekly, Tor., Ont., Aug. 6, 1960 "Alfred Pellan – Painter, Poet and Dreamer" Text by Herbert Steinhouse, photographs by Paul Rockett

Weekend Magazine, Vol. 10, No. 42, 1960 "Alfred Pellan: Lover Of Life And Art" by Bill Trent, Photos by John Max

La Presse, Mtl., P.Q., Jan. 14, 1961 "Les Beaux-Arts – Rétrospective Pellan" par Jean Sarrazin

Maclean's Magazine, Jan. 28, 1961 "Alfred Pellan – His art came like a blow" by Ken Lefolii

Hotel Publications, Tor., Ont., April 17, 1961 "Outstanding French-Canadian painter in Roberts Gallery Exhibition"

Toronto Daily Star, Apr. 22, 1961 "World of Art" by Robert Fulford

Globe & Mail, Tor., Ont. Apr. 22, 1961 "Art and Artists – Rare Love of Life in Modernist" by Pearl McCarthy

Toronto Telegram, Tor., Ont., Apr. 22, 1961 "Accent On Art – A Trail Of Achievement" by Paul Duval

Globe & Mail, Tor., Ont., May 19, 1962 "Pellan Says Art Decadent"

Le Maître Imprimeur, Novembre, 1962, Vol. XXVI, Numéro 11 "L'Exemple d'un Grand Artiste" par Paul Gladu

Toronto Telegram, Ont., Nov. 21, 1964 "34 Years Of Powerful Pellan" by Harry Malcolmson

Montreal '67, April, 1967 "Alfred Pellan – le libérateur de la peinture canadienne"

Le Devoir, Mtl., May 1, 1969 "Un cyclotron culturel en délire: image, son, danse, couleur" par Jacques Thériault

La Presse, Mtl., P.Q., Mai 13, 1972 "Alfred Pellan, lauréat de la SSJB de Montreal"

L'Action, Que., P.Q., Sept. 9, 1972 "Pellan: une puissance!" par Georgette Lacroix

The Gazette, Mtl., P.Q., Nov. 4, 1972 "Pellan: An exciting painter, an overwhelming spectacle" by Michael White

The Ottawa Citizen, Ont., Dec. 8, 1972 "Alfred Pellan, painter – Canada understands now" by Vivian Macdonald

L'Information Médicale Et Paramédicale, Mtl., P.Q., Dec. 19, 1972 "Consécration d'Alfred Pellan" par Paul Dumas

Financial Post, Tor., Ont., Jan. 13, 1973 "Arnold Edinborough - Greatness in art – with thoughts for our 29th Parliament" by Arnold Edinborough

The Gazette, Mtl., P.Q., May 15, 1974 "$15,000 – Pellan wins Molson Prize"

Montréal-Matin, Que., May 2, 1974 "Le cardinal Léger et Alfred Pellan honorés par l'Université de Montréal"

PELLEN, Jean

b. 1913

Born in Krefeld, Germany, he worked with Hans Greusech from 1939 to 1943 but is mostly self taught. Coming to Canada he settled in Toronto in 1954. He has shown his work in Toronto at Hart House, (1960) and the Upstairs Gallery (1961). He is represented in private collections in Toronto and Hamilton.

Reference
Information from the Upstairs Gallery

PELLERIN, Marthe

She studied form and colour at the University of Quebec school at Trois Rivières and took design studies in a private workshop with Louis Desaulniers. She was inspired by a trip to Mexico to create Navajo style tapestries. She took part in exhibitions in the Shawinigan region and in Montreal. She also creates fabrics for clothing, furniture, placemats, napkins, rugs, bedspreads and other items. Following a Rothman's tapestry exhibition at the Shawinigan town hall around 1965 she had the idea to develop a new technique for weaving. She has several pieces in Europe. All of her pieces are done by hand and are distinct individual works of art. Lives at Shawinigan-Sud, P.Q.

References
Le Nouvelliste, Trois-Rivières, P.Q., Mar. 28, 1974 "Marthe Pellerin: une véritable artisane artistique" par Michelle Guerin
Le guide des artisans créateurs du Quebec par Jean-Pierre Payette, Lapresse, Mtl., P.Q., 1974, P. 154

PELLERIN, Robert

b. 1948

A Shawinigan artist who started painting at age 6 or 7 and was encouraged by Mrs. Benoit Genest, art director at St. Joseph School in Shawinigan. He was painting in a modern style and was particularly interested in cubism. Also interested in theatre as a writer and comedian.

Reference
Le Nouvelliste, Trois Rivières, P.Q., Jan. 3, 1967 "Le peintre Robert Pellerin promis à une belle carrière"

PELLETIER, André

b. 1943

Born in Quebec, he is a graduate of the Ecole des Beaux-Arts, Quebec, and in his early work was influenced by the Cubists. He has executed some of his paintings by using his fingers when applying oils and has also used small brushes to achieve other effects. In 1972 his work was described as imaginative and influenced by science-fiction. His solo shows have been held at the Palais Montcalm, Que. (1969, 70, 72)

PELLETIER, André (Con't)

and Galerie Bénédek-Grenier, Que. (1973) also a three-man show at Galerie d'Art les Gens de mon Pays, Ste-Foy, Que. (1973); five-man show at Séminaire St. George-de-Beauce, Que. (1973). He studied History of Art at Laval University and Theatrical Art at the Ecole des Beaux-Arts, Quebec. He has been teaching classes in high school. His awards include: Prize from the Quebec Ministry for Cultural Affairs (1964); Award from United States Consul (1964); 4th Prize, Decorative Arts Section of Expo-Qué. (1965); First Prize, Drawing Section, Expo-Qué. (1967); 2nd Prize, Painting, Laval Univ. Competition (1969).

References
Le Soleil, Que., P.Q., Nov. 15, 1969 "Une expérience bien engagée" par Claude Daigneault
Ibid, Nov. 4, 1970 (photo of artist and his work)
Chronicle-Telegraph, Que., P.Q., Nov. 4, 1970 "Quebec Artist's Exhibit Officially Opened" (photo of artist and his work)
Le Soleil, Que., P.Q., Oct. 12, 1972 "André Pelletier expose 30 toiles qui font un monde de calme sous des couleurs vives" par Gislain Lebel"
Ibid, Mar. 24, 1973 "La peinture d'André Pelletier fait appel à l'imagination de l'inconnu" par Claude Daigneault
Canadian artists in exhibition, 1972-73, Roundstone, Tor., 1974, P. 168
Artistes du Québec par Irénée Lemieux, Editions Irénée Lemieux, Inc. Quebec, P.Q., 1974, P. 210-211

PELLETIER, Clement

b. 1949

Formerly an architectural student in Montreal, he turned to painting and set up a studio in Hull, Quebec and then in Ottawa in 1976. Described as an Automatiste he has produced several hundred paintings in mixed media, a good number of which have been sold. Planned a show in Montreal in 1976 with plans also for an exhibit in New York City.

References
The Ottawa Citizen, Ont., Jan. 19, 1976 "Entertainment – Artist on display"
Ibid, June 29, 1976 "Entertainment – Drop-in art – Studio home for visitors, color" by Robert Smythe

PELLETIER, Jacques

b. 1951

He studied at the Collège St-Louis-Maillet, Edmundston, N.B., and is known for his collages and drawings, one of which appeared on the cover of The Canadian Architect and publications of the National Arts Centre, Ottawa. He has exhibited at Galerie Colline, Edmundston, N.B. (1973) and a group show at the Centre Civique de Rimouski (1972). He lives in Edmundston.

References
The Canadian Architect, February, 1969
Canadian artists in exhibition, 1972-73, Roundstone, Tor., 1973
Fredericton Gleaner, N.B., Feb. 26, 1973 (photo of artist attending a group show in New Brunswick)

PELLETIER, Monique
b. 1941

She studied at the Ecole des Beaux-Arts with Jacques de Tonnancour and then became a teacher for the Catholic School Commission. In her own work she won a Quebec Provincial grant and scholarship in 1963 for further studies in France and won First Prize at the Salon des Moins de Trente Ans (1962). She was an artist of Galerie Agnes Lefort, Montreal in the 1960's.

Reference
> Visit to Galerie Agnes Lefort c. 1968

PELLETIER, Pierre

He studied Fine Arts at the University of Ottawa where he took classes in drawing, lithography, also both portrait and landscape painting and exhibited his work at the University (1965, 1966, 1973) and in Montreal at Galerie François Paris (1972) and Galerie Société des artisans (1972).

References
> *Le Droit,* Ottawa, Ont., Aug. 3, 1966 "L'exposition du jeune peintre Pierre Pelletier . . . décevante"
> Ibid, April 17, 1973 (photo of artist and his work and caption about his show at U. of O.)

PELLETIER, Regina (Mrs. Paul A. Pelletier)
b. 1898

Born in Claire, N.B., she started to paint at eleven years of age and continued throughout her life. Around 1950 she took lessons from a Viennese lady, attending her studio for six months. Her work was considerably influenced by the painting of Sister Ste. Louis of Congregation Bon Pasteur, Edmundston. She took a full course in wood carving and became active with the Federation of Canadian Wood Carvers. An artist working in a variety of fields she has not only carved in wood and painted in oils and tempera but has also worked with metals and leather. Her art, mainly realistic, has won prizes in several exhibitions. She has worked and studied with Dr. Paul Carmel Laporte and others. She is also a member of Cercle Artistique du Madawaska and the Edmundston Art Group. Living in Edmundston, N.B. in 1962.

Reference
> Document from artist, 1962

PELLETIER, Robert

A Montreal, P.Q., sculptor who created a 900 lb. statue of Louis Cyr, world famous strongman (1863-1912). The statue was erected on the corner of St. James and St. Antoine streets in Montreal where Cyr once patrolled a policeman's beat.

PELLETIER, Robert (Cont'd)

Surprisingly little information is available on Robert Pelletier who completed this important work.

References
> *The Montreal Star,* P.Q., June 8, 1973 "Statue honors 'Samson' Cyr" (photos of statue by Peter Brosseau)
> *Granby La Voix de L'Est,* Granby, P.Q., Jan. 18, 1965 "Monument Louis Cyr à l'Expo '67"

PELLIER, Robert

Born in Larochelle, France, he came to Canada and studied three years at the Ecole des Beaux-Arts, Montreal. By 1966 he had developed a new type of painting called "stratified", a new process for the conservation of colour. He exhibited his work at Sorel, Quebec (1966).

References
> *La Voix Métropolitaine,* Sorel P.Q., Mar. 15, 1966 "Exposition de peintures"
> *Le Courrier Riviera,* Sorel, P.Q., Mar. 16, 1966 "L'Homme de la Semaine"

PELLUS, Michel

b. (c) 1945

A Quebec painter of considerable ability who taught himself to paint in prison about 1972 where he has been serving a sentence for drug offences. Both his mother and father painted. His work was described by Virginia Nixon in *The Gazette* as follows, "Michel Pellus is a figurative painter, but in his flamboyant, brilliantly colored acrylics, the magic and the realism are two separate things combined in a highly distinctive and quite fascinating style. Pellus paints dream-like scenes in which uncannily realistic figures wander in fairy-land landscapes where trees, plants and clouds sprout and swell like globules of candy-painted cotton. They're fairy-tale landscapes laden with an atmosphere of menace." Up to 1976 he had painted 250 canvases drawing his models from magazines, newspapers, books, and television programmes which are then projected into his own imaginative world. Lithographs of his work are available from the Select Galleries Ltd., in Montreal. Exhibitions of his paintings have taken place at the Sadye Bronfman Centre in Montreal; the Manhattan Art and Antique Centre, New York City; the Kar Gallery, Tor.; Galerie Lukacs, Mtl; Galerie Colbert, Mtl.; Galerie Knobb-La Salamandre, Mtl. His canvases have been fetching an average of $2,000 each from collectors in Canada and the United States.

References
> *The Montreal Star,* P.Q., May 11, 1974 "Galerie Colbert"
> Ibid, Sat., Oct. 5, 1974 "Inmate finds art his outlet" by Don Braid
> *The Gazette,* Mtl., P.Q., July 31, 1976 " 'Typically Canadian' Aitkins shows magic realist style" by Virginia Nixon
> *Sunday Sun,* Tor., Ont., Nov. 7, 1976 "Convict is free only in his painting" by Sean McCann

PELLUS, Michel (Con't)

Montreal Matin, July 15, 1976 "Le bel univers intérieur d'un peintre: Michel Pellus" par Raymond Bernatchez
Weekend Magazine, Mtl., P.Q., Dec. 4, 1976 "Released Behind Bars" by Judy Dobbie
Calgary Albertan, Alta. (CP) Dec. 11, 1976 "Convict painter sees his reputation rising"

PÉLOQUIN, Roger (Pélo)

A painter-ceramist from Sorel, P.Q., he is known for his portraits, murals and wood sculptures in figurative and non-figurative styles. He has worked with Lucien Chabot, Jean Bertrand and Jean-Pierre Boivin of the Beaux-Arts but has developed his own art through a self-study programme. He has been influenced by Bernard Buffet and Amedeo Modigliani. He won 2nd Prize in 1956 for the "Painting" section also a mention for "Drawing" at the Exposition Artisanale de St.-Joseph-Tracy. In 1957 four of his murals were shown at the Montreal Spring Show. He established a workshop at St.Joseph-Tracy which was an attraction for visitors and a meeting place for artists. In 1970 he had great success with his pencil portraits of local personalities of Trois Rivières. In 1973 he executed bas-relief sculptures on the Olympic Games. His exhibitions include: Tranquille librairie, Mtl. (1954); Montreal Museum of Fine Arts (1956); Trail, B.C. (1957); Expo du Jeune-Commerce, Sorel (1958); Two-man show at Chateau des Gouverneurs, Sorel (1961); solo shows at Sorel Municipal Library (1970, 1973, 1974); Galerie des Trois A, Saint-Ours (1970); Summer Theatre, Saint-Ours (1973).

References
Le Courrier de Sorel, Sorel, P.Q., Apr. 9, 1959 "Roger Péloquin expose à St-Hyacinthe"
Le Sorelois, Sorel, P.Q., Apr. 9, 1959 "Roger Péloquin exposera ses peintures"
Le Progrès du Richelieu, Sorel, P.Q., Apr. 6, 1961 "Exposition de peintures au Château des Gouverneurs"
Le Nouvelliste, Trois Rivières, P.Q., Apr. 7, 1961 "M. Roger Péloquin" (photo of artist when he was director of 'La Palette' studio)
Le Sorelois, Nov. 18, 1965 "Expo dans la nature" (photo of sculpture by Péloquin)
Le Courrier Riviera, Sorel, P.Q., Feb. 9, 1966 "Arts — informations" par Robert Pellier (photo of Péloquin at work on a wood sculpture)
Le Nouvelliste, Mar. 15, 1974 "Le peintre Roger Péloquin expose à Sorel"
Ibid, Mar. 28, 1974 "Le peintre Roger Péloquin exprime le milieu sorelois"

PELTIER, Pierre

He held a show of his drawings at the Atelier de Réalisations Graphiques in Quebec City in April of 1975.

Reference
Pierre Peltier, Dessins, 28 au 11 avril 1975 (exhibition notice with skilfully executed cartoon in lower corner)

PELTOMAA, Arthur Matti
b. 1922

Born in Finland, he came to Canada in 1927, served in the Canadian Army from 1942 to 1946 and after his discharge he took a crash course completing Grades 10 to 13 in eight months and obtaining an honors average. He then studied art at McGill University, Montreal, Ontario College of Art, Toronto, under Jacobine Jones and Thomas Bowie; Danforth Technical School, Toronto for sculpture under Elford Cox then attended Teachers' College at North Bay and worked with sculptress Frances Loring. A former resident of Chippawa, Ontario and Niagara-on-the-Lake, he settled near Beamsville on thirty acres of wooded terrain along the Cave Spring Road. He has done wood carving, clay moulding, stone and welded steel sculpture as well as painting. Many of his wood sculptures were made from cedar, elm, maple and oak and occasionally black walnut. A show of his work was held at the Court House Theatre at Niagara-on-the-Lake (1965) and he has exhibited in art galleries in Toronto, Montreal, Hamilton and Buffalo also private showings in his studios. Over the years he has worked at every imaginable job from bush camp cook to university teacher. Later he became one of the few artists to make a living from his work. He has completed a number of commissions including sculpture decoration, using an Indian motif, for the Thunderbird Room of the Falls Way Hotel, Niagara Falls and has conducted classes for both children and adults in sculpture in high school and at McMaster University. More recently he has been employed as a Training and Development Officer for the St. Lawrence Seaway Authority. By 1969 it was estimated that two hundred pieces of his work had been sold to collectors across Canada and the United States. His work has been shown at the Art Gallery of Ontario and the Art Gallery of Hamilton. He built his own house on his property along the Cave Spring Road where he lives with his wife and children. He was planning in 1969 to open an art school on his property which he has converted into a beautiful park.

References
Advance, Niagara-on-the-Lake, Ont., Sept., 11, 1958 "Sculptor Open Studio in Niagara"
Evening Review, Niagara Falls, Ont., Oct. 29, 1958 "Niagara-On-Lake Man Has Wood Sculptures Exhibited"
St. Catharines Standard, Ont., Nov. 18, 1958 "Steady Hands, Artistic Sense Needed For Sculpture Work" by Gerry Wolfram
Hamilton Spectator, Ont., Sat., July 3, 1965 "Vicki Innes – talking of art – From oils to steel . . . "
St. Catharines Standard, Ont., Aug. 23, 1969 "Well-known Sculptor Applied Skills To Wooded Park Near Beamsville – Developing Outdoor Sanctuary For People" by Marg Furnival
NGC Info. Form rec'd 1960

PELZ, Bruno

He exhibited a piece of work, either a print or painting in the 35th annual exhibition of the Nova Scotia Society of Artists from April 10th to 22nd of 1961.

Reference
Note and reproduction of work in NGC Lib. artist's file.

PEMBERTON, Sophie

1869-1959

Born in Victoria, B.C. the second daughter of Joseph Despard and Teresa Jane (Grautoff) Pemberton. Her father was the Surveyor General for the Crown Colony of Vancouver Island. Sophie's talent developed from an early age and she exhibited her first work at the age of twelve. She studied at the Slade School of Art, London, England (c. 1892-c. 1896) and at the Académie Julian, Paris, France (c. 1897). She was awarded a Gold Medal in 1899 for being best student in painting out of all the students from twenty-seven ateliers in Paris. Returning to London, England, she shared a studio with Anna Nordgren, one of Norway's leading artists. The two artists sketched together in Brittany and elsewhere. In 1897 her painting "Daffodils" was hung in a commanding position in the Royal Academy annual show and the following year her painting "Little Boy Blue" was also accepted for showing at the Academy's annual show. An eventful year for her was 1904 when her "Un Livre Ouvert" was shown in the Paris Salon and praised by the *Journal des Débats*; her portrait "Bibi la Pure" was shown at the Royal Academy and noted in the *Illustrated London News* and another of her works was exhibited in the Louisiana Purchase Exposition in St. Louis, Missouri. Most of her life she lived alternately in Victoria, B.C. and in England. Her first solo show in Victoria was held in 1902 at Waitts Hall and was followed by showings at the Victoria Agricultural Show and in the Vancouver studio of James Blomfield. In 1906 she was elected an Associate Member of the Royal Canadian Academy. She married Canon Beanlands in 1905 and with him travelled to India where she continued to paint. By 1909 she was back in London and showed a collection of her Vancouver Island landscapes at the Doré Gallery. Between 1924 and 1947 she lived mainly in England and after the death of her first husband had married in 1920 Horace Deane-Drummond. She returned to Victoria in 1947 where a large exhibition of her work was opened at the Little Centre Gallery by Mrs. Charles Banks, wife of the then Lieutenant Governor. She spent her remaining years at her home on the shores of Oak Bay in Victoria. A retrospective exhibition of her work was organized in 1954 by Colin Graham, who was then Curator of the Greater Victoria Art Centre. The exhibition was held at the Vancouver Art Gallery where forty of her paintings were shown including portraits, landscapes, still lifes mainly in oils on canvas. Her subjects included scenes from Italy, France, India and British Columbia, and were assembled from collections of Victoria residents, Mrs. L.S. Duke, Mrs. A.L. Harvey, Mrs. H.R. Beavan, Major H. Cuthbert Holmes also from the Parliament Buildings, Victoria; Art Centre of Greater Victoria and from the collections of Mrs. D.O. Irving of Vancouver and of the Vancouver Art Gallery. Another show of her work was held in 1967 at the Art Gallery of Greater Victoria. In all, eighteen known solo shows of her works were held.

References

Sophie Pemberton Retrospective Exhibition, VAG, Van., B.C., 1954 (catalogue)

Globe & Mail, Tor., Ont., Nov. 3, 1959 (CP) "First B.C. Artists To Win Acclaim"

Colonist, Victoria, B.C., June 3, 1967 (article that Emily Carr overshadowed Sophie Pemberton)

Ibid, June 15, 1967 "Art Gallery – Smaller Work Sincere" by Ina D.D. Uhthoff

Creative Canada, Volume One, Reference Division, McPherson Library, Univ. Victoria, B.C./Univ. Tor. Press, Tor., 1971, P. 245

Painting in Canada: a history by J. Russell Harper, Univ. Tor. Press, Second edition (paperback) 1977, P. 217

PEMBERTON-SMITH, Freda (Frederica Augusta Pemberton-Smith)
b. 1902

Born in Montreal the daughter of Pemberton Smith and Muriel Gwendoline (Durnford) she received her art training chiefly in Montreal at the Barnes School of Art; the Monument National; the Ecole des Beaux-Arts; and life classes held under the auspices of the Royal Canadian Academy. Her main study was under Edmond Dyonnet at the Monument National for nine years. Her study period spanned a decade from 1922 to 1932 after which she worked briefly at commercial illustration. Her art career was interrupted by service with the Volunteer Aid Detachment (VAD) with the Canadian Army, 1939-1945, serving in England. Returning home she resumed her art career and joined the teaching staff of St. Helen's School, Dunham, P.Q., and also did some private teaching (1947-1955). Viewing a showing of her work in February of 1960 *The Gazette* noted, "Subjects for this well-known Montreal artist's present show were found in Newfoundland's old Avalon Peninsula. They include portraits, harbor scenes, fishing villages, seascapes and landscapes. All are painted with vigorous and observant spontaneity . . . . Miss Pemberton-Smith is successful in her invigorating and expressive smaller sketches, hastily painted with passionate intensity . . . . A large palette-knife portrait, 'Old Newfoundler,' (sic) remarkable for its monumental and relaxed quality. The artist has captured her subject's good-humored acceptance of a life of uncertainty and toil, as exemplified in the bespectacled and ruddy face of the retired fisherman." Carl Weiselberger for *The Ottawa Citizen* in 1965 noted, "Freda Pemberton-Smith opened an exhibition at Wallack's Art Gallery . . . . It is a curiously old-fashioned show. Oh no, her pictures are not too academic, too pretty, or too photographic. They are bright and bold and vigorous enough and some of her oils, pastels and watercolors have striking light effects and luminosity." From about 1953 to 1965 she worked mainly in oils with spatula, then she switched to water colours. She won a gold medal around 1920 for school-girl work submitted from one of her courses to the Royal Drawing Society, London, England and she won various other prizes during her study years. Her work has been shown in solo shows at the following galleries: Artlenders, Mtl. (1960); Argenteuil Art Association, Lachute, P.Q. (1960); Laurentian Hotel, Mtl. (1962); Memorial University Gallery, St. John's, Nlfd. (1964); Wallack's Art Shop, Ott. (1965) and in various juried shows including the Canadian Society of Painters in Water Colours (1973). She has also exhibited her work at Zwickers Gallery, Hal., N.S.; in Calgary, Alta.; and Alert Bay, B.C. She moved from Montreal to Vankleek Hill, Ontario in 1965.

References

The Gazette, Mtl., P.Q., Feb. 29, 1960 "Freda Pemberton-Smith's . . . " (show at Artlenders, Mtl.)

The Watchman, Lachute, P.Q., July 20, 1960 "Freda Pemberton Smith artist featured in next A.A.A. exhibit"

Ibid, Aug. 3, 1960 "Freda Pemberton Smith exhibits for the Argenteuil Art Association"

The Gazette, Oct. 6, 1962 "F. Pemberton Smith Show" by Dorothy Pfeiffer

St. John's Daily News, Nfld., Nov. 17, 1964 (photos of three of Ms. Pemberton-Smith's paintings)

The Ottawa Citizen, Ont., May 19, 1965 "Montreal painter's show 'old-fashioned' " by Carl Weiselberger

The Ottawa Journal, Ont., May 12, 1965 "One-Woman Art Show Worthwhile" by W.Q. Ketchum

NGC Info. Forms rec'd 1956; 1965; 1973

PENNER, Anna

Born in Russia, her father was well off so she was able to take painting lessons in her own home from an artist from Holland where her grandfather had been born. Her teacher sold his and her paintings in different European countries. At the age of sixteen she left Russia with her father and travelled to England and then to Canada. They landed in Quebec City then moved successively to Montreal, Winnipeg, Alberta and finally Vancouver, B.C. in 1946. She has painted a variety of subjects including animals and nature scenes which she painted on the spot. She sold some of her paintings in Hollywood, California and was in touch with the Watson Galleries of Montreal.

Reference

NGC artist's file in Library Documentation Centre – Letter dated Nov. 9, 1946 from Mrs. Penner to Watson Galleries.

PENNER, Mar

A Fort Erie, Ontario, weaver, she has created wall hangings which have been awarded prizes in juried shows in Buffalo, New York, and she has exhibited her work at the Cambridge Public Library in Galt, Ontario and elsewhere.

References

Cambridge Daily Reporter, Ont., Dec. 10, 1975 "Cambridge Forum"

PENNEY, Millicent
b. 1907

A Newfoundland artist, she studied painting during the period 1922-27; then full time studies at the Newfoundland Academy of Art (1949) and a month's private instruction in painting from Mrs. Ann Isaacs (1953). She was an active member of the Newfoundland Art Society (1925-27) and then St. John's Art Club (1940-55). In addition to her art studies she obtained her Teacher's Training Certificate (1925) and taught school for nine years (1926-35). Her early work was impressionistic in style but later she moved into abstraction and the use of acrylics. She has exhibited her paintings at the Royal Stores Building, Arts and Culture Centre, and the Memorial University Art Gallery all in St. John's. She lives at Long Pond not far from the main centre where she exhibits.

References

St. John's News, St. John's, Nfld., Feb. 23, 1965 "St. John's Painter Attains New Level in Group of Works" by Paul Sparkes

St. John's Evening Telegram, Nfld., May 28, 1969 "Acrylic paintings exhibited"

Clipping "Daily News" "Perspectives in art" by Rae Perlin (Exhibition at Arts & Culture Centre)

St. John's Evening Telegram, Nfld., June 13, 1969 "Art in progress" by Robert Percival

PENSON, Craig

b. 1957

A Prince George, B.C., artist who sponsors orphaned refugee children from the sale of his paintings. He paints a variety of subjects from landscapes to genre scenes. He has been donating his sales to the World Vision programme.

Reference
   Prince George Citizen, B.C., Aug. 11, 1976 "Paintings help under-privileged children"

PENTLAND, Cathy

She exhibited her paintings and drawings at the Merton Gallery, Toronto. She paints figures in landscapes and her work shows a possible influence of Matisse.

Reference
   Exhibition notice, Merton Gallery, with reproduction of her work.

PENTLAND, Mary Draper

b. 1902

Born in Rochester, N.Y., U.S.A., she has been always interested in art and took courses in art history at Wellesley College, Massachusetts, and at the University of Rochester. She received her Master's Degree in Geology from the University of Wisconsin, married Dr. Arthur G. Pentland, a geologist, in 1934 and came to Canada in that same year. She took a summer course in weaving at the University of British Columbia under Mary Meigs Atwater and a course organized by the B.C. Weavers under Karin Melander also design for craftsmen with Abraham Rogatnik. She has participated in the following exhibitions: Canadian crafts sent by the Canadian Government to the International Trade Fair, Poznan, Poland, 1958; International Craft Fair, Florence, Italy, 1962; Canadian Handicraft Guild, Montreal, 1958, 1963, 1967; National Gallery, Ottawa, Canadian Fine Crafts 1966-67; Vancouver Art Gallery; UBC Fine Arts Gallery; Stratford Festival, 1959, 1960, 1961; Henry Gallery, Seattle, N.W. Craftsmen, 1954, 1958; Canadian Pavilion, Expo '67. She lives in Vancouver where she is a member of the B.C. Weavers' Guild. She is represented in the collection of the Department of External Affairs (Canadian Embassy, Washington, D.C.) and was included in the Department's travelling exhibition of 1964.

References
   NGC Info. Form rec'd 1967
   Canadian Fine Crafts, Can. Govt. Pavilion, Expo '67 (exhibition organized by Moncrieff Williamson) P. 40

PENTZ, Donald

b. 1940

Born in Bridgewater, N.S., the son of Mr. & Mrs. Cyril Pentz, he studied at the Nova Scotia College of Art, Halifax (1960); Mount Allison University under Lawren

PENTZ, Donald (Cont'd)

P. Harris and David Silverberg (1963-66) where he was top student in his class and received his B.F.A. A self-taught musician he learned to play the piano, guitar, banjo, harmonica and piano-accordion. He worked with young people and served as waterfront director at summer camps sponsored by the YMCA in Halifax. He was appointed Assistant Curator at the Confederation Art Gallery in 1966 then moved to Ottawa in 1968 to become a scientific illustrator with the National Museum. His range of work includes cartooning, drawing in "magic realistic" style, painting and illustration. He became especially well known for his pen and ink drawings which were exhibited at the Wells Gallery first in 1968. He married Kathleen Walker of Aylmer, Quebec, in 1968, a fellow painting student at Mount Allison and they returned to the Maritimes in 1970 where he became a full time artist living at Pleasantville, Nova Scotia. In recent years he has done large abstract paintings in acrylic derived from geological and natural forms. Collectors have become interested in his work and he has enjoyed many successful solo shows. A few of his shows include: DesBrisay Museum, Bridgewater, N.S. (1967); Wells Gallery, Ottawa (1968, 1972); Travelling Exhibition by the Nova Scotia Museum of Fine Arts (1975); Manuge Gallery, Halifax (1976). He is represented in the following collections: Confederation Art Gallery and Museum, Charlottetown, P.E.I.; Owens Art Gallery and University Collection, Mount Allison Universty, Sackville, N.B. and St. Mary's University Art Gallery, Halifax, N.S. His awards include a Centennial Award for oil painting from the Maritime Art Association (1967) and a Purchase Prize from the Maritime Art Association (1973).

References

Guardian, Charlottetown, P.E.I., Sept. 8, 1966 "Centre Appoints New Assistant"
Tiessen/Pentz — Graphics, October, 1967, Owens Art Gallery/Mount Allison University (Exhibition Folder)
Chronicle-Herald, Halifax, N.S., June 16, 1967 (photo of work on exhibit at DesBrisay Museum)
The Ottawa Journal, Ont., Nov. 22, 1968 "Penz Shows At Wells Gallery"
The Progress-Enterprise, Lunenburg, N.S., Dec. 11, 1968 "Bridgewater Artist Success in Ottawa"
Halifax Chronicle Herald, N.S., Dec. 5, 1968 "Bridgewater Artist's Work On Exhibition In Ottawa" by Beverly Morin
Bridgewater Bulletin, N.S., Dec. 11, 1968 "Art exhibit opens at Ottawa"
Halifax Chronicle-Herald, N.S., May 6, 1970 "Goodbye Upper Canada, Hello Nova Scotia" by Beverley Morin
The Ottawa Citizen, Ont., Oct. 6, 1972 "Pentz exhibition"
The Ottawa Journal, Ont., Oct. 7, 1972 "Pentz exhibit at Wells"
Halifax Chronicle-Herald, N.S., Apr. 29, 1975 (large photo of Pentz's painting "Pacific Vein" in St. Mary's University collection)
Halifax Mail Star, N.S. Sept. 25, 1976 (photo of Pentz with pen and ink landscape on exhibit at Manuge Gallery)

PEPER, Ernst August Wilhelm
1883-1969

Born in Hamburg, Germany, the son of Mr. & Mrs. Heinrich Jurgen Peper, he became a sculptor under the direction of Prof. Friederich Heit at the Flensburg Academy of Fine Art, Germany. He took further studies under Prof. Hausmann

PEPER, Ernst August Wilhelm (Con't)

in Hamburg. He married Annie Muller in 1925 and at the invitation of the Globe Furniture Company of Waterloo, Ontario, came to Canada with his wife in 1928. With this company he carved statues and ornamentation until his retirement in June, 1958. He also completed work for churches and public buildings across Canada including the table in the House of Commons in Ottawa. He also did carvings for members of his family. He was survived in 1969 by his wife of Waterloo and son Heinz of R.R. 2, Petersburg, and two grandchildren.

References

Kitchener Waterloo Record, Ontario, May 30, 1969 "Ernst Peper, Sculptor, Dies at 86"
Galt Evening Reporter, Ont., May 31, 1969 "Sculptor Dies"

PÉPIN, Arthur
b. 1928

Born in Hartford, Conn., U.S.A., the son of J. Henri and Emilia (Michaud) Pépin of Victoriaville, P.Q., he studied two years at the Ecole des Beaux-Arts, Montreal and in France under S.W. Hayter and F. Springer in Grasse and Paris. An engraver and painter he is also a councillor in plastic arts for the School Commission of Chomedey where he lives just north of Montreal. He has exhibited his work at the Centre d'Art in Victoriaville, P.Q. He is a member of the France — Canada Association, Montreal, the S.A.P.Q. and the M.A.Q. He is represented in the collections of André Malraux, France and the Wong Foundation, New York City and the Quebec Delegation to Paris, France.

References

Victoriaville L'Union, P.Q., Aug. 19, 1969 "Prochaine exposition solo du peintre Arthur Pépin"
Ibid, Aug. 26, 1969 "Exposition solo du peintre Pépin"
L'Art Au Quebec Depuis 1940 par Guy Robert, La Presse, Mtl., 1973, P. 157-8
Vie des Arts, No. 56, Autumn, 1969 "Arthur Pépin et ses antiformes achevées"
NGC Info. Form dated 30 Jan., 1973

PÉPIN, Jean-Paul
b. 1894

Born in Montreal, P.Q., the son of Eugene Pepin and Blanche (Castonguay) Pepin, a musician. He attended the Montcalm and Plateau schools in Montreal. As a boy he scrounged supplies of paint from his father's store to give to artists so they would allow him to follow them around. He took drawing and the History of Art at the Monument National under a number of distinguished teachers including Franchère, St. Charles, Gill, Johnstone, Dyonnet and Hébert; life drawing at the Art Association of Montreal under Edmond Dyonnet; oil and landscape painting under E. Aubin and Jean-Baptiste Legracé also water colours under Legracé; engraving, lithography, drypoint under a teacher named Harris (possibly Robert Harris); sculpture under Louis-Philippe Hébert and Alfred Laliberté; wood engraving under Louis Jobin; also took a summer school course and attended the Ontario School of Art in Toronto. Perhaps best known for his landscapes Pepin by 1964 had done six thousand oils and water colours. He was compared to artists Marc-Aurèle Fortin and Clarence Gagnon. Much of his work was described as documentary especially in the recording of Montreal's old buildings. In this work he dispensed with the inconsequential detail and emphasized highlights by drawing the main lines in china ink and completing the work using the wash technique. He travelled from Nova Scotia to British Columbia in search of his subjects but was mainly interested in portraying the character of his native city. He completed about one painting a day and limited himself to smaller-size paintings up to 30 by 40 inches. Many of his paintings have been taken across the world by former Montrealers or persons wanting a memento of the city. He kept a record of the different types of work he did, a copy of which was deposited in the National Gallery of Canada Library Documentation Centre. The listing covers 8,875 works of all types including 100 lithographs, 200 engravings (views of Old Montreal), 50 portraits, 25 sculptures (portraits and bas-reliefs) and many landscapes of the Laurentians and other locations in Quebec and other provinces of Canada. He held more than 21 solo shows and the last on record in 1966 at Galerie Morency, Montreal.

References

La Presse, Mtl., P.Q., 19 avril, 1941

Ibid, 27 mars, 1941

Photo-Journal, Mlt., 27 mars, 1945 article by Roger Parent

La Patrie, Mlt., P.Q., 29 sept., 1945 article by Alphonse Loiselle

Le Canada Français, St. Jean, P.Q., 10 oct., 1945 article by D. France

La Patrie Du Dimanche, 1 oct., 1945 article by Roger Parent

Photo Journal, Mtl., 18 oct., 1945 article by Roger Parent

Le Devoir, Mtl., 8 avril, 1946 article by Jacques Delisle

Le Nouvelliste, Trois-Rivières, P.Q., 1946

Photo-Journal, 27 mars, 1947 article by Roger Parent

La Presse, 19 mars, 1947

Photo-Journal, 13 nov., 1948 article by Roger Parent

La Patrie Du Dimanche, 22 février, 1948 review by Marcel Hamel

Le Devoir, 26 février, 1948 review by J.G. Demombymes

Montréal-Matin, 1 mars, 1948 "Tradition et modernisme chez le peintre J.-P. Pépin" par Jacques Delisle

clipping – Montreal newspaper "City's Vanishing Landmarks – Jean Pépin's Life Devoted To Depicting on Canvas The Montreal of Old"

curriculum vitae, Jean-Paul Pépin, 1964 in artist's file NGCL Documentation Centre

PEPIN, Mary (née Sheila Mary Brock-Smith)

b. 1929

Born in Bellingham, Washington, U.S.A., the daughter of Harding Brock-Smith, she spent her early childhood in Vancouver. Her father's business took the family to Edmonton and later to Winnipeg. She attended school in Edmonton until Grade 11 then finished high school in Winnipeg. She attended art classes in Edmonton during the summers where she studied under H.G. Glyde and W.J. Phillips. She then studied two years at the Winnipeg School of Art under Joe Plaskett. In 1949 she went to Paris and took advanced studies in painting under Fernand Leger and during this period met a fellow Canadian, Jean-Luc Pepin who was a political science student at the University of Paris. She returned to Winnipeg and after finding commercial art too confining for her creativity she chose to earn her living by working in a bank while in the evenings she took private studies under Jack Markell. In 1952 she married Jean-Luc Pepin and moved to Ottawa where he had just become a professor of political science at the University of Ottawa. She continued with her painting and studied under Henri Masson. She became a member of the Ottawa Art Association and participated in its annual spring shows, winning the O'Keefe Prize in 1961 and 1962. She exhibited as well with the Canadian Society of Painters in Water Colour. Working in the media of oils, pen and inks, some mixed media and water colours she usually begins a painting with a sketch of her subject and then works from it to a final picture. Her subjects include portrait, figure and landscape, the latter receiving most of her attention in recent years. She has also combined wax crayon for colour accent, water colour for washes, and ink for linear effects. The wax crayon is applied and then the water colour wash over it. She often uses her oils thinly achieving a water colour effect. After her husband entered politics in 1963 she was afforded opportunities to travel with him on his various missions as a cabinet minister visiting Japan, Mexico and other Latin American countries. One of her shows in part was devoted to genre scenes she painted in Mexico. Viewing her work at Gallerie Fore in 1970 Sheila Bleeks of the *Winnipeg Free Press* noted, "The 31 oils, watercolors and pen and inks represent a wide variety of moods, techniques, and subject interest. Nature abounds in many scenes – trees in fresh spring green oils and trees stretching their strong naked limbs into the dull greys of an impending winter sky; wild flowers in large full bloom and hints of white blossoms in a vased bouquet; water, which complements many of her inhabited landscapes as well as her uninhabited ones, is a cold, wavy blue. The sharply-defining sketch lines of her watercolors are softened with gentle tints, which provide a striking contrast to the thick, vibrant swaths of her pallette knife work . . . . As goes her art, so goes Mary Pepin – sincere and dedicated to her work, spontaneous and warm in her feelings to others. It is significant that she should return to Winnipeg where she grew as a student of art in the capacity of a matured, accomplished artist." Her solo shows include those at the Robertson Galleries, Ottawa (1963, 1967, 1974); Caisse Populaire Saint-Frederic, Drummondville, P.Q. (1967); Gallerie Fore, Winnipeg (1970, also two previous solo shows). Mother of two children, Nicholas and Aude, she lives just outside Ottawa in Rothwell Heights with her family. Her husband has just completed a busy year travelling across Canada as a member of the task force on Canadian unity.

References

The Ottawa Citizen, May 3, 1963 "New MP's artist wife scores own success" by Carl Weiselberger

PEPIN, Mary (née Sheila Mary Brock-Smith) (Cont'd)

Ottawa Journal, May 6, 1963 "Mary Pepin Exhibits In Ottawa" by W.Q. Ketchum
Le Droit, Ottawa, May 18, 1963 "Mme Mary Pépin, peintre et femme de député" par Gertrude Lapointe
Ottawa Journal, Nov. 21, 1967 "Artist Mary Pepin A Gifted Artist" by W.Q. Ketchum
Le Droit, Dec. 2, 1967 "Deux femmes peintres exposent à Ottawa" par Denise Côté
La Parole, Drummondville, P.Q., Dec. 13, 1967 "Madame Jean-Luc Pepin s'adonne à la peinture"
The Investor, Winnipeg, Man., January, 1968 "Holds Second Art Show"
Winnipeg Tribune, Man., Sept. 25, 1968 (CP) Ottawa "Painting is her vocation, home and children her life" by Susan Becker
Le Droit, June 6, 1970 "Une impressionniste contemporaine: Mary Pépin expose à Winnipeg"
Winnipeg Free Press, Man., May 30, 1970 "Mary Pepin also works on the floor" by Sheila Bleeks (paints water colours on floor to prevent paints from running)
Winnipeg Tribune, Man., May 12, 1970 "'Knocks' part of art: Mary Pepin" by Susan Janz
Winnipeg Free Press, Man., May 11, 1970 (photo of Mary Pepin and husband at opening of her exhibition at Gallerie Fore)
The Ottawa Journal, Ont., Sat., Jan. 30, 1971 "Ottawa Artist (17) – Strives for 'Mood' of Subject" by Valerie Knowles
Le Droit, May 11, 1974 "Mary Pépin: arbres et saisons" par Michel Dupuy
The Ottawa Journal, May 10, 1974 "Ottawa scenes inspire Mary Pepin's canvases" by W.Q. Ketchum
NGC Info. forms rec'd 1952, 1965

PÉPIN, Michel

Originally from Shawinigan he has been active as a wood carver since 1974 in Saint-François-du-Lac where he is manager of the local Caisse Populaire.

Reference
Le Nouvelliste, Trois-Rivières, Que., Apr. 30, 1977 (photo of Pépin and his work)

PÉPIN, Yves

b. 1943

Born in Canada, he finished his studies in l'Institut des Arts Appliqués, Montreal in 1964. He participated in work for the Energy Section of the Canadian Pavilion at Expo '67 (1964-65). He then attended the Konstfackskolan in Stockholm, Sweden, where he worked on his own in the post-graduate section of the school obtaining two first prizes for his work. In 1967 he moved to France where he settled. He conceived in 1969 decoration with fibre glass and plastic for "La Fausse Suivante" of Marivaux at Limoges, France, and the same year also participated in the Concours Artistiques du Québec. He received a grant from the Canada Council and the Ministry of Cultural Affairs of Quebec in 1970 to continue his work. In 1972 he held a show at the famous Galerie Vetheuyl. His work of this period dealt with studies of trees of France through the aspect of light and movement and the resulting break-up of structures. His other shows include a solo at Maison des Etudiants Canadiens, Paris (1970); Salon des Réalités Nouvelles, Paris (1971); Maison de la Culture, Ostende, Belgium (1971); Centre Culturel Canadien, Paris (1971).

References
Zones – Yves Pépin biographical details for his show at Centre Culturel Canadien, 5, Rue de Constantine, Paris
Le Droit, Ottawa, Ont., Oct. 21, 1972 Paris (AFP) "Yves Pépin expose ses Gouaches '72"

PEPPER, George Douglas

1903-1962

Born in Ottawa, Ontario, the son of Charles George and Christie Ann (Biledo) Pepper, he attended Elgin Street Public School and the Ottawa Collegiate Institute where he matriculated (1919-20). He studied at the Ontario College of Art under Robert Holmes, J.E.H. MacDonald, G.A. Reid and J.W. Beatty and graduated in 1924, then studied a year abroad at the Académie de la Grande Chaumière, Paris, France and in Italy (1924-25). Returning home he settled in Ottawa where he was employed by the Parks Branch, Department of the Interior, Ottawa, as a map draftsman then later as a publicity artist with the Forestry Service (1925-31) while he also maintained his own studio. He submitted his paintings to a number of exhibitions including Wembley in 1925. In 1926 he was an invited exhibitor to the Group of Seven show at the Art Gallery of Toronto. He illustrated articles by Dr. Marius Barbeau which appeared in *La Presse* in 1925 and 1931, and he sketched in British Columbia in 1928. One of his paintings from this trip, "Totem Poles, Kitwanga" shared first prize at the Willingdon Arts Competition in 1930 with one of F.H. Varley's portraits of Vera. Both paintings were acquired by the National Gallery of Canada in 1930. He married Kathleen Frances Daly in 1929 and their long association as sketching partners and co-exhibitors produced many fine paintings, drawings, and prints. George Pepper was influenced considerably by the Group of Seven in that his landscapes were decorative realistic in presentation and strongly showed the natural rhythm of the land and stressed pattern possibilities in various elements. In 1932 A.H. Robson in his *Canadian Landscape Painters* noted, "George D. Pepper, of Ottawa, is one who paints with a powerful and rhythmic sense of line. His canvases show originality in both arrangement and viewpoint, and his decorative impulse translates the landscape into a bold arrangement of line and pattern." He was one of the twenty-eight painters who formed the Canadian Group of Painters as a successive movement to the Group of Seven. Members of this new group continued with the tradition of exploring Canada to its remotest regions. During a few months of each year he took time to seek out his subjects and with his wife Kathleen built a log studio in the Laurentians in Charlevoix County, Quebec, where they made local sorties from 1931 to 1959. His teaching career had begun in 1932 in Toronto at the Ontario College of Art as instructor in drawing and painting. He moved into the famous Studio Building on Severn Street with Kathleen and this was their Toronto base for seventeen years. He became a member of the Ontario Society of Artists in 1934. In his painting his work took on a " . . . choppy, vigorous rhythm" as explained by Paul Duval (*Four Decades*, 1972) and was well suited to portray the countryside he frequented in the Maritimes and the coast of Labrador. In 1938 he painted the canvas "Backyards", depicting row housing with the stark look of the depression (see *Four Decades*) and the next year exhibited his "Winter Sunlight, Hull, Quebec" in the Canadian Society of Painters in Water Colour section of the New York World's Fair. He painted many scenes of Hull with its numerous frame homes built after the great fire of 1900. In the early years he had been a reserve member of the Canadian Army's Governor General's Horse Guards, obtaining the rank of corporal in 1941. In 1943 he enlisted in the active army attached to the Directorate of History, Army Headquarters, Ottawa, and was officially appointed a Canadian War Artist in March of 1943. He painted training scenes in Western Canada and anti-aircraft defences in England but spent most of his service in North-West Europe depicting scenes, actions, and portraits of soldiers of the 2nd Canadian Division. Promoted to the rank of Captain he set about his duties with a flair that produced some of his finest work. He arrived in the front lines about thirty days following D-Day. In late 1944 while en route to a town near Antwerp, he and Captain George Engler discovered a German soldier in a slit trench and took him prisoner but while escorting him to their jeep their prisoner tried to take their firearm and was killed. The sound of the shot aroused other enemy soldiers in the area. The two men made for cover in a nearby ditch where Engler was killed and Pepper, with his escape cut off, had to remain hidden for ten days with no food. He finally managed to escape and was picked up by a British patrol. At home in Canada during that period he was listed as a casualty. Near the close of 1944 he exhibited with Capt. O.N. Fisher and Capt. W.A. Ogilvie at the Palais des Beaux-Arts in Brussels, their paintings of the Canadian Army's advance through France and Belgium (June-October, 1944). His last overseas exhibition was in "Canadian War Art" at the National Gallery, London, England. In 1946 a showing of "Canadian War Art" was held at the National Gallery of Canada, Ottawa. Some 161 of his works in oils, water colours, conte, pencil and ink were deposited in the National Gallery of Canada War Collection (later turned over to the Canadian War Museum). His experience as war artist resulted in the selection of his work for illustrations in various publications about the war including *The Canadian Army At War, Canada's Battle in Normandy* by Col. C.P. Stacey (1946), *The Canadian Army 1939-1945* by Col. C.P. Stacey (1948), and a commission for illustrations for *Men of Valour* by Mabel Tinkiss Good (1948) and two illustrations for *A Terrible Beauty* by Heather Robertson (1977). Following the war he returned to the teaching staff of Ontario College of Art to take up his duties again as director of the Drawing and Painting Department (1941-55) and then vice-principal of the College (1950-62) and supervisor of night school (1955-62); summers he was painting instructor at the Banff School of Fine Arts (1947 and other years). He painted in the company of his wife in Newfoundland (1951), St. Pierre and Miquelon (1951) and painted scenes of fishing operations from a trawler off the Grand Banks for a commission to decorate the offices of the Food and Agricultural Organization (United Nations) in Rome, Italy (1954); executed a 25-foot mural commissioned by the Government of Canada for the Department of Veterans Affairs (East Memorial Building), Ottawa (1955); spent a year in Spain and Morocco on sabbatical leave from O.C.A. and ten days sketching in the palace of the Caliph, Morocco. His wife Kathleen had been able to arrange their stay with the Caliph through a police captain after explaining her difficulty of finding sitters who were not believers that reproduction of their images in any form was sinful (1955-56); painted a mural for the Kootenay Park scenic dome car of the Canadian Pacific Railway (1956); served on the summer staff of the Banff School of Fine Arts (1957). In 1959 he was elected President of the Canadian Group of Painters and was earlier elected Academician of the Royal Canadian Academy (A.R.C.A. 1942, R.C.A. 1955) and member of the Canadian Society of Painters in Water Colour (1947). With Kathleen he made a three-month voyage in 1960 to the eastern Arctic aboard the Canadian Government ship *C.D. Howe*, where they drew and painted Eskimos and ice formations while also gathering information on Eskimo art for the Department of Northern Affairs. This was followed by their return to the North in 1961 where they spent seven weeks in an Eskimo settlement painting the Eskimos of Povungnituk. He accepted an invitation to adjudicate the annual Provincial Art Competition in Newfoundland (1962);

served on the summer staff of the Banff School of Fine Arts (1962) and painted at Moraine Lake and Lake O'Hara (1962). He suffered a heart attack and died in hospital in October of 1962. A memorial exhibition of his work was held in October, 1964 at the National Gallery of Canada with the selection, co-ordination and cataloguing of his work done by Major F.R. Wodehouse. The catalogue introduction was written by Dr. Charles F. Comfort who remembered his friend and colleague as follows, "George Pepper was a man of unquestioned integrity, both as a human being and as an artist. His manly bearing and abundant sense of humour, his staunch unwavering friendship and loyalties, are among the qualities of character that endeared him to all who knew him. He was well aware of the sweeping changes which were taking place in the world of art during his lifetime; he could discuss Impressionism or Cubism, or Abstract Expressionism of the post-war era. But he was a rational modern thinker; while his theories and practice as a painter took into account these movements, his art was flexible enough to admit an attractive lyricism and a breadth of treatment that gave it strength and spontaneity. It was stable enough to support the theory that the painter's responsibility was to represent the material world in accordance with the facts of vision. It was this rare combination of qualities that equipped him so well for his duties as a war artist." Pepper is represented in the following collections: Banff Library and Archives of Canadian Rockies, Alta.; Banff School of Fine Arts; Sarnia Public Library and Art Gallery, Ont.; London Public Library and Art Museum, London. Ont.; Willistead Gallery, Windsor, Ont.; Art Gallery of Ontario, Tor.; Hart House, Univ. Tor.; Nat. Gallery of Canada, Ott.; National War Museum, Ott.; Mount Allison Univ. Collection of Canadian Art, Sackville, N.B.; National Gallery of South Africa, Capetown; Hawke's Bay Art Society, Napier, New Zealand. He took part in many important national and international exhibitions (see *Creative Canada*).

References

Exhibition of Paintings, Etchings and Drawings by Kathleen Daly and George Pepper (exhibition catalogue sheet) May 9th to 14th, 1932

Canadian Landscape Painters by A.H. Robson, Ryerson, Tor., Ont., 1932 P. 178

A Century of Canadian Art, Tate Gallery, Lond., Eng., 1938, P. 27

Canadian Art, New York World's Fair, 1939, NGC, Ottawa, P. 15

Canadian War Artists – water colours and line sketches, Palais Des Beaux-Arts, Bruxelles, 18 November – 3 December, 1944

The Canadian Army at War, Canada's Battle In Normandy, 1946, P. 64, 68, 141, 154, 156

Men of Valour by Mabel Tinkiss Good, MacMillan, Tor., 1948 (15 illustrations by George Pepper)

The Canadian Army, 1939-1945 by Col. C.P. Stacey, King's Printer, Ottawa, 1948 (see page opp. page 246)

Canadian Drawings and Prints by Paul Duval, Burns & MacEachern, Tor., 1952, Plate 69

Canadian Paintings in Hart House by J. Russell Harper, Art Committee of Hart House, Univ. Tor., 1955, P. 58

A Painter's Country by A.Y. Jackson, Clarke, Irwin & Co. Ltd., Tor., 1958, P. 144

NGC Catalogue, Vol. 3, Can. School by R.H. Hubbard, NGC/Univ. Tor., 1960, P. 245-246

In Memoriam, Capt. G.D. Pepper, 1903-1962 (catalogue) by Major R.F. Wodehouse, NGC, Ottawa, 1964

Canadian Art, Vol. 20, No. 2, Mar./Apr. 1963 "George Douglas Pepper 1903-1962" by Lawren P. Harris

Mount Allison University, Sackville New Brunswick Collection of Canadian Art, 1965 (catalogue) No. 105

Check List of The War Collections by R.F. Wodehouse, NGC, Ottawa, 1968, P. 146-150

PEPPER, George Douglas (Cont'd)

The Hart House Collection of Canadian Paintings by Jeremy Adamson, Univ. Tor. Press, 1969, P. 103

The Art Gallery of Toronto, Paintings and Sculpture (Introduction by Martin Baldwin), 1959, P. 73

Art Gallery of Ontario, the Canadian collection by Helen Pepall Bradfield, McGraw-Hill Col. of Can. Ltd., 1970, P. 363

Creative Canada, McPherson Library, Univ. Victoria, B.C./Univ. Tor. Press, 1971, P. 246-247

Four Decades, The Canadian Group of Painters and their contemporaries, 1930-1970 by Paul Duval, Clarke, Irwin & Co. Ltd., Tor., 1972, P. 47, 81, 144

Painting in Canada, a history by J. Russell Harper, 2nd Ed. (paperback) 1977, P. 312

Canadian Art at Auction, 1968-1975 Edited by Geoffrey Joyner, Sotheby & Co. (Can.) Ltd., Tor., Ont., 1975, P. 155

A Concise History of Canadian Painting by Dennis Reid, Oxford, Tor., 1973, P. 178

Canadian Painting in the Thirties by Charles C. Hill, NGC, Ottawa, 1975, P. 25, 89

A Terrible Beauty, The Art of Canada at War by Heather Robertson, James Lorimer, 1977, P. 147, 217

The Impossible Dream (Banff School of Fine Arts) by Donald Cameron, Alcraft Printing and Bulletin Commercial Printers, 1977 (see 7th page of illustrations between P. 125 and 126)

Newspaper clippings

Ottawa Journal, Ont., Oct. 14, 1944 (CP) Tor. "Capt. G.D. Pepper Reported Missing"

The Toronto Telegram, Ont., Oct. 14, 1944 "Front Line Artist Reported Missing – Toronto Painter Kept So Close to Fighting Area Once Ahead of Troops"

Ottawa Journal, Ont., Dec. 12, 1944 "Capt. Pepper Shows Paintings in Belgium"

Windsor Daily Star, Ont., Mar. 17, 1947 "Art Program Is Described" (Capt. Pepper speaks to Windsor Art Assoc.)

Ottawa Journal, Ont., Oct. 23, 1964 "War Artist's Paintings At National Gallery" by W.Q. Ketchum

NGC Info. Form Jan. 12, 1959

Calendar, 1954, Rous and Mann Press Ltd. "Tobacco Patch"

PEPPER, Jack

b. 1905

Born in Prescott, Ontario, the son of Edward Pepper, designer and engraver of Ottawa, he took Saturday morning classes at Prescott from a local water colour artist, Mrs. Fleming. He then studied at the Ottawa Teachers' College; Ontario College of Art for applied design; Chicago for commercial art and at the Ontario University of Education for courses in arts and crafts. He taught for several years at the Arts Club, the Don Valley Club and summers at the Madoc School of Fine Art. After teaching art full-time for over forty years he turned all his attentions to painting. He has exhibited with the Royal Canadian Academy, the Ontario Society of Artists and the Montreal Art Association. Reviewing his solo show at the Kar Gallery, Toronto, in 1973 the *Globe & Mail* writer noted, "These are comfortable works that explore once more the familiar terrain of Canadian landscape: half-melted snow in forest glens, rushing brooks and waterfalls, gaunt windswept trees on windswept shores . . . . Pepper shows his versatility in a smaller group of paintings depicting old houses and barns. For variety he also includes one cityscape, a view of row houses on Cumberland Street." Pepper's work is restful, colourful, lyrical and skillfully executed. Has been on the Board of Management of the Todmorden Mills Historic Site and active with other community affairs. Lives in Toronto.

PEPPER, Jack (Cont'd)

References
> *Barrie Examiner*, Ont., Mar. 10, 1961 "Toronto Artist To Speak Here" (biographical notes on Jack Pepper)
> *Globe & Mail*, Tor., Ont., Sept. 15, 1973 "Jack Pepper" (review of his solo show at Kar Gallery, Toronto)
> Brochure – Jack Pepper (biographical notes and six reproductions of his work, one in colour)

PEPPER, Kathleen Daly (see DALY, Kathleen – Vol. One)

References (additional)
> *The Ottawa Morning Citizen,* May 10, 1932 "Daly/Pepper Exhibition Is Well Worth Seeing" by E.W.H.
> *Toronto Saturday Night,* Ont., Aug. 21, 1937 (photo of Kathleen Daly Pepper sketching two young Northern Quebec Indians)
> *Edmonton Journal,* Alta., Sept. 8, 1944 "Noted Torontonian Is Visitor Here – Famed Artist is Visitor Here" by Connie Ghostley
> *The Globe Magazine,* Tor., Ont., June 29, 1957 "An Infidel From Canada Paints Inside Morocco" by Kathleen Daly Pepper
> *The Toronto Telegram,* Ont., Aug. 27, 1960 "Accent on Art – At Last! Decent Display in The CNE Art Gallery" by Paul Duval
> *North,* March-April, 1962 "People of the North – An Album of Distinguished Paintings"
> *James Wilson Morrice* by Kathleen Daly Pepper, Clarke, Irwin, Tor., Ont., 1966
> *London Evening Free Press,* Ont., April 15, 1975 "Artists exhibit Canadian, European influences" by Janice Andreae

PERCIVAL, Robert
b. 1924

Born in Chesterfield, England, his family moved to Liverpool, England, where his father, a businessman, enrolled his only son in the Quarry Bank High School with the intention of seeing him become a businessman too. At the age of fifteen Robert contracted meningitis and after recovery found he had completely lost his hearing. Plans for his future had to be changed and he was enrolled in the Liverpool College of Art (1943-47). During this period the war had taken its toll of fifteen of the thirty former classmates at Quarry Bank High School. Deafness had made him dependent on others for communication. When an aunt left him an inheritance he decided to go it alone. He went to France where he studied at the Académie de la Grande Chaumière, Paris (1949-50). His inheritance was small and soon ran out. The balance of his stay in Paris was marked by financial difficulty and he simply existed with few extras. He met the challenge as well of having to lip read in a foreign language which did much to equip him with a superb self-confidence. Returning to Liverpool he became a commercial artist and executed murals in entertainment clubs in Liverpool and was decorating walls with black-light paintings long before they were avant-garde in America. He even inaugurated Liverpool's first Jazz Club and was closely involved with theatrical activities. He sketched many musicians and actors. He became a full member of the Liverpool Academy of Art and participated in the following exhibitions: "Paintings of the Nude", Manchester (1948); St. James Art Society, London (1949); "Five Painters", Liverpool (1950); Festival Open Show, Liverpool (1951); Fifty Years of British Art, Liverpool (1951); Liverpool Academy of Arts (1951-57); Merseyside and Manchester Artists (1955); Atkinson's Art Gallery (1955); City of Manchester Art Gallery (1955); City Art Gallery, Salford (1956) and held solo shows at Liverpool (1947, 1948, 1950); Manchester (1950) and London (1951). He came to Canada in 1963 and settled for five years in St. John's Newfoundland, where he did interior design for the Bells Club; painted a giant signboard of the city's central development (erected by the Seaboard Construction Company); made posters and sets for "The Unsinkable Molly Brown" put on by a local theatre group; became an official artist to the government of Newfoundland in the Historical Resources Division of the Department of Provincial Affairs where he worked on displays for the Aviation Museum, Gander Airport, the interpretation Centre at Port aux Choix and several other Newfoundland museums. In 1969 he was appointed Curator of Art at the New Brunswick Museum in Saint John. He continued with his own art and held solo shows at the University of New Brunswick's Ganong Hall, Saint John (1970) and a touring solo show organized by the Centennial Art Gallery, Citadel Hill, Halifax (1971) then on to Memorial University, St. John's, Nfld. (1972); Art Gal. St. Mary's Univ., Hal. (1972) then the show was enlarged to include paintings, drawings, constructions and sculpture by the N.B. Museum for showing at Confederation Art Gallery, P.E.I. (1972); N.B. Museum, Saint John (1973) and the Restigouche Art Gallery, Campbellton, N.B. (1974). The introduction of the travelling exhibition catalogue was written by Peter Bell, Curator of the Art Gallery of Newfoundland who described Percival's art as follows, "Bob Percival paints in two or three different styles. Though clearly related and unmistakably belonging to each other, they do suggest his varied needs as a painter. His drawings, for example, with the slashing expressionist strokes against the soft washed base, portray most movingly the pathos of threatened people, or the suffering of people in conflict with themselves. The intensity of their passion is so vividly expressed that one is reminded of Munch or Kathe Kollwitz. Very different, perhaps, is his art-nouveau treatment . . . which while preserving his sympathy with the subject, illustrates his formal qualities as a decorative painter. The female figure seems to become more important to Bob, and round shapes generally recur more frequently in his recent work." Percival also held solo shows at St. John's Nfld. (1967); Trinity College, Tor. (1968); Morrison Art Gallery, Saint John, N.B. (1971,1977); Nova Scotia Museum of Fine Art, Halifax (1971); U.N.B., Art Centre, Fred., N.B. (1971); Little Gallery, New Brunswick Museum, Saint John (1975). He was one of twenty Canadian artists commissioned to illustrate the Sunday Mass Book (the first prayer book of its kind published in Canada) for the Roman Catholic church. His subject for the commission was the founder of the Sisters of Charity (Grey Nuns), Marguerite d'Youville (1701-1771) who cared for the sick and poor of Montreal. Percival is represented in the following collections: Liverpool Walker Art Gallery, Liverpool, Eng.; Memorial Univ., Nfld.; University of N.B., Saint John; Univ. of N.B., Fred., N.B.; New Brunswick Museum, Saint John; and in many private collections in England and Canada. Lives in Saint John, N.B. Director, Saint John Arts Council; Director, N.B. Craft Assoc.; Director, Atlantic Provinces Art Circuit.

PERCIVAL, Robert (Cont'd)

References

St. John's News, Nfld., Nov. 30, 1965 "The Arts Page – Artist From England Working in St. John's"

Evening Times Globe, N.B., Nov. 15, 1969 "Museum Art Curator Appointed"

Ibid, Nov. 21, 1970 "Art Curator To Exhibit at UNBSJ Ganong Hall"

Ibid, Nov. 26, 1970 "An Exhibition of Paintings" (photo of Percival and his painting "Jenny")

Halifax Mail-Star, N.S., Sept. 10, 1971 "United States influence on Canadian artists too strong, claims curator" by Barbara Hinds

Evening Times Globe, N.B., Oct. 1, 1971 "Robert Percival Exhibition To Open At Morrison Art Gallery"

Ibid, Oct. 6, 1971 (photo of artist with his work)

Telegraph Journal, Saint John, N.B., Oct. 2, 1975 "Percival Exhibit To Open"

Ibid, Oct. 4, 1975 (photo of Percival with his work – "Hyper-realism" paintings to explore singularity of church facades)

Robert Percival (brochure), N.B. Museum, Saint John, N.B. (biographical sketch and an appreciation by Peter Bell)

Evening Times Globe, Saint John, N.B., April 30, 1976 "Percival Participates – Canadian Artists Illustrate Mass Book"

Art Collection, Canadian Catholic Conference, Ottawa, 1976 (catalogue of works commissioned for Mass Book illustrations)

Evening Times Globe, N.B., Sept. 14, 1977 "Morrison Art Gallery To Present Works By Percival"

Ibid, Sept. 21, 1977 (photo of Percival with his realistic study of a church "Winter Triptych")

Who's Who in British Art

PEREHUDOFF, William W.

b. 1919

Born in Langham, Sask., the son of Doukhobor farmers, he developed a serious interest in art and sketched at every available opportunity during his school years. At first he studied art by correspondence then at the Colorado Springs Fine Art Centre under Jean Charlot; in New York at the Ozenfat School of Art and the Carnegie Institute of Technology, Pittsburg. He worked as a meat-floor labourer for a time while he studied and taught art. He took care of the Perehudoff farm in his spare time. In 1951 he married artist Dorothy Knowles and they spent the following year travelling in France, Italy, England and America. Returning to Canada he studied further at the University of Saskatchewan Emma Lake Artists' Workshops under Will Barnet, Herman Cherry, Clement Greenberg, Kenneth Noland and Donald Judd. Even by 1949 his painting "Elevators" although a favourite subject of Western artists was presented in a "creative manner" in the words of Lucy Jarvis, Art Director, University of New Brunswick. By 1963 his expression of the prairie landscape now in more austere terms, caught the eye of touring American art critic, Clement Greenberg, who chose his "Fallow Land" for reproduction in his article "Clement Greenberg's View of Art on The Prairies." At this stage Perehudoff combined hard edge and abstraction of his subject, to portray the edge of a field, a scene he must have encountered daily when he was a wheat farmer. In 1969 his lyrical but representational pen drawings were a supplement to the photographs in Koozma J. Tarasoff's *Pictorial History of the Doukhobors* for which Perehudoff also did the design work. These illustrations were a delightful reminder that the artist had not abandoned his interest in illustration or his sense of history for his

PEREHUDOFF, William W. (Cont'd)

own people. By 1972 he had begun his large canvases based on the circle and bars, giving a personal expression to these elements through placement, colour, and shape. His work has aroused the interest of critics and collectors. His solo shows include: Mendel Art Gallery, Saskatoon (1962, 1965); Bonli Gallery, Tor. (1967); The Edmonton Art Gallery, Edmonton, Alta. (1972); Dunlop Art Gallery, Regina (1973); University of Saskatchewan (1974); Downstairs Gallery, Edmonton (1974); Noah Goldowsky Gallery, NYC (1974); The Waddington Art Gallery, Mtl. (1974); Saskatoon Public Library Art Gallery (1974); Wallack Galleries, Ottawa (1974). He did murals for the Intercontinental Packers Limited and the Saskatoon Public Library. He is represented in the permanent collections of: University of Saskatchewan, Saskatoon; Norman Mackenzie Art Gallery, Regina; Mendel Art Gallery, Saskatoon; Mendel Collection, Saskatoon; University of Calgary, Alta.; Edmonton Art Gallery, Edmonton; London Art Gallery, Ont.; The Saskatchewan Arts Board; Confederation Art Centre, Charlottetown, P.E.I.; The Canada Council Art Bank, Ottawa and in private collections in Canada and the U.S.A. He has participated in many important group shows including the Montreal Spring Shows, Canadian Biennials, Winnipeg Biennials and R.C.A. annuals. An Associate of the Royal Canadian Academy he lives in Saskatoon with his artist wife and three children.

References

Canadian Art, Vol. 6, No. 4, Summer, 1949 "Paintings From East and West" by C.H. Scott and Lucy Jarvis, P. 170

Ibid, March/April, 1963 "Clement Greenberg's View of Art on The Prairies" by C.G., P. 94

The Mendel Collection, forward by Eva Mendel Miller, Modern Press, Saskatoon, Sask., 1964 (catalogue for opening of the Mendel Art Gallery, Saskatoon), P. 46

Pictorial History of the Doukhobors by Koozma J. Tarasoff, Prairie Books Dept. of The Western Producer, Saskatoon, 1969 (design and ill. by W. Perehudoff)

Saskatchewan: Art and Artists, Introduction and Forward by Nancy E. Dillow, Norman Mackenzie Art Gallery/Regina Public Library Art Gallery, April 2 - July 31, 1971, P. 90,96

Artscanada, Feb.-Mar., 1971 "Some artists in Regina and Saskatoon" by Terry Fenton, P. 51

Ibid, early autumn, 1972 "William Perehudoff: recent paintings" by Karen Wilkin, P. 102

Canadian artists in exhibition, 1972-73, Roundstone, Tor., Can., 1974, P. 169

Major Saskatchewan Artists, The Mendel Art Gallery, 1975 (exhibition organized by Saskatoon Gallery & Conservatory Corp. and the University of Saskatchewan Alumni Assoc.) February, 1975, P. 18-19

Who's Who in American Art, 1976, R.R. Bowker Co., NYC, 1976, P. 435

NGC Info. Forms rec'd 1961, 1968

Newspaper clipping "Faces of Canada — This Artist Wheat Farmer Son of Quiet People" by Leon Kossar

PEREPELKIN, Sam

He has exhibited his paintings at the New Academic Building, Victoria College, University of Toronto (1974) and both paintings and drawings at St. Lawrence College, Kingston. His work has geometric aspects which are not unlike work done in relief by the Structurists.

PEREPELKIN, Sam (Cont'd)

References
    Flyer with reproduction of his painting, exhibition at New Academic Bldg., Victoria College, 73 Queen's Park Cresc., Toronto, Feb. 27 - Mar. 15, 1974
    Flyer with reproduction of drawing, exhibition at Art Gallery Kingston, St. Lawrence College, Kingston.

PERKINS, Arthur Alan
b. 1915

Born in Toronto, Ontario, he graduated from the Danforth Technical School in 1934 then entered the field of architecture where for the next thirty years he did design, planning, production and administration work. During this period he was developing his knowledge and skill at enamelling and related crafts and became known for his work through exhibitions where he won awards in 1962, 1963, 1965 and 1966. In 1967 his work was shown at the Canadian Government Pavilion at Expo 67. By 1968 he had established a home studio and decided to turn to full time enamelling and metal work. He retired from the architectural firm of Bregman and Hamann and with the aid of a Canada Council study grant he attended the Brookfield Craft Centre in Connecticut, U.S.A., where he studied enamelling and holloware techniques with Margaret Seeler, Francis Felton and John Fix. Over the years he has produced enamel paintings in rich colours, table accessories including bowls, pencil cups, wine goblets, wall plaques and wall assemblances and over sixty other different kinds of work. He is known as well for his printmaking. His one-man shows include: Cedarbrae District Library, Scarborough (1970); Shaw-Rimmington Gallery, Tor. (1970, 1971); Ontario Assoc. of Architects, Tor. (1971); Galerie des Artisans, Mtl. (1971); Craft Gallery, Tor. (1975) and has participated in numerous group shows since 1962 and more recently at the Scarborough Civic Centre, Scarborough, Ont. (1976). He has done teaching on a part time basis for a number of years at: Sir Sandford Fleming College (Haliburton School of Fine Arts); Centennial College of Applied Arts and Technology (1968, 1969); Georgian College of Applied Arts and Technology; Seneca College of Applied Arts and Technology; Prince Edward Island Craft School, Charlottetown and spent four years in the programme "The Artist in the School" sponsored by the Ontario Arts Council; and teaching for the Ministry of Community and Social Services; at the George Brown College of Applied Arts and Technology where he has been teaching enamelling; night school instructing in enamelling for the Toronto Board of Education. He has written a manual for instructors and teachers in enamelling techniques for the Province of Ontario Department of Education (1972); wrote a series of articles on The Craftsman in Business for the Ontario Craft Foundation publication. He has won an impressive number of awards including: Adrian Seguin Award for Excellence (1962, 1963); Quebec Association of Architects Award (1963); Helena Rubenstein Award of Excellence (1965); Canadian National Exhibition First Prize for Enamels (1966, 1967, 1968, 1969, 1970, 1971, 1972); Adelaide Marriot Award for Excellence (1969); Make (Mak) Contemporary Crafts Award (1971); "Editions 1" (printmaking award) from the Ontario Arts Council (1974); and was one of twelve Canadians whose work was chosen by an international jury to represent Canada in the World Craft Exhibition in which seventy-eight countries participated (1974).

PERKINS, Arthur Alan (Cont'd)

He is represented in the following collections: Cochran Murray Company (vitreous enamel, 1969); Confederation Art Gallery, Charlottetown, P.E.I. (1969); American Institute of Architects (enamel wall plaque, 1969); Cadillac Developments Ltd., Tor. (wall assemblance, 1971); Institute of Biocentric Psychology, Los Angeles, Calif. (wall assemblance, 1971); Crown Life Insurance, Tor. (wall assemblance, 1972); Ontario Institute of Studies (prints, 1973); Swiss Consulate, Mtl. (prints, 1974); Jean A. Chalmers collection (enamel wine goblets, 1974) and many private collections. He is a member of the Canadian Guild of Crafts (Ont.); Canadian Craftsmen's Council; World Craft Council (NYC); Ontario Society of Artists (1974); Society of Canadian Artists (1974); Craft Collaborative, Tor. (charter member, 1975). He lives in Toronto with his wife Reeva who is a goldsmith. They have one grown daughter.

References
   Canadian Fine Crafts by Moncrieff Williamson, Can. Govt. Pavilion, Expo 67, Mtl. 1967, P. 41
   Globe & Mail, Tor., Ont., July 25, 1968 "Architect becomes enamel craftsman" by Mary Jukes
   The Montreal Star, P.Q., Sept. 28, 1971 "Inside/Outside – Art isn't just something you hang on a wall" by Cynthia Gunn
   The Montreal Gazette, P.Q., Oct. 2, 1971 article by Shirley Raphael
   The Crown Crier, Tor., Ont., Crown Life Ins., 17 Mar., 1972 "A Hanging on the Seventh Floor"
   Charlottetown Patriot, P.E.I., June 9, 1973 "Successful craftsmen to conduct workshop" (Arthur and Reeva Perkins working as a team in Charlottetown)
   Kenora Miner & News, Ont., Mar. 5, 1976 "Renowned craftsman to appear in Dryden" (Alan Perkins exhibiting and demonstrating his work)
   NGC Info. Form rec'd (c.) 1975

PERKINS, Donald
b. 1933

Born in Scarborough, Ontario, he studied painting at the Ecole des Beaux-Arts, Montreal and at the School of Art and Design of the Montreal Museum of Fine Arts. He travelled in Europe and North America and has done several series of paintings including: a genre series on market life characterized by brightly costumed people moving among dense forms in a luminous tranquil environment; a series of landscapes in which he reveals a rich harmony of foliage and forms in a deep and solemn environment; a series on anguish and suffering showing the eternal ancient themes of human tragedy and predicament; dream, fantasy, symbolism and mystery series; love and affection series expressing the communion of persons. He works mainly in oils and tempera on panel and has exhibited his work in Montreal at the Dominion Gallery and the West-End Gallery. He has been Art Master of Lower Canada College, Montreal since 1964; Art Instructor of Weston School, Montreal; Art Instructor at St. Andrews, N.B. and tutors in drawing, painting and design. He lives in Montreal.

Reference
   Document from artist

PERKINS, Reeva

Working for a number of years as a successful goldsmith in her leisure time, she has been a partner with her husband, Arthur Perkins, enamelist, in running craft workshops. Exhibiting for many years she displayed her work in 1973 at the Master Craftsmen Exhibition held in Confederation Centre Art Gallery, Charlottetown.

References
> *The Globe & Mail,* Tor., Ont., July 25, 1968 "Architect becomes enamel craftsman" by Mary Jukes
> *Charlottetown Patriot,* P.E.I., June 9, 1973 "Successful craftsmen to conduct workshop"

PERLES, Barry
b. 1944

Born in Winnipeg he received his B.F.A. at the University of Manitoba where he studied sculpture and photography and won the Kenneth Finkelstein Prize for the best major sculpture done by a student during an academic year. Subsequently his sculpture was accepted for showing at the Ninth Winnipeg Biennial Show in 1964. He has exhibited his photographs on several occasions including a showing at the Centennial Art Gallery of the Nova Scotia Museum of Fine Arts, Halifax (1970). Lives in Winnipeg.

References
> *Winnipeg Free Press,* Man., Feb. 13, 1969 "Young Artists Show Promise" by John W. Graham
> *The Mail-Star,* Halifax, N.S., Feb. 7, 1970 "His pictures have wide vocabulary" by Barbara Hinds
> NGC Info. Form rec'd 1965

PERLET, Marion
b. (c) 1941

She began painting around 1964 and exhibited her work at Galleries Place Royale, Montreal (1966) and in Toronto in the window of Holt Renfrew on Bloor Street West, as a background for the store's own merchandise. Numerous enquiries about her work followed and an important Toronto collector wanted to arrange a solo show of her work for his friends and associates. Her work has been described as not merely good but brilliant. In 1975 her oil paintings and ink drawings were on exhibit at the New Academic Building, Victoria College, Queen's Park Crescent, Toronto. Her paintings bring to mind work by ancient Egyptian artists, art nouveau, Matisse and other intriguing sources.

References
> *Dimanche-Matin,* Mtl., P.Q. "Dans le vieux Montréal" (photo of the artist's work with caption)
> *Sunday Sun,* Tor., Ont., June 30, 1974 "Success – No. 1 – She's an artist who draws crowds. . ." by Simon Ford
> Exhibition notice with reproduction of her painting "The Egyptian Beauty", show at New Academic Bldg., Victoria College, Tor., Oct. 20 to Nov. 15, 1975

PERLIN, Rae

Born in St. John's, Newfoundland, studied painting with Samuel Brecher (1941-2, 46) and with Hans Hofmann in New York City (1947-48); Académie Grande Chaumière, Paris, Académie Ranson, Paris. Searches for the form and structure in subjects and is interested in all drawing media. In painting works in oils and acrylics and also water colours. Has been art critic with the *St. John's Daily News* (1960-71); *St. John's Evening Telegram* (1964-67) and has contributed to the *Book of Newfoundland, Vol. 4* (A history of art in Newfoundland) and illustrator of Paul O'Neill's *Spindrift and morning light, an anthology of poems* (1968). Lives in St. John's, Newfoundland.

References
>   *St. John's Daily News*, Nfld., Nov. 24, 1962 (reproduction of one of the artist's water colours)
>   *Spindrift and morning light: an anthology of poems* by Paul O'Neill, Valhalla Press, St. John's, Nfld., 1968
>   *Canadian Books in Print*, Univ. Tor. Press, P. 338
>   *Who's Who in American Art, 1976*, R.R. Bowker, New York & Lond., 1976, P. 435

PERLSTRAUSS, Ann

Born and educated in China she came to Vancouver to live in 1953 and studied at the Vancouver School of Art. She is known for her portraits and she took part in exhibitions of the Federation of Canadian Artists. She has received commissions from residents of Vancouver, San Francisco and other cities in Canada and United States. She held a solo show of her work in the Vancouver Museum (1964) and at that time had planned exhibitions in San Francisco and Los Angeles.

References
>   *The Province*, Van., B.C., May 22, 1964 "First one-man show arranged"
>   Ibid, Sept. 17, 1964 "Art work widens in scope" (photo of artist)

PERRAULT, Sister Beatrice

A Saskatchewan painter who exhibited her work at the Gallery on the Roof, Saskatchewan Power Corporation, in October, 1977.

Reference
>   Exhibition sheet, Gallery on the Roof, Saskatchewan Power Corp., Regina, October, 1977

PERRAULT, Gérard
b. 1903

Born in Montreal, P.Q. he attended McGill University and in 1922 went into art full time. He studied painting with Wilfred Molson Barnes at the Barnes School of Art, Montreal (1922-27); sculpture with Alfred Laliberté at the Monument National for one year; in New York City at the Art Students' League with Hans Flato and others where he studied drawing, painting and advertising art. He worked for several adver-

PERRAULT, Gérard (Cont'd)

tising agencies in that city. He returned to Montreal for a short period and sailed for Paris to study at the Académie de la Grande Chaumière recommended to him by Clarence Gagnon. While in Europe he travelled extensively in France, Belgium, Germany, Holland, Luxembourg, Scotland and England. He also studied the art of bookbinding, gilding and leather mosaics in Paris and London. Earlier he had won first prize for bookbinding at the Canadian Handicraft Guild show in Montreal (1927). He held his first solo show of painting in 1932. He returned to Europe for two years (1935-36) then returned to Montreal where he became a free lance artist. He held several private exhibitions of his paintings and fine bookbinding. His subjects in painting included Gaspé, Upper St. Lawrence and St. Jean Port Joli districts where he established a studio, art shop and home. He also painted in Mexico. By 1956 about two hundred of his paintings had been acquired by collectors. During World War II he served five years with the R.C.A.F. as commanding officer of University Air Squadrons and then personnel counsellor in Yorkshire, England, with the "Alouette" Squadron. Following the war he returned to Montreal where he became head of the Advertising Art Section of the School of Graphic Arts (1945-52). In 1960 he became director at the Centre d'Art at St. Jean Port Joli and up to 1965 was still its director. By 1965 he had held nineteen solo shows including those at: Cercle Universitaire, Mtl. (1951); Palais Montcalm, Que. City (1957); Seminar Room, Main Bldg., MacDonald College, Ste. Anne de Bellevue (1959) and at Galerie Montmorency (Mtl.); L'Art Français (Mtl.); Galerie Henault (Mtl.). He also participated in the Montreal Spring Shows (MMFA) and the Quebec Competition (Musée de Québec). Represented: Musée de Québec, The Granby Museum of Art and elsewhere.

References
La Patrie, Mtl., P.Q., Apr. 15, 1950 "La peinture – Gérard Perrault"
Ibid, Apr. 15, 1950 "Peintures et aquarelles du paysagiste Gérard Perrault"
Le Canada, Mtl., P.Q., Apr. 17, 1950 "Les Arts – Gérard Perrault, chez lui" par Rolland Boulanger
La Patrie, Mtl., P.Q., Apr. 10, 1951 "La peinture Gérard Perrault"
La Presse, Mtl., P.Q., Apr. 18, 1953 (photo of his painting "Coin du Banc" in coll. Musée de Québec)
Ibid, Apr. 26, 1952 (photo of his "Newport, Gaspésie")
Ibid, Nov. 9, 1957 "Exposition à Québec par Gérard Perrault"
Le Progrès Du Dag., Chicoutimi, P.Q., May 19, 1958 "Le peintre Perrault expose à Chicoutimi"
Le Soleil, Que., P.Q., Aug. 29, 1958 (photo of one of his coloured drawings of Percé Rock)
Lakeshore News, Pointe Claire, P.Q., Jan. 29, 1959 "Gerard Perrault painting exhibit at Macdonald"
Le Soleil, Quebec, P.Q., Aug. 14, 1965 "De l'inusité à St-Jean-Port-Joli" (photo of artist and his work) par Francine Robert
NGC Info. Forms rec'd Jan. 9, 1956; 1965

PERRAULT, Lise

A landscape painter from Saskatchewan who exhibited her work at the Gallery on the Roof, Saskatchewan Power Corporation, in October, 1977

Reference
Exhibition sheet, Gallery on the Roof, Saskatchewan Power Corp., Regina, October, 1977

PERRAULT, Suzanne Parent
b. 1924

Born in Montreal, P.Q., daughter of the late Lucien Parent, architect; drawing and painting were part of her home activities. She received her first formal art studies when attending Sacre-Coeur Convent, Montreal. Later she travelled to New York City where she attended the Art Students' League (1 yr.); then to Paris, France for the History of Costume at the Ecole du Louvre (1 yr.). She also studied ceramics and related crafts. Was living in Ste-Dorothée, Laval County near Montreal.

Reference
    NGC Info. Form undated

PERRÉ, Henri
1828-1890

Born in Strasbourg, Alsace, of French and Prussian descent, he studied art in Dresden and later took part in the rising in Saxony in 1849 and afterwards fled to the United States, living in Cincinnati and Chicago. He served for a time in the ranks of the Confederate army in the American Civil War. He came to Canada and settled in Toronto where he associated with members of the Ontario Society of Artists following its founding in 1872 and became a member. He spent his time between Montreal and Toronto and was considered a capable and careful artist in his prime who liked to paint woodland subjects. He made most of his living from teaching at the Ontario School of Art. He is represented in the National Gallery of Canada (RCA Diploma Coll.) by a peaceful rural landscape with two figures by a creek. He is represented in other collections including the Art Gallery of Ontario. Charter Member: R.C.A. He died a bachelor aged sixty-two in Toronto. (See J. Russell Harper's *Early Painters and Engravers in Canada*)

References
    Canada and Its Provinces, Vol. 12, Shortt & Doughty, 1914 "Painting" by E.F.B. Johnston, P. 605
    Canadian Landscape Painters by A.H. Robson, Ryerson, Tor., 1932, P. 52
    NGC Catalogue of Painting & Sculpture, Vol. 3 by R.H. Hubbard, NGC/Univ. Tor. Press, 1960, P. 407
    Early Painters and Engravers in Canada by J. Russell Harper, Univ. Tor. Press, 1970, P. 248
    Art Gallery of Ontario, the Canadian collection by Helen Pepall Bradfield, McGraw-Hill, Tor., 1970, P. 364
    NGC Lib. file on artist

PERREAULT, Gabriel
b. 1932

Born in Ste-Sophie, P.Q., he attended the Ecole des Beaux-Arts, Montreal, where he studied drawing under J. Simard, I. Senecal, Fauche, Charpentier; painting under J. de Tonnancour, Stanley Cosgrove; decoration under J. Simard and Maurice Raymond; modelling under Louis Archambault. He also studied the History of Art, History of Painting, wood sculpture, engraving and graphic techniques and advertising illustration. He graduated in 1955 with his teaching diploma in drawing. He has taught in Montreal schools and has shown his work at the Montreal Spring Show.

PERREAULT, Gabriel (Cont'd)

Reference
NGC Info. Form rec'd July 2, 1957

PERREAULT, Pierre
b. 1955

Born in Montreal, P.Q., a self-taught artist he started painting in 1972. Working in acrylics and oils he has produced landscapes, still lifes, figure studies and other subjects. He took a short course in enamelling on copper and has done work in this field. He is also known for his film work, photographs of the landscape and people of Quebec and poetry which he has combined for various presentations. He exhibited at the Musée National d'Art Moderne, Paris, France, 1977, as part of a touring company of visual and performing artists from Quebec. Lives at Lavaltrie, P.Q.

References
Biographical infor. from NGC Library (artist's file)
Le Devoir, Mtl., P.Q., January 21, 1977 (AFP) PARIS "Manifestations axées autour de l'oeuvre de Pierre Perreault"

PERRIER, Gordon B.
b. 1935

Born in Northern Saskatchewan, he grew up in Hamilton, Ontario and was greatly influenced by Madeline and Vincent Francis of Dundas, Ontario, professional artists. Mainly self-taught he began his formal training under Jean Wishart and Hortense Gordon at the Hamilton Technical Institute. Subsequently he studied at the Doon School of Fine Arts and at the Ontario College of Art. He has been influenced greatly by the work of Aba Bayefsky and Carl Schaefer and their approach to art. Primarily a water colourist he also paints in oils and is fascinated with the Southern Ontario landscape. He has done a great variety of other work including non-objective painting. From the age of sixteen he has been teaching art, first in Hamilton, Ontario and later in London, Ontario (1960-64); Chatham, Ont. (1964-66); travelled for a period in the U.S.A. and Mexico; returned to teach at the Dundas School of Art (1975) while also continuing with his painting in his free time. An artist producing fine work his solo shows include: Burlington Public Library, Burl., Ont. (1958); I.O.D.E. Provincial Headquarters, Hamilton, Ont. (1958); Shute Institute, London, Ont. (1961); Thames Theatre, Chatham, Ont. (1964, 1966).

References
The Hamilton Spectator, Ont., Apr. 26, 1958 "Weekend Art Chatter" by Ivan Vorres
Ibid., July 5, 1958 "Art and Reflections" (note about Burlington show)
London Morning Free Press, Ont., Dec. 20, 1961 "Gordon Perrier Surprises Art Critic" by Lenore Crawford
Chatham Daily News, Ont., Apr. 29, 1964 "Seeks His Own Identity, Artist Displaying Works"
Ibid, Ont., Sept. 26, 1964 "Course in Painting Commences Tuesday" by Red Lockwood
Ibid, May 20, 1966 "Sundays Best – Perrier's Art Display Attraction for 1,200"
The Hamilton Spectator, May 26, 1966 "City-born artist off to Mexico"
Welland Port Colborne Tribune, Ont., June 13, 1975 "Art Instructor Offers a Course"

PERRIER, Jean Richard Aimé

b. 1923

An enamelist he exhibited his work at the following places: Quebec Provincial Exhibition (1956); St-Hyacinthe (1956); Joliette (1956); University of Montreal (1956); Palais du Commerce, Montreal (1956); Canadian Handicrafts, Montreal (1956). An accomplished musician as well, he studied piano with Arthur Letondal, Yvonne Hubert and Helmut Blume; also studied at the New England Conservatory of Music, Boston.

Reference
    NGC Lib. artist's file, info. dated 1957

PERRIER, Louis

He is highly respected for his fine craftsmanship as a jeweller and believes his product can be both beautiful and functional. He often works in collaboration with designer Robert Wolfe. Perrier lives at Mont Saint-Hilaire, Quebec, where he has his studio.

References
    Le Devoir, Montreal, P.Q., Apr. 24, 1976 "Le joaillier Louis Perrier et la sociologie du bijou" par Viviane Simard
    Le guide des artisans créateurs du Quebec par Jean-Pierre Payette, La Presse, 1974, P. 138-139

PERRIGARD, Hal Ross

1891-1960

Born in Montreal, P.Q., from his earliest childhood he was interested in art and painted surprisingly good landscapes at the age of twelve. He attended life classes at the Royal Canadian Academy school where he received instruction from William Brymner and Maurice Cullen. He was however largely self-taught. He was known for his landscapes early and had a   painting accepted by the Royal Canadian Academy about 1913. Later he entered the field of design, graphics, decoration and illustration. He established a studio on St. Catherine Street West in Montreal but later moved to Westmount. His fine portrait entitled "Lalage" was exhibited in the Montreal Spring Exhibition in 1923 and was purchased by the National Gallery of Canada the same year. In 1932 he was noted by A.H. Robson in *Canadian Landscape Painters* as a brilliant artist, painting with fine colour and originality of design. His subjects also included seascapes and figure studies. Much of his inspiration for seascapes no doubt came from his summers spent in Rockport, Massachusetts where he had a studio from 1923 until his death. He did a number of murals for the Canadian Pacific Railway offices and hotels. One of his murals adorned the Laurentian Hotel in Montreal, others were done for oil, power, and aluminum companies and public buildings. In 1926 he won the R.C.A. mural competition to do a decoration for the women's waiting room in Windsor Station, Montreal. Sixty entries were submitted

PERRIGARD, Hal Ross (Cont'd)

for the competition and six artists were chosen for mural work at various places in the city. In 1939 he did mural work for the Canadian Pavilion at the New York World's Fair. Generally speaking Perrigard painted in a simplified realistic form, designed his work well and had a colourful palette. He worked in oils, water colours, pastels and charcoal. A sample of his book design and illustration work can be seen in Stephen Leacock's *Canada, The Foundations of its Future* published by The House of Seagram in 1941. His paintings were reviewed by *The Gazette* in 1948 as follows, "Hal Ross Perrigard . . . is holding an exhibition of his oils in the Arts Club . . . the collection revealing this Montreal artist's feeling for decorative arrangement and harmonious color. The works throughout are well composed, totally free of exaggeration and soundly painted. Landscapes are the favored subject, and these he treats at all seasons of the year." He was an active member of many art societies including The Arts Club of Montreal (1917); Rockport Art Association (1923); A.R.C.A. (1924); North Shore Artists Association of Gloucester; Artists Guild of Canada; Pen and Pencil Club, Montreal; and was in touch with the Beaver Hall Hill Group. He exhibited with the Ontario Society of Artists. His hobbies included woodworking and craft work with copper, brass, pewter and plastics. He became Director of Galleries of the Rockport Art Association (1930-35) and was on its advisory board. He died suddenly in his 69th year and was survived by his wife Pauline Bradley Perrigard, an amateur playwright, originally from Sherbrooke, Quebec, also by two brothers Stanley and Rev. George Perrigard of Montreal. His works are in the permanent collections of the National Gallery of Canada, Ottawa; the Musée du Québec and in private collections in Canada, United States, Hawaii, England, Holland, Belgium, Austria and elsewhere. The few known solo shows of his paintings include: The Arts Club, Mtl. (1948, 1950); The Gallery (Gemst Bldg.) Mtl. (retrospective show, 1962). His work was also handled by the Continental Galleries and Galerie de l'Art Français Montreal. He exhibited in group shows in many countries including the British Empire Exhibitions at Wembley.

References

Ateliers; études sur vingt-deux peintres et sculpteurs canadiens by J. Chauvin, Carrier, Mtl., 1928

Canadian Landscape Painters by A.H. Robson, Ryerson, Tor., 1932, P. 170

Canadian Geographical Journal, July, 1939 Vol. XIX, No. 1 "Canada's Participation in The World's Fair" by J. G. Parmelee, P. 93, 98 (middle photo)

The Gazette, Mtl., P.Q., Apr. 6, 1949 (photo of painting "Visiting" and caption)

Canada, The Foundations of its Future by Stephen Leacock, Seagram, 1941 (page decoration, cover design; ill's 150, 171, 195, 224 by H.R. Perrigard, A.R.C.A.)

Canadian Art, its origin and development by William Colgate, Ryerson, Tor., 1943, P. 237

The Gazette, Mtl., Apr. 17, 1948 "Hal Ross Perrigard Exhibits Landscapes"

Ibid, Oct. 7, 1950 "Hal Ross Perrigard Showing at Arts Club"

Ibid, Feb. 22, 1958 (photo of painting "The Bridge" and caption)

NGC Catalogue of Paintings and Sculpture, Vol. 3 by R.H. Hubbard, NGC/Univ. Tor. Press, 1960, P. 246.

The Montreal Star, Apr. 25, 1960 "Obituaries – H.R. Perrigard"

Ibid, Apr. 30, 1960 "In Tribute to Memory of Noted Local Artist" by R.H.M.

Ibid, Mar. 24, 1962 (retrospective show reviewed)

Canadian Art at Auction 1968-1975, Ed. G. Joyner, Sotheby & Co., Tor., 1975, P. 156

Document and letter from Pauline Bradley Perrigard, 1961

NGC Info. Forms 1920, 1943

Artists of the Rockport Art Association, 1956, P. 125